Y0-DEN-149

WITHDRAWN

The South
And Its Newspapers
1903-1953

*TO THOSE
WHOSE GENEROUS CONTRIBUTIONS OF TIME AND EFFORT
HAVE BUILT AND SHAPED
THE SOUTHERN NEWSPAPER PUBLISHERS ASSOCIATION*

Contents

I. **THE SNPA IS BORN**

Daily Newspapers in 1903 Form Association on a Broad Base, Avoiding Restrictive Policies which Had Been Fatal to Earlier Groups—Changing Newspaper Economics Provided Abundant Topics for Early Meetings.

II. **EXPLORING THE FIELD (1903-1913)**

South's Thriving Cities Shower Visiting Publishers with Hospitality and Proofs of Vigor, as SNPA Seeks Fields of Greatest Usefulness to Its Slowly Expanding Membership.

III. **DAILY NEWSPAPERS MATURE**

Southern Press is Strongly Represented in Nationally Organized Efforts to Reform Circulation Abuses and Improve Availability of Daily Newspapers for National Advertising.

IV. **THE SNPA AND WORLD WAR I**

Repeatedly Pledging Support to Nation's War Objectives, Publishers Battle Scaring Paper Prices and Unjust Postal Rate Schedules—Membership and Program Greatly Expanded Between 1918 and 1920.

V. **NEW SPHERES OF INFLUENCE**

E. W. Barrett Demonstrates Newsprint Made from Southern Spruce Pine—Association Sees Macon Printers' School Grow, Then Raises Funds to Endow Journalism Teaching at Washington & Lee—Many Tasks Prove Need for Professional Management.

VI. **ARE NEWSPAPERS INTERSTATE COMMERCE?**

Federal Trade Commission Asserts Jurisdiction over Advertising Practices in 1925 Complaint, Dismissed Six Years Later—Cranston Williams Named as SNPA Manager—Association Adopts Code of Ethics—The "Golden Age" Ends.

VII. **SURVIVAL IN THE LEAN YEARS**

Deepening Depression Brings Lower Newsprint Prices, Also Demands for Lower Advertising Rates—Dr. Herty Proposes Southern Newsprint Industry—Radio News Competition Stirs Publishers—SNPA Members Avoid Labor Strife.

VIII. **"EXPERIMENTS PERILOUS"**

Newspaper Honeymoon with New Deal Wanes—Sharp Words Exchanged in Writing Newspaper Industry Code Under NRA—SNPA Membership Grows and Dues are Raised 50 Per Cent to Meet New Service Demands —Southern Newsprint Mill Wins Association Approval.

CONTENTS—*Continued*

IX. THE SOUTH GETS A NEWSPRINT MILL

SNPA Committee, Undaunted by Disappointments, Wins Financial and Technical Backing for East Texas Plant—Association Membership Increased —Recession Hits Business, But Publishers Form New Plans for Regaining Lost Advertising Volume—Johnson Succeeds Williams as Secretary-Manager.

X. NEWSPRINT — AND A NEW SOUTH

Abundant Southern Forests, Seeded, Tended and Harvested as a Crop Provide Unfailing and Widely Distributed Source of New Wealth—Dr. Herty's Farsighted Pioneer Research Validated by Courageous Support of the South's Organized Publishers.

XI. THROUGH FOG OF WAR

SNPA Plans Support of New Paper Mills and Other Industries for New Prosperity in South, Also Continues Effort for Improved Newspapers—War-Travel Ban Prevents Annual Conventions in 1944 and 1945, as Association's Long-Held Hopes Approach Realization.

XII. ECONOMIC RENAISSANCE IN THE SOUTH — I

SNPA Seeks Permanence and Expansion of South's Industrial and Social Advances During World War II—Plans Second, Then Third, Newsprint Mill and Aggressive Program of Forest Conservation—Calls Publishers to Strengthen Editorial Staffs and Services to Meet Region's New Opportunities.

XIV. SNPA MARKS GOLDEN ANNIVERSARY

Coosa River Newsprint Mill Begins Production—Bowater of England Starts Construction of Tennessee Mill, with Moral but Not Financial Backing of SNPA—Association's Forestry Program Strengthened—Publishers Give New Attention to Operating Costs, as Korean Conflict Brings Quasi-War Economy.

XV. In RETROSPECT

Record-Breaking Attendance of More than 600 at Boca Raton Convention—50 Years Condensed into 50-Minute Review by President Jones—Trade and Daily Press Hail Occasion—Publishers Warned Against Complacency on Newsprint Supply and Television Competition.

EPILOGUE

INDEX

Foreword

This History of the Southern Newspaper Publishers Association has been long in the making. Its eventual production as a book became the aim of Walter C. Johnson during his service as secretary more than 30 years ago. With that in view, he guarded carefully a mass of items of seemingly transient interest that might clothe with the semblance of life the bones of the annual minutes and other formal records. Early annals that were lost in a flood before the Association had reached its 11th birthday have been partially replaced by diligent research in newspaper files and among men who still held memories of what had been done.

When the Fiftieth Anniversary of the Association's founding offered an appropriate moment for assembling the story, Mr. Johnson called to the task a man who had observed the SNPA with a friendly eye through much of its existence, from 1916 to 1944. As managing editor and editor of *Editor & Publisher* for more than 20 years, Arthur T. Robb realized the importance of the SNPA both to the South and in the broad national newspaper framework.

The growth of the SNPA closely paralleled the long-term industrial progress of the whole Southern region. That fact came sharply into focus from the immense mass of basic data, and it has governed to a large extent the form and content of this History. Almost from its inception, the SNPA sought to lead the South to the economic and social destiny that was clear to some Southern leaders half a century ago. In that respect, this story departs from the conventional pattern of newspaper association history. No other newspaper group had either the opportunity or the incentive of the SNPA to share and guide the industrial progress of its area. Development of the South's great natural resources inevitably increased the national importance of the region—and that was evident long before the astonishing expansion during World War II. Keeping pace with its people, the SNPA year by year assumed a larger share, through its committees and its individual members, in national newspaper activities.

Thus the traditionally conservative newspapers of the South long ago led in the establishment of sound circulation practices, in the elimination of deceptive advertising, in the organization of equitable relations with advertising agencies, and, of prime importance, in promoting the whole South as a primary market for nationally advertised goods. Later, SNPA voices were potent in obtaining fair second-class postal rates. Still later, the SNPA grew in national stature by the sensible moderation with which it presented the daily newspaper case in the long struggle over free press principles involved in the National Recovery Administration.

During the 1930's, when depression and the disappearance of many former newspaper advertisers kept newspaper incomes at a low level, the South escaped with few newspaper casualties and with almost no labor troubles. In part that may be attributed to the efforts of SNPA officers and committee heads to reconstruct a sound newspaper economic structure.

During the same troubled period, SNPA members, Southern scientists and industrialists tackled the formidable task of establishing newsprint manufacture in the South. Though the story of that uphill fight and its eventual successes fills many of these pages, this narrative makes no claim of completeness. Another volume could (and should) be written to preserve the record of that "achievement of the impossible," as many regarded it. The importance of Southern paper manufacture to the region and to the nation can hardly be over-rated; new techniques already brought to commercial practicability in the South can possibly make the United States independent of any non-domestic source for its massive paper needs.

To that end the SNPA in recent years has kept constantly before its members the transcendent importance of all measures for soil, forest, and water conservation. Great as these resources are throughout most of the South, the SNPA a decade ago recognized that they are not limitless. Views as to their most effective employment in the public interest differ widely. It is wholly probable that the members of the SNPA, through their news and editorial columns, will exercise the decisive influence in solving these interrelated problems in the broadest public interest. The SNPA and its members have been fully alert to this responsibility.

That last word comprises the "theme" of this History, so far as a History can possess a theme. Through more than half a century, SNPA members by their words and official acts have not limited themselves to the commercial concerns of the daily press. While those problems have never been minimized, they have not dominated SNPA counsels. From the early days when SNPA enthusiasts struggled with inadequate tools to open the South to the new national advertising, to the persistent efforts to found a Southern newsprint industry, the newspapers of the South have manifested a continuing concern, individually and as a group, for the welfare of their constituents.

As this narrative goes to press, the SNPA comprises more than 400 members the largest enrolment of any regional newspaper group. In several States, every daily newspaper holds SNPA membership. That is a token both of the regional homogeneity of the Southern press and of the effective cohesive force of the Association, developed by continuous service over many decades. We believe the story is a proud one, worthy of inclusion in the South's record of notable achievements. To those who brought it to pass, living and departed, and to perpetuation of SNPA responsibility to public and to press in the years ahead, the authors humbly dedicate this record of 1903-1953.

WALTER C. JOHNSON   ARTHUR T. ROBB

THE SOUTH
AND ITS NEWSPAPERS
1903-1953

*The Story of the Southern Newspaper Publishers
Association and its part in the South's
Economic Rebirth*

By WALTER C. JOHNSON *and* ARTHUR T. ROBB

GREENWOOD PRESS, PUBLISHERS
WESTPORT, CONNECTICUT

Library of Congress Cataloging in Publication Data

Johnson, Walter C
   The South and its newspapers, 1903-1953.

   Reprint of the 1954 ed. published by Southern Newspaper Publishers Association, Chattanooga.
   1. Southern Newspaper Publishers Association.
I. Robb, Arthur T., joint author. II. Title.
Z479.J6 1974   071'.5   78-136935
ISBN 0-8371-5407-3

Originally published in 1954 by The Southern Newspaper Publishers Association, Chattanooga, Tennessee

Reprinted in 1974 by Greenwood Press, a division of Williamhouse-Regency Inc.

Library of Congress Catalogue Card Number 78-136935

ISBN 0-8371-5407-3

Printed in the United States of America

The SNPA Is Born

Daily Newspapers in 1903 Form Association on a Broad Base, Avoiding Restrictive Policies which Had Been Fatal to Earlier Groups—Changing Newspaper Economics Provided Abundant Topics for Early Meetings.

NONE of the 34 men who founded the Southern Newspaper Publishers Association in 1903 was still alive in 1953. Therefore, the circumstances that brought this Association into being must be described from sparsely recorded memoirs, and from a few terse minutes and crumbling newspaper pages. For the rest of the Association's story, there is both record and human memory for foundation. One of the present authors attended the 1904 convention and has served continuously as an officer or director since 1913. Having enjoyed a personal acquaintance with every SNPA president, he can fairly claim, "much of this I saw and a part of it I was." His colleague in this record has known the SNPA as a reporter since 1916, and has chronicled at first hand many of the developments related in these pages.

The men who gathered at the old Piedmont Hotel in Atlanta on April 14, 1903, had no notion of making history. Their aim was to form a regional association to serve its members and the general welfare of the South, an association able to survive the internal strains of the newspaper business. Some of them had belonged to the Southern Press Association, which had been organized in 1880 with the primary objective of obtaining better telegraphic news service for newspapers. By no means incidentally, it also existed to produce friendly intercourse among Southern editors and publishers, and surviving records indicate considerable success in that function.

The objective of better news service was advanced when the Southern Press Association was, in effect, transformed into the Southern

Associated Press in 1891. The three national news services of the day were then engaged in a cut-throat struggle for supremacy and two of them would die in the process. Wisely, the Southern Associated Press cast its lot with the eventual survivor, and, becoming a part of the reorganized Associated Press in 1892, ceased as a separate organization.

During the troubled business period of 1893-1897 no regional newspaper association seems to have existed in the South. In 1898, a large number of those who had participated in the earlier organizations formed the Southern Publishers Association. While the purposes of this group were similar to those of the existing American Newspaper Publishers Association, and later of the SNPA, the Southern Publishers Association had one fatal defect. Its membership was limited to morning newspapers which took the Associated Press news service. Publishers who met those qualifications considered themselves a sort of newspaper aristocracy throughout the country. To them, the Associated Press appeared as a "franchise" analogous to the rights granted to local public utilities. They did their best to bar new competition by means which later generations would disapprove and abolish. They also looked down on the upstart evening newspapers which were gaining readers and prosperity, most of them without Associated Press membership. The Southern Publishers Association, reared on such a narrow and innately selfish foundation, held only three meetings and was heard of no more after 1901.

The needs it had been created to serve, however, increased with every year. Newspaper publication was entering a new era, with radical departures from the old. Machine type-setting had in recent years become essential to daily newspapers and many Southern newspapers were installing the new Linotypes in their composing rooms.

That made no hit with the old-time hand-compositors, who feared that the new monster might devour their jobs. They were wrong, of course, but the publishers had to face the new problem of keeping them employed and at the same time get full advantage of the great increase in production the machines afforded. Other machines, giant presses and automatic stereotype equipment, were coming on the market in 1903, and publishers eagerly sought reliable first-hand information on their performance. Larger newspapers, larger circulations,

The SNPA Is Born

and increased advertising revenues were already evident as a product of the new techniques.

Then, too, newspapers all over America were in the infant stage of soliciting national (and even local) advertising. Up to the turn of the century, few newspapers had sold their space systematically or aggressively. And few adhered strictly to the advertising rates that they published. Publishers realized the folly of numerous old newspaper practices, but, as individuals, felt powerless to change them.

Changes, then, were definitely in the air when the SNPA was organized. By meeting together and getting better acquainted with their fellows, progressive publishers believed that they could apply the experience and wisdom of many to the problems of the individual newspaper.

The old records do not tell in whose brain the basic idea of the SNPA originated. Reading between the lines, it can be deduced that the prime mover for the new and practical group of publishers was Franklin Potts Glass,[1] secretary-treasurer of the Montgomery Advertiser. Mr. Glass had been secretary of the Southern Publishers Association and had also been active in its predecessor, the Southern Press Association. He was at home in both editorial and business office duties, and unquestionably had well-defined ideas as to the function of a news-

---

[1] Mr. Glass is best remembered as president of the American Newspaper Publishers Association during World War I. He had fought the "paper trust" for many years in the interest of his newspapers. Cast as a leader of the nation's publishers in a war-time crisis, he saw the price of newsprint rise by leaps from $40 a ton to double and eventually treble that amount. Mr. Glass exercised great influence in the publishers' successful move to have the paper manufacturers' combination indicted for monopoly and restraint of trade, resulting in the dissolution of the Newsprint Manufacturers' Association. Mr. Glass maintained the publishers' right to bring down contract prices for paper, and under his Administration, the ANPA eventually arranged for the import of European tonnage, breaking the runaway market in 1921.

His stalwart resolution not to be cowed by apparently superior forces had many other exponents among successful Southern newspaper owners in 1903. Most of them had been born during the War Between the States. The older men recalled years of hardship and back-breaking poverty. Many had also gone through several "boom and bust" cycles in local attempts at recovery. They were fighters. Their editorials straddled no fences. News columns often indicated ignorance or disregard of libel laws. If the code duello, which had ended several Southern editorial lives in earlier times, no longer prevailed, even after 1900 the fire-breathing editor had to beware of an angry subscriber with a gun. On the whole, it was a generation to be admired—far from faultless, but generally free from the ruthless avarice that marked so much of American business life toward the end of the Nineteenth Century.

paper trade association. In the editorial chair of the Montgomery Advertiser, he had stepped into the shoes of W. W. Screws, one of the South's spiritual mainstays in the hard hours of Reconstruction. Mr. Glass was a worthy successor. He was also one of the first Southern editors to recognize that free journalism must have a sound economic foundation, and by 1903, he was giving much of his attention to the Advertiser's business affairs. A few years later, he became associated with Victor H. Hanson in the publication of the Birmingham News. While Mr. Glass exemplified the old journalism of the South, Mr. Hanson was the salesman who was to become the dominant type among newspaper executives in the coming quarter-century. The combination soon made the Birmingham News one of the South's great newspapers.

When Clark Howell, Sr., editor and general manager of the Atlanta Constitution, called the meeting to order in the Piedmont Hotel, Mr. Glass was named temporary chairman, with Henry Harrison Cabiness of the Atlanta Journal as temporary secretary. The first order of business was appointment of a committee on permanent organization. The speed with which the committee reported suggested that Mr. Glass had done effective spade work beforehand. The full report of the committee, adopted with minor changes, provided:

"The committee on permanent organization recommends the formation of an association to be known as

"The Southern Newspaper Publishers Association.

"And that the membership be confined to daily newspapers of Virginia, North Carolina, South Carolina, Georgia, Alabama, Mississippi, Louisiana, Texas, Tennessee, Arkansas, Kentucky, and Florida.[2]

"We recommend annual meetings, time and place to be selected by the executive committee.

"We recommend the following officers: President, vice-president, secretary-treasurer, and an executive committee of seven members, besides the president and secretary, who will be ex-officio members of the executive committee.

"The term of officers shall be for one year.

---

[2]Oklahoma was added after it was admitted to statehood in 1907, and West Virginia in 1923.

The SNPA Is Born

"The objects of this association shall be to promote the business interests, harmony, and prosperity of its members. It is not antagonistic to any national organization but it hopes to be an auxiliary to such national newspaper publishers' association as will work in harmony with it. It is not the purpose of this organization to interfere with the internal management of the offices of its members.

"Discussions of all topics of interest or profit to newspapers are invited.

"The annual dues shall be fixed by the executive committee not to exceed $60 per annum.

"Respectfully,

F. P. Glass
T. T. Stockton
J. C. Hemphill
Robert Ewing
H. H. Cabaniss"

This terse and simple document holds several points of interest. Two of the five signers represented evening newspapers, a clear sign that the restrictions of the older associations no longer applied. In defining the new association's objects, the committee emphasized that it desired harmony with other national newspaper publishers' groups. The only national newspaper associations at that time were the ANPA and the Associated Press. The ANPA, established in 1887, was just then entering a new and aggressive phase under the direction of Lincoln B. Palmer and the Southern publishers wisely foresaw many opportunities for useful co-operation with it. The final sentence of the paragraph seems an indirect reference to the Associated Press and an invitation to publishers who did not love the AP rules.

Southern publishers who had helped to found the new AP in New York a year or two earlier understood the need for the stringent code which gave the AP rights to all local news and provided severe penalties for violation of numerous rules. They understood that creation of a successful co-operative news service demanded the cession of some individual rights. To survive and operate effectively the AP as a whole had to have the power to restrain and punish individual newspapers which set their own advantage over that of the organization. The AP occasionally had to interfere in the affairs of its member newspapers. But some publishers, including a number in the South, chafed at this AP discipline. Some had remained out of the former Southern Publishers Association because it seemed to be too closely affiliated with the AP. The new SNPA avoided that weakness.

After adoption of the organization plan, the association tendered the presidency to Mr. Glass, who refused on the ground that a man more closely associated with the business of newspapers should be chosen. H. H. Cabaniss was then named president, with Mr. Glass as secretary-treasurer, and the executive committee was constituted as follows:

Robert Ewing, New Orleans Daily States (evening); Rufus N. Rhodes, Birmingham News (evening); D. A. Tompkins, Charlotte Observer (morning); J. C. Hemphill, Charleston News and Courier (morning); Edgar M. Foster, Nashville Banner (evening); T. T. Stockton, Jacksonville Times-Union and Citizen (morning); A. R. Holderby, Richmond Times-Dispatch (morning).

Since Mr. Cabaniss was associated with an evening paper, four places on the executive committee of nine were thus held by evening newspaper people. That was a big step forward, but only a few years passed before the SNPA ignored all distinctions between morning and evening newspaper members.

The convention ratified the committee's provision for annual dues and authorized the secretary-treasurer to employ an assistant when the business of the association warranted, the salary to be paid out of annual dues.

Lacking any further formal program, the meeting discussed shop topics and concluded their initial session with an address by Governor Terrell of Georgia.

Fifty-two members and guests assembled at the Piedmont Driving Club in the afternoon for a barbecue, marked by speeches emphasizing the serious purposes of the new association. Among the speakers was A. R. Holderby of the Richmond Times-Dispatch, who described the recent merger of the two Richmond dailies and offered, though he admitted his youth in the business, to supply some pointers on newspaper consolidations.

The SNPA Is Born

Newspapermen present at the organization meeting included:

Atlanta Constitution—Clark Howell, T. J. Kelley, J. R. Holliday, and Chris C. Nichols
Atlanta Journal—James R. Gray, H. H. Cabaniss, Charles D. Atkinson
Atlanta News—Col. John Temple Graves and Charles Daniel
Augusta Chronicle—E. B. Hook
Birmingham Age-Herald—E. W. Barrett, Ross C. Smith
Birmingham Ledger—James J. Smith
Birmingham News—Rufus N. Rhodes
Charleston News & Courier—J. C. Hemphill
Charlotte Observer—D. A. Tompkins
Columbus (Ga.) Enquirer-Sun—C. I. Groover
Jacksonville Times-Union & Citizen—T. T. Stockton
Louisville Courier-Journal—Bruce Haldeman
Louisville Post—Eugene Knott
Macon News—R. L. McKenney
Macon Telegraph—C. R. Pendleton, P. H. Campbell
Montgomery Advertiser—F. P. Glass, Victor H. Hanson
Mobile Register—Paul E. Rapier
Montgomery Journal—F. H. Miller
Nashville Banner—E. M. Foster
New Orleans States—Robert Ewing
Raleigh News & Observer—F. B. Arendell
Richmond Times-Dispatch—A. R. Holderby
Savannah News—Col. J. H. Estill
Shreveport Times—Louis N. Brueggerhoff

A critical examination of that roster would disclose that morning papers in Chattanooga, New Orleans, Houston, Galveston and Dallas, hitherto prominent in publishers' meetings, were not represented. It seems likely that they did not wholly approve of the new venture and intended to watch its progress before giving it their undeniable strength. They joined within a few years and bore their full share of SNPA responsibilities.

As the first convention ended, the publishers present were convinced that they had founded an organization that would live. In that they were right. They had laid down the framework on which a useful trade association could be constructed. They realized that the association would grow and, naively, they authorized the secretary-treasurer to employ an assistant to be paid out of annual dues. They did not understand yet that dues of $5.00 per month provided for no such organization as a paid staff, or that the schedule of dues barely met the needs of rudimentary service. It must be remembered, however, that $60 per annum was a big jump ahead of the $10 dues that had been assessed by the earlier Southern associations.

Operating on that tight budget, it is not surprising that Mr. Glass reported at the second meeting, in Nashville on June 7, 1904, that the membership numbered only 32. That itself was a gain of one-third over the initial membership and it probably represented zealous missionary work by the secretary-treasurer and others. With no record of association achievement to point to, new members had to be recruited on friendship and faith—and they would be for some years to come.

Some meaty topics came before the second SNPA convention. President Cabaniss focused attention on newsprint, which, with labor relations, constituted the publishers' most urgent problems. Mr. Glass immediately emerged as a spokesman against the paper makers. He had made a satisfactory contract with an independent mill, he said, and he would not resume relations with the "paper trust." The paper manufacturers' recent combination was then under investigation by a Congressional committee and SNPA members listened with interest to excerpts from the investigators' reports.

J. C. Hemphill of the Charleston News and Courier commented that too much newsprint was being used, that newspapers were printing too much matter. None of the members is reported as agreeing with that judgment, but it is probable that some sympathized privately. (A conversation with Adolph S. Ochs in the New York Times office in 1919 is recalled, in which Mr. Ochs deplored the necessity for a daily edition of the Times larger than 32 pages). Some of the old-timers didn't wholly welcome the expanded production of the new Lintoypes and high-speed presses.

When Mr. Hemphill proposed that the president name a committee to consider the newsprint problem and report at a later meeting, two of the three appointed to the committee argued that the ANPA was doing everything that could be done with the current paper situation. But the Association directed that the Committee should act under its instructions. Its members were Edgar M. Foster, Nashville Banner; A. R. Holderby, Richmond Times-Dispatch, and F. G. Gray, Atlanta Journal.

The Nashville Banner's report of the meeting gives no details of the discussions on labor. One can guess that they centered on compensation for Linotype operators and on the International Typographical Union's campaign for an eight-hour day. In many shops, Linotype operators worked on piece scales rather than on salary. A man who developed unusual skill on a well-kept machine could produce enough type in a week's work to give him more pay than the editor or business manager drew. At this SNPA meeting and many another, publishers anxiously compared piece scales prevalent in various offices with their own. They also discussed the possibility of printers' strikes and kept an uneasy eye on New York, Chicago, and other big cities where the unions were more militant than they had been in the South. And in 1904, they also canvassed the possibility of using oil rather than gas in heating Linotype metal pots. Those who had tried oil reported its use impractical.

Victor H. Hanson of the Montgomery Advertiser opened the discussion on "What is the best way to handle foreign agencies in order to secure rates and get along smoothly?" The question of employing representatives in New York and Chicago also had its innings, for this plan of soliciting "foreign" or "national" advertising was still new. The advertising solicitor, in general, was a fairly recent arrival in newspaper ranks; Henry L. Mencken is authority for the statement that so important a newspaper as the Baltimore Sun did not employ any solicitors until about 1904.

A question that has often arisen in newspaper meetings was raised by A. E. Gonzales of the Columbia State. It concerned the right of a newspaper to reject objectionable copy offered by an advertiser who had a contract with the newspaper. A characteristic answer came from the fiery Major E. B. Stahlman, publisher of the Nashville Banner. The convention adopted his resolution that advertising contracts should include a provision that the space contracted for should be used "for the purpose of advertising its business in a legitimate way and in such form as shall not be objectionable to the publisher."[3]

After a renewal of the print paper discussion, Major Stahlman, Secretary-Treasurer Glass and President Cabaniss constituted a committee to visit the paper mill operated by the Kansas City Star and to gain other information on the topic, "Can Southern Dailies Act Jointly in the Purchase of Paper?" Even to ask that question in 1903 required considerable courage. Its practical answer, in unpredicted form, would not arrive until 1940 for the SNPA—but the germ of the idea seems to have been present from the beginning.

The newsprint committee, which had been sent back for an amended report, again told the meeting that the best course for the SNPA was complete co-operation with the ANPA. The committee also requested that SNPA members answer a circular questionnaire on newsprint matters.

But the meeting wasn't all sternly business. In the middle of the opening session, the publishers adjourned to accept a treat of champagne offered by Sidney Lucas, a Nashville innkeeper well and favorably known to newspaper people. And at the end of the meeting, after discussing whether to charge baseball clubs and theatres advertising rates for their notices, the publishers went to the Nashville ball park, presumably as guests of the management.

The concluding dinner at the University Club was presided over by Major Stahlman. Among the numerous speakers was W. E. Mansfield, Southern representative of the International Paper Company. Even though his employing company frequently offered a target for publisher criticism, Mr. Mansfield held the friendship of many Southern publishers for decades and was succeeded by his son Laurence in the same kindly relationship.

Officers and executive committee members named at the 1903 meeting were all re-elected, despite the provision that their terms should

---
[3]Major Stahlman served on important committees of both the SNPA and the ANPA during the next 25 years, and when he rose to speak on any topic affecting newspapers, his hearers looked for fireworks. Positive in all his convictions on newspaper affairs, he scorned middle-of-the-road solutions. His interest in the SNPA continued until his death in 1930, at the age of 87, after he had attended several conventions in a wheel chair. His grandsons have ably carried on for the SNPA in a manner that would have evoked his approval.

The SNPA Is Born

be for one year. President Cabaniss, who had moved from Atlanta to the Augusta Chronicle, is one of seven SNPA presidents to serve more than one year.[4]

---

[4]Henry Harrison Cabaniss was distinctly a Southern gentleman of the old school. He had been one of the most active members of both the Southern Press Association and the Southern Publishers Association, but he appears to have dropped out of SNPA affairs after returning to the Atlanta Journal from the Augusta Chronicle. His association with the Journal was maintained until the end of his life in 1934, but not in a position that brought him to the fore. He is remembered by William Cole Jones, retired associate editor of the Journal, as "a shining example of the Old South's sociability and courtesy. He overflowed with anecdotes of quaint characters and prominent people, and abounded in genial humor. Frequently he would drop into my office and chat at length about Dickens, of whom he was a tireless reader. His personality might be summed up in Shakespeare's lines:
"'I count myself in nothing else so happy
As in a soul remembering my good friends.'"

Exploring The Field (1903-1913)

South's Thriving Cities Shower Visiting Publishers with Hospitality and Proofs of Vigor, as SNPA Seeks Fields of Greatest Usefulness to Its Slowly Expanding Membership.

THE FIRST decade of the Southern Newspaper Publishers Association history might be called exploratory. The earnest men who brought it into being in 1903 knew that concerted thought and, sometimes, co-operative action was essential to the continued healthy development of newspaper publication. How to achieve those ends offered a problem in which few of them had experience. Probably not more than half a dozen of the SNPA pioneers belonged to the American Newspaper Publishers Association and knew the techniques it had already evolved for finding facts and indicating individual or joint action. Less than half a dozen had been in the center of events out of which the Associated Press had evolved in 1900.

Familiar to all was the pattern of association activity that had been followed by the preceding Southern Press Association, Southern Publishers Association and the several State press associations. That scheme called for annual meetings, with a prepared program of topics, a sight-seeing trip (preferably on calm waters), a banquet or two, plenty of good fellowship, and a little gentle politicking over the election of officers for the ensuing year. In general, that formed the pattern of the early SNPA meetings. The South's thriving cities bid lustily for the privilege of entertaining the visiting publishers. Local publishers and chambers of commerce believed that lasting good could be derived from the widespread publicity that member newspapers would give the annual assembly. National prohibition had not yet become more than a wishful dream of great employers, and local prohibition, if it existed, went into seclusion when the newspaper people met.

Exploring The Field (1903-1913)

Twenty-five publishers were recorded as attending the third annual SNPA convention at Charleston, S.C., May 2-4, 1905. President H. H. Cabaniss and Secretary Frank P. Glass rendered pleasing reports of the association's progress at the opening session, which also received a resounding address by Mayor Rhett. His Honor's remarks, carried *in extenso* by the Charleston News & Courier and Evening Post, reviewed the city's history since its establishment in 1670, its alternating periods of prosperity and decline, its triumph over war and reconstruction, its survival of a devastating earthquake in 1886 and of the formerly perennial blocking of its magnificent harbor by the silt of its great rivers. But in 1905, the Mayor declared, Charleston's harbor received more imports than all of the Atlantic ports South of and including Norfolk. And the 20th Century was bringing many more commercial and industrial glories.

"I welcome you, therefore, to the city of the 18th and 19th centuries," Mayor Rhett concluded. "To her historic halls, her churches, and her homes, her monuments, and her knightly people. And I welcome you likewise to the city of the 20th Century, just budding into one of the nation's busiest ports, with her harbor the deepest on our South Atlantic Coast; her suburban country one of the garden spots of the world, and her people alive with confidence and energy."

President Cabaniss, in his equally eloquent and courtly response, did his best to keep the city and his members reminded that their meeting had a serious purpose. He emphasized that the association was one of business managers rather than of editors and that the work of the convention would be to discuss and attempt to solve the vexing problems confronting those upon whose shoulders the management of the newspapers rested.

Secretary Glass continued the business note by reporting on the association's 1904-1905 progress, reading a list of the topics to be discussed at the next day's session, and recommending that the membership dues be reduced. His suggestion was enthusiastically carried. When it is recalled that these dues had been fixed in 1903 at a maximum of $60 per annum, present-day observers will understand (a) that the Southern press still did not appreciate the potential field of its association; and (b) that a $5 bill remained a highly important item in Southern newspaper economics. Mr. Glass probably wished to attract new members to whom any expenditure for association membership presented a formidable obstacle.

The meeting broke up at noon for a trip around the harbor on the government steamer Wisteria, visiting historic Fort Sumter, the big coast-defense guns and the new Navy dry dock. This trip ended in time for visitors to attend the Sally League baseball game between the Charleston Sea Gulls and the Jacksonville Jays. The evening was devoted to a reception at the Commercial Club, with dancing, music and refreshments.

Back to business the next morning, the Association buckled down to the discussion of 40 topics, all of which, we are assured by newspaper accounts, received due attention. None of the reporters, alas, considered any one of these topics worthy of record for present or future readers. If minutes of this meeting were kept, they probably perished a few years later with other association records in a storm which swept Mobile.

When election of new officers came up on the agenda, Mr. Cabaniss declined a third term. He had, apparently, retired from the Augusta Chronicle and had not yet returned to Atlanta Journal, the newspaper which he had guided in its infancy and with which he would be associated until his death in 1934. His retirement brought forth one of the graceful and appreciative resolutions so often met with in Southern press annals.

Colonel J. C. Hemphill of the Charleston (S.C.) News & Courier was elected president, with G. J. Palmer, of the Houston (Texas) Post, vice-president, and Frank P. Glass, of the Montgomery (Ala.) Advertiser was elected secretary-treasurer.

The executive committee comprised: D. V. Tompkins, Charlotte Observer; T. T. Stockton, Jacksonville Times-Union; Thomas R. Waring, Charleston Evening Post; J. H. Estill, Savannah Morning News; Colonel Robert Ewing, New Orleans States; Rufus N. Rhodes, Birmingham News; Edgar M. Foster, Nashville Banner.

Exploring The Field (1903-1913)

After electing W. B. Philips of the Louisville Courier-Journal and Gilbert D. Raine, Jr., of the Memphis News-Scimitar,[1] to membership, and deciding to meet at Montgomery, Ala., in 1906, the convention ended its function with a banquet at the Hotel Charleston, with Governor Heyward as principal speaker. The banquet's decorative features included cigars tied with long white satin ribbons, upon which were reproduced the day's headlines of the Evening Post and the News & Courier, which, concluded the Post, "made the ribbons very handsome souvenirs for the publishers to take home with them."

When the SNPA gathered in Montgomery on May 15-16, 1906, entertainment features were less dominant. Mr. Glass, on his home grounds, provided a business program that included speakers of national newspaper prominence and a provocative sequence of topics. More than 50 members were reported as present in the new Exchange Hotel, then just opened, when the Acting Mayor of Montgomery and Major W. W. Screws, editor of the Advertiser and dean of Southern journalists, extended the city's welcome. The opening session was adjourned for a barbecue at Jackson's Lake, across the Alabama River, followed by a trolley ride through the city and suburbs. Business held the stage on the first evening. Secretary-Treasurer Glass reported a gratifying increase in membership and a treasury balance of $424.74. Most of the evening was given to discussion of business topics.

An address by S. S. Rogers, business manager of the Chicago Daily News and president of the American Newspaper Publishers Association, enunciated some sound newspaper philosophy.

"Advertising is one of the most important features of newspaper management," Mr. Rogers said, as quoted by the Montgomery Advertiser. "It is most important, nevertheless, that it be regarded as merely the by-product, and not the object of the newspaper. Before everything else, the owner should remember that he is publishing a

---

[1] The father of Mr. Raine was publisher of the News-Scimitar. He had only recently purchased the Morning News and the Evening Scimitar. Walter C. Johnson who had been secretary-treasurer of the News played an important part in handling many of the details incident to the merging of the two papers. Following the merger he was named business manager. Mr. Johnson recalls an invitation for the News-Scimitar to join the newly formed Southern Newspaper Publishers Association and be represented at the meeting to be held in Charleston, S. C. As he was busy organizing the affairs of the News-Scimitar, it was suggested that young Raine attend the convention.

newspaper. It is hard to remember this when the returns from readers are so small, and when advertising pays so well, as it does in the cities, it is difficult to maintain the proper balance."

One regrets that the reporter did not give more space to Mr. Rogers' wisdom, for it is certain that the able head of the ANPA did not capsule his ideas into the platitudes just quoted. Invitations had been extended also to Melville E. Stone, general manager of the Associated Press, and to General Charles H. Taylor, publisher of the Boston Globe, but it is probable that these features on the program did not materialize.

Topics discussed at the business meeting included:

Classified advertising.

Obligations of the non-advertising business community toward the press, with special reference to the legal and medical professions.

Returns from newsdealers.

Newsprint from cotton stalks, a "new process" explained by St. Elmo Massengale, then a rising advertising agent in Atlanta.

The coupon method of securing classified advertising.

Advertising agency discounts.

Effects of magazine, street-car and billboard advertising upon newspapers.

Post Office department construction of the lottery law.

With the Montgomery Commercial Club as host, the association's banquet guests heard Governor W. D. Jelks respond to the toast: "Alabama". Addresses also were made by Mr. Glass, President Hemphill, and V. H. Hanson.

The annual election resulted as follows:

President, Frank P. Glass, Montgomery Advertiser; vice-president, Edgar M. Foster, Nashville Banner; secretary-treasurer, Victor H. Hanson, Montgomery Advertiser. Executive Committee—Major J. C. Hemphill, Charleston News & Courier; Rufus N. Rhodes, Birmingham News; T. T. Stockton, Jacksonville Times-Union; George F. Milton,

EXPLORING THE FIELD (1903-1913)

Sr., Knoxville Sentinel; J. R. Gray, Atlanta Journal; and M. K. Duerson, Lynchburg News.

Norwood A. Richards, Mobile Item, and Walter Meyrick, Beaumont Enterprise, were elected to membership.

Richmond was selected as the 1907 meeting place.

Listed as attending the Montgomery meeting were:

Major Hemphill; F. P. Glass, E. S. Noble, and V. H. Hanson, Montgomery Advertiser; G. J. Palmer, Houston Post; R. L. McKenney, Macon News; J. J. Smith, Birmingham Ledger; Paul E. Rapier, Mobile Register; Edgar M. Foster, Nashville Banner; J. H. LaCoste, Charleston News & Courier; George F. Milton, Sr., Knoxville Sentinel; T. T. Stockton, Jacksonville Times-Union; R. H. McMaster and George M. Kohn, Columbia State; C. W. Ufford, Birmingham News; J. G. Morris, Charleston Post; M. K. Duerson, Lynchburg News; H. H. Cabaniss, Atlanta Journal; J. R. Ross and J. P. Caldwell, Charlotte Observer; E. W. Barrett and J. L. McRae, Birmingham Age-Herald; J. A. Davis, Albany (Ga.) Herald; C. I. Groover, Columbus Enquirer-Sun; Max Hamburger, Mobile Herald; Edward O'Connor, Mobile Item; and Horace Hood, Montgomery Journal.

If that roster is a bit short of the "fifty" reported at the opening session in Montgomery, the reporter may be pardoned for his enthusiastic exaggeration. It may not have been as great as it appears, for at this meeting there is noted the beginning of "trade" interest in SNPA gatherings. Among the outsiders introduced to the publishers were representatives of the Hoe and Goss printing press companies, as well as St. Elmo Massengale, mentioned above as the exponent of a "new" source for print paper. In years ahead, the SNPA conventions would attract notable gatherings of machinery and supply representatives.

Despite the distractions of the Jamestown Exposition, commemorating the establishment of Colonial Virginia in 1607, the SNPA made further progress toward a solid organization at its Richmond meeting, May 22-24, 1907. Again, attendance was reported as "approximately 50." Assembling in Richmond, the publishers held their business meeting aboard the steamer Pocahontas en route from Richmond to Norfolk. On the way down James River, the publishers stopped briefly at Jamestown Island and inspected the historic ruins of the first English colonial site on American soil.

Guest speakers included Medill McCormick, then an editor of the Chicago Tribune, and St. Elmo Massengale of Atlanta. Newspaper reports state that Mr. McCormick (later he would be United States Senator from Illinois) spoke on "the technical side of newspaper work." Mr. Massengale's subject was the "relation of the advertising agency to the newspaper publisher." And, again, one laments that the reporters of 1907 found no detailed account of these talks newsworthy.

As the Pocahontas slipped through Hampton Roads to her Norfolk dock, the U.S.S. Alabama (then in the 13-inch gun battleship squadron of the Atlantic Fleet) fired a 12-gun salute in honor of President Frank P. Glass.

Mr. Glass retired as president and was succeeded by Edgar M. Foster of the Nashville Banner. J. P. Caldwell, editor of the Charlotte Observer became vice-president, and Victor H. Hanson, now advanced from advertising manager to business manager of the Montgomery Advertiser, was re-elected secretary-treasurer. The executive committee was constituted with J. C. Hemphill, Charleston News & Courier; M. K. Duerson, Lynchburg News; Leland Rankin, Richmond News-Leader; Curtis B. Johnson, Knoxville Sentinel; and W. H. Jeffries, Birmingham Age-Herald.

Recognition of the Association's responsibilities appeared in the re-definition of the secretary-treasurer's duties and the assignment of a salary to the office. No sum is mentioned, but it is probable that the rate of $200 per annum was established at this meeting, to remain fixed for most of the next decade.

At this meeting also, the SNPA sorrowfully noted the final illness of Colonel J. H. Estill, editor of the Savannah Morning News. Colonel Estill, who died shortly after the meeting closed, had been associated with Southern publishers' organizations since 1880, when he became president of the Southern Press Association. His wisdom and calm judgment had guided his own generation and its successors through many an organization crisis.

EXPLORING THE FIELD (1903-1913)

Sightseeing through the Exposition grounds (a tour in which automobiles figured prominently for the first time in Southern convention annals) and a banquet at the Exposition in the evening concluded the 1907 convention.

With the energetic and witty Edgar M. Foster, business manager of the Nashville Banner, at the helm, the recorder of SNPA history looked for reports of important and original action in the sixth convention, held at Charlotte, N. C., May 19-20, 1908. Foster was then, and for many years thereafter, one of the most effective members of the association—a practical newspaper administrator who helped to frame many of the Association's major policies.

But, with the minutes of the meeting lost and only meager press reports of its actions available, the tale of 1907-1908 remains largely in the region of conjecture. By May, 1908, the country's business was still trembling from the effects of the "money panic" of the previous autumn. Undoubtedly the advertising receipts of the Southern press had suffered, even though circulation remained relatively steady. The panic was of too short duration to have caused many cancellations of newspaper subscriptions. And probably few Southern editors realized that the seed of that "bankers' panic" was located in the South. Not until the Stanley Congressional investigation in 1911 would it become known that a complex battle in Wall Street ignited the panic and had resulted in the absorption of Tennessee Coal & Iron by the United States Steel Corporation, in an era when President Theodore Roosevelt was swinging the Big Stick of anti-trust prosecution. The publishers had troubles enough of their own, and the intrigues of high finance were better screened in 1907 than in recent years.

Among the publishers' troubles on which the convention acted was the perennial problem of more and cheaper newsprint. In 1908, practically all of the newsprint used by American publishers came from domestic mills, the majority of which were located in New England and New York. Newsprint prices had been fairly stable for several years, but publishers who watched the paper industry closely knew that trouble lay ahead. Most of the domestic mills had been built near streams which provided an adequate power supply and convenient transportation for pulpwood logs. Most of them stood in or near forests which had promised an apparently inexhaustible supply of wood when the mills were built. But, with the wasteful forestry methods of the day and a steadily increasing demand for paper, the nearby forests were largely waste lands by 1907 and the mills drew their pulpwood from increasingly distant sources. The vast Canadian forests were available for development and some mills had already imported both pulpwood and woodpulp from Canadian lands. The drawback to that lay in the duty levied by the United States on such imports. Sooner or later, the publishers reasoned, the higher costs of transportation and the tariff would be added to the cost of the paper delivered to their pressrooms.

Following the lead of the American Newspaper Publishers Association, the SNPA in 1908 called upon Speaker Joseph G. Cannon and the Congress to end the delay in the enactment of the Stevens Bill, repealing the duty on woodpulp and print paper imports. That may be regarded as the opening step in a campaign of several years—a sustained effort by the publishers which took many forms and the ultimate result of which was to create, with United States capital, a great Canadian newsprint industry beyond the reach of American authority. But that's another story, to be told elsewhere in these pages.

Another action of the Charlotte convention endorsed the creation of the Appalachian and White Mountain Forest Reserves—a constructive effort initiated by Theodore Roosevelt to conserve what remained of the nation's forest resources.

J. P. Caldwell, editor of the Charlotte Observer, was elected president, succeeding Mr. Foster. Rufus N. Rhodes of the Birmingham News, was named vice-president, and Mr. Hanson was again re-elected as secretary-treasurer.

Robert W. Brown of the Louisville Times was elected chairman of the executive committee, with the following members: J. C. Hemphill, Charleston News & Courier; F. W. R. Hinman, Jacksonville Times-Union; Curtis B. Johnson, Knoxville Sentinel; Edgar M. Foster, Nashville Banner; and Fred Seely, Atlanta Georgian.

After examining the sparse record of accomplishment during the first six years of the SNPA, the critical reader might well ask whether the association had justified the hopes of its founders. An annual

Exploring The Field (1903-1913)

banquet, sight-seeing, perfunctory discussion of shop topics, adoption of resolutions with no follow-through machinery—did these constitute sufficient reason for the assembly of newspaper people from all over the South? We cannot doubt that this question arose among the publishers then. The answer must have been "yes".

The SNPA was still exploring its field. The heritage of good fellowship at annual meetings afforded an ever-widening circle of personal acquaintance. If the discussion of topics in open meeting was generally perfunctory—and not all of it was—a publisher could get down to cases with his friends in private. Every newspaper had its own collection of questions to which the publisher and his staff had found no ready answers. The public or private pooling of experience often suggested a new line of thought, a new approach, to their solution.

In the nation at large, as among newspapers, the period 1900-1910 was marked by social and economic groping. The new and gigantic aggregations of capital in industry had become an established part of American life, but many in politics and journalism realized that their power had to be controlled in the public interest. The mechanism of those controls provided most of the political thunder in the first decade of the Twentieth Century. Mr. Roosevelt shouted of "busting the trusts"; magazine publishers amassed fortunes by exposing the evils of corporate finance (and earned from Roosevelt the euphonious title of "muck-rakers"); Congress in 1907 attempted to give powerful teeth to the long dormant Interstate Commerce Commission. But in 1907, the "trusts" remained unbusted. The agricultural South and Middle West continued to groan of inequitable tariffs and still more poignantly against discriminatory freight transportation rates. In brief, the opening of the century was a period for study and discussion, not decision. Business in that decade was what military writers of later date would call "fluid", meaning that no one knew precisely what was happening at any moment or what might happen tomorrow. And that was no less true in Wall Street than it was in Chattanooga or Atlanta.

To an even greater degree that was true of the publishing business. Within the decade, new machines multiplied the mechanical capacity of newspapers. New circulation techniques were developing. New features were attracting to newspapers people who, apparently, had done no reading in their earlier years. Most important, a new species of advertiser had emerged since the century opened.

Prior to 1910, daily newspapers had published little of the new "national" advertising. Magazines had energetically promoted the idea of prestige to be gained by self-styled "national" advertising for the infant automobile industry and a growing number of packaged and branded food, drug and cosmetic products. Although the old-line patent medicine advertisers and their agencies understood the importance of local newspapers in putting a product into the hands of the consumer, the new crop of advertising agencies placed the bulk of their appropriations in the weekly and monthly magazines. Not yet understood was the necessity of keying "prestige" advertising to the retail market.

Few newspapers had taken their own medicine of advertising at that time. The minority which had employed space in trade journals claiming to reach the advertisers and advertising agencies offered circulation figures—which, with few exceptions, received small credence from the buyers of space. Sworn or audited figures on circulation belonged to the future. So did credible records of advertising volume. So did all market statistics, except the decennial census figures. The "tools" of effective advertising, as they are known in 1954, did not exist for newspapers in 1909.

All the more remarkable, then, was the action of the SNPA at its Birmingham meeting on June 15-16, 1909, in naming a "special committee to present the Southern field and its resources most attractively to the big advertisers of the North and West." That was the beginning of regional (and national) promotion of the daily newspaper as the golden key to the marketing of nationally advertised merchandise. While the extant records do not indicate who advanced this proposal and argued it into adoption, a fair guess would attribute it to one or more of the three publishers named to the special committee: James M. Thomson, New Orleans Item; A. F. Sanford, Knoxville Journal & Tribune; and Edgar M. Foster, Nashville Banner.

The idea proved to be a year or two ahead of its moment in 1909. Intensely proud as they were of the South's commercial strides, it is probable that the publishers didn't quite know how to transfer that feeling to words on paper. It is also plausible that some of the rugged

Exploring The Field (1903-1913)

individualists didn't cotton to the idea of spending their own money in an effort which might benefit others (including competitors) more than it would themselves. If the committee's labors produced no concrete result during the 1909-1910 twelve-month, the seed it planted didn't die.

That advertising itself had attained new importance in the thinking of Southern publishers is indicated by the list of 1909 convention topics:

How to get advertising, what to do with it after it is secured, how to make it most effective and valuable to the advertiser.

The attitude of the newspaper toward billboard and other outdoor advertising.

How to stimulate the reading of advertisements.

What leeway should the news department be given in free write-ups of theatrical attractions?

Elimination of objectionable advertising.

Ramifications of advertising rates.

Political advertising.

Whisky and beer advertising in prohibition states.

The association also discussed the establishment of a news bureau in Washington to gather and transmit government news and features of particular attention to Southern readers. The preoccupation with *news* that had been noted in the earlier Southern associations never lapsed. While this proposal died at birth, it foreshadowed a demand for specialized regional news that the Associated Press and other wire services would eventually obey and serve. The AP already had added another wire for Southern service and SNPA members at this meeting were asked for comments on its merits.

That questions other than those of mechanical production stirred in Southern newspaper minds of 1909 appears from these topics:

What can employers do, and how, to keep their employees loyal, satisfied and contented, working every day of each week?

Do newspaper managers generally carry liability insurance, and when employees are hurt, does the office carry the injured employee on the payroll while absent? If so, for how long?

Do members give their employees annual vacations? If so, for what period and on what conditions?

The desirability of arriving at the relative value of trades employed in newspaper offices, so that in negotiating increased wages, one class of employees may not gain an advantage over another.

We do not have a transcript of what members said on these questions. The fact of their inclusion in the program suggests that some Southern publishers stood well in advance of the day's prevailing ideas on employer-employee relationships.

Circulation problems received a whole afternoon, with spirited dispute on the relative values of comic supplements and magazine supplements as circulation builders, and the never-ending debate on the merits of voting and premium contests.

General Rufus N. Rhodes, publisher of the Birmingham News, was elected president (he would be the first SNPA head to die in his term of office). Curtis B. Johnson, already a rising figure in Southern newspaperdom, was named vice-president, and Victor H. Hanson of the Montgomery Advertiser, added another year to his long service as secretary-treasurer. To the executive committee were named:

John Ross, Charlotte Observer; A. F. Sanford, Knoxville Journal & Tribune; W. H. Jeffries, Birmingham Age-Herald; Frank G. Bell, Savannah Morning News; F. W. R. Hinman, Jacksonville Times-Union; and A. E. Clarkson, Houston Post.

Mobile was selected for the 1910 meeting-place.

Appropriate tribute was paid to the memory of General Rufus N. Rhodes, the late president, when the association met at Mobile, May 10-11, 1910, with Vice-President Curtis B. Johnson in the chair. Even though the newspapers of Mobile collaborated with the Federal government in providing extraordinary sight-seeing opportunities in the historic city, the publishers completed a down-to-earth business program.

Exploring The Field (1903-1913)

The opening business of the meeting, however, revealed again that the Southern editors and publishers had not yet arrived at full comprehension of their association's possible functions. Secretary-Treasurer Hanson ruefully reported that not one member had taken up his offer to serve as a clearing-house for employment matters. He also reported that individual newspapers had not supported the plan for advertising the South prepared by the committee appointed the previous year and endorsed by the executive committee.

It would not have been in true character for the positive Hanson to let the advertising project die on that note, and he did not. Arrangements had been made with *Printers' Ink*, he continued, for a "Southern Edition",[2] and he hoped that individual newspapers would take space in this edition at their own expense to advertise their own wares and add to Southern prestige. It was impossible, he said, to undertake any large expenditure from the small general treasury.

The opening session, held in the Vineyard of the Cawthon Hotel (one of the city's numerous scenic entertainment spots), cleaned up the topics relating to circulation practices. With a majority of those present at this session representing morning papers—others arrived later—it is not surprising that pre-dated editions of evening newspapers were frowned upon as an invasion of the morning field.

Robert W. Brown, managing editor of the Louisville Times and also representing the Courier-Journal, summarized the Southern distaste for the comic supplement: "Ordinarily, to intelligent people, it is an abomination, but the children want it and it is a necessary evil."

Mr. Brown and Frank P. Glass (who always kept his finger in the editorial pie) agreed that magazine supplements which included local features and pictures were excellent circulation builders. Mr. Brown also stressed the value of local and out-of-town society news.

Sports extras increased circulation, the majority agreed, with the reservation that in some cities the apparent increase was at the expense of earlier editions.

Mr. Hanson, who had transferred his activities from the Montgomery Advertiser to the Birmingham News, reported that the latter had

---

[2]Apparently this plan did not work out in 1910, probably for lack of adequate publisher support. After 1912, the SNPA used paid space in Printers' Ink, Editor and Publisher and other trade publications.

had excellent experience with circulation contests. So, declared Mr. Glass, had the Montgomery Advertiser.

Sight-seeing filled the remainder of the first day, with automobile trips around the city and suburbs, a dinner at the Mobile Yacht Club, and a variety of individual amusements in the evening.

Bright and early the next morning, the publishers boarded the Revenue Cutter Winona for a trip around Mobile Bay and to Fort Morgan, then a major Coast Artillery post. "Security" and "classified" had not entered the government vocabulary in 1910 and the visitors saw everything that Fort Morgan had to offer—great 12-inch rifles shoving their snouts over the parapet and dropping back into hiding, and stub-nosed mortars in the routine that would be theirs if enemy vessels risked wooden decks in the Gulf of Mexico. The visit had the blessing of Secretary of War John Dickinson, to whom the publishers addressed a graceful resolution of gratitude. The Treasury also was thanked for the courtesies of the cutter Winona.

During the leisurely cruise down Mobile Bay the association members continued their business meeting. By-laws prepared during the previous year were turned over to the executive committee with directions to make necessary amendments, and print.

Curtis B. Johnson was advanced to the presidency. Robert W. Brown, of the Louisville Times, became vice-president, and Victor H. Hanson, of the Birmingham News, reluctantly took another term as secretary-treasurer. On the new executive committee were A. F. Sanford, Knoxville Journal & Tribune, chairman; Frederick I. Thompson, Mobile Register; W. M. Clemens, Memphis News Scimitar; Mason C. Brunson, Charleston News & Courier; and Edgar M. Foster, Nashville Banner.

Vice-President Brown extended an eloquent invitation on behalf of "Marse Henry" Watterson, famed editor of the Courier-Journal, and Bruce Haldeman, its publisher, to Louisville as the 1911 meeting-place. He won out over an equally spirited plea for Knoxville by A. F. Sanford of the Journal & Tribune. Mr. Sanford settled for a year's postponement.

Although some of the publishers wanted a heavy program of business discussions, the convention cities generally were chosen on the

Exploring The Field (1903-1913)

prospect of entertainment—and Louisville offered the illustrious Pendennis Club and a superior "wine of the country", among other means of diversion.

Despite all the distractions the publishers covered considerable ground in their discussions aboard the Winona. Some of the conclusions reported in the Mobile Register's account of the meeting will indicate the relatively elementary problems that worried the newspapers four decades ago:

The circulation manager cannot afford to pay cash commissions for soliciting credit subscriptions.

Afternoon newspapers can facilitate early delivery by establishing sub-stations.

Premiums do not pay as circulation-getters because old subscribers complain of discrimination.

Newspapers should not let agencies outside of their own organization prepare and collect for special editions.

Many newspapers, among those present, declared that they were advertising their value as media.

A majority declared that they favored the flat advertising rate. (Possibly they did, in theory, but in practice few newspapers in the South or anywhere else in America then put the theory into daily use.)

Frank P. Glass reported that the Montgomery Advertiser had installed scales in its pressroom and required daily reports on white paper use from the foreman. Its close check on paper consumption had not only reduced white and printed waste, but also had recovered considerable sums from carriers for paper damaged in transport.

It was agreed that Linotype machines and presses should be depreciated, for sound accounting, at 10 per cent annually.

No SNPA member had yet installed Monotype machines, which were thought to be useful for tabulated work.

And, led by Mr. Brown of Louisville, the publishers agreed that larger salaries ought to be paid to reporters and other editorial workers.

A provocative budget of questions on classified advertising was referred to the secretary for assignment to qualified members who would answer them at the 1911 meeting.

If any of the publishers present when the SNPA met in Louisville, June 13-14, 1911, had been endowed with the veil of a prophet, he could have made his fortune in a few years. The shape of things to come was indicated in several matters that came before that meeting, which, regardless of lavish entertainment, set a fine record of business accomplishment.

The past also attained recognition when the publishers rose to return the greetings of the venerable Marse Henry Watterson, whose youth had been journalistically adventurous before most of his 1911 audience was born. Colonel Watterson had been a Confederate soldier and editor, flitting from town to town with his press, a handful of type and a bundle of paper whenever Yankee bayonets got too close. Almost the last of the old-time "personal journalists" (the South still had a few in harness), Colonel Watterson thought there was room for improvement in newspaper performance.

"One shortcoming," he said, "seems to be lack of respect for respectables. Improvement might be made even in the South, which is the last stronghold of chastity in journalism, by improving the self-respect of the newspaper."

Another journalistic great who was serving his last decade of more than half a century in journalism, Melville E. Stone, general manager of the Associated Press, also advanced some constructive criticism. He expressed regret that the trend of modern journalism was toward the trivial and inconsequential, and declared that a newspaper should do something more than amaze, excite, and amuse its readers. There is an obligation on newspapers, he said, to instruct as well as to entertain, to give serious consideration to the problems of the country and to give distinction to Journalism by having ideas and expressing them.

"There are people in this country who really want to think and their demands should be met," Mr. Stone advised. "A newspaper that is edited for mere amusement, that is filled with tittle-tattle, scandal and what is termed 'human interest' stories must prove substantially a

Exploring The Field (1903-1913)

failure. Exciting and sensational features should be treated with a proper relation to other things."[3]

Much more proximate of events to come lay in the Association's resolution favoring the ratification of reciprocity with Canada. The Association resolved:

"That we urge the Senators from the Southern States to vote for the Canadian reciprocity bill now before the Senate. We request this: First, because we believe that the reciprocity measure will prove beneficial to all the people of the United States. We also urge the Southern Senators to support the measure on account of the provisions in the bill regarding print paper and wood pulp, not because we are asking special legislation for our own benefit, but because we believe these measures to be fair to the manufacturers of print paper in this country as well as to the newspapers, for the reasons so clearly elucidated by the President in his Chicago speech. The exactions to which the newspaper publishing industry of the country has been subjected are so manifest that one of the foremost Republican opponents of the reciprocity measure, who submitted a minority report to the Senate yesterday opposing the bill, conceded that the publishers have been subjected to extortions and have been forced to conduct their business under conditions which are intolerable. This Senator, as a member of the finance committee, had heard all of the evidence submitted to that committee, and his conclusion is added evidence of the justice of this portion of the reciprocity bill."

The fate of the Canadian reciprocity move was to affect newspapers for many years of the future. The bill did pass the American Congress, including the provisions on print paper and woodpulp that the publishers desired. By American law, Canadian paper and pulp then could enter the United States free of duty. The publishers had swung a hostile or indifferent public opinion to favorable action on a measure which had originated in Canada and which had little direct appeal to the average American voter.

It was another story across the border. Sir Wilfrid Laurier, the brilliant and able Quebec statesman who had vigorously promoted reci-

---
[3]Even then, we learn from the history of the Associated Press, Mr. Stone was cautiously discussing with Kent Cooper, who would succeed to his place many years later, the broadening of the Associated Press report to bring "human interest" features into their proper relation with other things. Mr. Cooper would put the thought into action during the fabulous Nineteen-Twenties.

procity with the United States, could not put it through the Canadian Parliament and was soundly defeated on the issue in a general election. The agricultural Prairie provinces warmly favored the plan, but the railroads and Eastern industrial interests feared loss of business to the United States. Laurier's popularity waned in his native Quebec because of his "militaristic" policies—he had founded the Canadian Navy and wanted to equip Canada for the assistance of Britain in the always-impending European war. And, in many Canadian hearts at that time there prevailed the feeling that if closer relations were to be achieved with any State, it should be with Britain, rather than the U.S.A.

Consequences were not long delayed. The Newsprint Manufacturers Association, which included the principal suppliers of paper to American dailies, did not constitute a trust in any sense of the word, but it most certainly did exist for the purpose of restrictive trade agreements and the fixing of prices. With their basic raw material growing more and more expensive as domestic mills had to haul pulpwood from increasingly distant forests, with newsprint on the free list, and with the publishers manifesting the ability to influence Federal legislation, many paper manufacturers decided to shift their operations across the border as rapidly as possible. Not all did so, of course.[4]

They would soon be moving the larger part of their production into a field where Congressional investigations and the future Federal Trade Commission could not reach. Beginning with 1914, the price of newsprint would climb at first gradually and then with giddy leaps until the basic contract price stood at more than three times the level of 1911. That was one of the shadows cast by convention events of 1911.

Another was an economic-ethical discussion in which leading parts were assumed by Victor H. Hanson, Edgar M. Foster, and Frank P. Glass.

[4]The Great Northern Paper Company, at East Millinocket, Maine, belonged to the manufacturer's association, but followed divergent operating and sales practices in several important respects. Its forestry policies had been prudently intelligent—40 years later, it is still cutting trees on the same Maine woodlands it harvested then. On the sales side, it apparently valued the friendship of its customers equally with their dollars. Great Northern did not join the exodus to Canada. It continued to serve many important Southern dailies throughout the next troubled decade, with mutual satisfaction.

Exploring The Field (1903-1913)

Mr. Hanson proposed that advertising of whiskey and beer be charged 50 per cent more than the commercial advertising rate. Mr. Foster emphatically disagreed. If such advertising is objectionable, he contended, the publisher should reject it outright instead of soothing his conscience by a penalty rate.

Prohibition sentiment was growing through America in those days, under the able generalship of the Anti-Saloon League—sponsored by earnest church people and financed by large employers for obvious reasons. Many publishers and editors who did not reject alcohol in their own lives favored more stringent regulations of the liquor traffic, even to the extent of prohibition, as good public policy. Rejection of liquor advertising or penalty rates sometimes implemented that policy.

Mr. Glass joined the critical chorus with a blow at fraudulent patent medicine advertising. Newspapers should refuse advertisements of nostrums with claims that taxed ordinary credulity, he said, and they should also reject "suggestive" advertisements. And an unnamed advertising agency representative told the meeting that advertisements of a medical nature had declined 60 per cent in volume during the three years just closed.

These disapproving glances at medical and liquor advertisements may be taken as early tokens of the reform movement which would sweep the publishing business within the next five years. For more than a generation patent medicine advertising had furnished publishers in many small and large cities with a large part of their cash income. These shrewd merchandisers contracted for newspaper space in large quantities. In earlier years (and possibly as late as 1911) some of them bought more than they needed and sold the excess to other advertisers at a generous profit. As a general rule, they paid the publishers a sizeable sum in advance of publication, and, also generally, their purchases were at less than card rates.

Reference has been made to the emergence of a new class of national advertisers between 1900 and 1910. These advertisers were, indeed, a different breed of cats than the merchants of laxatives, "cures", tonics (which, with a mighty alcoholic content, brought contentment to sufferers in prohibition areas), and a wide array of remedies for "female weakness" and general debility in the male.

Newspaper solicitors who called on the motor manufacturers and other purveyors of class merchandise in the new dispensations, got a cold reception. In cities all over the country, solicitors told the publishers that newspaper columns must be "cleaned up" if newspapers wished to participate in the new fortunes then being spent in magazines. These new and ethical advertisers wanted no association with the shabby patent medicine vendors. Many of them didn't care to offer their wares in proximity to liquor or beer advertising. So the publishers craving this unattainable revenue had sound economic reasons backing ethical revulsion to their old medicine friends. The latter had been also under the fire of the new Federal Food & Drug Administration, led by Dr. Harvey W. Wiley, for the past three years. It was, indeed, "time for a change."

Still another forecast, of somewhat longer range, was that of President Curtis B. Johnson in his opening speech. Mr. Johnson possessed a sinewy grasp of business fundamentals and he marshalled an array of statistics for his fellow publishers and their guests to demonstrate the commercial progress already attained in the South.

The South's great development during the past 40 years and the great change in money values make it pointless to quote Mr. Johnson's figures in this record. He exulted in the construction of two dams, near Chattanooga and Knoxville, at a total cost of $6,000,000 to produce an aggregate 85,000 horsepower, but he could not be expected to visualize the tremendous water-power developments that the next three decades would bring to the industrial and rural South. Nor could he foresee that the 1910 value of Southern farm products (nearly $2,000,000,000) would be quadrupled before 1950, and that Texas alone in 1950 would produce greater crop values than were credited to the whole South when he spoke at Louisville.

Calling upon his colleagues to promote and share in this material advance he concluded:

"The opportunity is now ripe for us to look to the future with believing eyes, and, by expanding editorial and news departments, to cope with this general progress and make Southern newspaperdom the peer of the entire American press. No great work has ever been accomplished without honest effort. We cannot instill confidence in our greatness unless we believe in it ourselves. There must be unanimity of purpose if we are to advance rapidly. The promotion of the South as a whole should be the ambition of all."

Another straw in the winds of the future came in the speech of George C. Hitt, business manager of the Indianapolis Star, who averred that the public should be informed about the management and conduct of newspapers.

"The greatest asset of a newspaper is its character," he said. "A newspaper should have a character which will stand the lime-light. There should be no deceit and no false statements or attitudes. The man who tells an untruth about the circulation of a newspaper is no better than the man who uses shortweight scales."

A little more than a year later, Mr. Hitt's principle would be enacted into Federal law, requiring newspapers to publish semi-annual sworn statements of their circulation and ownership. Little opposition to this corrective measure appeared either in the daily or newspaper trade press. Newspapers, in fact, gave marked and indispensable support to advertiser and agency efforts to go beyond the legal requirements of sworn circulation within the next two years. And in 1914 the Audit Bureau of Circulations would arrive, to unite and supplant the earlier organizations, and, with broad newspaper support, to provide the long-desired accurate measurement of newspaper circulations.

The 1911 record is disappointingly bare of reference to the newspaper advertising of the South that had been proposed in the two preceding conventions. Curtis Johnson's address demonstrated both the need and the opportunity for united exploitation—but, as has been noted before, the novelty of the co-operative idea and the well-developed individualism of publishers retarded the project. Within a few years, however, it would attain creditable dimensions.

Robert W. Brown, Louisville Times, was elected president. Victor H. Hanson, Birmingham News, was rewarded for his long service as secretary-treasurer by advancement to the vice-presidency, and George W. Brunson, Greenville (S.C.) News, became secretary-treasurer.

The executive committee included: W. M. Clemens, Memphis News-Scimitar; Frederick I. Thompson, Mobile Register; Curtis B.

Johnson, Knoxville Sentinel; A. F. Sanford, Knoxville Journal & Tribune; F. W. R. Hinman, Jacksonville Times-Union; and Robert S. Jones, Asheville Citizen.

An atmosphere electric with the "do something" spirit attended the tenth annual SNPA convention at Knoxville, June 4-5, 1912. Newspapers and local leaders took full advantage of the newspaper meeting to gain support for the National Conservation Exposition, scheduled for Knoxville in 1913. And the Association itself, stronger by the addition of 20 new members in the previous year, stepped out resolutely in its own behalf.

Speakers at the annual banquet pulled out all stops in their missionary work for the Knoxville area and the Conservation Exposition. The exposition, nominally national in scope, had as its special intent the development of the South along lines designed to make its resources perpetual sources of wealth. The SNPA endorsed the project, urged its support by all commercial bodies in Southern cities and States, and appealed to Southern members of Congress to pass an appropriation bill of $400,000 for Federal participation.

Possibly energized by the dynamism of its hosts, the Association acted upon its oft-discussed campaign of advertising the South. A committee headed by J. R. Holliday of the Atlanta Constitution proposed that the Association use its own funds and supplement them by calling upon the membership, if necessary, for an effective all-South promotion campaign. His committee members included Curtis B. Johnson, Knoxville Sentinel; John A. Park, Raleigh Times; F. C. Withers, Columbia State; and J. B. Wintersmith, Louisville Courier-Journal.

The committee's report was adopted, calling for the expenditure of $400 for a campaign in *Printers' Ink*, and authorizing the executive committee to spend not more than $750 for additional advertising of the region. The germ planted in 1909 had at last become a plant—not a giant Sequoia by any standard, but a living entity which would grow and prove to many publishers that they, too, could prosper by advertising.

The publishers addressed Congress also on the subject of postal rates and their resolution is quoted here:

Exploring The Field (1903-1913)

"RESOLVED, that the members of the Southern Newspaper Publishers Association, in convention assembled, express themselves as unalterably opposed to the Postmaster General's recommendation to Congress, which proposed to increase the second-class postage rate on newspapers from one cent to two cents a pound.

"RESOLVED FURTHER, that each member of the Association be requested to write the Congressmen and Senators in his State and urge them to compass the defeat of the recommendation."

That was in 1912—a year in which the United States government spent a total of $689,881,000 and took in $692,609,000, according to the World Almanac. Then, as now, the Post Office piled up an annual deficit, but several years more would pass before the publishers, under SNPA prodding, would ask how the Post Office kept its books. The 1912 recommendation to Congress of a 100 per cent increase in second-class rates was the first of many attempts to make newspapers pay a larger share of postal costs. The SNPA was to be a powerful force in keeping Congress aware of the purposes for which second-class postage had been created and in holding rate increases within tolerable bounds.

The Association marked by resolution its respect for the late Major J. P. Caldwell, editor of the Charlotte Observer, who had been its president in 1908-1909.

Victor H. Hanson, Birmingham News, was elected president, A. F. Sanford, Knoxville Journal & Tribune, vice-president, and George W. Brunson, Greenville News, secretary-treasurer (re-elected). To the executive committee were named: Robert W. Brown, Louisville Times; F. W. R. Hinman, Jacksonville Times-Union; Edgar M. Foster, Nashville Banner; Daniel D. Moore, New Orleans Times-Democrat; Curtis B. Johnson, Knoxville Sentinel; J. R. Holliday, Atlanta Constitution; W. M. Clemens, Birmingham News; A. R. Holderby, Richmond Journal; G. J. Palmer, Houston Post; R. S. Jones, Asheville Citizen; Elmer E. Clarke, Little Rock Arkansas Democrat; James J. Smith, Birmingham Ledger; and F. C. Withers, Columbia State.

It will be seen that the executive committee had been increased from the seven provided in the original organization. The 13 members of the 1912-13 committee represented eleven of the 12 States then in the Association. No Oklahoma newspaper had yet been admitted and West Virginia was not included in SNPA territory until 1923.

New members elected during the 1912 meeting were Columbia (S.C.) Record, Nashville Democrat, Augusta Herald, Raleigh Times, Bristol (Va.-Tenn.) Herald-Courier; Tampa Tribune, Little Rock Democrat, and New Orleans Daily States. Since Colonel Robert Ewing of the Daily States had attended the first meeting of the SNPA in Atlanta, helped to draft the plan of organization, and served on the first executive committee, it seems probable that the paper had dropped its membership during the decade.

In any case, New Orleans won the 1913 convention in a brief contest with Norfolk, offering not only its own famous attractions but the prospect of a trip to the newly opened Panama Canal as bait.

A good time was had by all in New Orleans. That's an inescapable conclusion after reading what the Daily Picayune and the Evening Item wrote of the publishers' meetings. Even the reporters enjoyed spoofing the visiting publishers, noting, for instance, that the second day's session on January 17, 1913, started two hours late. Due to slow trains, a number of the publishers did not arrive in time for the convention's opening on January 16, and the first morning session was devoted entirely to the affairs of the Southwestern Association of the Associated Press.

Even though AP family affairs form no part of this chronicle, it might be noted that Charles Patrick Joseph Mooney, managing editor of the Memphis Commercial Appeal, put the AP show on the road with this remark:

"I have no serious complaints to make, except—."

Then he proceeded to demand that the AP furnish him the news, all the news, regardless of what it cost. Speaking of Associated Press correspondents and editors throughout the country, he said:

"Instead of getting the news, they are checking up wires and figuring where postage stamps can be saved. Now, we want the news; we want it as cheaply as we can get it, but we want it."

Of interest as minor landmarks in newspaper progress were reports that the AP was planning to send complete box scores of all major

Exploring The Field (1903-1913)

league baseball games with the opening of the season, and a complaint from an evening paper member that early Saturday markets crowded important news off the wire. The AP management representatives also reported that a new trunk wire had been set up between Louisville and New Orleans, cutting out the relay at Atlanta.

No afternoon session was held on January 16, because of the press of social functions arranged by the hospitable Orleanians.

Approximately 150 newspaper people were present on January 17, when the two Associations resumed business sessions, according to the New Orleans newspapers. Although the Daily Item reporter hinted that some of the members had kept unduly late hours the previous evening, there is no sign of prevalent ill health in the discussions.

Responding to an inquiry by George M. Kohn, representing *Printers' Ink,* the Association voted to continue to buy one advertisement monthly in that publication. Apparently no report on this activity was rendered at the convention.

The question of medical advertising still provoked heated interest.

"The big, clean newspapers are getting on a magazine basis," said James M. Thomson, publisher of the New Orleans Item. He declared that the Item was black-listing patent medicine advertising.

John Stewart Bryan, publisher of the Richmond Times Dispatch, said that his newspaper had ceased to solicit whisky advertising and was publishing very few advertisements for such products. He added that "beauty hints typed to resemble news" had also been eliminated. G. J. Palmer, business manager of the Houston Post, noting that readers should be credited with intelligence, asserted that "no newspaper wants to carry fraudulent advertising."

Frank P. Glass, of the Birmingham News, inquired whether any newspaper accepted pay for a fraudulent advertisment after it had published such an advertisement inadvertently. "A score arose and gave him the proper answer," wrote the flippant reporter for the Daily Item.

Col. Robert Ewing, of the Daily States, and J. R. Gray, of the Atlanta Journal, agreed that commissions should not be paid for local advertisements.

Clark Howell of the Atlanta Constitution informed the members that the competing newspapers of Atlanta had discovered the virtues of unity when their pressmen struck in sympathy with the striking pressmen of Chicago. Similar unity would prevail after the convention, he said, when the Atlanta newspaper business managers intended to act in concert on advertising rates. How this concord would be arranged the convention did not learn. The meeting adjourned at 1:30, under the pleading of "Uncle Dan" Moore, of the Daily Picayune, chairman of local arrangements. The time had come for a luncheon at the Country Club, followed by a boatride around the harbor. In the evening, the members were guests of the Falstaffians Ball at the French Opera—one of the great social events of the New Orleans winter season.

A. F. Sanford of the Knoxville Journal and Tribune was named president, and was succeeded as vice-president by F. W. R. Hinman of the Jacksonville Times-Union. William M. Clemens of the Birmingham News was elected secretary. The executive committee comprised: Curtis B. Johnson, Knoxville Sentinel; Robert S. Jones, Asheville Citizen; Edgar M. Foster, Nashville Banner; Victor H. Hanson, Birmingham News; George W. Brunson, Greenville News; Daniel D. Moore, New Orleans Picayune; Elmer E. Clarke, Little Rock Arkansas Democrat; G. J. Palmer, Houston Post; Walter C. Johnson, Chattanooga News; James M. Thomson, New Orleans Item; R. W. Brown, Louisville Times; and A. R. Holderby, Richmond Journal.

What might be called "unfinished business" of the New Orleans convention came before the executive committee at its meeting in Birmingham on November 17, 1913.

The Committee was not altogether happy with its venture into association advertising. True, 15 of the 18 pages arranged for had been published; of the amounts pledged by the members interested, $745 had been paid to the Association, leaving a balance unpaid of $210. *Printers' Ink* had been paid $650 of the sum collected. The committee voted to notify *Printers' Ink*, "without any reflection on *Printers' Ink* or the campaign", that it would have to collect the rest of the money, "that the SNPA, as an association, cannot lend itself to the collection of accounts for any particular trade publication."

Exploring The Field (1903-1913)

Then the committee went into a lengthy discussion of the proper method of advertising the South. A motion by Victor Hanson, seconded by Walter C. Johnson, of the Chattanooga News, called for the appointment of a new committee of five to work out a promotion and publicity plan. Upon its adoption, Curtis B. Johnson was named chairman, with authority to select his own associates. This committee would meet in Knoxville soon after the New Year.

That was one vital turning point in the SNPA annals. With a year's experience in association advertising, financed by the pledges of individual members, the SNPA got down to formulation of a definite plan of advertising the South. This event also marked the initial association activity of Walter C. Johnson. His name would henceforth appear continuously on SNPA letterheads for more than 40 years.

Another vital crisis in the Association's activity arose with the action of the executive committee on the 1914 convention. W. L. Halstead of the Atlanta Constitution sat with the committee by invitation. He was requested to consult with his Atlanta associates as to whether March 16-17, 1914, would be satisfactory dates for the meeting in Atlanta.

Next, the committee declared that it believed entertainment features in Atlanta should be so arranged as to leave the hours from 10:00 A.M. to 5:00 P.M. each day free for business sessions, that the actual business of the convention should not be subordinated to social features. The committee also commented favorably on Victor Hanson's suggestion that papers be prepared dealing with subjects of live interest in the making of newspapers, in advance of the Atlanta convention.

With those decisions, substantially made effective in March at Atlanta, the Southern Newspaper Publishers Association began a new era. The time of "exploring the field" for useful functions was over. The publisher members could now see the road that their trade association must travel. Meeting only once a year in convention, they had at last determined that no precious moment of the annual meeting should be wasted in amusement. The famous hospitality of Southern cities would henceforth be extended after business hours.

Daily Newspapers Mature

Southern Press is Strongly Represented in Nationally Organized Efforts to Reform Circulation Abuses and Improve Availability of Daily Newspapers for National Advertising.

THE SOUTHERN Newspaper Publishers Association officers knew that newspapers stood on the threshold of a new phase of existence when they called for "strictly business" in the Atlanta convention. They did not know, and could not have known, that 1914 would be a fateful year, not only in newspaper operation, but in the history of the nation and the world. It may be said, with truth, that the years 1901-1913 belong in the Nineteenth Century; what happened in 1914 and thereafter makes earlier events almost irrelevant to this tale of present-day journalism.

When the publishers met at the Ansley Hotel, Atlanta, on March 16-17, 1914, President Alfred F. Sanford fretted in a Knoxville hospital, recovering from an appendectomy. Secretary-Treasurer William M. Clemens was confined to his Birmingham home by a minor ailment. Both prepared annual reports, which were read, respectively, by Vice-President F. W. R. Hinman and by A. E. Clarkson, of the Houston Post, acting secretary.

The President put into concrete forms the results of more than a decade's trial and error by the Association—the decision upon definite fields in which it would operate profitably and without duplicating the work of other publishers' associations. The most immediate need, he found, was presentation of a four-point program to potential newspaper advertisers:

First—emphasize the growing wealth, resources and purchasing power of the South.

Daily Newspapers Mature

Second—emphasize to newspaper advertisers not in the South that they are overlooking a great field.

Third—Demonstrate to magazine advertisers that general magazine conditions do not apply to the South; even if they use newspapers nowhere else in the United States, they should do so in the South.

Fourth—Work out a plan whereby Southern local dealers handling nationally advertised goods can be induced to co-operate with Southern publishers by advising manufacturers that they will find it profitable to use Southern newspapers in preference to relying entirely on magazines, and urging the newspaper policy on those whose goods they handle.

As a strategic program, that was sound but elementary, even in 1914. The report of the Secretary-Treasurer would reveal that the Association, as then organized, did not possess the tactical resources to execute even that simple program effectively.

Mr. Clemens' report noted the policy on collection of assessments for the advertising campaign, reported in the previous chapter. He added that if the Association, as a body, undertook a general campaign, the Secretary's office should handle collections and remittances. He advised the members that if the work of the SNPA was to become broader and more efficient, as it ought to be, the Secretary should be "a man whose time is worth something." He did not believe that the $200 allotted for the Secretary's salary would attract such a man.

Despite his discontent with the salary, Mr. Clemens had attempted to expand the association's service during his term. He had asked members to furnish data on departmental costs, trying to arrive at some compilation of cost of composition per page and the relation of that factor to contract rates for advertising. Few newspapers responded.

Many publishers undoubtedly wanted this information and could have used it effectively, but few kept their accounts in a form which made it easily available. The Inland Daily Press Association had made a similar effort in 1911 and a decade later would make statistics of this nature one of its major services to members.[1] Its early effort had also produced little.

---
[1] The Inland (1887-1950) by Elizabeth Lamb (Page 20)

THE SOUTH AND ITS NEWSPAPERS

Mr. Clemens also sought to give the SNPA a basic fund of information on labor matters, inquiring of members in a postcard questionnaire which of their departments were unionized. In his personal experience, Mr. Clemens had learned that this information, of itself, had little value in wage scale negotiations. It was no more than a start toward equipping the Southern publishers with economic information of inter-city and regional value in dealing with the major unions, which had well organized information services. Mr. Clemens considered that the Southern publishers would do well to supplement by their own efforts the work of the special standing committee of the ANPA, then directed by H. N. Kellogg.

Two New York City executives appeared at the Atlanta convention —both of them men of unusual distinction in metropolitan journalism. The first speaker was Jason Rogers, publisher of the New York Globe;[2] the second, Don C. Seitz, business manager of the New York World.

Mr. Rogers covered the whole gamut of newspaper problems in his 40-minute talk. A breezy, humorous speaker, he packed plenty of good practical advice into his anecdotal address. For example:

"The mere presentation of news is not enough for present-day success; the newspapers which have made the most headway during recent times have given the people what they want in the way of light entertainment, interesting information, and a complete summary of the news."

Getting to the subject in which his audience had an immediate vital concern, Mr. Rogers said:

"In order to place the matter of co-operation clearly before you, I want to state that United Newspapers (which I organized until it

---

[2]Jason Rogers was *sui generis*. Unlike most men bearing the title of publisher at the time, he owned no stock in the New York Globe. His genius lay principally in promotion. He pioneered many efforts to make newspapers more effective as advertising media—groups which offered audited circulation at a joint package rate; a sliding scale of rates, based on day-to-day circulation guarantees; advertising columns purged of undesirable copy. He wrote several books setting forth principles of newspaper management and accounting, which remained standard, and without competition, for many years. In 1919 he took the lead in organizing the Publishers' Buying Corporation, which furnished newsprint to small city publishers during the post-war runaway paper market. During the period 1914-1920, he was a perpetual candidate for president of the American Newspaper Publishers Association, but the conservative majority of that body would have no part of his "radical" leadership.

had a membership of over 400 papers) was subsequently merged with the Daily Newspaper Club and National Newspapers to form the Bureau of Advertising of the American Newspaper Publishers Association. . . . I, for one, believe that the work of developing more advertising is the most important function the ANPA can perform . . . . At the present time, the Bureau of Advertising represents a potential (income) of about $30,000 a year, every dollar of which is spent for the preparation of advertising talks, the gathering and distribution of information, and conferring with advertisers regarding prospective campaigns. If sufficient additional newspapers become subscribers to raise the revenue by $20,000 or $30,000 more per year, its efficiency would be so much greater."[3]

Hopping to his other pet hobby, audited circulation, Mr. Rogers combined history with advocacy of his latest organization for the industry—the Gilt Edge Newspapers.

"This," he said, "is a simple matter of gathering together quarterly statements of circulation, subject to verification, in a summary which is mailed to some 4,000 general advertisers and agencies. The cost is $5 per year per paper. It is open to any newspaper which will sign the plan pledging itself to support the policy adopted as the basis of organization. When the Advertisers' Audit Association is fully organized the Gilt Edge Newspapers will probably recognize it as the single authoritative auditing body to verify the circulations of its members. This new organization will do away with the necessity of sending out the numerous and varied statements demanded by the different agencies; it completely eliminates the directory makers and in many other ways makes for efficiency and economy."

The Advertisers' Audit Association referred to by Mr. Rogers was one of the abortive efforts which preceded the organization of the Audit Bureau of Circulations in 1914. His own Gilt Edge Newspapers

---

[3] Mr. Rogers correctly estimated the potential value to newspapers of the Bureau of Advertising, which had been created at the ANPA convention the previous April. During the next two decades, it performed well on a limited budget. It was, unquestionably, a major force in gaining recognition of the daily newspaper as an effective medium for national advertisers and in furnishing newspapers with statistical ammunition against magazine competition. By 1935, however, the spectacular rise of radio and newspaper losses during the Great Depression, compelled the adoption of new theories and new methods, backed by adequate finance. During the 1940's, the Bureau was for the first time performing to the full the functions which Jason Rogers wished to give it in 1914.

was another auxiliary effort to unite newspapers with advertisers and advertising agencies in a group which would render reliable audits of newspaper circulation.

Other speakers at the 1914 SNPA meeting had their doubts on these early auditing efforts. Some charges were made, without evidence, that auditors were ignorant or dishonest in their relations with newspapers belonging to the A.A.A. And some publishers considered that the semi-annual affidavits of circulation required by the Post Office should be sufficient for the advertisers. Mr. Rogers argued convincingly that the audits of the new Bureau, as planned, would give newspapers far greater advantages than would be present in a mere affidavit of gross circulation. Mr. Rogers also offered the Southern publishers the privilege of printing the daily front page "advertising talks" written for the New York Globe by William C. Freeman—an example of the "Stone Age period" of newspaper promotion, but considered effective by advertising leaders in 1914.

Don C. Seitz, a man from Maine who had come through the editorial departments of several large and small newspapers to become the effective top man of the New York World, still considered himself an editorial man despite his title of business manager. He had been the confidant of Joseph Pulitzer during the great publisher's active association with the World's direction and he had kept the absent and ill Pulitzer in touch with administration during the last 18 years of his life. Not yet had he attained fame as biographer and historian,[4] but he was recognized throughout the nation as a thoroughly competent newspaperman.

Mr. Seitz laid down the dictum that "an editorial ideal cannot conflict with good business if the office is honestly and properly managed. If you haven't got a good editor, you can't have a good paper; if you haven't got a good paper, you can't get circulation; and if you haven't circulation you can't have any business; therefore, the beginning and the end, the Alpha and Omega, of a newspaper shop is a good editor. It's the things the reporters write and the things you have the courage to print that make the paper."

---

[4]Seitz wrote authoritative biographies of Joseph Pulitzer and Horace Greeley, also of General Braxton Bragg, C.S.A., and a little-known work, "The Also Rans," men who missed election to the Presidency of the United States. The biographies of Pulitzer and Greeley are on file in the Southern Newspaper Library at Chattanooga.

Daily Newspapers Mature

In that connection Mr. Seitz paid tribute to his audience.

"You gentlemen in the South," he said, "operate in the most delicate field in the world for newspapers. You are in sensitive communities, with time-honored habits, not all of them good habits. You have to contend against those habits, against fierce politics, strange antagonisms which do not exist in the North, and I marvel at the way you have overcome them and the way newspapers have grown in the Southland in the last ten years. It proves that there must have been somebody with courage and ideals, who could stand by a purpose, and get out a paper under difficult financial conditions, against public opinion until you changed most of that opinion, until you softened the country, made it less suspicious and broader-minded. I have read editorials in Southern newspapers in the last two or three years that would have led to a great deal of difficulty twenty years earlier. That shows that communities realize newspapers aren't solely a business affair, that they stand for something living, a living purpose that has meaning. Otherwise they could not exist."

From Mr. Seitz's inspirational heights, the convention turned to the practicalities of promoting classified and circulation. Many Southern papers at that time carried little classified advertising and they naturally cast green eyes toward the bulging want ad columns of those that did. One publisher related that his competitor offered a 30-cent half-pound box of chocolates as a premium for every 25-cent want ad—but had brought about no bull market in candies. The consensus was that such schemes generally cost more than they produced.

As a general rule, classified advertising departments of the SNPA membership operated with a minimum of expense and personnel. Edgar Foster of the Nashville Banner, reported that three girls did nothing but take want ads by telephone (a novelty in 1914) and that carrier boys collected for the ads when they delivered the next day's paper. The boys received a nickel for each 25-cent want ad collection. Losses were negligible, Mr. Foster said. Mr. Hinman reported that the Jacksonville Times-Union paid a man $15 a week to collect want ad charges, which sometimes amounted to $60 or $75 a day.

Back to the truth in advertising crusade, Marshall Ballard of the New Orleans Item related that the paper had gained a number of reputable national advertising accounts after establishing a code which eliminated most of its patent medicine advertising. Advertising rates on national copy had been increased 10 cents a line, he said, and, although linage was slightly off from the previous year, money income was running 15 to 20 per cent higher. Revenue lost by dropping the medical copy, Mr. Ballard estimated, was $27,000 to $30,000.

Another editor, M. W. Connolly of the Memphis News-Scimitar, related that his paper had eliminated liquor advertising to the amount of about $100,000 over a four-year period, in addition to much of its profitable patent-medicine advertising. Although readers apparently approved, Mr. Connolly could point to no other gain by the reform.

Not all the publishers gave unqualified approval to the summary ouster of the old proprietary medicine stand-bys. George J. Auer, advertising manager of the Atlanta Georgian, thought that the reform movement backed by the Associated Advertising Clubs of America should have the support of all publishers, as a matter of good business. But W. T. Anderson of the Macon Telegraph (always a strong-minded dissenter from the fad of the moment) didn't go along. He thought nobody suffered by the advertising of good whisky, and he saw no reason to throw out the advertising of all proprietary medicines because some offended. He was for exercise of the same judgment in the advertising department that the public expected of the editorial department, with one code of ideals prevailing for the whole paper.

Another man who often demonstrated in SNPA counsels that he didn't think in current slogans was A. E. Clarkson of the Houston Post. He believed there had been "entirely too much talk" about disreputable advertising. He thoroughly favored censorship of advertising claims and the refusal of advertising that might mislead readers, but, he said:

"I have a great deal of respect for the publisher who quietly refuses to accept certain advertising because, for any reason, he deems it improper to place before his readers. I don't appreciate nearly so much the publisher who takes column after column of space, telling how good he is, when his real purpose is to discredit his competitor. In trying to do this, he discredits advertising as a whole."

J. R. Holliday of the Atlanta Constitution agreed with Mr. Clarkson.

Another Atlantan of long distinction in the SNPA brought the meeting back to the warm subject of audited circulation. Enthusiastically, Charles D. Atkinson of the Journal described the new day in advertising, with special reference to the organization of the Audit Bureau of Circulations, then in progress.

"The idea is progressive," declared Mr. Atkinson. "The plan is feasible. The possible good to be accomplished is great. The question marks are as to details of operation, cost to newspapers, salaries of officers, perquisites of promoters, and adequacy of newspaper representation upon the board of control. Approaching these, as they surely will, with mutual confidence, and the common purpose to make the purchase of newspaper space as fair and as easy as the buying of postage stamps, there should be no serious doubt as to the value of such an audit association, alike to publishers of newspapers and to users of advertising space. The Atlanta Journal has signed an application for membership."

So, it shortly developed, had a number of other SNPA members, some with misgivings. Publishers who have gone through the frequent economy waves of the past 40 years may find it hard to credit that major Southern newspapers believed that 15 per cent unpaid circulation was a proportion that advertisers should accept and pay for as a necessary element of newspaper production. Several publishers objected that the proposed ABC audits would deprive them of credit for unpaid copies sent to correspondents, advertisers, city employees, etc. But, it must be remembered that newsprint in 1914 cost about $40 a ton on the publisher's sidewalk, and that few publishers had ever before closely analyzed their circulation figures.

Generally akin to the idea of improving the effectiveness of newspaper advertising, but new to SNPA discussions, was the suggestion by Walter C. Johnson, the young and progressive general manager of the Chattanooga News, that newspapers should work closely with retail dealers. So-called merchandising co-operation had been standard newspaper practice for many years, with numerous temporary abuses, but in 1914 it was practically brand-new in the South. Its ramifications would fill many a page of future SNPA proceedings.

Of similar intent was a paper submitted by James H. Allison, then advertising manager of the Nashville Tennesseean-American. This paper featured a column in its Sunday edition, called "The Firing Line" and addressed to traveling salesmen, manufacturers and wholesalers. In addition to developing interest in the paper's advertising columns for the wares made and distributed by its readers, the column produced a considerable volume of small-space copy from jobbers and wholesalers in Nashville area.

With the decks cleared of topics, the meeting buckled down to its principal business—the formulation of a policy of advertising the South. The committee appointed the previous November and the membership as a whole at last realized that this task could not be done in desultory fashion. Mr. Halstead's lengthy report boiled down to a few simple facts:

The previous year's campaign had not been adequate. It didn't tell the story that all of them knew could be told. Granted that any advertising was better than none at all, Southern newspapers could get better value than they had received by spending money to learn definite facts upon which convincing copy could be based. The committee had no plan to present, at the moment. It did suggest that an advertising fund be raised, with members contributing $5.00 for each thousand of their newspaper's circulation. With a total circulation of about 1,000,000 for all SNPA member papers, it should be possible to raise $5,000. Of this $1,000 could be spent for research, paying an experienced part-time man for the job. The remainder could be used to buy space in *Printers' Ink, Editor & Publisher, The Fourth Estate* and other trade journals which claimed to reach the national advertiser. A suggestion that some money be spent on broadsides or circulars to be distributed by individual members ran into stiff opposition.

After an unusually thorough discussion, the Association voted to continue the committee, with instructions to prepare a plan for submission to the membership by mail, with its recommendations for assessments on individual members. When Victor Hanson called for a show of hands by those present, twenty-two newspapers signified their approval, with no negative votes.

Daily Newspapers Mature

The idea of selling the Southern newspapers as an advertising "package" received brief discussion, but was considered impractical. For the present, it was enough to put advertisers on notice that the South offered many profitable and largely unexploited markets.

Then the members got into a lengthy but amicable wrangle on the question of recognizing Southern advertising agencies. The ANPA had for several years policed this field effectively, requiring strict credit qualifications before recognizing an agency as entitled to commission from newspapers. The SNPA did not set up any such stringent code, but on an exchange of opinions and information on advertising agencies which operated in Southern cities, compiled a list of about a dozen to which it suggested SNPA members extend commission privileges. It was all extremely informal, probably unnecessary in view of the ANPA activity that covered the whole country, and it would involve the SNPA in unforeseen legal difficulties a decade later.

F. W. R. Hinman, publisher of the Jacksonville Times-Union, who had presided at the Atlanta meeting, was named president. The able and active W. R. Halstead, of the Atlanta Constitution, was rewarded for his labors by election as vice-president. William M. Clemens of the Birmingham News again became secretary-treasurer. The executive committee was elected as follows: A. R. Holderby, Jr., Richmond Journal; Robert S. Jones, Asheville Citizen; A. E. Clarkson, Houston Post; Elmer E. Clarke, Little Rock Arkansas Democrat; Walter C. Johnson, Chattanooga News; D. D. Moore, New Orleans Times-Picayune; A. F. Sanford, Knoxville Journal and Tribune; Edgar M. Foster, Nashville Banner; Victor H. Hanson, Birmingham News; W. T. Anderson, Macon Telegraph; Curtis B. Johnson, Knoxville Sentinel; George A. McClellan, Jacksonville Metropolis.

Asheville, N. C., was selected as the 1915 meeting place. No one placed any significance on that choice in 1914, but it marked another milestone in SNPA progress. Henceforth the Association would do no more "shopping around" for its convention seats, with rival cities holding out tempting offers of entertainment. With one exception, all meetings for the next ten years would be held in Asheville. Isolated from metropolitan distractions amid the grandeur of the Great Smoky Mountains, the bustling little city let Nature purvey its entertainment.

Less than six months after the publishers departed from Atlanta, a fanatic's bullet in distant Bosnia ignited a war that changed the face of civilization. Even before the armies clashed on the Marne and the Danube, American business trembled in bewilderment and shock. Plans for expansion and promotion gathered dust for many months, and among them lay the optimistic program of the SNPA for organized advertising of the Southland.

Another madman's bullet had deprived the SNPA of its president a few months before the 1915 convention, which met at Grove Park Inn, Asheville, on June 14 and 15. F. W. R. Hinman, publisher of the Jacksonville Florida Times-Union, had embarked on the Clyde Liner Mohawk for a business trip to New York, and was strolling on deck when a maniac shot and killed him. Several other passengers were injured before the killer was overpowered and disarmed.

The executive committee, meeting shortly after the tragedy, sent the Association's sympathy to Mrs. Hinman and her children. The committee, disregarding doubts as to its powers over the Association's funds, also rendered immediate financial aid to the bereaved family, and asked the membership for additional contributions. According to normal procedure, the vice-president would have been advanced to the vacant chair, but when the committee met, it found that the Association had neither president nor vice-president. W. R. Halstead of the Atlanta Constitution had left the paper and SNPA territory.

W. T. Anderson of the Macon Telegraph was then elected president and Robert S. Jones of the Asheville Citizen vice-president.

Much of Secretary-Treasurer Clemens' report, naturally, dealt with these emergencies. He reported also that the past year had been "one of the most successful and prosperous in the Association's history, and but for the war, which reduced promotion and advertising to a minimum, might have been one of the most active." The treasury balance had reached the unprecedented height of $861.43.

But he had to report "no progress" on the advertising campaign which had been so bravely approved at the 1914 convention. Publishers who had not been present at that meeting did not react favorably to the proposed assessment plan. The advertising and executive committees had not been able to round up support that they considered sufficient for "a big Southern representation."

At the invitation of President Hinman, the committee had listened to a sales presentation by James Wright Brown, president of *Editor & Publisher,* the previous September. Mr. Brown, a former Southern publisher, had owned the trade journal for about two years and had progressed mightily in establishing it as the newspaper voice in advertising circles. He proposed that the members of the SNPA buy a weekly page in *Editor & Publisher* to advertise the South, his publication (and not the SNPA) to be responsible for solicitation and collection. The committee endorsed the proposal without committing any member to participation—but there was no campaign in 1914-15. The committee also relieved the membership of pledges which had been given at the Atlanta convention.

Southern newspapers, like most American business, shied away from future financial commitments until they could see more clearly through the fog of war. The pocket nerve was paralyzed temporarily. Another year would have to pass before the healing currents of British and French and Russian war orders revived the vigorous thinking that Serajevo had dampened.

Mr. Clemens' report cited another instance of the frustration that marked 1914-1915. An economic result of the European conflict was felt more immediately in the South than elsewhere in America. Europe had stopped buying Southern cotton, which piled up in docks and warehouses while the market price shrank almost to invisibility. The Birmingham Rotary Club proposed an obvious palliative—the stimulation of domestic consumption of cotton products. The Club asked the aid of newspapers, through the SNPA, in the publication of publicity stories, and the Secretary's office passed the request along without comment. Although many Southern newspapers agreed to print the publicity, the campaign did not come to pass. For the moment, no one could be found to gather the facts and write them convincingly! Later, a nationwide publicity effort on behalf of the Southern cotton industry would be completely effective.

Reporting that six new members had been elected by the officers during the year, the Secretary asked that they be seated at once in the 1915 convention. They were, as follows:

The South and Its Newspapers

Greensboro (N.C.) News, E. B. Jeffress; Tampa (Fla.) Times, L. D. Reagin; Roanoke (Va.) Times, W. E. Thomas; Charlotte (N.C.) Observer, J. V. Simms; Winston-Salem (N.C.) Journal, N. L. Cranford; Asheville (N.C.) Gazette-News, W. A. Hildebrand.

After a brief review of the Association's advertising program, the following committee was directed to investigate and report at the next day's session for "final settlement:" W. B. Sullivan, Columbia (S.C.) Record; W. C. Dowd, Charlotte (N.C.) News, and Walter C. Johnson, Chattanooga News.

Then a recess permitted the publishers an automobile ride through Asheville and its attractive surroundings, next to enjoy a dinner given by F. L. Seely, formerly publisher of the Atlanta Georgian and now proprietor of the Grove Park Inn. The single speech at the dinner was delivered by Wilbur W. Fry of N. W. Ayer & Son, then the nation's leading advertising agency, on "The Newspaper and National Advertising."

While the committee wrestled with the thorny advertising program, the Association tackled a wide range of topics. R. S. Carver, of the Jacksonville Florida Metropolis, related that until recently that paper's accounting had been limited to showing "what came in and what went out," the owner taking the balance. Under a system he had installed, the paper had an accurate picture of costs from day to day in each department.

President Anderson decried the idea that newspapers should rely upon advertising revenue for their entire profit. The public, he said, should pay enough for subscriptions to meet *all* expenses and to account for more than half of the paper's net profit. No newspaper, he declared, could be sold for less than $5.00 per year.

Answering questions, Mr. Anderson said that he considered 2 cents per line per thousand circulation a fair average advertising rate in the North, and 3 cents per line per thousand in the South. The "milline rate" had not yet edged its way into newspaper dictionaries. National advertising should pay more than local, Mr. Anderson believed, because it reached newspaper subscribers beyond the daily range of the local retailers.

Daily Newspapers Mature

A. F. Sanford of the Knoxville Journal & Tribune proposed that newspapers eliminate premium rates for theatrical and other amusement advertising, treat such matter as news and abolish the free reading notices that custom dictated. His mail poll of SNPA members indicated, he said, that most of them published serial stories based on current movies as an inducement to advertisers, without any feeling that the stories had circulation value.

Curtis Johnson of the Knoxville Sentinel outlined his newspaper's method of continuous check on time-space advertising contracts, maintaining uniform use of contract space by advertisers and avoiding short-rate troubles.

E. B. Jeffress of the Greensboro News, one of the "freshman" members, raised a question created by the recently enacted Federal income tax. How should newspapers report income on circulation obtained by contests, with subscriptions running over several years? Walter C. Johnson gave the common-sense answer that his policy was to prorate this subscription income as it was earned.

F. L. Seely, the convention's host, invited the publishers to come back next year for their convention. A former newspaperman, he thoroughly believed in advertising and the hotel had spent $50,000 to attract guests during the two previous years. So much did he want the convention business, he said, that he would take advertising in payment for his services. He also urged a golf tournament on adjacent links as a convention accessory and offered to donate a prize cup. So persuasive was his argument that the Association voted to hold not only the 1916, but also the 1917 convention, at Grove Park Inn. Rival claims of Jacksonville and Columbia for succeeding conventions were graciously waived. And Mr. Seely was voted honorary membership in the SNPA.

Then came the report of the advertising committee. First, it was recommended that the oft-approved co-operative advertising campaign be undertaken; second, that a committee be appointed to raise funds, and prepare copy; third, that the basis of co-operation be fixed at $3.00 per thousand circulation, with a minimum of $15.00 and a maximum of $60; the "name of each member entering therein to appear in connection therein."

When Walter C. Johnson pointed out that the $60.00 maximum made it likely that the funds so raised would not exceed $2,500 per annum, and that the maximum should be raised to $100 to assure adequate money, the report, so amended, was adopted. Choice of advertising media was left to the committee, which again included W. B. Sullivan, W. C. Dowd, and Walter C. Johnson.

Reduction of the assessment from $5.00 to $3.00 per thousand, it was thought by George M. Kohn, who had done most of the spade work on the 1912-1913 campaign, would attract members who considered the $5.00 rate excessive.

Mr. Seely's proposed golf feature was put in the hands of a committee comprising Mr. Seely, George W. Brunson, W. B. Sullivan, A. F. Sanford, and Robert S. Jones.

A number of elementary questions submitted by members evoked off-the-cuff answers. Varying opinions were expressed on the desirability of paper cores for newsprint rolls. The Macon Telegraph did not deliver papers free to employees' homes, but charged half-price, even to the publisher. Nor did department stores get free copies from the business-like Macon daily. Several members declared resolutely against publication of free reading notices requested by advertising agencies. Agreement was general that competing newspapers should agree not to belittle each other publicly.

When election of officers came up, W. T. Anderson, Robert S. Jones, and W. M. Clemens were continued as president, vice-president, and secretary-treasurer, respectively. To the executive committee were named:

Victor H. Hanson, Birmingham News; D. D. Moore, New Orleans Times-Picayune; F. G. Bell, Savannah News; Robert W. Brown, Louisville Times; Elmer E. Clarke, Little Rock Arkansas Democrat; G. J. Palmer, Houston Post; M. K. Duerson, Lynchburg News; John A. Park, Raleigh Times; Charles D. Atkinson, Atlanta Journal; W. A. Elliott, Jacksonville Florida Times-Union; Edgar M. Foster, Nashville Banner; Robert Lathan, Charleston News & Courier.

Then Curtis B. Johnson proposed that "in view of his services to the Association," Walter C. Johnson be elected second vice-president. The constitution provided for no such office, but the simultaneous vacancies of the previous winter in the presidency and vice-presidency evidently impressed the members with the need for another step in the succession.

In any case, no one objected to a motion to suspend the rules and create the new office, to which Mr. Johnson was elected by acclamation. Neither he nor his colleagues realized that the "services to the Association" thus recognized were only the first marks on the longest page in SNPA annals.

Fierce storms raged over the South and disrupted railroad service as the Southern publishers assembled for their 14th annual convention at Grove Park Inn, Asheville, N.C., July 10-12, 1916. Storm clouds were gathering over the newspaper business, too, and the early arrivals at Asheville decided to give the delayed members time to participate in discussion of several important questions. With Secretary-Treasurer W. M. Clemens among the storm-bound (he had moved to the Mobile Item during the year) Walter C. Johnson was asked by the president to assume the secretary's chair. After he had presented to President W. T. Anderson a gavel of mountain laurel, the gift of the Chattanooga Rotary Club, the convention took a roll call, approved the appointment of auditing and nominating committees, elected three new members, and adjourned to the afternoon. Members from the Deep South had not yet arrived, so another adjournment deferred the convention's real business until the next morning.[5]

Anticipating a heavy program, the executive committee had scheduled an unprecedented three-day session. Now the convention would have to get two days' business into one. Another evidence of the Association's rising importance appeared in the novel exhibits of newspaper machinery on one of the Inn's porches. With the recent reorganization of the Intertype Corporation, competition had stirred the old-established Mergenthaler Linotype Company to massive efforts

---

[5] Heavy rain fell throughout the convention and Asheville itself suffered slight damage from floods on July 11 and July 16. Convention attendants who did not leave promptly after the adjournment on July 12 found themselves pleasantly marooned for most of a week. W. T. Anderson and his party got as far as Hendersonville, N.C. by train on their homeward journey and stayed there, flood-bound, for three days. Then they returned to Asheville by automobile and at length departed by train for Macon via Murphy, N.C. During another wait at Murphy, the publishers and their families crowded the little country hotel, with the gentlemen sleeping on pallets in the corridors. A number of publishers arrived at Grove Park Inn after the convention had closed, and with no business to transact, it is a fair guess that poker, etc., received some expert exposition.

to hold its market. Both of these companies and the relatively new Lanston Monotype Machine Company had their officers and top-grade salesmen at the convention to demonstrate new models and write orders.

Matters of routine nature occupied the opening session. P. C. McDuffie, president of the Atlanta Ad Men's Club, presented a paper on "Insurance Advertising", evidently a field which few Southern newspapers had yet exploited. A committee was appointed to interest underwriters and insurance companies in a general campaign of advertising.

Russell R. Whitman, managing director of the Audit Bureau of Circulations, informally addressed the meeting and answered numerous questions. Within two years, it appeared publishers had realized that their pre-A.B.C. circulation practices had been incredibly expensive.

H. C. Adler, publisher of the Chattanooga Times, evidently knew the circulation discussions would turn on cost and revenue-production, and he spelled out the Times' operation with actual figures. Charging the entire cost of white paper to circulation and a fair proportion of other production expense, Mr. Adler demonstrated that the Times had gained a profit of $1,257 on its circulation in the first six months of 1916. The A.B.C. had marked several phases of the Times' system "100 per cent," he reported.

F. C. Withers of the Columbia State had also come armed with his figures, showing a 1915 profit on circulation of $20,899.93—and better results expected in 1916.

The figures of the two papers could not be compared, of course, for expense items differed in several important respects. Uniform newspaper accounting still lay several years in the future.

Discussing the question of percentage of advertising to news in an average daily issue, W. T. Anderson delivered a wide-eyed encomium on practices of the Scripps-McRae Newspapers, which, he said, would not publish larger than a 16-page paper (with 1500 column inches of advertising) unless the additional advertising added up to 350 inches. The Cleveland Press, he said, would not print more than 24 pages under any conditions. Advertisers didn't get whatever space they ordered, but whatever the paper allotted to them. Not many Southern publishers enjoyed such affluence or such command over their advertisers. Mr. Anderson's Macon Telegraph published 60 columns of news daily, sometimes more, never less, regardless of advertising volume.

Victor H. Hanson and Marcellus E. Foster, editor of the Houston Chronicle, agreed that pictures make circulation. The Chronicle used two columns daily, Mr. Foster said. He differed sharply with Mr. Adler's view that news was the only important function of a newspaper. Mr. Foster wanted the newspapers to encroach on the magazine's entertainment field as fully as possible.

A number of publishers explained their employment of advertising mat services, then comparatively new as a newspaper tool. Once introduced to local advertisers, these services quickly became indispensable. Practice differed considerably with respect to charging for special advertising cuts made for local retailers.

These and a few other topical questions filled the morning session. The brief summaries throw a light on newspaper thinking and newspaper dimensions in the days before paper costs doubled and trebled, and before advertising volume reached its war-time peak. The afternoon session dealt extensively with newsprint—the biggest storm cloud that was gathering on the newspaper horizon.

When the paper discussion opened, only a minority of those present appeared to realize that big trouble lay ahead. Then the members learned by an exchange of individual information some of the portentous facts:

No newspaper had been able to contract for future tonnage at the early 1916 price of $40 per ton or less.

Some publishers whose contracts had expired during 1916 found quotations varying from $2.20 to $2.50 per lb., plus freight, on contracts for less than their entire needs.

Spot market purchases revealed prices up to $80 per ton, plus freight.

Metropolitan publishers either owned mills or guaranteed the profits of their regular suppliers, and thus were assured of paper, but the comparatively small Southern consumers enjoyed no such protection.

Questioned by a member, Senator Luke Lea, then publisher of the Nashville Tennesseean, stated that no active steps had yet been taken on newsprint by either the Department of Justice or Congress.

Proposed remedies included changing from 7 to 8 column make-up, as had been proposed several years earlier at an ANPA convention by John Norris, of the New York Times.

Increased circulation and advertising rates were considered inevitable by several members—none of whom could have been expected to prophesy how greatly both would have to be increased for mere survival by 1922.

Greater care in handling paper in rail transit and in pressrooms would eliminate much waste, one publisher testified.

Close supervision of free copies, to advertisers and others, had several champions as an economy measure.

Recommendation of the American Newspaper Publishers Association that free publicity be refused was noted, without comment by any member.

Since no clear principle or policy emerged from the discussion—nor could one have been expected—the chair informally recommended that the by-laws be amended to provide for appointment of a white paper committee, to canvass the situation and co-operate with the ANPA. The committee comprised F. G. Bell, Savannah News; Alex B. Kohn, Charleston Evening Post; D. D. Moore, New Orleans Times-Picayune; R. L. McKenney, Macon News, and G. J. Palmer, Houston Post.

Representative and able as that committee was, it would find the paper situation developing too rapidly and radically during the next year to be controlled by its limited resources.

Turning to Association accomplishments of 1915-16, the members reviewed the co-operative advertising campaign with satisfaction, and voted that it be carried forward for the next year. The following committee was placed in charge of this effort: Charles H. Allen, Montgomery Advertiser; Walter G. Bryan, Atlanta Journal; and James H. Allison, Nashville Tennessean-American.

With copy prepared gratis by St. Elmo Massengale, the Atlanta advertising agent who had become familiar with SNPA problems, the campaign had included 22 pages in *Printers' Ink* three pages in *Editor & Publisher,* one page each in *The Fourth Estate* and *Judicious Advertising,* plus 16,000 copies of a booklet. The committee hoped that a larger fund would be made available for the next year's advertising, possibly $3,500 or $4,000. With a rate of $5.00 per thousand of circulation, the committee recommended a minimum assessment on participating members of $30 and a maximum of $125.

Another matter of far-reaching importance came before the SNPA for the first time at this meeting—an effort to have the proposed $20,000,000 nitrate plant of the Federal Government constructed in the South. The Association went on record as favoring Muscle Shoals, Ala., for the "location of this vast and important enterprise." Copies of the resolution were sent to President Wilson and the Secretary of War. While a minority of publishers hesitated to commit the Association to endorsement of a specific site for the hydro-electric plant, the majority backed the decision of the Army engineers on Muscle Shoals. Unheralded, that marked the beginning of a new era for the South.

A novel feature of the banquet that closed the convention was installation of telephone headsets at each plate. The American Telephone & Telegraph Company had recently completed its first coast-to-coast connection and the diners thrilled to the roar of the surf on the Pacific Coast brought by Mr. Bell's miracle.

Unanimous endorsement was accorded the slate of the nominating committee, as follows:

President, Robert S. Jones, Asheville Citizen; first vice-president, F. G. Bell, Savannah News; second vice-president, D. D. Moore, New Orleans Times-Picayune; secretary-treasurer, Walter C. Johnson, Chattanooga News.

Executive committee—Victor H. Hanson, Birmingham News; Edgar M. Foster, Nashville Banner; Curtis B. Johnson, Knoxville Sentinel; James H. Allison, Nashville Tennessean-American; A. F. Sanford,

Knoxville Journal and Tribune; G. J. Palmer, Houston Post; W. T. Anderson, Macon Telegraph; W. A. Elliott, Jacksonville Florida Times-Union; Robert Lathan, Charleston News & Courier; Elmer E. Clarke, Little Rock Arkansas Democrat; W. E. Thomas, Roanoke Times; W. B. Sullivan, Charlotte Observer.

With extraordinary prescience, the nominating committee had moved Walter C. Johnson from the comparatively idle vice-presidency to the strategic office of secretary-treasurer. He succeeded W. M. Clemens, who had moved during the year from the Birmingham News to the Mobile Item and then to the executive direction of the Mobile Chamber of Commerce and Tourist Bureau. After a difficult year, Mr. Clemens turned over a balance of about $1,100, or nearly $1,000 more than he had inherited three years earlier. But, alas, many of his SNPA records had been destroyed by the storms that had ravaged the South a few days earlier.

If the Southern editors and publishers did not wholly pierce the veil of the future in their 1916 convention, they had abundant company in America. Paper manufacturers in the East and in Canada continued to meet ever so often, considered their rising costs, and decided that the expanding newspaper industry could stand another hike in prices. They had the paper, the publishers needed the paper in ever-increasing quantity—and had not the law of supply and demand been enacted to meet such a situation? Three thousand miles across the Atlantic, a brightly uniformed galaxy in Berlin weighed their great gamble—if they could strangle Britain and France by unlimited submarine warfare, would or could the United States bring its unquestioned power to bear in time to affect the result of the war in Europe? And in New York, Chicago, and Washington, Democrats in sober tweeds and serge decided that they would re-elect President Wilson with the slogan "He kept us out of war."

Whether or not the Southern editors believed that Mr. Wilson had kept war from America, they and their publishers worked hard for his re-election. Sympathizing with the allied cause,[6] the Southern press, in the main, supported Wilson as the exponent of continued peace.

---
[6]Propaganda for War, by H. C. Peterson. University of Oklahoma Press, Norman, Okla. 1939. Page 167.

But, before the Southern newspaper people met at Asheville, July 9-11, 1917, the chimera of continued peace had vanished. American regulars had landed in France a few days before. Conscription had been enacted for the first time since 1863, and throughout the South camp sites had been selected for the training of the National Guard and the as yet unborn National Army. The hydro-electric plant at Muscle Shoals, approved by the SNPA in 1916, was under construction. Long dormant shipyards in Southern harbors worked around the clock to build cargo vessels faster than German U-boats could knock them out. If the American war tempo had not reached its peak in July, 1917, (and, of course, it hadn't) the South was abreast, and probably ahead, of the rest of America in answering the call to arms. At the same time, the Southern newspapers exercised vigilance to defend their rights, against the ruthless "supply and demand" credo of the paper makers, against discriminatory postal charges, and against war censorship.

The paper situation had developed at cyclone speed since the 1916 meeting. Then, with justified skepticism, the publishers had heard propaganda of a shortage of paper in the United States. By July, 1917, they heard and many of them believed that the shortage of paper had truly become world-wide. Whether that was true or false, few publishers could ascertain. What they knew, beyond any doubt, was that their paper bills had doubled during the past two years. They knew also that they needed more paper than they had ever before ordered, to keep pace with the surging demand for newspaper advertising. The influx of new advertisers that might have been expected on the heels of the "truth in advertising" campaign of recent years had been greatly accelerated by the war-boom prosperity of 1916. Many newspapers had to pay dearly for paper bought outside of their contract arrangements. They had seen contract prices jump with few intermediate steps from $40 to $80 per ton, plus freight charges, with spot market prices obeying only the law of what the traffic would bear, and they could see neither a limit in the demand for newspaper advertising nor in the prices that the shrewd makers of paper would exact if no restraints were imposed.

"Restraints" of any kind on business came as a novel and repugnant concept to publishers in 1917. Neither then nor 20 years later did they think kindly of Federal controls. If the paper mills had taken the long view in 1917 and foregone the quick profits to be squeezed out of emergency conditions, it is doubtful that the Southern Newspaper Publishers Association would have enacted this resolution at its 1917 convention:

"Resolved, that the Southern Newspaper Publishers Association, representing 105 leading daily newspapers of the South, in convention assembled, unqualifiedly approves and strongly urges the immediate adoption of the complete plans of the print paper committee of the American Newspaper Publishers Association to empower the Federal Trade Commission by legislative enactment to control the production of newsprint paper, to pool its distribution, and to fix its price.

"This action is absolutely necessary to conserve the best interests of our government and our people under the present extraordinary emergency."

Behind that Macedonian cry lay several more or less visible factors. If all mills in the United States and Canada capable of making newsprint had been employed in its production, at a reasonable rate of profit, the demands of United States and Canadian papers for newsprint could have been met. Within the past few years, however, a number of United States mills had shifted from newsprint to other paper products marketed at a higher margin of profit. It is probably true that many of these mills could not profitably produce newsprint at $40 or $50 per ton. Although they could have been converted back to newsprint for spot market production at $80 or more per ton, some of the manufacturers preferred to keep them off the market, thereby creating a potential shortage, to the advantage of the mills that remained on newsprint. Throughout the newsprint industry ran the sentiment that the newspapers deserved no sympathy—they had kept political pressure on the paper makers to the extent that newsprint production was no longer an attractive operation, and they had driven many of their suppliers into Canada, beyond the reach of Federal regulation or political duress. Mills which might have made newsprint or woodpulp found handsome profits and satisfied customers for their sulphite and other products among the ammunition manufacturers.

During the previous year the publishers had exercised what they considered great diligence in paper saving. News and feature content

Daily Newspapers Mature

had been reduced, advertising had been restricted by many, margins had been shaved and columns increased from 7 to 8 per page within existing or smaller paper roll-widths. At the same time they pressed paper manufacturers and the Federal Trade Commission to agree on a fair price for paper, which newspapers could accept as a basis for future operations. The Federal Trade Commission had set a price early in 1917—$62.00 per ton—which pleased the majority of publishers, but met only cold stares from the paper industry. At that time the Federal Trade Commission lacked powers of enforcement, and the paper makers, many of them operating from Canada, saw no reason to bow before a Federal Government stuffed club.

So, having reluctantly and vainly sought Government intervention toward a voluntary price agreement, the baffled and angry publishers now asked for Government intervention with legislative teeth.

At the same time, the SNPA called for enactment of the Walsh and Reed bills by Congress, believing that the "adoption of such measures insures the release and development of the water power resources of our country and promises release to the newspapers of the country from the oppressive condition brought about by the newsprint manufacturers' trust."

On another front, the SNPA demanded fair treatment for newspapers by the Post Office. Rates on second-class matter had stood unchanged for many years. Congress had enacted special treatment for newspapers and other publications in 1879, granting admittedly low rates in order to foster the spread of information throughout the land. Now, in 1917, with the government facing unprecedented expenses in arming for war, it was no longer tolerable that millions be diverted to meet Post Office deficits incurred by serving the nation's press and its readers.

Under the leadership of Major E. B. Stahlman, publisher of the Nashville Banner, the SNPA looked behind the details of the postal deficit. They found, according to Major Stahlman's report, that newspapers caused a relatively small part of the red ink postal balance. Agreeing that higher rates should be imposed, the SNPA urged enactment of the McKellar amendment to the War Revenue Bill, providing for a sliding scale of rates by geographic zones, preserving the rate of one cent per pound in the first, second and third zones (under 300 miles from the point of mailing) and also continuing the free-in-county circulation for newspapers provided by existing law. In a resolution addressed to Senator Simmons of the Senate Finance Committee, the Association declared:

"The Southern Newspaper Publishers Association .... unanimously passed a resolution expressing the keenest sympathy with the Government's needs in the present extraordinary financial situation, the most cordial willingness to co-operate in raising the necessary additional revenues and their desire to stand their just and fair proportion of increased taxation. The convention, however, unanimously voiced the opinion that the proposed extra tax on the net revenue of newspapers which does not apply to other lines of business is unjust, unfair and discriminatory.

"In reference to the proposed increase in second class postage rates, this Association believes that it had no place in a revenue bill and that the proper rate or rates should be determined by an impartial investigation. If, however, an increase in postage rates is absolutely necessary at this time, this Association believes that the only fair and equitable basis is the zone system, the theory of which is fully outlined in Senator McKellar's amendment with the present rate applying for the first 300 miles, and increasing rates for larger distances in proportion to the cost to the Government for services rendered publishers."

"Fair and equitable" as this proposal might have been under ordinary conditions, it could not meet the nation's financial needs under war conditions. Few Southern dailies would have been adversely affected by its enactment, and the same could be said of newspapers in other regions, excepting the great metropolitan press. Nationally circulated magazines (large and small) and a limited number of metropolitan dailies sent copies beyond the 300-mile radius and would have had to swallow the higher mailing costs or pass them to subscribers. In any case, the new revenue to the Post Office would not have been important in reducing the deficit. Uncle Sam needed the money, and after a long rear-guard action by all publishers' associations, he got it by an increase in all second class rates in 1918. Postal rates would remain a sizzling question in SNPA conventions for many more years.

DAILY NEWSPAPERS MATURE

Internally, the Association had prospered greatly in 1916-17. After earning an extraordinary citation from President Robert S. Jones, Secretary-Treasurer Walter C. Johnson read a list of 35 new applicants for SNPA membership, a 50 per cent gain during the year and a tribute to the Secretary's vigorous missionary labors. Among the latter could be listed a great increase in the frequency of Association bulletins, keeping members informed on a wide variety of current affairs.

In advertising the South, the Association had abandoned its old uncertainty. By 1917, the report of the advertising committee had become routine—to be read, approved, and the committee reappointed with instructions to continue its good work.

Russell R. Whitman of the Audit Bureau of Circulations again visited the convention, explained improved service methods, and commended the Association for its splendid growth. He added that 73 of its 105 members had joined the Audit Bureau.

"Truth in advertising" received another fillip from Arthur G. Newmyer, business manager of the New Orleans Item and vice-president of the spirited Associated Advertising Clubs of the World, which had added a special department for newspapers. The A.A.C.W. then was at work with other associations on a set of rules governing the publication of advertising, Mr. Newmyer told the Southern publishers.

The increased strength of advertising agencies in the South appeared in the formation of a new Southeastern Advertising Agents Association at Asheville while the publishers were meeting. After an exchange of views, the SNPA named a committee to frame official recognition of the new organization and to co-operate with it for mutual interests.

F. G. Bell of the Savannah News advanced from first vice-president to president. James H. Allison, Nashville Tennessean, was named first vice-president, and Charles H. Allen, Montgomery Advertiser, became second vice-president. Walter C. Johnson, Chattanooga News, continued as secretary-treasurer. To the executive committee were named:

Victor H. Hanson, Birmingham News; W. A. Elliott, Jacksonville Florida Times-Union; Edgar M. Foster, Nashville Banner; Curtis B.

Johnson, Knoxville Sentinel; R. S. Jones, Asheville Citizen; F. C. Withers, Columbia State, S. L. Slover, Norfolk Ledger-Dispatch, Marcellus E. Foster, Houston Chronicle; Arthur G. Newmyer, New Orleans Item; Harry Giovannoli, Lexington (Ky.) Leader; W. T. Anderson, Macon Telegraph; Walter G. Bryan, Atlanta Georgian.

The SNPA and World War I

Repeatedly Pledging Support to Nation's War Objectives, Publishers Battle Soaring Paper Prices and Unjust Postal Rate Schedules — Membership and Program Greatly Expanded Between 1918 and 1920.

WHITE paper continued to hold the stage at Asheville when the SNPA convened for the 16th time on July 8-10, 1918. The Federal Trade Commission had recognized the emergency so earnestly described by the SNPA the year before, and had legally fixed the price of newsprint at $62.00 per ton. Although that marked a better than 50 per cent advance over base prices of 1914, publishers welcomed the stability produced by official regulation. Paper makers sullenly bowed to the inevitable. And the SNPA heard warnings of 1918 convention speakers from both sides of the fence that paper would cost more, much more, before long.

Under orders of the War Industries Board (compliance with which was more or less voluntary, with no penalties for disobedience) paper consumption had been reduced considerably. Reading the bare record a generation after 1918, a cynic might conclude that the publishers' acceptance of Federal regulation was compelled by economic necessity, but that reading of events would completely miss the spirit that guided the nation, and especially the SNPA members, in those stirring days. By July, 1918, some of war's realities were comprehended in the United States. More than 2,000,000 young men had gone into military training. Two American divisions and part of another had been in major battles, and the casualty lists already published knocked into oblivion the quaint notion that American arms and dollars, rather than American bodies, would be our major contribution to Allied victory. Within a week after the SNPA members left Asheville for home, American troops would form the largest part of the Allied forces in the decisive Second Marne battle. But when the publishers met, the Germans had not yet been beaten and no one predicted that the war would end before the year was out. Every prospect indicated a long and bitter fight, with every American resource needed for eventual victory.

Almost the first business transacted by the convention was this resolution introduced by Victor H. Hanson, adopted, and sent to President Woodrow Wilson:

"The Southern Newspaper Publishers Association, in convention assembled at Asheville, N.C., on this eighth day of July, 1918, goes on record as expressing its profound belief in the justice of the cause of America in this war; its sincere admiration for the manner in which the President and his advisers and co-workers have conducted the various branches of the government during the war; and its entire confidence in the future of this country, whether in war or in peace, under the masterly guidance of our President.

"This Association pledges itself to carry this devotion into action, no matter what the cost, no matter what the sacrifices may be asked of it; that it pledges its entire membership to undivided devotion to the principles for which our heroic army and navy are battling; that it pledges the fullest possible use of the newspapers under control of its members to the support of the Government in prosecuting this war until complete over-mastering military victory brings peace again to the world."

Part and parcel of that spirit of devotion to victory was the will to resist rulings by war-created bureaus which might impair the newspaper's function in the national effort. The new schedule of postal rates on second class matter had been in effect for only a week. As enacted, it exemplified Congressional urgency in seeking new revenue sources rather than a studied effort to deal fairly with the publishing business. The SNPA legislative committee, headed by Major E. B. Stahlman, had fought hard for adoption of the zone rate schedule proposed by Senator McKellar of Tennessee, and would continue to do so. The publishers saw no justice in rates which charged daily and weekly newspapers so much per hundred pounds for a distance of 40 miles, and charged no more for the same weight of magazines that might be carried 3,300 miles. President Bell pointed out that the new system of charging zone rates upon the advertising portions of newspapers imposed new costs on publishers and on governments which, in the case of the Savannah News, totalled $12, against an additional revenue of $1.04 gained by the government under the new schedule.

In obeying the wishes of the War Industries Board for paper economy, the publishers sought the guidance of the Association's committee on conservation of white paper, headed by Charles 1. Stewart of the Lexington (Ky.) Herald. They also welcomed the advice of M. Koenigsberg, general manager of the International Feature Service, then making great progress toward its later eminence. Mr. Koenigsberg went to Asheville with the mission of convincing the Southern publishers that the suggested elimination of comics, magazines and other newspaper features as an economy measure would be impractical and dangerous.[1]

Nothing would play more into the hands of the Germans than the elimination of comics and magazine features, declared the speaker. A smiling foe is always dangerous. The Germans sought to conquer the minds and wills of their adversaries, and that intent could not be better served than by depressing the spirit of our people.

"A publisher can render no better service than by extending circulation and providing matter which shall lighten the hearts of the people," Mr. Koenigsberg concluded. "Morale is essential to victory. We are an emotional people and on more than one occasion our sense of humor alone has saved us."

In not dissimilar vein, Lincoln B. Palmer, manager of the American Newspaper Publishers Association, addressed the convention on "The Newspaper's Part in Winning the War."

"If the newspapers of America had had in 1860 the relative circulation they now have," he said, "There would have been no Civil War."

Mr. Palmer pointed out that present-day newspapers had performed a vital function in uniting public opinion and had co-operated with the government regardless of sacrifice. In somewhat plaintive tone, however, he remarked that the government paid for everything it received, except advertising.

---

[1] King News. By M. Koenigsberg. Frederick A. Stokes Co. New York, 1941.

Turning to the inescapable topic of paper, Mr. Palmer told his audience that some paper mills had inflated their costs (and sales prices) by purchasing wood and pulp from wholly owned subsidiaries at fancy prices. He predicted higher prices after the war—$80, $100, $120, or even more per ton—unless the publishers brought about free competition in the newsprint industry. One method he mentioned implied the encouragement of new mills by the pooling of publishers' contracts and the provision of a cost-plus profit to the mills.

Jason Rogers, of the New York Globe, once again addressed the convention, with a proposal for a "new national newspaper organization." Apparently, the fertile-minded Rogers wished to organize a federal form of newspaper association, including state groups, the SNPA and other regional bodies. Many SNPA members by this time knew of Mr. Rogers' dissatisfaction with ANPA methods and procedures, and, correctly or not, suspected that he wanted an organization in which his ideas would receive a more attentive hearing. Among those ideas was included the pooling of paper contracts, which he would put into temporary and limited effect a year or two afterwards, with dramatic effect on the newsprint market. In 1918, the SNPA just listened politely.

They listened, attentively, to W. C. Powers, representing the Great Northern Paper Company, who appeared before the convention by invitation of Secretary Johnson. Mr. Powers believed the Federal Trade Commission had erred in fixing the newsprint price of $62.00. That price tended to discourage production, creating a shortage and potential panicky conditions, he said. Answering questions, he stated that a price of $72.00 maximum at mill would have been fair and to the best interests of publishers and manufacturers. Although some of the latter would have netted large profits from a $70 rate, 90 per cent of the mills would have found only a living margin at that price.

Great Northern, the speaker declared, had fixed a $60 price for its customers, and he believed that it had been a wrong guess under the circumstances; it did not guard the mill against a steady rise in costs under war conditions.

Freight shipping facilities had greatly improved in recent months, with cars available on three to five days' notice, but grave shortages were anticipated for the coming winter. He asked the publishers to urge upon the War Industries Board the importance of having no freight embargoes against newsprint. To guard against paper shortage in the South, Mr. Powers said that his company had stored 1,100 tons of newsprint at Norfolk, whence it could be quickly shipped to any Southern publisher facing an emergency. Unfortunately, much of this paper had been damaged in transit.

Mr. Powers advised publishers to increase subscription rates, to eliminate non-essentials (such as comics and magazines) and to reduce returns from newsdealers. He asserted that the white paper involved in returns accepted by New York City newspapers would supply all the needs of Great Northern's customers in the South.

That a paper mill executive considered it advantageous to talk in such terms to Southern publishers, in the existing seller's market, evidences the growing importance of the SNPA as a major newspaper organization. No longer could the Association be regarded as a fraternal-social body which met once a year for a get-together and some incidental business chit-chat. By 1918, the SNPA had developed year-round functions of constant importance to its membership. Like the newspaper business as a whole, it had suddenly matured, grown to adult commercial stature.

Secretary-Treasurer Johnson must have put in many a long working day in those war years. As general manager of the flourishing Chattanooga News, he had all of the problems that war operations created for his fellow members. In addition, he carried on extensive correspondence for the Association, issued frequent Bulletins, and kept up a continuous campaign for new members. In 1917, he had reported 35 new applicants for membership, increasing the Association's ranks by 50 per cent; in 1918, he presented 22, among them papers of current and future importance which had passed up earlier bids to join. Wartime operations had made membership in some such organization practically indispensable to all publishers, and the SNPA rose effectively to its new opportunities. Most of the members recruited during World War I remained on the rolls.

Mere increase of numbers at the old dues added to the Secretary's burdens without providing means for carrying the added load, and the 1918 convention unanimously voted a new scale of dues, based on circulation, and ranging from $15 to $40 per year. It was estimated that the new schedule would provide a total of $2,955, an increase of $1,300 over the previous year. It was the Association's first suit of "long pants" and it would soon be outgrown.

Technical topics in 1918 seem to have centered on experience with dry mats. The Association had heard varying opinions of this equipment in earlier years, notably from the effervescent Jason Rogers of New York. Always ready to try something new, Rogers' New York Globe had experimented for several months with dry mats some years earlier. He had then reported on the trials and advised the SNPA against general adoption of the dry mat until (1) its price had been greatly reduced, and (2) until improved techniques had been developed for control of shrinkage.

Now the shrinkage factor had assumed new importance. Under control methods developed by the Wood Flong Co. and in numerous newspaper plants, shrinkage was uniform and in a horizontal direction, enabling the use of narrower newsprint rolls and thereby saving up to 2 per cent in paper consumption. Also, the mats were now "made in America," whereas the early products had come from Germany. Nelson Maynard, superintendent of the Wood Flong Co., informed the Southern publishers that 120 dailies had adopted dry mats exclusively, eliminating the old wet-mat process, and none had abandoned the innovation.

That was one of the topics on which the SNPA kept its members currently informed between conventions by frequent Bulletins.

The genesis of regular SNPA Bulletin service and the experiments with dry mats deserve more notice than this History has so far accorded them. When the European War began, publishers lost their German source of dry mats, which many had been hopefully trying. Several newspapers helped to finance a group of Massachusetts people in manufacture of American dry mats at Worcester. When the topic came up at the 1916 convention (it had been discussed at earlier meetings), F. C. Withers, business manager of the Columbia State, offered to undertake experiments with the American product. The State's stereotype foreman, a Scot, had used dry mats in the "old country." Marcellus E. Foster of the Houston Chronicle agreed to give the mats a trial in his plant. And Walter C. Johnson, newly

The SNPA and World War I

elected as secretary-treasurer of the SNPA, decided to test the mats in the Chattanooga News plant.

Mr. Johnson recalls that he had difficulties. The News' stereotypers, like those in most other shops, resisted the new device. For generations, the stereotypers had held tightly the trade secret of mixing the paste with which wet mats were made and they were reluctant to see this asset made technically obsolete. "The things won't work," they told Mr. Johnson, and they did everything possible to prove their verdict, even breaking the mat machine on which the mats were rolled. In an "executive session" with the stereotypers, Mr. Johnson made it plain that some people would be out of jobs if a good plate wasn't produced, and he would not be one of the jobless. He must have been convincing, for good plates began coming from the stereotype room. The other two experimenters also finally achieved their tests, and returned reports to the SNPA secretary.

Rather than wait for the next convention with this news of immediate interest, Mr. Johnson decided to incorporate the reports of Messrs. Withers and Foster with his own in a Bulletin to all SNPA members. In type, the reports made six pages. To fill out an eight-page format, Mr. Johnson wrote a suggested 10-point program of activities that SNPA members might undertake, and filled the eighth page with news of what members were doing. The immediate response from members indicated general approval of the 10-point program, one of its points being publication of a weekly Bulletin. That was in the final week of January, 1917, and there have been few weeks in the intervening 36 years in which a Bulletin has not been issued. Covering an almost unlimited range of affairs, the Bulletins have been in fact, if not in name, a regional trade journal for Southern dailies.

Another evidence of the Association's maturity appeared in the activity of the Legislative Committee. Reports extant in 1953 did not indicate the genesis of this body; almost certainly it came about in 1917, when the war-time postal rate situation demanded the unremitting attention of newspaper organizations. Headed by Major E. B. Stahlman, the committee included Col. L. J. Wortham, Fort Worth Star-Telegram; A. F. Sanford, Knoxville Journal and Tribune; James M. Thomson, New Orleans Item, and Urey Woodson, Owensboro Messenger. All of these men possessed at least one common quality—the intimate acquaintance and friendship of Members of Congress and the Senate from their home States. They knew the newspaper story at first hand, and their chairman also had an excellent working knowledge of railroad operation, a major factor in postal transportation. But, although they poured their pleas eloquently into Congressional ears in 1917-1918, their logic did not prevail against the government's urgent need for money. Later efforts of SNPA legislative committees, including one or more of these publishers, would produce more pleasant results. When Major Stahlman asked to be relieved from the committee in 1918, for business and personal reasons, the Association turned a polite but unhearing ear. The committee received a vote of thanks and instructions to carry on for another year.

Sixty newspapers supported the Association's advertising campaign during the year, using a total of 33 pages in *Printers' Ink, Editor & Publisher, The Fourth Estate, Newspaperdom,* and *Associated Advertising*. The old difficulties with copy and technique had become only dim memories. Now the Association had the co-operative services of several Southern advertising agencies, with St. Elmo Massengale, of Atlanta, again winning high praise for his co-ordination efforts. Collections from members for the advertising assessment were practically 100 per cent, indicating that the advertised claims of Southern prosperity had abundant factual background.

This committee also received the thanks of the Association and was constituted for the coming year with Walter G. Bryan, Atlanta Georgian and American, chairman; James H. Allison, Nashville Tennessean; and Charles H. Allen, Montgomery Advertiser.

Deciding against a change in administration in the midst of war, the Association re-elected officers as follows:

President, F. G. Bell, Savannah News; first vice-president, James H. Allison, Nashville Tennessean; second vice-president, Charles H. Allen, Montgomery Advertiser; secretary-treasurer, Walter C. Johnson, Chattanooga News.

Executive committee—Victor H. Hanson, Birmingham News; Edgar M. Foster, Nashville Banner; Curtis B. Johnson, Knoxville Sentinel;

The SNPA and World War I

Robert S. Jones, Asheville Citizen; F. C. Withers, Columbia State; W. T. Anderson, Macon Telegraph; W. A. Elliott, Jacksonville Florida Times-Union; S. L. Slover, Norfolk Ledger-Dispatch; Marcellus E. Foster, Houston Chronicle; Arthur G. Newmyer, New Orleans Item; Harry Giovannoli, Lexington Leader; Walter G. Bryan, Atlanta Georgian.

Guns had ceased their thunder in Europe, the A.E.F. was coming home, and America basked in peace and such prosperity as had never been enjoyed by any land—or so Americans naively thought as the SNPA gathered in unprecedented numbers for its 17th convention at Asheville, July 7-9, 1919. Sharing the dream of endless plenty amid the quietly massive splendors of Grove Park Inn were members of the Southern Division of the Associated Press, the executive board of the new American Association of Advertising Agencies, and the Southern Council of the A.A.A.A. Despite numerous clouds on the horizon (some of them considerably larger than the hand of a man) the assorted conventioners proclaimed the past year's achievements as the heralds of a new era for the South and the nation.

Amid new plaudits for the untiring activity of Secretary Johnson, the Association hailed the growth of its membership to 157 newspapers—95 evening and 62 morning, with a total circulation of 2,546,348. In the past three years, 68 new dailies had joined, including every newspaper in Tennessee. Receipts for the year had far surpassed estimates, reaching $3,200, and the Association had the healthy balance of $2,000 cash on hand.

On top of that proof of new affluence, the Association learned that its members had invested $7,000 in advertising the South during the previous year, with 85 newspapers participating. Copy had appeared in *Printers' Ink, Editor & Publisher, Associated Advertising*, and dailies in the South. In tune with the spirit of the times, Walter G. Bryan, as chairman of the advertising committee, expressed his belief that the 1919-1920 campaign should run to $10,000 or more. Newspapers throughout the South had enjoyed great gains in advertising, he reported.

Looking back three decades, it is easier to see the whole picture more clearly than it was in 1919. Prior to 1914, no nationwide record of newspaper advertising volume existed. Individual newspapers had kept their own figures by varying unit measurements; probably most of them kept similar tab on the records of their nearest competitors. Special representatives in New York, Chicago, and Atlanta, knew in 1919 that their billings of general advertising had increased mightily since the start of the war-orders prosperity. Advertising agencies also knew that the number of their accounts and the volume of space bought had trended steadily upward. But few newspaper people in 1919 realized that the total volume of advertising in newspapers had doubled between 1914 and the year after the war's end.

Only in a vague way did they realize then that a considerable volume of this advertising had resulted from war-time excess profits taxes; logically, the Treasury Department had decided that advertising costs should be allowed as a normal business expense. Possibly to the Treasury's amazement, many business firms determined that it would be wiser to buy advertising than to pay excess profits taxes out of the new war-generated income. And probably to the amazement of many of the advertisers, their reckless ventures into newspaper and magazine advertising has worked wonders in opening new markets and increasing total sales. What had begun as a shrewd tax-avoidance device had blossomed into a new and essential implement of commerce.

Nobody worried much about the moral issue. Publishers hustled to get the newsprint, for the height of the new advertising flood proved impossible to calculate in advance. Advertising agencies, which had had a Topsy-like growth in the preceding decade, saw the vital necessity for the establishment of standard practices in their own ranks—uniform commissions and discounts from publishers, for example—and for publication rates and definition of mechanical requirements that bore some semblance to a standard. All of those factors, some new, some old, agitated the publishers, editors, and advertising men in session at Asheville.

Some of the publishers voiced thoughts that evidenced new worries. Composing rooms found it difficult to locate enough Linotype operators to set the type that the influx of advertising and news features required. Wages had risen during the war and continued their upward swing. Unionized employees had done fairly well, as usual, and some of the publishers expressed concern that editorial and other "white collar" employees should also receive better pay. It should be made plain that no Southern publisher mentioned holding down the pay of the editorial and clerical people; they wished to keep these departments in a fair pay ratio with the unionized crafts. And there was a forecast of another trend—open shop employment in the mechanical departments of several Southern newspapers was discussed with considerable interest.

In that general era of good feeling, however, it was natural that the publishers should again open their meeting with a tender of good wishes to President Wilson, then just returned from his fateful part in the Paris peace conference. The SNPA in its telegram, signed by Frank G. Bell, president, expressed the belief that "the mission which took him to Europe will bring enduring peace and prosperity to all the world."

No such kindly sentiments, however, went to Albert G. Burleson, the Texan Postmaster General who had blocked the publishers' campaign for equitable postal rates and referred to newspapers as "grafters", seeking special privilege under the law. The chorus of denunciation included even Marcellus E. Foster, editor of the Houston Chronicle, who, reluctantly conceding that Burleson was a Texan, declared, "he is in office by appointment and could not be elected to any office within the gift of the people of that commonwealth."

Major E. B. Stahlman, chairman of the Legislative Committee, told his fellow publishers that the fight for fair postal rates would have been won if the committee's facts had received the backing of other publisher groups. Eastern papers had lacked interest in the campaign, he said, and the magazines had opposed the Southern stand, which had been supported by the Inland Daily Press Association and twice by the ANPA. Existing rates and those proposed by the Postmaster General were neither honest nor fair, in Major Stahlman's view.

He and his committee of stalwarts were instructed to keep up the fight for another year.

Uncertainty ruled the newsprint situation. With the end of the war the Federal Trade Commission's price fixing powers lapsed and several investigations of newsprint supply and price ground to a slow stop for lack of funds. Paper manufacturers now were quoting new contract prices at three-month intervals, and each quarter witnessed a new advance. Fortunate publishers were paying $80 per ton in mid-1919; those with less solid mill connections paid more, and spot market prices spiralled dizzily. In truth, few publishers had any reason to be cheerful, but, with the competition of brighter topics, newsprint prospects received comparatively little attention at this convention.

Several proposals which came before the Southern Newspaper Publishers Association in 1919 had no precedents. L. B. Palmer of the ANPA had made a wistful remark to the SNPA in 1918 that the government paid for all services it received—except advertising. Now came Thomas H. Moore of the Bureau of Advertising with the news that the Navy had had notable success with its post-war campaign for recruits, through newspaper advertising, and that the Army, putting free publicity aside, planned a similar recruiting effort. The generous space which commercial firms had made available for Government advertising of Liberty Bonds, etc., had opened government eyes to new possibilities. In passing, let it be recorded that Josephus Daniels, long-time editor of the Raleigh News and Observer, and Secretary of the Navy since 1913, had not pressed the case for advertising and was astonished when a Congressional committee member suggested that the Navy advertise for the men it needed.

Then there was James O'Shaughnessy, silver-haired and silver-tongued former Chicago editor, who made a missionary fight for the new American Association of Advertising Agencies, of which he was Executive Secretary. His first goal was the up-grading of commissions paid by publishers, a subject upon which exact information had been scarce and often conflicting. At a joint meeting of the SNPA, the executive council of the A.A.A.A., the Southern council of that body and a new group of Southern Farm Paper Publishers, O'Shaughnessy turned on all of his charm, and argued for a universal 15 per cent commission, and also for refusal of any commission on advertising space bought directly by a national advertiser, without agency intervention. On the same subject, William H. Johns, president of the A.A.A.A., pleaded with the publishers to refuse commission on such advertising even though it meant the loss of the business. While that agency "demand" affected comparatively few newspaper advertisers, those it aimed at included several names well revered in most newspaper offices—the old stand-by patent medicine firms which had survived the purge of recent years. Radical as the A.A.A.A. proposal seemed at first glance, it attained acceptance of almost all of the nation's dailies within the incredibly short period of two or three years. According to A.A.A.A. testimony, Southern publishers showed the "greatest improvement" in their agency relations.

Jason Rogers of the New York Globe again attended. He had become almost an annual fixture at SNPA meetings, but this time he offered something brand new and of such interest that he spoke for more than an hour. He described his "standard accounting system", which he and some expert accountants had evolved from forms supplied by 50 newspapers. Rogers had recently published his book on "Newspaper Building", embodying this system and a mass of other data of interest to the publishers of that day. The book, in fact, enjoyed considerable popularity over many years. The SNPA in 1919 couldn't get too much of his breezy wisdom.

Also indicating the newspapers' preoccupation with production worries was the proposal of W. T. Anderson that a school be established with SNPA aid for the training of composing room apprentices. The typographical union rules limited the number of apprentices in newspaper shops—one boy to every five or even more journeymen. The union claimed that it did not want boys to be used on work that should be done by competent printers, but the publishers feared, reasonably, that the union's real goal was to restrict the number of qualified printers so that their individual earning power would be increased. Whatever the strategy, the immediate situation saw the South's newspapers with too few printers for the work to be done and the prospect of still fewer in the future.

Walter H. Savory, general sales manager of the Mergenthaler Linotype Company, described the company's training schools in New York, Chicago, New Orleans and San Francisco, with smaller courses in established technical schools. Urey Woodson, of the Owensboro Messenger, approving Mr. Anderson's proposal of a school in the South, argued that men trained in the big city schools often remained in the high-wage metropolitan centers and did not return to their old fields. And Col. L. J. Wortham of the Fort Worth Star-Telegram urged the "education" of legislators to the end that Linotype instruction would be given by all vocational and technical schools.

Out of that discussion eventually came the SNPA program of training young men at the Southern School of Printing, at Nashville—an effort of many years' duration. In 1931 the present Southwest School of Printing was established in Dallas, Texas, as the Southwest Vocational School, by members of the Texas Newspaper Publishers Association, with the cooperation of a group of members of the SNPA in Texas.

Reiterating its demand that second class postage rates be adjusted in keeping with the service rendered and the cost of that service to the government, and calling for the principles of the McKellar zone rates, the Association also asked that Major E. B. Stahlman be named on the Postal Committee of the American Newspaper Publishers Association in place of George McAneny, New York Times, who had recently resigned.

The annual election also set a new precedent—the election of a woman publisher to the executive committee for the first time. The pioneer was Mrs. Lois K. Mayes, of the Pensacola (Fla.) Journal, who had taken an active part in the 1918 and 1919 convention debates.

James H. Allison, first vice-president, who had moved from the Nashville Tennessean to the Fort Worth Record during the year, was advanced to the presidency. Another Texan, Marcellus E. Foster, of the Houston Chronicle became first vice-president, and W. A. Elliott, of the Jacksonville Florida Times-Union, second vice-president. Walter C. Johnson, Chattanooga News, continued as secretary-treasurer. Executive committee members, in addition to Mrs. Mayes, were: Victor H. Hanson, Birmingham News; J. L. Mapes, Beaumont Enterprise; Charles I. Stewart, Lexington Herald; F. G. Bell, Savannah News; E. B. Jeffress, Greensboro News; M. K. Duerson, Lynchburg News; Elmer E. Clarke, Little Rock Arkansas Democrat; V. C. Moore, Raleigh News & Observer; D. D. Moore, New Orleans Times-Picayune; W. W. Holland, Spartanburg Herald & Journal; A. F. Sanford, Knoxville Journal & Tribune.

A deceptively bright sunshine of prosperity still warmed the nation and especially its newspaper people in the summer of 1920. Two Ohio publishers had just been nominated for President. One would succeed to the burdens that had stricken down Woodrow Wilson and was to die in office, disillusioned and unhappy; the other, turning resolutely from political defeat to continued distinction in journalism, would, within a few years, own two of the strongest dailies in the SNPA membership. Those frowns and smiles of Fate were hidden from men in 1920. Businesswise, newspapers continued to enjoy a torrent of advertising, of which no end seemed to be in sight. Although some already felt the pinch of rising costs, few anticipated, and none mentioned the probability that scores of newspapers would balance their books in red a year or two hence. The Southern press would fare somewhat better than newspapers in other regions in post-World War I adjustments, and it is possible that the activities of the SNPA should be credited for a part of that strength.

The 1920 convention at Asheville, July 19-21, produced the largest attendance and the greatest volume of talk of any SNPA meeting then of record. Questions engaging the members included newsprint prices and future supplies, postal rates, relations with the Audit Bureau of Circulations, the school for printers, the Association's advertising campaign, and, also an address by the British Ambassador which counseled the editors to set their sights on preserving world peace by honest reporting and comment on world news.

Permanent headquarters of the Association had been established at Chattanooga during the year, with Walter Johnson dividing his energies between his duties as secretary-treasurer and as general manager of the News. Membership had had its greatest increase during 1919-1920 and now stood at 230 dailies. The secretary's office had issued 27 regular Bulletins, five special Bulletins, 4,136 form letters and 3,359 personal letters. Mr. Johnson reported a treasury balance of $1,195.76 and recommended that dues be raised $5.00 per year. The committee on dues went a little beyond that figure, and fixed a new sliding scale ranging from $15.00 to $75.00 according to circulation. This committee also recommended, and the membership approved, a raise for the diligent secretary-treasurer. His pay from the Association went in one jump from $200.00 to $600.00 per annum.

Newsprint developments the previous autumn had sounded alarm bells throughout newspaperdom. The new quarterly price announcements of leading paper manufacturers meant that newspapers would pay $100 or more during early 1920, with the prospect that still higher prices would follow. The American Newspaper Publishers Association hurriedly called a special convention in New York to decide on measures of salvation. The SNPA held a similar convention in Birmingham during November, 1919. Both conventions outlined stricter measures of economy and counseled their members against competitive bidding for spot market paper. The price of spot paper by that time had soared to $200 and more per ton—it would top $300 before the crazy spiral reached its peak. Metropolitan newspapers were bidding against each other for comparatively small lots of paper, to supplement their contract supplies and to provide safe reserves in their own basements. Small dailies and weeklies, accustomed to buying rolls or sheets for little more than their current needs, were the immediate victims of the resulting squeeze. Their slim cash resources could not stand the drain of paper prices multiplied three or four times above "normal" levels. They had shared in the great advertising upsurge to only a minor degree, and they had neither the will nor the know-how to make advertising and circulation prices match their sky-rocketing costs. Late 1919 and early 1920 had seen many of them close their doors with fatal finality.

Another step had been taken by publishers during the American Newspaper Publishers Association convention in April, 1920. This was formation of the Publishers Buying Corporation, with Jason Rogers of the New York Globe and William J. Pape of the Waterbury (Conn.) Republican among the moving spirits. In the words of Rogers, its aim was to "solve the print paper situation for the smaller newspapers of the country by direct action." No longer did newspapers look to the Federal government for help in the runaway price situation. Their views on that were definitely expressed by Charles I. Stewart, chairman of the SNPA newsprint committee, when he told the 1920 convention that "nothing but disaster to the publishing business and misfortune to the public need be expected in the event of governmental interference."

President Pape appeared before the SNPA in 1920 to explain the purposes of the Publishers Buying Corporation and read a telegram from Jason Rogers, chairman of its executive committee, in which 300 tons of spot newsprint were offered at a price of $210 per ton. Although the SNPA expressed no official approval of the co-operative venture, it is beyond doubt that some of its members joined and benefitted by the next year's operations. The PBC, starting with approxi-

The SNPA and World War I

mately 100 members, had enrolled 250 before the paper crisis tapered off in 1922.

SNPA action on newsprint in 1920 pledged co-operation with the Special Committee of the ANPA (appointed at the emergency convention in November) and conferred similar powers on the SNPA newsprint committee. Both of these special committees promulgated specific measures for paper economy, to keep demand within the limits of probable and vaguely defined supply and to build reserves against the expected peak advertising demand of October, 1920. Chairman Stewart took a long view of the newsprint prospect in his 1920 report. The law of supply and demand was indeed operating in its usual elephantine manner; the rising price curve of recent years had attracted new capital to newsprint manufacture and the product of new mills in Canada would be coming on the market within two or three years. Since that promised no early relief, the most practical course open to newspapers was continued drastic conservation of paper.

On the positive side, Mr. Stewart counseled increased advertising rates and provision for their revision on 30 days' notice, co-operation with the ANPA in efforts to work out more flexible contracts on national advertising, and "sympathetic consideration of every means for the creation of a newsprint industry in the South."

On Mr. Stewart's recommendation, the Association adopted resolutions calling upon Washington and the railroad managements to hasten an increase in motive power and cars, expressing opposition to governmental operation of the transportation system and the coal mines, and governmental regulation of the size of newspapers. Apparently, what the newspapers had seen of government railway operation during the war had confirmed their natural antipathy to government intervention in private business.

The advertising committee's report was delivered by Arthur G. Newmyer, aggressive business manager of the New Orleans Item, for Chairman Walter G. Bryan had been rewarded for his good work on Hearst's Atlanta Georgian & American by assignment as publisher of the New York American. Mr. Newmyer reported enthusiastically on the previous year's campaign, carried on with the aid of the Southern Council of the A.A.A.A. Thomas E. Basham, of Louisville, who had spearheaded the A.A.A.A. council's co-operative effort with the publishers, was voted a $500 bonus. The convention also broadened the powers of the advertising committee and made its chairman ex-officio a member of the executive committee. It also voted to increase the advertising assessment to $10 per thousand circulation, and set aside 1 per cent of the advertising fund as compensation to the secretary-treasurer for his increased labors.

Collin Armstrong, speaking for the A.A.A.A., again adjured the publishers to uphold the hands of the advertising agencies which were building solid newspaper prosperity, by refusing commissions to direct advertisers and "house" agencies. He called for "unreserved co-operation of publishers" with the A.A.A.A. in its efforts to place newspaper advertising upon a high and profitable plane.

Still another index of the intensified interrelationship between newspapers and advertising organizations appeared in the address of Stanley Clague, managing director of the Audit Bureau of Circulations. Now well past its swaddling clothes stage, the ABC came under increasingly critical scrutiny from publishers. Newspaper executives no longer suspected the integrity of its auditors, but they noted that new rules set by the ABC tended to decrease the circulation which newspapers could report as net paid. Mr. Clague stanchly defended the rules as designed for the best interests of newspapers, declaring that tons of newsprint would be conserved for productive service when the publishers cut off circulation six to twelve months in arrears, from which they derived no revenue. The managing director did not refer to the other grievance generally held by publishers —that newspapers, paying the largest share of the Audit Bureau's costs had only a 10 per cent representation on its board of directors.

Presaging a much more active participation of newspaper publishers in the shaping of ABC policy, the Southern publishers adopted this resolution:

"We recommend that the SNPA make provision for and appoint a permanent ABC committee, this committee to be authorized to solicit proxies of SNPA membership and handle with other press associations, and take such steps as they deem advisable to secure their co-operation to the end that the greatest harmony may be maintained in the ABC and that publishers' interests may be protected in any laws of rules contemplated or passed by the directors of the ABC."

The cognate topic of postal rates continued to arouse indignation. Although the McKellar zone system amendment had been accepted by the Senate, it was not yet law, the convention heard from Col. Louis J. Wortham, of the Legislative committee. The iniquitous program fathered by Representative Claude Kitchin of North Carolina and Postmaster General Burleson remained in force. Colonel Wortham urged publishers to work for its repeal, not so much for the money value involved, but to maintain the principle that there should be the widest possible diffusion of knowledge among the people at the minimum of cost. He denied emphatically that newspapers' use of the second-class privilege cost the government $70,000,000 a year.

Rosy reports on the progress of the apprentices' school established with SNPA blessing the previous year at Macon, Ga., were made by President Allison. W. T. Anderson, publisher of the Macon Telegraph, headed the SNPA committee in charge of this activity and the school itself was under direction of his brother Eugene, characterized by Mr. Allison as a "born teacher." A start, at least, had been made toward overcoming the shortage of printers. This, and other questions concerning labor, held the Association in a long executive session with Henry N. Kellogg, chairman of the Special Standing Committee of the ANPA. The Association also named a committee to consider conditions in the photo-engraving craft, possibly with the idea that another school for apprentices might be undertaken.

A plea that the Southern newspapers would enrol voluntarily in the ranks of international peace-makers featured the only social session of the busy 1920 meeting. It was voiced by Sir Auckland Geddes, British Ambassador to the United States, and it fell upon the receptive ears of men and women who still hoped that World War I had not been fought wholly in vain. The objectives of Woodrow Wilson's statesmanship commanded universal sympathy and editorial support in the South of 1920.

Marcellus E. Foster, the pungent and scholarly editor of the Houston Chronicle, was elected president. W. Anson Elliott, of the Jacksonville Florida Times-Union moved up to the first vice-presidency, and was succeeded as second vice-president by Charles I. Stewart, of the

Lexington Herald. Walter C. Johnson, Chattanooga News, was again named secretary-treasurer, with increased pay and responsibilities. To the executive committee the following were elected, with each of the States now represented by a member:

Frederick I. Thompson, Mobile Register and Item; J. N. Heiskell, Little Rock Arkansas Gazette; Mrs. Lois K. Mayes, Pensacola Journal; J. C. Harrison, Augusta Chronicle; Urey Woodson, Owensboro Messenger; Arthur G. Newmyer, New Orleans Item; Thomas M. Hederman, Jackson (Miss.) Clarion-Ledger; John A. Park, Raleigh Times; E. K. Gaylord, Oklahoma City Oklahoman; B. H. Peace, Greenville (S.C.) News; E. Munsey Slack, Johnson City Staff; J. H. Allison, Fort Worth Record, and R. E. Turner, Norfolk Virginian-Pilot.

For the first time, the Association named a complete slate of major committees before the convention adjourned. A year-round program was placed in charge of these men:

Newsprint—Charles I. Stewart, Lexington Herald, chairman; J. C. Wilmarth, W. W. Weaver, F. C. Withers.

Legislative—Urey Woodson, Owensboro Messenger, chairman; Col. Louis J. Wortham, Major E. B. Stahlman, John Stewart Bryan, A. F. Sanford, E. B. Jeffress, and Rorer James.

Printing School—W. T. Anderson, Macon Telegraph, chairman; Harry Brown, George R. Koester, Col. Harry M. Ayers, W. W. Barksdale, Harry Giovannoli, M. Botts Lewis, Park W. Walker.

Photo-Engravers—A. W. Burch, Charlotte Observer, chairman; E. W. Barrett and R. E. Hughes.

Audit Bureau of Circulations—P. T. Anderson, Macon Telegraph, chairman; D. D. Moore, Roy G. Watson.

Traffic—Frank G. Bell, Savannah News, chairman; W. W. Holland, J. W. Hayes.

Program—Edgar M. Foster, Nashville Banner, chairman; P. M. Burdette, Charles P. Manship, Edward J. Paxton, and E. Taylor.

New Spheres of Influence

E. W. Barrett Demonstrates Newsprint Made from Southern Spruce Pine—Association Sees Macon Printers' School Grow, Then Raises Funds to Endow Journalism Teaching at Washington & Lee—Many Tasks Prove Need for Professional Management.

AFTER seven years of truly phenomenal progress, the Southern Newspaper Publishers Association might have welcomed a static period in which past proficiency might be reviewed and future paths charted. No such opportunity arrived in the early Twenties. The brief post-war depression solved no old problems and presented several all its own. Second class postal rates remained practically unchanged after 1919, but newspaper publishers contented themselves with approving postponement of scheduled increases in the schedules. If the existing status was unfair, as many considered it, newspapers had become accustomed to its working, and they feared that any new legislation might raise rather than lower their costs. The post-war decline in national advertising had interrupted the SNPA advertising effort, but it increased the members' concern with all proposals of the multiplying associations of advertisers. The price of newsprint reached its peak in 1921 and almost immediately began a gradual descent. While the price remained at its highest, the SNPA witnessed a demonstration by one of its oldest members that good newsprint could be made from plentiful Southern wood at a cost probably lower than that of Northern mills. The Macon School for Printers flourished, sought new finance from the SNPA and also from the ANPA, with the idea that the latter might support schools in other areas. Possibly inspired by this venture into education, the SNPA also undertook to raise endowment funds for the rehabilitation of the journalism school at Washington & Lee University, Lexington, Virginia, at which the beloved General Robert E. Lee had sought to establish instruction for journalism during the late 1860's. In good times and bad, membership continued to increase. It had grown from 61 in 1916 to 250 in 1923. Ambitious members proposed a code of conduct, with teeth that would punish infractions of rules for business operation. And, by 1923, the volume of correspondence, etc., that passed over the desk of Walter C. Johnson as Secretary-Treasurer convinced him and his fellow officers that a full-time manager was needed. Not even the industrious and wiry Johnson could carry the double burden of managing a newspaper and seeing to the wants of 250 Association members.

A token of the Association's broader scope appears in the size of the printed proceedings of the 1921 convention—72 pages of solid eight-point type, 25 picas wide. The proceedings were recorded in shorthand and transcribed by Miss Vocie Hines (now Mrs. Vocie Fawkes) who was at the time an employee of the Chattanooga News and Mr. Johnson's secretary. This meeting probably set a new record for range of subjects covered, but it was a record that would be surpassed year after year. For several reasons (that quickly lost whatever importance they might have pretended), the Association shifted its 1921 convention locale from Grove Park Inn, on the hills above the city, to the Battery Park Hotel, in the heart of downtown Asheville.[1]

Of outstanding interest at the 1921 meeting was a demonstration by Edward W. Barrett, publisher of the Birmingham Age-Herald, that Southern pine trees could be converted into standard newsprint of excellent quality and, probably, at a cost less than that of Northern wood. Mr. Barrett had asked fellow publishers at the 1920 convention to let him know whether they had pine trees in their area from which newsprint might be made. He heard from only one publisher, but went ahead on his own judgment that good paper could be made from

---

[1] F. L. Seely's program of making Grove Park Inn unforgettably distinctive included rules of conduct for his guests that verged on the monastic. Neatly printed signs in all rooms cautioned the occupants against making any unnecessary sounds after bedtime. Although the SNPA members and guests at conventions have always been notably decorous (by any business convention standards), several groups enjoyed a game of cards after business hours, and they resented the Inn's conventual restraints. The SNPA returned to Grove Park Inn for the 1922 meeting and several later conventions, until the membership outgrew its meeting and sleeping facilities.

trees that grew in Alabama and other Southern States. He selected a tree which he called "Southern spruce pine," and described as having a thinner bark than ordinary pine, only a trace of resin and turpentine, and only one inch of heartwood in an eight-inch bole.

He submitted his idea to paper-making friends. Some of them, for example, John Marshall of the Great Northern Paper Company, discouraged the effort. Mr. Marshall, respected and admired by many SNPA members, believed that Mr. Barrett planned to make the paper wholly of ground wood, with no sulphite content, and emphatically advised him not to throw his money away. One Canadian paper-maker, Mr. Robert Clade, agreed with the Birmingham publisher and suggested that he ship a quantity of the wood north for trial in an established mill.

Two carloads of wood, about 50 cords, were shipped to the Defiance Paper Company's mill at Niagara Falls (which at the time was in receivership and not producing for the trade), made into paper, and used for printing the June 20 issue of the Age-Herald, which Mr. Barrett proudly exhibited to his colleagues. The paper company's report, he declared, indicated that the "wood grinds easily, is fully equal in fiber and other respects to Canadian spruce, went through a 90-inch Pusey & Jones machine at a speed of 420 feet a minute without difficulty, and met the tests for standard newsprint completely." He was advised also that the price of Southern spruce pine delivered to a mill in the South would be about one-quarter of the cost of Canadian spruce delivered to a mill at Niagara Falls or other Northern points. Southern coal was cheaper than Northern coal, he said, and the water of the Warrior River was adaptable for paper manufacture.

While the publishers admired the acceptable printing qualities of the experimental sheet, Mr. Barrett asked the views of the paper-mill representatives at the convention. W. E. Mansfield of the International Paper Company remarked that "you can make wood pulp out of any kind of wood," and reminded the publishers that a mill in South Carolina had been making paper from pine for many years, but, like the Northern mills, had to go further and further from the mill site for its wood supply. Mr. Barrett replied that he knew of that operation and others, but that his present experiment employed an entirely different variety of wood.

Mr. Mansfield then thought his company might have overlooked an opportunity and asked that some of Mr. Barrett's wood be shipped to an International mill for further experiment. In a pleasant exchange between Mr. Barrett and Mr. Marshall, the latter remarked that he might be asking Mr. Barrett for a job. Mr. Barrett explained Mr. Marshall's previous misunderstanding of the project, and stated that the paper before this convention had been made of 70 per cent ground wood, 30 per cent sulphite pulp, a composition that made a grade of paper somewhat superior to that in general use by the Southern publishers at the time. (A copy of the June 20, 1921 issue of the Age-Herald is on file in the office of the SNPA at Chattanooga, Tennessee.)

Genuinely stirred by the prospect, several members proposed the appointment of a committee and the reimbursement by the Association of Mr. Barrett's expenses in the experiment. The Birmingham publisher declined any reimbursement, declared that he would continue his research and urged his fellows to do likewise. Then, if the facts warranted, they could consider establishment of a newsprint mill in the South. Mr. Barrett finally received the Association's hearty thanks, and the hope that he would share his achievement with the Association "one year hence."

But, alas, that bright promise was not realized "one year hence" nor for many another year. Mr. Barrett died suddenly in 1922 and his dream died with him. He had discouraged the appointment of an SNPA committee, which might have picked up the project and carried it to a successful conclusion in the flush 1920's. Most of the details had been kept in Mr. Barrett's brain, and apparently, no other publisher had taken his advice on parallel research. The conservation, development and utilization of Southern forest resources, one of the SNPA's most important undertakings in later years, would lie dormant until Dr. Charles H. Herty revived it a decade later.

In another quarter of the publishers' firmament, distant lightnings flickered a warning of labor difficulties. The eight-hour day had been generally accepted in the printing industry for more than a decade.

New Spheres of Influence

Now there were signs that the printers wanted a shorter work week. Job printers in New York City had, the previous year, shut down many shops by a "vacation", (read "strike") on behalf of the 44-hour week. Newspapers had not been affected then but ITU spokesmen had clearly indicated that the 44-hour week stood high on the union's agenda. On the other side, publishers were aware that important groups of employers felt that "union labor needed a lesson," a part of which would be substantial reduction in the high wages generated by war employment and high prices. Within two years that cause would assume portentous dimensions in many industries.

The SNPA in 1921 expressed itself briefly as favoring the principle of the eight-hour day and pledging its membership collectively and individually to do everything possible for its retention. Neither then nor later did the SNPA join in any "union-busting" program. Some of its members had been printers and held ITU cards. A minority (which included some of the Association's most influential members) looked upon unions as an unwarranted interference in employer-employee relationships and forestalled organization in their plants by human and humane contacts with employees of every grade. "Paternalistic" they were called then and later, but they made the idea work in their own plants and were content to let others follow their individual patterns.

The publishers did unite, however, in pledging support to the school for typesetting machine operators established two years earlier by the Andersons at Macon. According to W. T. Anderson, the Telegraph's publisher, and his brother Eugene, active head of the school, ample equipment had been assembled. Linotypes, Intertypes, and Monotype machines traded in by SNPA newspapers for new equipment were shipped by the manufacturers to the Macon school and reconditioned at school expense. On the 28 line-casting machines and 8 Monotypes, some 75 students had been trained during 18 months' operation. Most, but not all of them, had come from Southern homes. SNPA members and other publishers had given or pledged support of about $10,000 a year for three years, which Mr. Anderson believed adequate. Tuition fees averaged $150 per student, and Mr. Anderson advised against a lower fee, as likely to attract an inferior class of student.

W. T. Anderson saw two developments as most desirable. First was more adequate support of the school by SNPA members, in sending young people to the school for training, and by publicity in their newspaper columns to create public opinion favorable to the school's "graduates." Second, he favored the establishment of similar schools in other territories, supported by the American Newspaper Publishers Association.

Without hesitation, Mr. Anderson (himself an ITU card-holder) conceded that the school's trainees were not wholly competent job printers. They could operate a machine when they left the school, and, according to the experience of numerous publishers, they developed into capable operators within six months, if they were not discredited by the foreman and other union printers before they had had a chance to prove their worth. The school had had no difficulties with the typographical union and looked for none, he said. At that early stage, he estimated that three or four out of every ten students became union members after getting permanent employment.

His efforts were commended and the Association pledged its members to send at least one student each to the school during the next year. They also agreed to give the school publicity in their columns.

Apparently, the membership saw no inconsistency in that promise with their denunciation earlier in the meeting of the free publicity demands of automobile and amusement advertisers. The free publicity story has many complexities, the pious utterances of publishers in convention assembled often squared badly with their performances at home, but it was a question on which the SNPA as a body did not match the hysterical conduct of a few other newspaper groups. In principle, they deplored the idea that an automobile dealer should get a half-column or so of factory publicity with every piece of paid advertising, but a number of them "whipped the devil around the stump", rationalizing the free space when a sizable contract hung in the balance. When no advertising, present or potential, was involved, most publishers of 1921 seem to have tossed the propaganda on the floor. Practice varied on amusement publicity. As noted in an earlier chapter, some publishers printed serial condensations of current motion picture stories without believing that they had substantial reader interest. Others undoubtedly capitalized their enterprise, promoting new readers by the publication of stories which popular films brought to public notice. It seems probable that this device originated with Captain J. M. Patterson of the Chicago Tribune and New York Daily News,[2] which would indicate that it had at least passing merit as a circulation-getter.

That the Southern publishers did not differ from their brethren in other parts of the country in talking one policy and acting another is plain from the fact that free publicity remained a constant ingredient of newspaper conventions year after year. All recognized that potential advertisers kept up a constant effort to get themselves or their products mentioned in news columns as a cheap substitute for paid advertising. They also knew that some of these efforts carried news of great public interest. The announcement of a new price schedule or a new line of models by Ford or General Motors, for example, had to be printed as news, regardless of its commercial value to the manufacturer. Beginning with the war, the number of "worthy causes" demanding editorial space for fund-raising efforts had multiplied many times. Occasionally, these combined "space-mooching" with propaganda, but no publishers' association resolution could completely bar newspaper doors against them. Through the chinks that could never be sealed, free publicity of many kinds (including propaganda for worthy and doubtful causes) seeped into news columns.

With unquestionable logic, the publishers viewed their promised publicity for the Macon school as justified in the public interest. The school would train scores of young people in a useful craft. It would help to assure newspapers a supply of workmen which, apparently, could not be made available from existing sources. The school's work did not clash with the true interests of newspapers' unionized employees, and school graduates who measured up to union qualifications frequently obtained union membership without going through the prescribed five years' apprenticeship.

High principles of public interest were maintained by the SNPA in its 1921 discussion of a proposal that Congress repeal the 1912 requirement that daily newspapers publish sworn statements of circu-

---

[2] An American Dynasty, by John Tebbel. Doubleday & Co., Inc. Garden City, N.Y. 1947. Page 92.

lation twice a year. Stanley Clague, Managing Director of the Audit Bureau of Circulations, had brought this idea before various newspaper associations, with varying success. Disclaiming any wish to benefit the Audit Bureau by the move, Mr. Clague told the convention that the sworn statements required by the Post Office had no value for the advertiser. Whereas the ABC presented a completely informative analysis of circulations, the Post Office statement offered a gross and indefinable figure. Occasionally, it had been proven that the sworn statements by newspapers were deliberately falsified.

SNPA speakers, led by Major E. B. Stahlman, publisher of the Nashville Banner, advocated that the law stand unchanged. Its principal purpose was to inform the public as to the ownership of newspapers, and that information, all speakers agreed, should be public knowledge. Major Stahlman pointed out that newspapers which did not belong to the ABC and which made false statements under oath would not be induced to join the Bureau by lack of legal compulsion to make sworn statements.

During the discussion, the special ABC committee appointed at the 1920 meeting reported that it had voted against changing publisher representation on the ABC board at the previous October convention. Their aim, as expressed by President M. E. Foster, was to continue the ABC as a body which would serve the advertiser, the newspaper's customer, by furnishing essential information on newspaper circulation. That interest would be best served by insuring the continued control of the Bureau's operations by the advertiser, without increasing the publishers' voice.

The convention voted after an exhaustive discussion against repeal of any part of the 1912 law, but held that the "government should stand ready on occasion to verify by audit sworn circulation statements if the same are questioned or disputed by reputable persons or organizations acting in good faith."[3]

---

[3]With all but a negligible number of small newspapers now enrolled in the Audit Bureau of Circulations, the sworn statements of circulation have lost most of their one-time importance. During the 1940's, the law was amended to require their publication only once a year. Proceedings against newspapers for false statements of either ownership or circulation have been rare and of little effect. The original law provided no specific penalties for its violation. The Post Office apparently has lacked funds and legal facilities for institution of perjury proceedings in cases where offense might have been proven. The marked preferment displayed by advertisers for publications submitting their performance to ABC audit long ago starved out the circulation liars.

NEW SPHERES OF INFLUENCE

Discussion of postal rate legislation, for a change, took little convention time. Chairman Urey Woodson reported that the Legislative Committee was watching Washington, where the periodical publishers were said to be quietly working for repeal of the existing zone rate legislation. The Association adopted and telegraphed to members of the Congressional postal committees this terse resolution:

"Resolved, That the Southern Newspaper Publishers Association approves the proposed postponement of increase in second-class postal rates, which would become effective July 1, 1921, and approves the effort to secure the separation of newspapers from other classes of second-class matter."

With a Republican President and Republican majorities in both Senate and House, the predominantly Democratic Southern publishers had lost their former intimate contacts with department and committee heads, few of whom were Southerners under the Harding administration. The Legislative Committee, however, continued its vigilant and useful labors on national affairs.

Also of short duration was the discussion of photo-engraving matters. A. W. Burch, business manager of the Charlotte Observer, reported for the committee named in 1920 that a school could be established in Charlotte, but that such action probably would be unnecessary. Attempts of the photo-engravers' union to establish the selling price of engravings had been ruled illegal by the courts and Mr. Burch predicted early abandonment of restrictive efforts by the union.

Quite otherwise was the reception of a proposal that the SNPA endorse the establishment of a chair in journalism at Washington & Lee University as a memorial to General Robert E. Lee. Instruction for journalism had been a favored occasional topic at newspaper conventions for nearly five decades. In 1872, Whitelaw Reid, editor of the New York Tribune, had laid out a practical curriculum before the New York State Publishers Association, for possible adoption by New York University. And in 1903, Joseph Pulitzer, proprietor of the New York World, had outlined the program to which he would give effect after his death in 1911 by endowment of the Pulitzer School of Journalism at Columbia University. Prior to that date, Dr. Walter Williams had established a school at the University of

Missouri, with the hearty co-operation of the Missouri Press Association, and had already gained national recognition for both the "practical" and the "professional" standards it maintained. During the ensuing ten years or so, a number of schools of journalism had sprung into being, mostly in the Middle West. If any collegiate instruction for journalism existed in Southern universities before 1921, its operation attracted little attention.

Most SNPA members knew, vaguely or otherwise, that General Lee had attempted to found a school of journalism at Washington College, Lexington, Virginia, when he assumed the presidency of that small and war-ravaged institution after the War Between the States. One historian relates that the General informed the board of trustees in June, 1869, that "a limited number of boys can receive instruction in the printing office of Messrs. Lafferty & Co., in this town, for the present, without charge or cost to the college." Scholarships offered that summer included tuition and all college charges, with the condition that each student should labor one hour per day in the line of his profession. Although many new newspapers arose in the Reconstruction period in small Southern communities, the response to General Lee's call was meagre. General Lee's death in October, 1870, probably slowed acceptance of his idea, which, admittedly, was far ahead of its time. Washington & Lee catalogues continued to offer the instruction until 1878.[4]

What General Lee probably had in mind was the production of practical printer-editors who would help lift his people from the despair and poverty produced by the war. Differing from some of his most eminent colleagues and opponents on the battlefield, General Lee nursed no prejudices against newspapers. He realized their importance on both sides of the Potomac during the War. His program would have educated members of the typographical union (to which he appealed for help in finding candidates for the scholarships) for higher responsibility as community leaders.[5]

In presenting for adoption a resolution prepared by President Foster, these ambitions of General Lee were cited by Clark Howell,

---

[4]The Daily Newspaper in America. By Alfred M. Lee. The Macmillan Company, New York. 1937.

[5]R. E. Lee. By Douglas Southall Freeman. Vol. IV-page 425. Charles Scribner's Sons, New York. 1935.

Sr., publisher of the Atlanta Constitution and chairman of the committee for the project. The resolution, unanimously adopted, read:

"*Whereas*, General Robert E. Lee, the matchless leader of the Confederate armies, had the foresight and wisdom as a no less able educator to recognize the place of the editor in modern civilization and established at Washington College in 1869, a generation ahead of his times, the first school of journalism in America, which was discontinued eight years after his death for lack of funds; and

"*Whereas*, it is proposed that the editors of the South, by a simultaneous appeal for popular subscriptions, re-establish and endow the Lee Memorial School of Journalism at Washington & Lee University as their tribute to the founder of journalism as a learned profession: and

"*Whereas*, the press associations of various states and the president of the University have requested the Southern Newspaper Publishers Association to undertake the management of this patriotic enterprise,

"*Be It Resolved:* (1) That the Southern Newspaper Publishers Association heartily endorses this movement, hereby undertakes the responsibility of its management, and welcomes this opportunity to focus the gaze of the whole South upon the matchless character and services of her ideal hero.

"(2) That its president is hereby requested to appoint a central committee of seven members, of which he shall be one, who shall appoint state committees, select the date of the simultaneous appeal, and, as the representatives of the Southern editors, carry this patriotic enterprise to a successful conclusion.

"(3) That the president of the University be requested to act as consulting member of the central committee and to supply to the press, in preparation for the campaign, all needed information."

The modest General Lee might have jibbed at some of the flattering adjectives, but he would have welcomed both the intention and the active support of the publishers. The latter saw the fund-raising to its successful conclusion, as provided. More than that, they have given the school and education in general constant aid and encouragement.

Aside from Mr. Barrett's contribution, the convention's newsprint discussions mirrored the year's improvement in the situation. "Improvement" may cause a lifted eyebrow by readers who remember 1920-1921, since its principal cause was a sharp and sudden drop in the advertising flood. Operations of the Publishers' Buying Corporation and the decision of the big-city publishers to stop bidding for small lots of spot paper had checked the ascension of spot market prices at somewhere in the neighborhood of $300 per ton. In October, 1920, importation of a relatively small lot of German newsprint, with more promised from Swedish and Finnish mills, completely routed fears of a shortage. These imports had been arranged by the American Newspaper Publishers Association, under the guidance of Samuel P. Weston, former publisher of the Seattle Post-Intelligencer. Before 1920 ended, spot market purchases commanded lower than contract prices.

According to the report of Chairman Charles I. Stewart, hopes of some paper mills for a price of $150 per ton in 1921 were shattered. Instead, International Paper Company and other producers announced that they would cut tonnage of contract customers by 20 per cent, and International also allocated 10,000 tons to be distributed to newspapers without contracts. Mr. Stewart's committee arranged for allocation of some 2500 tons of this newsprint to Southern dailies. Before the process was ended, the paper manufacturer offered to take these small newspapers on as contract customers.

Available tonnage of Canadian and domestic mills exceeded the current demand by mid-1931, and several large manufacturers were offering contract tonnage at $95 per ton. Other mills, notably the Great Northern, which had treated the publishers fairly throughout the artificial crisis, were quoting $100 per ton and their customers sought no reduction. Mr. Stewart warned the publishers that the so-called "world-wide shortage of newsprint" had been created by propaganda in the interest of abnormally high prices, and advised that contracts for an adequate supply with a dependable manufacturer constituted the best possible insurance against future crises. He concluded on a note that publishers often struck in later years—"the interests of the newspaper publishers and the newsprint manufacturers are mutual."

The same decline in newspaper advertising linage (which was comparatively short-lived and not so disastrous as had been feared) caused no reduction in the "Sell it South" advertising campaign that had been planned for 1920-1921. In fact, the committee approved adequate campaigns in several trade journals plus a number of insertions in strategically situated daily newspapers outside of the South. Total appropriations to November 1, 1921, for space and art work amounted to $19,331.25, against current collections and reserves of $20,829.77. Under the chairmanship of A. G. Newmyer, a strong SNPA committee worked smoothly with a committee representing the Southern Council of the AAAA in preparing the campaign. The committee sought and received the editorial co-operation of the Southern dailies in combating Northern misconceptions of Southern business conditions, 114 SNPA newspapers filing editorials of this character with Mr. Newmyer. The committee urged continuation of the advertising through 1922 on a similar scale.

During the 1920-1921 year the Association stiffened its hitherto informal procedure for recognition of advertising agencies in its territory. Again working in close co-operation with the AAAA and, on its own, gathering a mass of data on agency credit, it recommended the recognition of some 29 agencies, refusal of recognition to another 24, and temporary withholding of recognition from one agency. The gist of the committee's report appears in this dogmatic paragraph:

"We emphatically state that if this work is to be truly effective, the entire membership of the SNPA must pledge itself not to grant, or to allow its special representatives to grant, agency commission to anyone not specifically recognized by this Association; and furthermore, in the absence of definite action by this Association, it must be agreed to inform all agencies that commission will be withheld for not longer than six months to allow for definite decision on their qualifications by this Association. Unless such support is granted, your committee feels its work valueless—for individual action by the membership on such matters is unfair alike to publishers and to agencies of real character and standing."

The good intentions of that dictum cannot be questioned. Its adoption indicated, however, that the 1921 membership of the SNPA had forgotten one of the principles stated at its establishment 18 years earlier—non-interference with the internal conduct of its members' business. This convention action and those in succeeding years led to proceedings against the SNPA a few years later by the Federal Trade Commission—proceedings which were dropped in 1930 because the pre-New Deal government decided that newspapers, not being in interstate commerce, lay outside the Trade Commission's jurisdiction. The Federal Trade Commission, however, found no evidence that the SNPA had ever taken any action under the terms of this or similar resolutions. Walter Johnson as secretary, and later Cranston Williams as secretary-manager, recognized the impracticality of Association action in disciplining members. The resolution's powers were never invoked.

Another 1921 project also involved some such internal interference, but afforded vitally necessary assistance to members in the growing complexity of labor relations.

This contemplated the establishment of a special standing committee on labor and the employment of one or more experts to assist publishers in relations with the newspaper unions.

This important policy took form in the following resolution, hammered into shape in the course of a lengthy discussion:

"*Resolved,* That to promote a fair scale of wages to be paid by members of the SNPA and establish fair working conditions, one or more wage experts be employed by the Board of Directors, whose duties shall be:

"First—To prepare, with the advice and approval of the Board of Directors, a standard form of contract to be entered into between members of the SNPA and such employees as they may wish to contract with.

"Second—To formulate a mutually fair scale of wages to be paid by the different papers to their different employees, this scale to be based on the size of cities and living conditions in each.

"Third—To be present and assist any employer in renewing contracts with any employees.

"*Resolved further,* That we will not enter into any contract without consulting the said wage expert of the SNPA.

New Spheres of Influence

"*Resolved further,* That if the expense of the said wage expert cannot be paid out of the ordinary funds of said SNPA, the Board of Directors be requested to prorate the additional expense among the publishers of said organization.

"*Resolved further,* That the incoming president is hereby authorized to name a special standing committee on labor, and that the directors of the SNPA and the Labor Committee are authorized to take all action necessary to carry on the purposes of these resolutions, including the making of assessments to meet all necessary expenses."

Sharp-eyed readers will have noted the resolution's mention of the "Board of Directors." When the change to this form of organization from the old Executive Committee took place existing records do not indicate. The roster of officers, etc., published in 1936 designates an executive committee through 1921-1922 and begins calling it a board of directors with the 1922-1923 listing. In fact, if not in name, the board appears to have been constituted at the 1920 convention, when, for the first time, one member was named for each State in the Association. The change certainly became formal when the Association set up was reorganized at the 1922 convention.

Officers elected in 1921 were:

President, W. A. Elliott, Jacksonville Florida Times-Union; first vice-president, Charles I. Stewart, Lexington Herald; second vice-president, Arthur G. Newmyer, New Orleans Item; secretary-treasurer, Walter C. Johnson, Chattanooga News.

Board of directors—Frank H. Miller, Montgomery Journal; J. N. Heiskell, Little Rock Arkansas Gazette; E. Taylor, Miami Herald; Charles D. Atkinson, Atlanta Journal; Urey Woodson, Owensboro Messenger; Robert Ewing, New Orleans States; T. M. Hederman, Jackson Clarion-Ledger; A. W. Burch, Charlotte Observer; E. K. Gaylord, Oklahoma City Oklahoman; Robert Lathan, Charleston News & Courier; Mrs. Edith O. Susong, Greeneville (Tenn.) Democrat-Sun; Marcellus E. Foster, Houston Chronicle; Charles P. Hasbrook, Richmond Times-Dispatch.

There must have been something in the air of the early 20's that caused newspaper people, in convention assembled, to promulgate codes of conduct and provide more or less effective means of their enforcement. Best known of the "codes" adopted during that period is the Canons of Journalism published by the new American Society of Newspaper Editors in 1923, which set standards of editorial conduct that no decent newspaperman could reject. President Harding gave to the world his code of ethics for the Marion Star, and Dean Walter Williams of the University of Missouri School of Journalism issued "The Journalist's Creed." Both are unimpeachable. The Newspaper Advertising Executives Association in 1921 also defined broad standards of practice governing newspaper advertising.

Within a year or two, the American Society of Newspaper Editors was to measure the unethical conduct of a member by the Canons of Journalism yardstick, and, regretfully, to find that it could not act because his sins had been committed before the adoption of the Canons. The member resigned from the Society, without publicity.

The Associated Press, of course, had fined and otherwise punished members for infractions of its rules over many years, but such matters were held strictly in the family and offenders were spanked privately in the woodshed. The Audit Bureau of Circulations occasionally suspended a publication which did not comply with its standards, but did so without fanfare. Up to 1922, however, the record reveals no instance of an association of newspaper publishers prescribing rules for its membership, with penalties for their violation. Most, if not all, of them (including the ANPA) operated on the principle stated in the organization of the SNPA—no interference with the internal affairs of their members.

But, such was the climate in 1922, no one seems to have been shocked by the *Editor & Publisher* headline over the SNPA convention story. Arthur Robb, who wrote the head over the telegraphed report by John F. Redmond, then managing editor of Editor & Publisher, remembers no sense of disbelief or disapproval of the innovation. The headline proclaimed, in 30-point caps:

S.N.P.A. WILL PUNISH RULE-BREAKING MEMBERS[6]
—o—
Standards Will be Drawn and Secret Grievance Committee Will Enforce Them—New Organization Plan Adopted—Stewart President, Newmyer Board Chairman

---

[6]Editor & Publisher, July 15, 1922.

New Spheres of Influence

The dispatch related that new standards of conduct for newspaper associations had been set by the SNPA in amending its constitution and by-laws to the effect that members who broke rules, regulations, or the spirit of regulations would be subject to penalties in the form of fines, censure, expulsion "or other punishment." A grievance committee would hear evidence and fix penalties. Punishment would be inflicted only for violation of rules, regulations and resolutions to be adopted in future, with the full knowledge that they carry a penalty. Included in the list of possible violations would be infraction of standards of practice that the SNPA might adopt pertaining to advertiser and agency relations, ethics, etc. Punished members would have the right of appeal to the convention, but between the action of the grievance committee and the convention, the sentence would stand. The regulations and standards of practice which might be violated must have been adopted by a two-thirds vote of members present at a convention and must also have been notified to all members by registered mail.

The reporter commented that the action was believed to be the first of its kind ever taken by any American newspaper body, and related that it arose from complaints that some SNPA members were granting commissions direct to advertisers, cutting rates, allowing agencies to split commissions, competing unfairly, disregarding association policies, etc.

Definition of advertising and agency practice was referred to the committee on agency relations, which was authorized to draw up standards of agency recognition, agency practice, advertiser co-operation, etc.

Procedure was further strengthened (and complicated) by an agreement with the AAAA, represented at the convention by Collin Armstrong, of New York, that complaints against agencies would be registered with that body. Mr. Armstrong invited specific complaints about AAAA members who demanded free publicity, undue co-operation advertising accounts, special position without extra compensation to the newspaper, rate-cuts, etc. Mr. Armstrong, grim of visage but gentle of speech, had done an extremely effective job in recent years, in conjunction with James O'Shaughnessy, executive secretary of the AAAA, converting hundreds of newspapers to the agency way of thinking on problems of mutual interest. On net balance the newspapers en masse were the gainers by reforms which established rational relationships between circulation and advertising rates, standardized rate cards, established equitable standards for advertising agency commissions, discouraged agency demands for free publicity and other favors that tainted the advertising atmosphere. He and his associates must be recognized as major factors in the moral urge that actuated the 1922 convention.

Another prime mover whose name must be starred was Arthur G. Newmyer, business manager of the New Orleans Item. Aggressive and articulate, Mr. Newmyer had been active for more than a decade in the Associated Advertising Clubs of the World and its predecessor organizations. In his own newspaper activities and in many appearances before newspaper groups, he had kept to the fore the banner of "truth in advertising."

When the SNPA assembled at Asheville (back once more in Grove Park Inn) July 10-12, 1922, Mr. Newmyer brought forward his plan of reorganization with the avowed purpose of "putting more life into the association." Without question, the philosophy of enacting codes that meant what they said and provided penalties for violation, can be attributed mainly to his crusading spirit. His organization plan did, indeed, give new strength to the SNPA skeleton, which, as these annals have shown, had been altered ad lib. to meet conditions as they arose.

The Newmyer plan abolished the vice-presidencies, which, in recent years, had provided a gradual succession to the presidency for men who had displayed interest and leadership. The president would now be elected without regard to his previous offices, by vote of the convention. Second-in-command would be a chairman of the board, to be elected by the directors, one representing each State in the Association. The secretary-treasurer would be continued as a co-ordinating officer with the president, the board chairman and the directorate. Each director would be assisted by a state committee of five members, sub-chairmen for news, legislation, business office matters, labor, and advertising. Two general chairmen would be named by the president, one to have charge of news matters and legislation, the other of business office, labor and advertising affairs. The effect would have been establishment of five standing committees, representing all states, and headed by the two general chairmen. The latter would be responsible to the president and the board of directors.

As presented by Mr. Newmyer in enlarged chart form, the plan looked attractively feasible. It was adopted, but before the "ayes" had died away, the unregimented publishers decided to add committees not provided in the chart. The grievance committee and the committee on agency relations could not be fitted into the Newmyer framework and they were appointed by the incoming president on a confidential basis; their names were known only to the president and the board of directors. It was also decided to name a separate committee to handle advertising campaigns conducted by the Association. Neither of the two general chairmen provided in the table of organization was named before the convention adjourned.

Nobody doubted the advantages of a change in the frame of organization. Within six years the Association's membership had more than quadrupled and its activities had taken many forms that none had imagined in 1916. In Mr. Newmyer's concept, the Association would theoretically be equipped to deal with many other matters, and to apply salutary discipline. Thirty years later, it appears probable that few of the members who approved the plan had thoroughly analyzed its implications; with the national instinct for democratic self-government, they adopted the whole, applied what they needed at the moment, and left the rest to the future.

One future activity that was considered essential was renewal of the "Sell It South" advertising campaign. After six years of uninterrupted advertising gains, newspapers in 1920-1922 ran into many successive months in which they "didn't beat last year." That discouraged a number of SNPA members who had contributed to previous advertising campaigns and they declined participation in the 1921-1922 project, so earnestly approved the previous summer. And, with newspapers operating as they did in 1922 (and for long thereafter), it is altogether likely that the loss of only a small proportion of their national advertising volume meant the wiping out of their profits. Members who had paid their assessments got them back from the discouraged advertising committee. But 1922-1923 should be a different story, they resolved. It wasn't.

Once more the convention affirmed its devotion to the Lee Memorial School of Journalism at Washington and Lee and prodded the members to get busy on the local campaigns for funds that had been approved in 1921. The advertising doldrums had evidently stilled activity along that line also.

Organization of the special standing committee on labor had not been fully accomplished, either. The new labor committee, with each State represented, was empowered to keep members advised at all times, through the secretary, of local labor conditions, to collect the assessments approved in 1921, and to appoint field representatives, if necessary.

The convention voted to tax each member $1 for each composing machine in his shop to help support the Macon printers' school, which had been promised similar aid from the American Newspaper Publishers Association after January 1, 1923. Such assessment would assure a permanent fund of $9,000 for the school. Any relations between the school and the International Typographical Union were disapproved.

Some old straw was rethreshed when the convention approved compensation of advertising agencies by payment of commissions by publishers, rather than by the fees of the clients served by the agencies. Payment of commissions direct to advertisers and the splitting of commissions between agencies and their advertiser clients were opposed.

Second class postal rates ranked high on the 1922 agenda. During the past year a loose confederation of organizations representing newspapers, magazines, trade journals and other publications had taken the name of the American Publishers Conference, with the mission of working toward postal rates acceptable to all publishers. The conference favored the Kelly bill, sponsored by a Pennsylvania publisher sitting in the House of Representatives, which would have cut second class rates back to the 1919-1920 schedules. The SNPA heard an address by Frederick W. Hume, executive secretary of the National Publishers Association (magazines) and representing the American Publishers Conference. The brilliant and persuasive Hume, with long experience in Washington lobbies, once more told the Southern publishers what they had heard years before from Major E. B. Stahlman and other members of the Legislative Committee—that the Post

Office did not have any rational basis for its second class charges. Hume was out to make certain that the SNPA, with its many close friendships in Congress, would be in his corner when the Kelly bill came up in December. He won a pledge of support from the convention, which suggested that Mr. Hume or another conference representative attend the meetings of Southern state press associations and inform them of the postal rate situation. As Mr. Hume put it, publishers were paying $33,000,000 more a year than they paid in 1917 for postal service; all other war revenue measures affecting other industries had been revoked or amended, but the war-time postal rates remained on the books.

The SNPA, however, did not put all of its eggs into the American Publishers Conference basket. Its able Legislative Committee asked and received approval of a fund of $5,000 to be raised among the membership by the directors to finance its work in Washington, which had broadened to include many matters besides postal rates. It was now watching tariff laws, taxation proposals and censorship attempts, and believed the day was near when the SNPA should have permanent representation at the Capitol.

Near the 1922 convention's close, another of those tiny premonitory signs appeared, as they did at so many SNPA meetings. President W. A. Elliott discussing the value of radio broadcasting to newspapers, said that the Jacksonville Times-Union had noted no direct benefits from its station, but he believed it was a good means of keeping the name of a morning paper impressed on the public mind during the hours when the paper was not for sale on the streets. This was, almost certainly, the first comment by a newspaper publisher on the potential value of a radio broadcasting adjunct. Few newspapers had then given more than passing thought to radio as a mass communications medium, and the number of newspaper-owned stations in 1921-1922 could have been counted on the fingers of one hand. The first commercially sponsored radio advertising program would not go on the air of WEAF, New York, until September 7, 1922, several months after the SNPA meeting.

Under the new organization, Charles I. Stewart, Lexington Herald, became president. He had been first vice-president. Mr. Newmyer, who had been second vice-president, became the first chairman of the board of directors, elected by the latter body. Walter C. Johnson,

Chattanooga News, continued his seemingly perpetual assignment as secretary-treasurer. The new Board of Directors was constituted as follows:

F. Harvey Miller, Montgomery Journal; Elmer E. Clarke, Little Rock Arkansas Democrat; W. A. Elliott, Jacksonville Florida Times-Union; Major Clark Howell, Jr., Atlanta Constitution (the first appearance of Major Howell in the SNPA command); W. W. Stouffer, Louisville Post; Arthur G. Newmyer, New Orleans Item; T. M. Hederman, Jackson Clarion-Ledger; Josephus Daniels, Jr., Raleigh News & Observer; E. K. Gaylord, Oklahoma City Oklahoman and Times; R. C. Siegling, Charleston News & Courier; Mrs. W. W. Barksdale, Clarksdale Leaf-Chronicle; Roy G. Watson, Houston Post; Major Allen Potts, Richmond News-Leader.

Before the Southern publishers assembled (in wholly new surroundings) for their 1923 meeting, general business had stopped dragging its feet. Advertising had resumed its upward course, keeping time with the march of "prosperity" that would continue without interruption into 1930. After a not too fruitful year since the 1922 convention, the Southern Newspaper Publishers Association assembled at the Greenbrier Hotel, White Sulphur Springs, W. Va., July 9-11, and made its first order of business complete organization under the plan adopted in 1922.

White Sulphur Springs had been a favorite resort of many Southerners over a stretch of years that antedated the War Between the States, but until 1923 it had lain beyond SNPA territory. With the admission of five West Virginia newspapers, the Association had at last attained its full geographical scope, and its convention in the Greenbrier's stately halls witnessed its preparation for a new scale of activity.

Retiring President Charles I. Stewart set the new pace by proposing that new officers be elected early in the convention so that organization of the complex committees provided in the 1922 table could be accomplished before adjournment. Mr. Stewart had experienced the difficulty of filling committee places by correspondence, and though he would have no place in the new organization (he had left the newspaper business) he wished his successor to have his "cabinet" posts filled before the members left for home.

New Spheres of Influence

As the father of the 1922 scheme, it was fitting that Arthur G. Newmyer, promoted during the year to associate publisher of the New Orleans Item, should have the honor of putting it into full effect. He did so, to the last place on every committee, within forty-eight hours of his election as president. Nobody had any question concerning the office of secretary-treasurer; Walter C. Johnson had to remain, but he made it emphatic that the office now needed the services of a full-time professional manager.

Several names appeared for the first time among the directors, together with a number of veterans. The new slate was:

Victor H. Hanson, Birmingham News; Elmer E. Clarke, Little Rock Arkansas Democrat; W. Anson Elliott, Jacksonville Florida Times-Union; Major Clark Howell, Jr., Atlanta Constitution; Harry Giovannoli, Lexington Leader; Colonel Robert Ewing, New Orleans States; Major Frederick Sullens, Jackson (Miss.) News; H. Galt Braxton, Kinston Free Press; E. K. Gaylord, Oklahoma City Oklahoman and Times; George R. Koester, Greenville Piedmont; Major E. B. Stahlman, Nashville Banner; Major Allen Potts, Richmond News-Leader; Roy G. Watson, Houston Post; and W. Guy Tetrick, Clarksburg (W. Va.) Exponent.

Mr. Hanson became chairman of the board. Edgar M. Foster, business manager of the Nashville Banner, was appointed general chairman of the business office committees, and Major John S. Cohen, editor of the Atlanta Journal, general chairman of the news and legislative affairs committees. Sub-chairmen of the "standing" committees provided by the 1922 plan were named as follows:

Business Office—Charles Allen, Montgomery Advertiser.

Labor—J. W. Bowen, Birmingham Age-Herald.

Advertising—James E. Chappell, Birmingham News.

News and Legislative Affairs—These committees were combined as one body under the direct chairmanship of Major John S. Cohen, who also served as chairman of the committee on the Washington & Lee School of Journalism.

Each of the above committees had a full quota of members representing every State.

Membership of the grievance and agency relations committees was held confidential. New special committees were constituted for traffic (a question of newly important status) and on printing schools.

Major Stahlman headed the traffic committee, which comprised Col. Robert Ewing, New Orleans States; Urey Woodson, Owensboro Messenger; E. B. Jeffress, Greensboro News, and John A. Brice, Atlanta Journal.

Expiration of the SNPA contract with the printers' school at Macon, Ga., as of October 1, 1923, stirred up the whole question of educating young printers. The discussion, in executive session, stemmed from the wish of some members to have schools established in other cities of the South and to divide SNPA financial support among these and the Macon institution. That was a development to be anticipated, for the $9,000 or $10,000 made available annually to the Macon school by the contributions of SNPA and ANPA publishers stood as a bright target for technical schools which had enjoyed moral but not financial support from the publishers. After deciding to renew the Macon contract, the Association named a committee to investigate the claims of other schools for association approval and support. Mr. Woodson headed this committee, in association with Colonel Ewing, M. E. Foster, Major A. Potts, and Harry Giovannoli.

Not difference but solid unity of opinion marked the publishers' decision on the next educational item—completion of the task undertaken two years before for the endowment of the Lee Memorial School of Journalism at Washington & Lee University. Major Cohen reported receipt of pledges totaling $38,000 from and through newspapers of the South. Upon a proposal that the balance to complete the publishers' pledge of $50,000 be raised at the convention, more than $13,000 was promised within five minutes. P. T. Dodge, president of the International Paper Company and of the Mergenthaler Linotype Company, celebrated his July 11 birthday by starting the list with $2,000. Many of the members and guests who had previously contributed to the fund rose in their seats with additional pledges. This was the first of many proofs during the next three decades that Southern newspaper interest in Southern education meant deeds and dollars, not mere kind words.

New Spheres of Influence

The generous Philip T. Dodge also addressed advice to the publishers from both of his industrial thrones. Even though his International Paper Company had been damned as "the trust" by a generation of publishers, SNPA members also recalled that it had made available 10,000 tons of paper during the recent crisis for newspapers without paper contracts. That had been a sound stroke of business and 10 years or so later, it would have been called "good public relations." Some of both qualities marked his 1923 advice to the SNPA that publishers should not depend too greatly on foreign sources for their newsprint supplies—foreign, on this occasion, applying only to European suppliers. Mr. Dodge added to his store of publisher goodwill by referring to the assistance Mergenthaler Linotype Company had given to the education of printers. Its donations of machines alone amounted to a $500,000 value, he said.

In tune with the educational atmosphere came an address by Major George L. Berry, president of the International Printing Pressmen's and Assistants' Union. Major Berry noted that his union was the only one of the five international printing craft unions which had not broken off international arbitration relations with the American Newspaper Publishers Association. He told the SNPA that any proposal by union or publisher which affected the cost of newspaper production and did not give full consideration to the rights of the other party must be considered immoral.[7]

As already noted, 1923 prices of newsprint had rebounded slightly upward and SNPA leaders took steps to help the membership keep paper consumption under control. Members were asked (in a resolution introduced by Major Stahlman) to inform the secretary of their paper use in a stated period when conservation rules were in force, with their average circulation in that period, compared with similar reports for corresponding periods in 1923 and 1924.

---

[7]Strained relations had existed for several months between the New York local of Major Berry's union and the city's daily newspapers. A strike had been threatened by local officers and several minor walkouts had delayed production of one or more Manhattan newspapers. Major Berry stood firm against a strike as the remedy for the local's well-founded grievances, and during the SNPA convention at White Sulphur Springs gave Arthur Robb a statement for publication that he would disband the New York local if it resorted to an unauthorized strike. Despite this published warning, the local struck early in September, 1923, preventing individual publication of the New York dailies for about 10 days. Major Berry kept his word. Local No. 2 was disbanded and reorganized by the I.P.P.&A.U., which made a new contract with the New York publishers. Normal relations were resumed after a year and have continued unbroken.

Appointment of a traffic committee, noted above, marked the new concern of publishers in the rise of railroad freight rates on newsprint. Prior to 1914, freight charges had bothered few publishers. The majority of newsprint contracts had quoted prices for delivery of the paper with freight paid from the mill to city of publication. After 1914, the rule had been "f.o.b. mill", but in the war years publishers were more concerned with the rising cost of transportation. Now the railroads were seeking higher rates, through change of classification and other devices, which would have increased the cost of paper three cents to eight cents per 100 pounds, adding 60 cents to $1.60 to the $80 or so per ton that Southern newspapers paid on 1923 contracts. The traffic committee was authorized to co-operate with other traffic bureaus to head off this "unjust freight increase", and, if necessary, to appear before the Interstate Commerce Commission to place the "active support of the Southern newspapers squarely beside the work of the traffic bureaus of the South in this fight."

A hearing conducted by an examiner of the I.C.C. was held in Atlanta. At this hearing which extended over a period of almost two weeks, representatives of traffic bureaus and shippers put in an appearance. Although Secretary-Manager Johnson's knowledge of the freight rate structure was limited and he owed a duty to his newspaper, he took time out to attend and testify for Southern newspapers. As a result of coaching by a freight rate expert and listening to the testimony of others for several days, he was ready when called. He, therefore, obtained a liberal education in the intricacies of freight rates. Incidentally, the decision of I.C.C. was in favor of the shippers. The savings to newspapers, which at the time were paying the freight bills, were considerable.

Express rates on transportation of printed papers were also on the rising escalator and had been for the previous year or two, especially in Tennessee. In the old days, some newspapers and railroad companies had had a friendly arrangement. The papers published local railroad schedules daily and charged for the space at card rates. In payment for the advertising the railroads carried newspapers gratis, almost entirely within the State where they were published. In some localities this relationship continued after the American Express Company (later the Railway Express Agency) took over this class of railroad business. Now the American Express Company had set a rate of $1.00 per 100 pounds for intra-state transportation of newspapers regardless of distance carried. The SNPA resolution requested newspapers to take steps to have this rate cancelled and an intrastate limit of 50 cents per 100 pounds established, by action of State railway or utility commissions.

Once more the postal rate situation was reviewed by Colonel Robert Ewing, Major Stahlman, and Frederic A. Hume of the American Publishers Conference. And again the Association voted to cooperate with the latter organization in its efforts to adjust second class postal rates downward.

A recent action of the Canadian Parliament alarmed the publishers. It empowered the Dominion government to make regulations prohibiting the export of pulpwood from freehold and privately-owned timberlands. Apparently this was a Canadian move on the politico-economic chessboard, with the implicit purpose of forcing more and more of the newsprint industry to the Canadian side of the border. According to the SNPA resolution, United States manufacturers then imported about 1,000,000 cords of pulpwood from such Canadian lands, and the loss of this source would put some mills out of business, destroy employment opportunities, and add greatly to the newsprint bill of United States newspapers. Protesting against the step, the SNPA requested the American Secretary of State to lay before the Dominion government the consequences of Canadian action along this line, with the warning that "it could only be regarded as an unfriendly act, inevitably bound to seriously disturb the cordial entente that has been so long maintained."

There is no record that Secretary of State Hughes took either the resolution of the Canadian Parliament or that of the SNPA seriously. It is not at all likely that he employed the portentous words of the SNPA, for the idiom of diplomacy gives "unfriendly act" a grave connotation that was scarcely warranted by the occasion.

Retiring President Stewart received the thanks of the Association for his long labors as committee chairman and officer, and was elected to honorary membership, with the hope that he would return to the newspaper field. In his farewell, Mr. Stewart warned publishers that news and editorial departments should be strengthened.

"There is not," he said, "the proper appreciation on the part of the average newspaper publisher of the real value of the high-class reporter, and the compensation offered for reportorial work is rarely sufficient to attract first-class material. Many newspapers pay compositors more than they pay reporters, although the reporter is one of the most important means of contact between the publication and the public. A definite course by this organization, looking to a higher standard of reportorial service, would be not only a service to its membership and the communities they represent but also the pursuit of sound business policy."

Without a dissenting vote the Association adopted the report of the advertising agency relations committee appointed in 1922. This report embodied a thorough study of the subject and laid down policies to be followed by SNPA members. The report included a list of "recognized" agencies in Southern territory. It also included a list of advertisers, some old and consistent users of newspaper space, which employed no advertising agency but demanded that they be paid the agency commission. The report recommended that the agency commission be denied to these firms. It also stated rules for "cooperation" to be rendered by newspapers on advertising accounts, accepting the Code of Practice adopted in 1921 by the National Association of Newspaper Executives (later known as the Association of Newspaper Advertising Executives). The report also recommended that the troublesome question of "differential" between national and local advertising rates be resolved by making the rates on national advertising exceed local rates only by the amount of the advertising agency commission.

In conclusion, the committee report, submitted by Arthur G. Newmyer as chairman, noted that "its findings are merely a recommendation to our membership and that to secure decisive action on this report, the Association must act in convention assembled."

The convention did act, accepting the scholarly document with a minimum of discussion and no dissent. One may speculate 30 years later whether the members recognized that this could be one of those actions which they had bound themselves to obey, under penalty, by the constitution and by-laws adopted in 1922. In theory, the committee's philosophy was unassailable; the code of conduct it laid down was one that the great majority of Southern publishers wished to follow. But—in denying commission to "direct" advertisers who had received it from newspapers for many years, it attempted to upset an accepted trade custom by an arbitrary fiat. The "direct" advertisers did not take this blow at their privileges supinely, as would appear within the next year or two.

In a lighter vein, the publishers looked forward to a pleasant innovation. John Stewart Bryan, publisher, and Major Allen Potts, business manager, of the Richmond News-Leader, promised their colleagues that they would read daily reports of their activities, delivered by airplane from Richmond within an hour or so of each day's adjournment. The author recalls a long afternoon and evening wait at the edge of the Greenbrier golf course with Mr. Bryan, Major Potts, Col. Hierome L. Opie, editor of the Staunton Leader, and J. Roy Flannagan, the reporter who had written the story for the News-Leader. The sun had disappeared behind the Western ranges and Mr. Bryan had gone to dinner when sharp eyes caught the airplane edging over the long ridge to the Eastward, an hour or two, or maybe three, behind schedule. A score of publishers rushed to the plane as it landed, with the pilot cheerily explaining that he had had a mad chase for gasoline fit for an airplane engine after a landing at Clifton Forge, and the News-Leader's extra was delivered to the Greenbrier dining room by as distinguished a group of carriers as ever any newspaper boasted. While any claim to a "first" must be put forward delicately, it is probable that the SNPA in 1923 was the first newspaper gathering to read an air-delivered account of its day's proceedings.

Are Newspapers Interstate Commerce?

Federal Trade Commission Asserts Jurisdiction over Advertising Practices in 1925 Complaint, Dismissed Six Years Later—Cranston Williams Named as SNPA Manager—Association Adopts Code of Ethics—The "Golden Age" Ends.

PROSPERITY reigned over most of the South in the years between 1924 and 1930. Even the ravages of the boll weevil in the cotton belt were received as a disguised blessing, compelling Southern farmers to turn their land at last to other crops. Although a number of prominent SNPA journalists had to miss the 1924 convention because of their efforts to name a "successor to Jefferson" at the endless Democratic convention in New York, many Southern publishers purred contentedly under the Coolidge calmness.

Newsprint troubles had faded. Plenty of paper could be had at fair prices for the growing demands of circulation and advertising. Labor disputes troubled few Southern dailies. Postal rate regulations continued to boil and bubble and to elicit annual warnings from the Legislative Committee, and traffic matters kept the headquarters office in a small blizzard of correspondence. The Association at last accepted Walter C. Johnson's urging that the SNPA needed a full-time manager and he made an excellent choice for that post. Mr. Johnson was rewarded in 1925 by election to the Presidency, and then advanced to Chairman of the Board. All in all, the picture was one of normal, placid progress.

When trouble came, it arrived from a totally unanticipated quarter. It will be recalled that the SNPA in 1922 had adopted strict rules of conduct for its members in payment of commissions to advertising agencies and in withholding such commissions from concerns which employed no agencies. Implicit in the SNPA code was the idea that members would apply its provisions uniformly, with no exceptions, as a duty to their common tie of SNPA membership. Shadowy penalties for violation of the code were enacted casually and without extended debate by the Association in 1922 and 1923.

Among the large advertisers affected by the withholding of commissions were numbered several which had received substantial discounts from newspaper card rates for three or four decades. In the last quarter of the 19th Century, newspapers had welcomed their patronage. They constituted bread-and-butter income for hundreds of publishers, buying space in large quantities and frequently paying cash in advance. Money in the bank was then worth a sizable discount. As newspapers grew more prosperous, however, many bucked at what had become an established practice. When the American Newspaper Publishers Association was organized in 1887, its primary reason for being was reform of the chaotic payments of commission to advertising agencies and direct advertisers. Reports rendered at its early meetings indicated that discounts allowed by publishers ranged all the way from 10 per cent to 75 per cent from card rates, with 20 per cent the prevalent allowance by metropolitan newspapers.

The early Twenties saw much of this confusion eliminated by parallel action of publishers' associations and the newly reorganized American Association of Advertising Agencies. The SNPA action in 1922-1923 had been an honest effort to banish its remnants, to recognize the function of the advertising agency and to fix a uniform compensation for its services, and at the same time to protect the advertising agency flanks from erosion by splitting of commissions and payments to firms which employed no agency service. The reform had its place in the general purge of unethical advertising practices.

When SNPA members sought to comply with their own code by refusing commission to some old and powerful advertisers, they touched a sensitive ganglion. Many of these old customers marketed proprietary medicines and they had gained considerable experience in dealing with government in the previous 20 years. They had come through numerous jousts with the Federal Trade Commission since its establishment in 1914. Now they turned that knowledge to advantage.

Quietly they directed the Federal Trade Commission's eye to newspaper association practices. Did not these constitute action in restraint of trade, in effect a conspiracy among newspaper associations and their members against the interests of established and reputable firms?

Apparently the legal minds of the Trade Commission thought a case might be made. Then they considered procedure. Under a lengthy line of decisions, it appeared that the courts would not consider newspapers or advertising as interstate commerce. If that were true, the Trade Commission had no jurisdiction. So in drafting the complaint that was served in January, 1925, the Trade Commission lawyers laid stress on "type parts"—the transmission across state lines of type, matrices, and engravings from advertising agency and advertiser to publishers. That, they argued, constituted interstate commerce and gave the Commission jurisdiction over the rules by which publishers sold their space. Also involved were the AAAA, the American Press Association (representing small dailies and weeklies), and the Six-Point League of New York (an association of newspaper representatives) in addition to the ANPA and the SNPA.

Publicly, the SNPA and other respondents proclaimed the certainty of their vindication and pointed to the unquestionable honesty of their intentions and performance. Privately, they worried. They suspected then, and would learn later, that once newspapers were established as part of interstate commerce, many Federal fingers would itch for regulatory power. The Trade Commission move failed. It was abandoned in 1930, on the finding that jurisdiction was lacking. By 1930 the advertising agency system was impregnably established. In theory, it had been subjected to many apparently valid objections; in practice, it worked. One by one, the old direct advertisers changed their operations to include advertising agency service. Also, by 1930, publishers, advertisers and the government had more serious worries than type parts in interstate commerce.

But in the years between, the South and Southern newspapers progressed handsomely. Membership in the SNPA hovered around the 200 mark, with publishers looking to the headquarters office for extensive categories of advice and assistance. The faithful and tireless Walter C. Johnson finished his 9th year as secretary-treasurer in 1924 and informed his colleagues that employment of a full-time manager could be deferred no longer. He would stay on as secretary-treasurer for the next year, if they requested, and train the new man. The 1924 convention heeded President Newmyer's advice, authorized the employment of a salaried manager, re-elected Mr. Johnson by acclamation and then staged a surprise party. The modest Secretary-Treasurer received a Swiss watch with a gold chain and a locket holding pictures of his wife and their two children. Mrs. Johnson, giving so much of her husband's time and her own interest to the Association, was presented with a full 160 piece silver service in a mahogany chest.

The inscription engraved in the watch case read:

"Walter C. Johnson—For years of unsefish service to Southern journalism, this testimonial is presented with the respect and love of his fellows in the Southern Newspaper Publishers Association July 3, 1924".

Not all the 1924 activities carried out that brotherly note. The question of SNPA support for the Georgia-Alabama Business College, operator of the Macon Printers' School, had smouldered through the 1923 convention. It flamed in 1924. An objective report by Harry Giovannoli, of Lexington, Ky., outlined the school situation. During the years 1920, 1921, and 1922, the Georgia-Alabama Business College, operator of the school, had received in tuition for printer-students a total of $73,370. It expended for instruction, etc., a total of $37,225, indicating a profit to the college of $36,145. The publishers saw no reason to continue the SNPA subsidy to a school operating for profit. The machinery manufacturers who had made available the equipment for the school disapproved the idea of furnishing machines free to a profitable institution.

In an impassioned address W. T. Anderson, of Macon, who had led the SNPA into the school experiment, decried as unjust the clamor over the school's small profits. He declared that the school had met an urgent need of the publishing business—the training of young men as printers in a time when the typographical union had drastically limited the number of apprentices—that that need still existed. The school had trained 1,000 printers, he said, at an average cost to SNPA members of $3 per man, and at an even lower cost to publishers in other parts of the country who had helped support the enterprise. The average annual profit, he said, amounted to no more than the salary of the head machinist who kept the equipment in order.

Mr. Giovannoli's report advised that the school idea not be abandoned, but made no recommendations for its continuance. The profitable Macon School was definitely debarred from further use of the SNPA name, and the Association voted to "create or continue" the operation of a school of printing on such terms and arrangements as a new committee should determine.

The situation distressed many Association members. W. T. Anderson and his brother Eugene were popular and respected. The membership understood that the Andersons had embarked on an experimental enterprise, of which no one could accurately predict the outcome or the cost of operation. With SNPA approval they had set their tuition fees at a level designed to attract serious and ambitious students, and to discourage drifters. Enrollment had passed expectations, due largely to the encouragement of prospective students by SNPA publishers. The subsidies by SNPA and ANPA newspapers had been granted in the years before it was established that the school could earn a profit on tuition fees alone. But when the pros and cons were balanced, it was plain that the Association could not continue to subsidize an organization operated for and at a profit. Support was withdrawn by the 1924 convention, as well as the use of the SNPA name in connection with the school. That critical step was accomplished without dissension. The Macon Telegraph remained an SNPA member and the Anderson family continued active in Association affairs.

Eventually, SNPA and ANPA support went to the Southern School of Printing at Nashville, with the ANPA also contributing to schools in Dallas and other cities, and the question stirred no further crises in the SNPA. It was finally settled in 1925.

The SNPA advertising campaign proceeded at full speed in 1923-1924, with the purchase of trade journal and newspaper space to the amount of $15,000 and the contribution of member newspapers' space valued at nearly $100,000 during the year.

The Federal Trade Commission action had not taken form when the 1924 convention considered another elaborate plan of governing relations among advertising agencies and publications. This called for organization of an Association of Agency Relationship, to be directed by three advertising agents, three newspaper publishers, two magazine publishers, one farm paper publisher, one business paper publisher and one managing editor. It would define requirements to be met by agencies from whom alone publishers would accept national advertising with the agency commission allowed. The A. of A.R. would investigate the qualifications of agencies and recommend to the board of control the acceptance or rejection of applicants. It would also supervise operations of agencies through district managers and a staff of auditors. Informal approval was said to have been given the plan in discussions with the ANPA, the AAAA, and other groups, and the convention authorized the president to seek the official cooperation of these bodies in organization of the proposed group. Unlike the Audit Bureau of Circulations, this group would have a majority of publishers on the board of control, and that fact may have been its most attractive feature for many publishers. Before its organization could be effected, the Federal Trade Commission complaint brought to a sharp stop newspaper ambitions to police the advertising agency business. No more was heard of the A. of A.R.

Political maneuvers complicated the postal rate situation in 1923-1924, the SNPA heard from its doughty legislative war horses, Colonel Robert Ewing and Major E. B. Stahlman. The SNPA and the American Publishers Conference had backed a new rate bill introduced by Representative Kelly, providing lower second-class charges. Then Mr. Kelly added an amendment increasing the pay of postal employees and saddling second-class matter with the added financial burden. These measures passed, despite newspaper opposition, but were vetoed by the President. An ANPA effort for rate reductions died in conference.

Major Stahlman warned that a report adverse to newspapers might be expected from a committee then investigating second-class rates and postal costs and urged the publishers to get their case before Congress in emphatic and irrefutable terms. His views were later supported by Frederic W. Hume of the American Publishers Conference.

The old question of choosing a meeting place took a new form in 1924, with an invitation from George B. Lindsay, publisher of the Marion (Ind.) Chronicle and president of the Inland Daily Press Association, for a joint SNPA-Inland meeting at West Baden, Ind., in 1925.

While this underscored the increasingly cordial relationships between the two great regional newspaper associations, majority sentiment looked askance at meeting outside of Dixie. The decision rested with the Board of Directors, and the 1925 meeting remained in Asheville.

The name of W. M. Clemens, former Secretary-Treasurer, absent for several years from SNPA chronicles, appeared again in 1924. Mr. Clemens, then managing editor of the Knoxville Journal and Tribune, proposed a code of ethics for adoption by the SNPA. Codes of ethics enjoyed popularity in the early Twenties. The Canons of Journalism had been adopted in 1923 by the American Society of Newspaper Editors. President Harding had published his code for the Marion (Ohio) Star. Dean Walter Williams of the University of Missouri School of Journalism had recently promulgated one for journalism in general. And when Mr. Clemens rose to advocate his declaration for the SNPA, W. T. Anderson of Macon asked that consideration be given to the code published several years earlier by his Macon Telegraph. Mr. Clemens argued that a code was necessary because of the advent of the "cold-blooded business man" in the publishing business.

Adjournment was near. The Association liked the code idea, but wisely determined that haste was not required. With Mr. Clemens as chairman, a committee on code of ethics was appointed and the matter went over to 1925.

A long-range forecast of future SNPA interest in Southern agronomy could be discerned in the enthusiasm with which the 1924 convention greeted a paper by John A. Davis, business manager of the Albany (Ga.) Herald. The boll weevil had struck the Georgia cotton fields with the destructive force of an Egyptian plague—the 1923 crop of 600,000 bales represented a loss of 1,400,000 bales from the average of normal years, or nearly $200,000,000. The Albany Herald's county had suffered even more disastrous losses, and the Herald assumed the task of restoring the farmers' confidence. The paper adopted the direct attack—find out how to control the pest, then educate the farmers to apply the remedy, then get the community's business men to convince the farmers that all must stand together to combat adversity. Apparently the extermination measures caused some inconvenience to the boll weevil, with a little improvement in crops expected for

Are Newspapers Interstate Commerce?

1924. Clark Howell, Sr., F. G. Bell, both Georgia publishers, and Col. Robert Ewing of Louisiana, went beyond Mr. Davis' counsel, by declaring their advocacy of diversified crops as the primary need of Southern agriculture. Already this idea had been adopted in Deep South areas where the weevil damage had been extensive.

Arthur G. Newmyer won unanimous re-election as president, with Victor H. Hanson again serving as chairman of the board. As already reported, Walter C. Johnson was returned for his final term as secretary-treasurer. Board members elected were:

Alabama, Mr. Hanson; Arkansas, Elmer E. Clarke; Florida, Ross A. Reeder; Georgia, Major Clark Howell, Jr.; Kentucky, Harry Giovannoli; Louisiana, Col. Robert Ewing; Mississippi, T. M. Hederman; North Carolina, H. Galt Braxton; Oklahoma, E. K. Gaylord; South Carolina, F. C. Withers; Tennessee, Wiley L. Morgan; Texas, Marcellus E. Foster; Virginia, Major Allen Potts; West Virginia, W. Guy Tetrick.

Before another year arrived, the Board acted upon the convention mandate to employ a full-time manager. Cranston Williams, of Greensboro, Georgia, began work at the Chattanooga Headquarters on October 1, 1924. He had just resigned as secretary to Senator William J. Harris, of Georgia, and behind that Washington experience, he packed several years of country newspaper work. He had enlisted in the Regular Army when the United States entered World War I, and was discharged as a captain after service in France with the A.E.F. He soon learned the SNPA ropes under the wise guidance of Mr. Johnson, and his calm wisdom, expressed in soft Georgian intonations that fell sweetly on the ear, would be with the SNPA for the next 15 years.

With the Federal Trade Commission complaint offering a brand new experience to the Association and its members, one might have looked for blazing comments on the case at the 1925 convention. It was barely mentioned—once in President Newmyer's report, once in that of Manager Williams. The membership had placed its individual legal cares in the hands of James F. Finlay, of Chattanooga, attorney for the SNPA, and refrained from oratory.

While business affairs received their due attention, the Association gave much of its 1925 convention at Asheville to what might be called the spiritual side of the newspaper business. For the first time in its 23-year history, the SNPA was honored by the presence of Adolph S. Ochs, who had been the mainspring of Southern newspaper organizations before he purchased the New York Times in 1896. Other bright lights of contemporary journalism at the meeting included Josephus Daniels, editor of the Raleigh News and Observer, former Secretary of the Navy and future Ambassador to Mexico; C. P. J. Mooney, managing editor of the Memphis Commercial Appeal, and Robert Lathan, editor of the Charleston News & Courier, 1925 winner of the Pulitzer prize for the best editorial of the year.

When the committee on code of ethics presented the results of its year of consultation, no one was amazed to hear its phrasing challenged by the militant Daniels and the Mooney who had scourged the Ku Klux Klan out of West Tennessee in 1923. The committee's draft proposed that newspapers abstain from "destructive" criticism, but accepted Mr. Daniels' objection that it was sometimes necessary to criticize destructively in order to bring about constructive results. When the committee proposed that "editors may be justified sometimes in defying libel laws in the public interest," Mr. Mooney pointed out that the Association and its editors would scarcely wish to record themselves as favoring defiance of any law—and the committee found new words for the idea.

With the adoption of the code, the Association members agreed to give it publicity in their columns and post it in their offices. As a part of the Association's history and as an expression of the principles accepted by Southern newspapers in 1925, its text has a place in this record. Amended in minor details after its submission by Chairman W. M. Clemens, it read:

"A newspaper's first duty is to print the news honestly and fairly to all, unbiased by any other consideration, even its own editorial opinion.

"Its second duty is to construe honestly and fairly, in its editorial columns, happenings at home and abroad, that the people may realize their full benefit under a republic and require of public officials faithful performance of the duties entrusted to them as servants of the people. It must protect its readers, insofar as may be reasonably possible, from evil influences in public life and from dishonest or misguided persons who, through its advertising columns, might seek to mislead or exploit its readers.

"Lastly, its duty is to itself, and its stockholders; for unless a fair return on their investment is yielded, the publication must cease and, with it, its opportunity to be of any service to the public.

"In furtherance of these duties, we hold these principles to be compatible with both high ideals and sound business conduct of a successful, prosperous and useful newspaper:

"1. SERVICE to the community, the state, our country and to civilization. Our criticisms shall be constructive. Our columns, whether editorial, news or advertising, must be governed by the public welfare; no other consideration for the suppression of news is defensible, nor should advertisements detrimental to the public be accepted.

"2. FAIRNESS to its subscribers, its advertisers, its competitors and the public. Recognizing honest differences of opinion exist, we may vigorously maintain our own position without denouncing others as dishonest or unfair. Under no circumstances must we countenance the use of our columns to vent personal spite nor permit innuendo, often more deadly than direct charges. We should not be deterred by consequences to ourselves in speaking out boldly in the public interest, but unfairness in any cause is an unforgivable sin. We regard it as unwise to underestimate our competitors, unethical to disparage them and dishonest to misrepresent them.

"3. DECENCY, which should be the guiding star in the printing of news, editorials, advertising and all feature articles or illustrations. Even though, at times, pruriency, morbidness and a desire for sensationalism may seem to be in demand by the reading public, it is a newspaper's duty to keep its own columns decent and thus strive to hold steady the public mind in the path of right, morality and the service of God. 'Is it fit to print and be read by my own mother, wife, or daughter?' should be the test, rather than 'will it sell more papers?' Let us be enterprising without being sensational.

"4. CONSIDERATION for the unfortunate and the guiltless victims of the faults of others. Since publicity is the greatest deterrent of crime, we must expose fearlessly and without favor the names of law-breakers, but we should protect the names of members of their families and other associates. No story justifies needless damage to a good reputation nor wanton pain to the innocent.

"5. RESPECT AND TOLERANCE for those of different religions, races, and circumstances of life. Ridicule may bring only pain to them, but its author cannot escape real injury in loss of respect in which he is held by the public and by himself.

"6. HONESTY in our dealings with our readers, our advertisers, our employees, our competitors, and all with whom we do business; to give a dollar's value for every dollar received and to pay a dollar for every dollar's worth of service. We should do no less and be expected to do no more.

"7. TRUTH, first, last, and always, to the limit of our ability; to be as accurate as human fallibility on the part of others as well as of ourselves will permit; to willingly mislead none and to be fair to all. There are two sides to every story. Let us tell both. If we do anyone an injustice, we should correct it at once, whether the injured person demands it or not. Though temporary prosperity may be achieved by violation of some of these ideals, we conceive it our duty to hold steadfast to these principles, and believe permanent success will reward their faithful performance."

Mid-century critics may wrinkle sensitive noses and call this code platitudinous and uninspired. It is. Several individual editors present at its adoption could have done a better job of literary craftsmanship. Some would undoubtedly have used more forceful language. And some would have thrown the whole matter in the scrap-heap as a waste of time and paper. In the main, this code was written by William M. Clemens, an enthusiast who would have made a great salesman but who laid no claims to writing style. He recognized in the journalism of the day some trends against which he thought the weight of SNPA influence ought to be thrown. As the code came before the Asheville meeting, the Scopes evolution trial a few miles away in Dayton, Tenn., lent currency to sneers at religious beliefs firmly and devoutly held in the South with Henry L. Mencken leading the chorus. In New York, two new tabloid journals, the Mirror and the Graphic, had worse than scraped bottom in salacious bait for circulation. The metropolitan press as a whole, and many others, had

Are Newspapers Interstate Commerce?

apparently discarded the standard "Is it fit to print and be read by my own mother, wife or daughter?", and Mr. Clemens' code found a strong echo among Southern newspaper people who adhered to an old and fine American tradition. The code would have been the better for more polishing, but the SNPA members accepted its spirit rather than its framework and approved it "as is" rather than incur further delay. The draft, of course, bears the marks of piecemeal amendment and hastily phrased ideas, but it can be accepted as an extempore expression of Southern journalism in 1925.

Equally sincere and equally lacking in forensic elegance was the address of Adolph S. Ochs to his old companions of the South. Mr. Ochs was preaching heresy when he told the SNPA:

"The all-pervading tendency for distinctly high-grade newspapers is to overemphasize the importance of swollen circulation and their number of lines of advertising. My opinion is that this is of little substantial value. It may be a matter of pride to claim progress and supremacy along these lines, and to provoke the envy and jealousy of competitors, but is quantity of circulation and advertising the only true measure of the merits of a newspaper? And do such claims impress the intelligent reader and the wise advertiser? Isn't it probable that all this is over-valued; in fact, in its final analysis, that it is harmful? Take, for instance, the amount of advertising linage—what does this disclose? In the matter of circulation, a newspaper with very large circulation does not, by its numbers, indicate the quality of its reading matter or the 'pulling power' of its advertising columns.

"From my standpoint, I should regard it as a distinct disadvantage for a high-class newspaper in a competitive field to endeavor at any price to maintain supremacy in advertising and circulation. The desire to attain that position and the pride of holding it, coupled with the fear of the bad impression its loss might entail, would certainly influence the newspaper in the exercise of its rules for admission of advertisements and for maintaining rates. In the wild chase for numbers, appeals would be made for new readers who could be attracted only by features which may overburden the paper and really prove a blemish on its quality and its attraction to its legitimate news-reading clientele."

At that moment, Mr. Ochs' New York Times had recently attained leadership in advertising over its principal competitor, the Morning

World, long the top dog in the morning field. In circulation, too, the Times was steadily edging up on the World's lead and would soon go out in front. The Times did not feature those advances in its promotion and within less than six years, Mr. Ochs would sincerely lament the passing of the New York World as a competitor. He practiced his own doctrine, but many other newspaper leaders found attentive ears in advertising circles for dubious statistical claims to leadership. Mr. Ochs took an unusual line, too, in his advice that publishers closely investigate the sources of all syndicated feature material and guard against "very subtle propaganda, the promotion of private interest, etc." A few years later the Federal Trade Commission would reveal widespread organized efforts to get public utility matter printed in newspapers as syndicated features.

On postal rate procedures, Mr. Ochs again bucked the tide. The SNPA legislative strategists for several years had united with the American Publishers' Conference, representing magazines and other publications, in presenting to Congress, a postal case for all publications. Mr. Ochs declared that the Post Office was mistaken in its estimates of the cost of handling newspapers. He urged that the Post Office encourage the widest possible circulation of metropolitan newspapers, to make the best products of journalism available everywhere, thus knitting the country more closely.

"I believe the first step in that direction should be to give daily newspapers a special classification and remove them from the classsification of weeklies and periodicals," he argued, "as they require different service."

Nonetheless, the SNPA reaffirmed its affiliation with the American Publishers' Conference and called again for downward revision of second-class postal rates, which had not followed the post-war decline in other service charges. Mr. Ochs was elected an honorary life member. He attended several subsequent conventions.

Finis was formally written to the SNPA sponsorship of the Macon School of Printing, along the lines of the 1924 discussions, and the case for the Southern School of Printing, at Nashville, already receiving ANPA support, was presented with eloquent gestures by E. B. Mickle.

Are Newspapers Interstate Commerce?

Most gratifying was the report of Major John S. Cohen, editor of the Atlanta Journal and chairman of the Lee Memorial School of Journalism Committee. Upwards of $80,000 had been pledged for the School, he said, and Washington & Lee University had announced that classes in journalism would open the following September, under the direction of Prof. Roscoe B. Ellard, then head of the school of journalism at Beloit College, Wisconsin. That marked concrete progress on the program approved by the 1923 convention; much remained to be done, Major Cohen counseled.

Without comment, the 1925 convention approved the report of Secretary-Treasurer Johnson on the American Inter-Regional Newspaper Council which had been formed a few months earlier by the executive heads and standing committee chairmen of the SNPA, the Inland Daily Press Association, Northwest Daily Newspaper Association, New England Daily Newspaper Association, Pacific Northwest Newspaper Association, and Canadian Daily Newspaper Association. The SNPA representation at the organization meeting included Mr. Johnson, Ross A. Reeder, F. C. Withers, Major Powell Glass, Colonel Urey Woodson, Harry Giovannoli, Wiley L. Morgan, Cranston Williams and James F. Finlay. The council, designed to afford closer contact among the directing heads of regional newspaper organizations, had no authority to bind its members on any subject. This idea, originated by a proposal of the Inland Association's president in 1924, had little noticeable impact on SNPA activities.

Nine years of intelligent drudgery in the secretary-treasurer's office with magnificent results were rewarded when Walter C. Johnson was seated as president for 1925-1926, receiving back from President Newmyer the gavel made from laurel wood grown on Lookout Mountain, that he had presented the year before. Mr. Newmyer became chairman of the board, and Wiley L. Morgan, business manager of the Knoxville Sentinel, moved into the secretary-treasurer's post. Cranston Williams was retained as manager. The new board of directors was constituted as follows:

Alabama, Victor H. Hanson; Arkansas, John S. Parks; Florida, Frank B. Shutts; Georgia, John A. Brice; Kentucky, Harry Giovannoli; Louisiana, A. G. Newmyer; Mississippi, Frederick Sullens; North Carolina, John A. Park; Oklahoma, E. K. Gaylord; South Carolina, Robert

Lathan; Tennessee, C. P. J. Mooney; Texas, M. E. Foster; Virginia, M. K. Duerson; West Virginia, W. Guy Tetrick.

The 1925 convention also noted a marked increase in interest in the annual golf tournament, directed by Col. Walter H. Savory of the Mergenthaler Linotype Company. Prizes for members and guests were donated by supply and equipment firms and most of the member contestants carried away some trophy.

"Strictly business" was the program to be expected from President Johnson during 1925-1926, and strictly business it was. The president, and Manager Cranston Williams, kept headquarters operating with a minimum of friction. Nationally, business continued to boom; it had not yet attained its spectacular phases that marked 1927-1929. Calvin Coolidge sat in the White House with a velvety grip on the throttle and government caused publishers few headaches. Labor disputes were rare. Postal rates remained static, with little immediate probability of an increase and none at all of reduction.

That paragraph could almost stand as an SNPA report for the year had it not been for the Federal Trade Commission's complaint. The SNPA was told by its attorney, James F. Finlay, that the Association would call 100 witnesses to prove that it had not acted in restraint of trade in interstate commerce. Lincoln B. Palmer, general manager of the American Newspaper Publishers Association, and James O'Shaughnessy, executive secretary of the American Association of Advertising Agencies, also reported on the suit in executive session. These speakers and several SNPA Directors emphasized, however, that the Trade Commission action must be taken seriously. An adverse decision would wreck the structure of national advertising, they warned, and would also subject individual newspapers to liability for damages under the Sherman Anti-Trust Law. All declared that while no adverse decision was expected, the cost of defense would be heavy. Ample funds would be needed for legal fees and expenses.

Later in the year the publishers were destined to receive startling proof that vigilance was essential to victory. Before testimony had been heard, counsel for the defendant organizations moved the dismissal of the complaint for want of jurisdiction. Three members of the Commission over-ruled the motion and announced their action as a "unanimous" decision. One of the two absent members, Commissioner William E. Humphrey, promptly rose from a sick bed to register his views in public disagreement. He declared:

"There is not, in my judgment, a single fact, either in the record or in the argument of counsel, to justify making the various newspapers parties to this action."

The other Commissioner, Frederick I. Thompson, publisher of the Mobile Register and News Item and an SNPA member, was absent from the "rump" decision and declined comment.

The 1926 convention mourned the recent passing of Edgar M. Foster, business manager of the Nashville Banner, past-president of the SNPA and for 24 years a power on most of its important committees. Mr. Foster's report on the 1925-1926 advertising campaign, completed just before his death of June 20, 1926, showed more than $21,000 available for this purpose, with much of that sum already committed for newspaper and trade journal space.

Complaints were registered by the editorial and business affairs committee chairmen of insufficient co-operation from the membership. Little progress had been made in assembling cost data on newspaper operating departments, after a two-year effort. Although the Inland Daily Press Association had built information of this kind into one of its key membership services, Southern publishers remained indifferent to these statistics. On the editorial side, the committee could make no award of the cash prize provided in the will of the late George F. Milton, Sr., publisher of the Chattanooga News, for the editorial most effective in the cause of international peace. It is hard to believe that no Southern editor commented significantly on the Locarno treaties, submitted in December, 1925, to the League of Nations and marking the re-entry of Germany into the European family of nations—but the committee reported no entries worthy of the award, which was deferred for a year.

C. P. J. Mooney, executive head of the Memphis Commercial Appeal who insisted on the title of managing editor, produced a typically unorthodox but practical suggestion during the discussion of free publicity. He found little agreement with his idea that newspapers should give not free publicity, but advertising credit to new enterprises in their communities.

"Don't give them free notices," he counseled. "Give them advertising space, $250 worth or so, and you'll be surprised how often your investment will be repaid. Treat them as a bank or a supply house would treat them. They are assets to your city. Don't put the item on the books at all. If they come through, they are friends and advertisers. If they fail, you don't have to charge it off the books."

Mr. Mooney also roused dissent by his opinion that professional big league baseball received too much space outside of its playing cities. Goodwill and circulation could be gained, he advised, by giving prominence to local amateur and semi-professional athletics.

Mooney, always an individualist and *sui generis,* could often win on formulæ that would bankrupt another newspaper. He would die as he had lived, dramatically and in harness, at his desk in the midst of completing a newspaper consolidation in Memphis a few months later, and his salty wit and wisdom would be missed by SNPA members.

Walter C. Johnson completed his long cycle in office (or so he thought) by stepping up to chairman of the board. He was succeeded as president by the ebullient John A. Park, publisher of the Raleigh Times. Wiley L. Morgan of the Knoxville Sentinel remained as secretary-treasurer, and the following directors were elected:

Alabama, Victor H. Hanson; Arkansas, John S. Parks; Florida, Herbert Felkel; Georgia, Clark Howell, Jr.; (his father declined a nomination); Kentucky, Urey Woodson; Louisiana, Leonard K. Nicholson; Mississippi, Frederick Sullens; North Carolina, Charles A. Webb; Oklahoma, E. K. Gaylord; South Carolina, W. W. Holland; Tennessee, M. Stratton Foster; Texas, A. E. Clarkson; Virginia, Junius P. Fishburn; West Virginia, W. Guy Tetrick.

The convention closed with an informal decision to celebrate its 25th birthday by meeting in Atlanta, scene of the first convention in 1903.

Socially, the silver anniversary celebration left nothing to be desired. The golfing publishers and guests trudged and carved divots in the footprints of Bobby Jones on Atlanta's magnificent courses. Everybody went out to Stone Mountain and viewed the gigantic likenesses of Confederate heroes taking form under the chisels of Gutzon

Are Newspapers Interstate Commerce?

Borglum. An old-fashioned barbecue with all the Southern trimmings set the stage for a memorial oration by Josephus Daniels on the Fourth of July, with a plea for revival of the ancient editorial virtues. An outdoor banquet and dance at the Piedmont Driving Club, under lantern-decorated trees, released a flood of journalistic reminiscence. Several SNPA presidents of the early years sat on a dais presided over by James B. Nevin, editor of the Atlanta Georgian, and among them, Henry H. Cabaniss, first SNPA president and the Nestor of Southern newspaper organizations, received a silver cup from President Johnson.

But while the newspaper publishers of Atlanta and the city's business men unrolled the red carpet, serious minds in the SNPA recorded statistics and decisions of ominous portent. The nation's commerce had rolled through 1926 and into 1927 in flood tide, and the leaders of every major trade publicly declared confidence for the future. Every month of 1927 had seen new records set in newspaper advertising linage. Radio competition had arrived, but few publishers accorded it importance. Newspaper circulation totals stood at an all-time peak. And yet, the newspaper business was displaying symptoms that should have been disquieting.

One of these was the marked increase in newspaper consolidations since 1925. In city after city, newspaper competition had been diminished either by merger of two newspapers under one ownership with continued operation of both, or by suppression of the weaker unit. In the report of Secretary-Treasurer Wiley L. Morgan, 27 combined operations including a total of 54 newspapers were listed, some of long-standing, the majority of recent creation. The SNPA expressed concern because such newspaper members often paid less in combined dues than they would have paid as individual newspapers, under the sliding scale based on circulation.

"In the interest of financing expansion of SNPA work, you may see fit to revise upward the schedule of dues as applicable to both single and dual ownership and operations," Mr. Morgan advised.

That was done, the old maximum of $100 a year being replaced by a sliding scale ranging from $80 to $250, with dues payable quarterly.

Another rumble that should have indicated hidden trouble came in the report of the advertising committee. After noting that $16,000 had been expended in newspapers and trade papers to advertise the

South, the committee recommended that the campaign be wound up with fulfillment of existing commitments. It was felt that $16,000 did not allow for adequate exploitation of the Southern market and it was also reported, with apparent resentment, that the campaign had been financially supported by only half the membership. So this co-operative effort, which had been maintained for most of the previous 15 years, went by the board, with no more than a "hope" that it would be revived with the support of a substantial majority.

Few newspaper publishers (few business leaders of any stripe, for that matter) concerned themselves with underlying causes in the frenetic Twenties. The immediate parties to a newspaper consolidation knew that conditions under which they had operated as individual enterprises no longer afforded profits to all. They saw the prosperous leading newspaper get an ever larger share of the market's advertising, with less and less going to the trailing papers. The loser could not cut basic operating costs to eliminate red ink without crippling his operation. Consolidation wiped out blocks of administrative payroll and often permitted large reductions in operating staffs, with profits coming immediately and automatically.

Up to the end of World War I, many small Southern cities had been served by three or even four daily newspapers. Even in the most prosperous years, newspaper revenues alone could not keep all of them profitable. Generally speaking, one made handsome profits, the second paper gave its owner a comfortable income, and the third and fourth papers relied upon job printing or political friends for their bread and butter. The high-cost post-war years had killed most of the marginal operations, leaving all but the largest cities with one morning and one evening newspaper. Now the mid-Twenties were demonstrating that even two newspapers could not survive as competitors in most communities.

Advertising practices accelerated the trend toward newspaper mergers. Retail merchants, anxious to get 100 cents in value out of every advertising dollar, concentrated their appropriations in newspapers that could prove local circulation supremacy, with occasional crumbs to the runners-up, and often not that. National advertising followed a similar practice. A newly founded newspaper could not hope for any national advertising patronage until it had demonstrated its vitality for a year or more. Representatives of "second" papers in all but the largest cities seldom could get their journals on a space-buyer's list after a campaign had been put into execution.

Those conditions provided little meat for convention debates in 1927. Publishers who survived found no fault with the system; those that didn't had no forum for protest. No successful SNPA member apparently saw in these circumstances a valid reason for the non-support of the co-operative advertising campaign by half of the Association's members. They didn't contribute either because they couldn't afford the outlay, or because they found in it no prospect of increasing their own advertising income.

Another factor should be mentioned, even though it found no voice in the 1927 programs of the SNPA or of any other newspaper body. Analysis of newspaper advertising volume and newspaper advertising rate structures proved beyond doubt that newspaper prosperity of those days rested on a foundation of sand. Successful newspapers earned profits because their advertising volume increased year after year between 1924 and 1930. Advertising rates did not increase proportionately with growing circulations, as publishers pursued the will-o-the-wisp of volume. Operating costs rose fantastically in the late Twenties, with newspapers granting wage increases to unionized employees almost on demand—a strike must not interfere with bonanza operations. Simple arithmetic proved that a loss of as little as 10 per cent of the swollen advertising revenues of 1927-1929 would put most of the country's most profitable newspapers immediately into the red. When the depression inflicted its blows in 1930-32, advertising losses quickly went beyond 10 per cent, and newspapers which earned profits in those years were few indeed.[1]

In addition to these ground-swells, the SNPA in 1927 had to cope with the perennial Federal Trade Commission complaint. Many thousand words of testimony had been taken during 1926, and President Park had gone about the country warning newspaper organizations of the perils to which the action exposed them and their members. Chairman Johnson and Manager Williams and Attorney Finlay had spent many hours, extending into months, in guarding SNPA interests,

---

[1] "Budgeting a newspaper to reduce costs when business decline threatens." By Samuel P. Weston. Editor & Publisher, March 19, 1927, April 9, 1927. "Advertising control at rates insuring unit profit is advised." By Samuel P. Weston. Editor & Publisher, September 19, 1931.

and hope was held out to the convention that a committee of eminent members might be able to convince the Trade Commission that the suit should be dismissed, so far as it affected the Southern press. The convention also clarified its policy toward advertising agencies in this resolution:

"WHEREAS the advertising agency method which was in existence many years before the organization of the SNPA had proven a valuable and economical method of obtaining national business for newspapers, therefore,

"BE IT RESOLVED that this Association express itself as approving the agency method, which is not to be construed as meaning that the Association recommends that any definite amount of commission be paid."

The careful legal thinking that distinguished the above marked a safe path of retreat from the ill-considered stand taken in 1922 on agency policy and commissions. It also marked an affirmation of the original principle that the SNPA would not interfere in the internal conduct of members' business. But more than three years would pass before the Washington lawyers relaxed their grip and accepted the basic contention of the SNPA that the Trade Commission lacked jurisdiction over advertising.

The postal situation received its usual review and the SNPA reaffirmed its position that war-time rates should be repealed and that the Association continue its co-operation with the American Publishers Conference and all other organizations interested in the reduction of second-class postal rates.

Colonel Robert Ewing's valiant service as head of the legislative committee was rewarded by his election to the Presidency. The rotund Falstaffian figure of the New Orleans States' publisher had been prominent in almost every meeting of the Association since 1903. His political acquaintance and acumen had been especially valuable in preventing the enactment of legislation that publishers regarded as inimical to their best interests. In the year just ahead, he would see his many years of argument in Washington crowned by Congressional repeal of the war-time postal rates.

President John A. Park took the automatic step to the chairmanship of the Board. Secretary-Treasurer Wiley L. Morgan had retired from newspaper work and in voting for his successor, the Association separated the offices. That of Secretary was combined with the duties of Manager, with Cranston Williams holding both titles. The new treasurer was none other than Walter C. Johnson, and the Association rejoiced that it had found the means of retaining him in executive office.

Several new names appeared on the Board of Directors, which included:

Alabama, Victor H. Hanson; Arkansas, John S. Parks; Florida, Herbert Felkel; Georgia, John A. Brice; Kentucky, Harry Giovannoli; Louisiana, Leonard K. Nicholson; Mississippi, James H. Skewes; North Carolina, J. B. Sherrill; Oklahoma, E. K. Gaylord; South Carolina, B. H. Peace; Tennessee, James G. Stahlman; Texas, Marcellus E. Foster, (who had returned to active newspaper work as editor of the Houston Press); Virginia, Junius P. Fishburn; West Virginia, H. I. Shott.

Marked for future fame among the new directors was James G. Stahlman, who had been introduced to the membership a year or two earlier by his grandfather as "heir apparent." The old Major surrendered reluctantly to the infirmities of age and gave personal attention to the training of the young man in all departments of the Nashville Banner. "Jimmy" would soon become a power in SNPA affairs, win two terms as president, and move on to two noteworthy years as president of the American Newspaper Publishers Association.

With its accustomed regard for the graceful amenities, the Association in 1927 awarded honorary life membership to Walter H. Savory, vice-president of the Mergenthaler Linotype Company and noted in SNPA circles for his stern handicapping of the annual golf tournaments.

Colonel Ewing's persuasiveness and the choice of Houston for the 1928 National Democratic Convention brought the annual meeting of the SNPA to the Edgewater Gulf Hotel, near Biloxi, Miss., June 21-23, 1928. Many of the publishers participated as delegates or correspondents at the Houston convention and moved directly thence to their own business meeting.

As noted above, President Ewing happily reported that the closing hours of Congress had enacted new postal rates, returning to the 1920 schedules in the postal zones of most interest to the daily press.

Giving full credit to Chairman Urey Woodson of the Legislative Committee and to Major E. B. Stahlman and Manager Cranston Williams for their part in the postal victory, the forthright Colonel Ewing rapped the American Newspaper Publishers Association sharply for its reluctance to co-operate with the SNPA and other associations affiliated with the American Publishers Conference. The venerable Major Stahlman attended this convention in a wheel chair, placed beside the president's desk, with Colonel Ewing solicitous that his old comrade should share as fully as possible in the meeting. He did.

A new plan for promotion of the South on a much more ambitious scale than the Association had ever attempted was presented by Colonel Luke Lea, publisher of the Nashville Tennessean. Such a campaign, involving a total appropriation of more than $300,000, could be worked out by the SNPA in co-operation with Southern railroads and publicity corporations. Although some prominent SNPA members supported the proposal, a vigorous protest came from Major Stahlman, who recalled his old-time battle ardor in a 20-minute speech.

Major Stahlman denounced the plan as leading to a weakening of newspaper independence. He protested against entangling alliances with business and entered specific complaints against certain utility corporations, mainly on the ground of their allegedly abnormal profits from the consumers' purse. Major Stahlman and John S. Parks, publisher of the Fort Smith (Ark.) Southwest American and Times-Record, joined in warning the publishers of the perils in such an alliance. They noted that only recently newspapers had been embarrassed by revelations before the Federal Trade Commission concerning activities of publicity agents for the "power trust."

Since Colonel Lea had presented no specific plan for approval, the Association voted that a committee ascertain whether utility and other corporations would co-operate and also learn what advertising agencies would suggest for promotional themes.

Are Newspapers Interstate Commerce?

Even though the Labor Committee chairman, H. C. Adler of the Chattanooga Times, reported that the past year had produced no strikes or other disturbances, the Association voted to establish a Labor Department to co-operate with similar activities of other associations. It was felt that the labor relations of SNPA member newspapers needed more specialized attention than it had been possible to obtain from the special standing committee of the American Newspaper Publishers Association.

Although newsprint questions drew practically no attention in June, 1928, traffic problems involving freight charges on paper shipments were reported by Secretary-Manager Williams, who had added this activity to those of his busy office. They entailed frequent conferences with the traffic executives of other newspaper associations and of the principal newsprint manufacturers and consumed considerable time. So did the prolonged hearings of the Federal Trade Commission's advertising complaint, still hanging fire. Treasurer Johnson reported an excellent response by the membership to the higher schedule of dues. Free publicity, circulation and advertising rates came in for spirited discussion, but the prevailing sentiment seemed to be that newspapers were doing right well in 1927-28.

Colonel Ewing was re-elected president and all other executive officers were retained. The new board of directors continued to bring its annual infusion of new blood to association activities, with the following members:

Alabama, Victor H. Hanson; Arkansas, John S. Parks; Florida, L. Chauncey Brown; Georgia, P. T. Anderson; Kentucky, Urey Woodson; Louisiana, Leonard K. Nicholson; Mississippi, L. P. Cashman; North Carolina, W. C. Dowd, Jr.; Oklahoma, E. K. Gaylord; South Carolina, F. C. Withers; Tennessee, James G. Stahlman; Texas, James L. Mapes; Virginia, Junius P. Fishburn; West Virginia, Robert L. Smith.

All newspaperdom vibrated during the summer of 1929 with the Federal Trade Commission revelation that the International Paper Company had financed the purchase of numerous daily newspapers, including four in the South. William LaVarre, young explorer, and Harold Hall, a former Scripps-Howard Newspapers executive, had borrowed from the paper company the funds with which they had bought the Columbia (S.C.) Record, the Spartanburg (S.C.) Herald

& Journal, and the Augusta (Ga.) Chronicle. They, and other publishers who had received similar aid, had declared that the transactions had been nothing more than good business. The paper company had loaned money at rates considerably lower than those available from banks in the frenzied speculative conditions then prevalent. In return, it had asked no more than a contract for paper supply from the publishers it had assisted. With new Canadian production flooding the newsprint market, paper manufacturers were fighting hard to sell tonnage.

Nevertheless, there was widespread suspicion that the International Power & Paper Company was interested more in friendly newspaper support for its power ambitions than in a market for its paper. Southern publishers, especially, harked back to the warning sounded in 1928 by Major Stahlman and John S. Parks against too intimate relations between newspapers and public utilities. In the light of later developments, it would appear that the paper company and its president, Archibald R. Graustein, were primarily interested in assuring a market for newsprint, with a friendly atmosphere for their power projects a by no means negligible by-product. In mid-1929, however, many newspaper people cocked a suspicious eye at any activity of a public utilities concern. They were ashamed and embarrassed by revelation that newspapers had either been willing tools or dupes of public utility propagandists in many sections of the country even though Southern newspapers and the SNPA had come through the Federal Trade Commission investigation creditably.

In such a thunderous atmosphere, then, the Association returned to Asheville for its 27th annual convention, July 4-6, 1929. Colonel Ewing had been ill for most of the previous year and, in his absence, Chairman John A. Park took over the presidential functions. John D. Ewing, publisher of the Shreveport Times, however, acting in his father's behalf, presented a terse resolution on the disturbing topic which, as unanimously adopted, read:

"BE IT RESOLVED by the Southern Newspaper Publishers Association in convention assembled that the purchase of newspapers by interests affiliated or identified with the power and newsprint or similar industry is contrary to sound public policy and to sound journalistic policy and is a menace to a free press and free institutions of these United States."

Are Newspapers Interstate Commerce?

Present but silent in the convention hall was William LaVarre. Outside, in the spacious lobby of the Grove Park Inn, President Graustein of International Power & Paper, and Mrs. Graustein, chatted with publishers and awaited an invitation to address the meeting which was never accorded. The SNPA had made its stand clear and wanted no dilution.

With the members well stirred up on the question of propaganda, Chairman Park obtained a rousing adoption of his resolution, signed by nine leading SNPA members, condemning free publicity and pledging members to its extermination so far as that might be possible.

The gigantic advertising campaign proposed the previous year had been the subject of several conferences with South, Inc., a group of promotion-minded business leaders, but Colonel Luke Lea could report no substantial agreement to the SNPA. The avalanche of the depression, then only a few months in the future, would smother this project beyond recall.

Slight progress was noted toward the establishment of a Labor Department, also approved in 1928. The South continued to be free of strikes, but several speakers warned that the future might not be so serene. Harvey J. Kelly, chairman of the ANPA special standing committee, told the publishers that wage increases would go far over current levels if publishers did not organize to combat inordinate demands. Among these he included the typographical union's proposed campaign for the five-day week. The past decade's payroll increases had been accompanied, he said, by a steady decrease in production per man, except where publishers had kept their composing rooms on a piece scale compensation basis.

Charles A. Webb, publisher of the Asheville Citizen and chairman of the open shop division of the American Newspaper Publishers Association, told the publishers how his division had assisted struck newspapers in other parts of the nation, and declared that help could be supplied to publishers who wished to operate open shop plants.

Getting down to establishment of an SNPA Labor Department, G. J. Palmer, general manager of the Houston Chronicle and labor commissioner of the Texas Daily Press Association, favored the appointment of regional labor commissions for several sections of the SNPA territory. Individual publishers could not expect to resist successfully the organized and informed pressure of the international unions. No immediate action was taken.

The long-standing apathy of SNPA members toward cost accounting disappeared in a flash when J. A. Blondell, treasurer of the Baltimore Sun, laid before the convention details of the Sun's budgeting system. Costs were mounting steeply in 1929 and some publishers may have anticipated that the long reign of prosperity was near its end. Whatever the reason, Mr. Blondell's story commanded so much interest that a special evening session had to be arranged for a thorough exploration of the topic by interested executives.

Only a handful of Southern editors and newspaper women entered their year's work for cash prizes of $200 in each category under the provisions of the will of the late George F. Milton, Sr. The donor's son, publisher of the Chattanooga News, had considered asking court approval for revision of the bequest to the estate for the benefit of other heirs, but withheld action pending another effort by the SNPA to arouse interest in the prizes. The fund in 1929 amounted to $5,000.

Radio received passing attention again. Half a dozen publishers said they operated stations; one, who had embarked on the enterprise for constructive promotion of his newspaper and his city, reported that station advertising revenues paid expenses and justified the operation. Radio did not yet loom as a threat to national advertising revenues.

Shop topics, especially those related to economical operation, aroused more than usual interest at this convention; otherwise, the publishers gave little evidence of concern for the economic future.

Considerable interest was manifested in an exhibit of the teletypesetter, arranged by the Southern Bell Telephone Company. This device, which would assume great importance in newspaper production 20 years later, had been developed largely under the sponsorship of Frank E. Gannett, publisher of a number of New York State newspapers and for a time owner of the Winston-Salem Sentinel.

John S. Parks, publisher of the Fort Smith Southwest American and Times-Record, was elected president—the first Arkansas man to hold this office. Colonel Ewing became chairman of the board, Mr. Johnson was returned as treasurer, and Cranston Williams as secretary-manager.

ARE NEWSPAPERS INTERSTATE COMMERCE?

The 1929-1930 board of directors was named as follows:

Alabama, Victor H. Hanson; Arkansas, Kirtland A. Engel; Florida, L. Chauncey Brown; Georgia, Clark Howell, Jr.; Kentucky, W. B. Hager; Louisiana, Leonard K. Nicholson; Mississippi, L. P. Cashman; North Carolina, W. C. Dowd, Jr.; Oklahoma, E. K. Gaylord; South Carolina, F. C. Withers; Tennessee, James G. Stahlman; Texas, James L. Mapes; Virginia, Junius P. Fishburn; West Virginia, Colonel J. H. Long.

Urey Woodson, who had retired from the ownership of the Owensboro (Ky.) Messenger during the year, was voted an honorary life member.

Before the Association again convened in Asheville June 30-July 2, 1930, the chill winds of depression had dulled the glow of business prospects. A mid-year poll of the membership had turned down a proposed revival of the co-operative advertising campaign. Suspensions and consolidations, numerous during the year, had again cut into the income from dues, and Treasurer Johnson had to report, for the first time, an excess of expenditures over income. The Federal Trade Commission complaint had faded from the scene, the Commission declaring that it was without jurisdiction, but also that if jurisdiction had been found, the complaint had no basis as it applied to the SNPA and its members. Newsprint moved back into the picture, with the over-expanded Canadian mills trying to get on an even keel via some uneven price adjustments and with the publishers stoutly resisting. And postal matters, quiescent in recent years, again came to the fore with a portent that the Post Office would soon have to increase its charges.

Certainly the onrushing depression put an edge on the words addressed to the SNPA by John Benson, permanent president of the American Association of Advertising Agencies. He discussed free publicity, and told the publishers he agreed with them in disliking puffs and handouts that lacked news value. In fact, advertising agencies would rejoice if all newspapers abolished all free publicity, good, bad and indifferent, he said. But so long as editors found news value in free publicity, advertisers, agents and publicity makers would continue to furnish it.

Once again he raised the question of the differential between advertising rates charged to national advertisers and those paid by retail stores. He cited the new linage compilations of Media Records to prove that half of the advertising revenue of important newspapers came from national accounts and that retail advertising volume had been shrinking in recent years. Why, then, he asked, penalize the newspaper's best customer?

His address in some phases recalled that of Adolph S. Ochs before the 1925 convention, especially in his deprecation of newspaper claims to advertising and circulation supremacy in their fields. He pointed out that quality of circulation had been diluted in the mad scramble for volume. He also charged that publishers had printed advertising at a loss, to gain volume, that they had not played fair with their readers by accepting copy, from both national and retail accounts, which offered spurious claims and values.

"Competition is the bane of American business," Mr. Benson declared. "It is eating the heart out of industry. It has brought on an era of profitless prosperity and of over-stimulation from which we are now suffering acutely. The same tendency has invaded the newspaper and the advertising business. We are all too anxious to be big. Seventy-five per cent of the selling effort employed is futile, in my opinion; it creates no new business; it offers no information; it solves no problems; it just yaps and snarls and undermines. It forces weak publishers to strong-arm their weakness and strong publishers to yield to any kind of pressure."

Mr. Benson concluded with a tribute to newspaper advertising:

"Its possibilities are unlimited, I think, if we agents will learn better how to use it and you publishers will give us a more responsive medium, a fair rate structure, and an equitable chance to compete."

Newspaper executives reviewed the retail-national rate differential from several viewpoints. Some explosive data on abuses which had been noted in the frantic final days of the 1929 boom were laid before the meeting by Leslie M. Barton of the Chicago Daily News, speaking on behalf of the Association of Newspaper Advertising Executives. The discussion ended with the adoption of the ANAE code covering charges on retail and national copy and the appointment of an SNPA committee to consider the whole question and report at the next convention.

Up to the 1930 convention, newspaper advertising volume had declined only slightly, if at all, from the 1929 figures. Retail advertisers, especially, had kept the advertising pressure on in an effort to move goods to buyers who were already committed beyond safe limits by boom-time installment purchases. Leslie Barton had told the convention that the total cost of advertising in some lines had ceased to bear any relation to the value of the merchandise to be sold. That had been especially true of radio receiving set advertising in late 1929. Profitable national advertising had declined, though not to an alarming degree, but the bulk of the volume printed by newspapers in early 1930 no longer supported the previous rate of profit. The danger signals were flying plainly.

So the SNPA listened attentively to a plan devised by the separately owned newspapers of St. Petersburg, Fla., to minimize uneconomic competition for advertising and circulation. Major Lew B. Brown, of the Independent, and Paul Poynter, of the Times, got together on December 19, 1929, and decided, first, to call a halt on their expensive and needless contest for circulation leadership. Next, they agreed to joint representation in the national advertising field. Then they appointed an adjustment board, with a representative of each newspaper and an independent third party, to serve as secretary and referee, paid by both papers, to decide controversies but to have no control over business and editorial operations of either paper. A new rate structure encouraged the use of both newspapers by national advertisers. A new deal was worked out with the competing special representatives of both papers, keeping both firms on a flat fee plus year-end commission basis, with special inducements for the sale of the market rather than the individual papers. After six months' experience, this strange scheme seemed to be working well; amended from time to time it would carry these papers through the depression years.

It was a time for plain talk and the publishers got more of it from Frederic A. Tilton, Third Assistant Postmaster General. His address was lengthy, bristling with figures, and aimed at convincing publishers that they stultified their own case by opposing the Post Office program for higher rates on first-class matter. Mr. Tilton, an accountant on loan to the Post Office Department, presented his statistics convincingly and the publishers, applauding, voted to print his address for separate distribution to the whole membership. Although Mr. Tilton did not forecast an increase in second-class rates, the country's financial situation a year later served as a reason for abolishing the reduced schedules that had been enacted only two years previously.

Newsprint was reviewed by Colonel Ewing. Several circumstances irked the newspapers. They had expected a substantial reduction from the price of $65 per ton prevalent in 1928. They received announcement of a reduction of only $1.00 for 1929. At the same time it became generally known that International Paper Company had contracted with the Hearst organization to supply its titanic paper needs at $57 per ton. When newspapers sought to have that rate accorded to all, the provincial governments of Quebec and Ontario intervened. Premier L. A. Taschereau of Quebec and Premier G. H. Ferguson of Ontario had organized the large producers of Canada as the Newsprint Institute of Canada. All except International agreed to restrictive control measures. Mr. Taschereau in 1929 brought pressure on International and on the Hearst newspapers for renegotiation of the contract at a higher price than $57. In February, 1929, this contract was adjusted to provide a $62 price in New York, and International promptly offered other publishers five-year contracts at that figure.

This caused a considerable rumpus at the 1929 convention of the American Newspaper Publishers Association. E. K. Gaylord, publisher of the Oklahoma City Oklahoman and an SNPA director, charged that the paper committee, headed by S. E. Thomason of the Chicago Journal, had "lulled the publishers to sleep while allowing the price of newsprint to be raised." Mr. Gaylord also alleged that Elisha Hanson, ANPA counsel in Washington, had represented the International Paper Company before a Congressional Committee, and before another committee had opposed a Senate investigation of newsprint prices and monopoly.

Mr. Thomason defended his course with eloquence. He told the convention that he had organized, with John Stewart Bryan of the Richmond News-Leader, the Bryan-Thomason Newspapers, holding stock in the Tampa Tribune and the Greensboro (N.C.) Record. Then, wishing to return to Chicago, where he had been for many years general manager of the Tribune, he had bought the dying Chicago Journal with Mr. Bryan as his associate. This transaction was financed with assistance from the International Paper Company. The paper firm had offered to market without commissions $2,000,000 in debentures and preferred stock of the Journal if Mr. Thomason would sign a 10-year newsprint contract at the prevailing market price and issue International 10,000 shares of Journal common stock. The latter would be sold back to the publishers over a five-year period at graduated prices. Mr. Thomason declared that this stock represented only one-ninth of the common stock which the Journal could issue. He also stated that he had told the ANPA board of the situation and offered to resign as chairman of the paper committee. His offer had been declined. He declared that the ANPA paper committee had been warned by the Department of Justice not to enter into any price-fixing agreements with the Canadian paper makers.

Other ANPA members had defended Mr. Thomason, but Frank P. Glass of the Birmingham News and a former president of SNPA, who had battled the paper companies bitterly a dozen years before, expressed his disapproval. Mr. Thomason and his committee got a vote of confidence and the ANPA refused to adopt a resolution offered by Colonel Ewing, repeating the sense of the resolution he had offered to the SNPA in 1929. But, reluctant as they were to reprimand the paper committee, the ANPA membership agreed in general that newsprint company finance was bad medicine for newspapers.

The Federal Trade Commission inquiry into the subject of newspaper finance by paper companies kept the pot boiling during the summer of 1929, and more heat was added in the Fall. Two large Canadian mills announced a $5 per ton increase for 1930 and attempted to have other members of the Newsprint Institute of Canada fall into line. Under threat of Federal action instigated by a special convention of the ANPA, International announced that it would continue the $62 price through 1930. Other companies reluctantly followed suit. Then, with the ANPA paper committee under the chairmanship of William G. Chandler, of the Scripps-Howard Newspapers, the publishers heard a proposal from the Newsprint Institute of Canada that three-and-a-half year contracts be signed, setting a New York price of $62 in 1930, $64 for 1931 and 1932 and $65 in 1933. Mr. Chandler's committee approved. Important publishers shared with the Canadian provincial premiers and the principal newsprint manufacturers the wish that the paper industry be stabilized to the ultimate advantage of all.

That was the situation in mid-1930, when Colonel Ewing reported. Not everyone realized then that the Canadian newsprint situation, with peak production at a moment when United States demand was sharply declining, had passed beyond any such rescue measures. The curious effort of the publishers to maintain paper prices—curious, indeed, in the light of long-sustained efforts in the opposite directions—was doomed to failure.[2]

As might be expected, labor relations had occupied much of the SNPA board's attention during the troublous winter months and the situation had been thoroughly canvassed at several board meetings. A committee headed by J. L. Mapes, Beaumont Enterprise & Journal, reported at the 1930 convention, but was not yet ready to chart a complete course for the Association's labor set-up.

President Parks and all other officers were re-elected and the new board included the following:

Alabama, James E. Chappell; Arkansas, Kirtland A. Engel; Florida, L. Chauncey Brown; Georgia, Clark Howell, Jr.; Kentucky, W. B. Hager; Louisiana, Leonard K. Nicholson; Mississippi, James H. Skewes; North Carolina, Don S. Elias; Oklahoma, E. K. Gaylord; South Carolina, F. C. Withers; Tennessee, James G. Stahlman; Texas, James L. Mapes; Virginia, Powell Glass; West Virginia, J. H. Long.

Thus ended an era—a six-year period in which newspapers appeared to be enjoying the most fabulously profitable operation in all history.

In later years, annalists have accepted Westbrook Pegler's ironic "Golden Age of Wonderful Nonsense" as the pat and complete description of those times. The Southern Newspaper Publishers Association could look back on them without many twinges of conscience. If it hadn't recognized all of their perils, it had spoken its mind plainly on those that its membership saw. Its ultimate policy had been sound in the Federal Trade Commission proceedings on advertising. It had led and won the fight for equitable postal rates. It

---
[2]History of the American Newspaper Publishers Association. By Edwin Emery. University of Minnesota Press, Minneapolis, 1950.

had been successful in resisting what it considered an unreasonable proposed increase on freight rates on newsprint. It had warned of the growing danger of free publicity and propaganda. It had provided a concrete example of practical efforts to end cut-throat competition between newspapers. Its membership faced the same hardships that would beset all America in the years ahead, but in those years, with initiative that's rare in any business group the SNPA would undertake the creation of a new paper industry in the South and would carry it to accomplishment despite financial and spiritual depression.

Survival In The Lean Years

Deepening Depression Brings Lower Newsprint Prices, Also Demands for Lower Advertising Rates — Dr. Herty Proposes Southern Newsprint Industry—Radio News Competition Stirs Publishers — SNPA Members Avoid Labor Strife.

ALL PUBLISHERS knew by the end of 1930 that the golden days were over. Throughout 1931 many hoped, against judgment, that business would recover and go forward over the old rails, and they hailed every flutter as a harbinger of returning prosperity. In that they had plenty of distinguished company. Before 1932, even the most optimistic had to concede the undeniable. With few exceptions, newspapers balanced their 1932 accounts in red ink, and took great pride in holding staff reductions to a minimum. Almost all had to impose at least one pay cut, and three successive reductions of 10 per cent in white collar salaries became essential for most newspapers before the dreary 1932 twelve-month closed. Unionized crafts generally maintained basic pay rates, and eased the depression's impact on their membership by "share the work" programs.

Southern newspapers, like all others in the country, had seen their linage decline in every classification during the first six months of 1931. They had also experienced a slight shrinkage in circulation. But, reading the reports of officers and committees and the annual proceedings of the 1931 convention at Asheville, June 29-July 1, twenty-two years afterwards, the searcher will find few accents of despair. President John S. Parks, concluding his second term, larded his annual report with not-too-grim humor. Secretary-Manager Cranston Williams noted that the past year, with its successive business crises, had greatly increased the number of calls upon headquarters for assistance to members. Treasurer Walter C. Johnson found cause for gratification in the fact that few members had fallen delinquent in dues, that membership remained steady at nearly 200, and that quarterly payment of dues seemed a satisfactory arrangement in an era of declining income.

What might have seemed an ominous portent (it didn't work out that way) was the rise of interest in the Association's "protection fund", which had been discussed in executive session the year before, and adopted with little fanfare. Only a minority of Southern newspapers had operated under union shop conditions in their mechanical departments during the 1920's. A few Southern publishers actively promoted the open shop, in co-operation with the Open Shop Department of the American Newspaper Publishers Association. The majority of newspapers which did not have contractual relationships with the international printing trade unions appeared indifferent to union membership of their employees during the prosperous years. The depression's advent coincided with, and possibly stimulated, an effort of the International Typographical Union to push organization of Southern newspaper composing rooms—and put an end to the unconcern of publishers in numerous cities.

Approximately one-third of the SNPA membership had subscribed to the protection fund between the 1930 and 1931 conventions. To them it represented a financial reserve in the hands of the Association with which to defend newspapers against unwarranted aggression by labor unions. Translated from that clipped formula, which is quoted from the 1931 convention story in *Editor & Publisher* of July 4, the idea of the protection fund was that a newspaper which did not wish to accept contract provisions demanded by a union and thereby incurred a strike, would receive SNPA assistance for continued publication. Secretary-Manager Williams rendered much advice and aid in labor negotiations both to Association members and to non-members in the South during the 1930-1931 year. His office also reported giving prompt assistance, the nature of which was not detailed, in a strike at Orlando, Fla. This was the only labor disturbance experienced by Southern newspapers during the year. There were comparatively few strikes in SNPA circles throughout the depression; whether the protection fund, by the mere fact of its existence, contributed to that happy condition must remain a matter of individual opinion.

The newsprint market received surprisingly little discussion at the 1931 meeting. Throughout the past year, it had been marked by much sub-surface seething, as the Canadian manufacturers strove vainly to maintain their price levels in the face of shrinking demand and expanded production. Probably the majority of publishers believed that the price trend was inexorably downward, with no good to be anticipated from convention talks or resolutions. Probably not many of those present at Grove Park Inn realized at the moment the importance of the first appearance before an SNPA meeting of Dr. Charles H. Herty, with his proposal that Southern publishers explore the immediate possibilities of establishing a newsprint industry in the South. Dr. Herty's address and its momentous consequences are detailed at length in Chapter X. They are mentioned here to indicate the erection of the most important signpost in the career of the Southern Newspaper Publishers Association.

Another topic which would engross newspapers in the years to come—radio competition—merely flickered briefly at the 1931 meeting. Harold H. Anderson, an associate of Dr. George H. Gallup (who specialized in newspaper research at that time, before seeking fame as a political pollster) heartened the publishers with the results of a "radio survey."

Newspapers, said Mr. Anderson, had little to fear from radio as a competitor. While radio was undoubtedly suited to the advertising of certain firms, its general applicability as an advertising medium was doubtful. Publishers could determine for themselves without difficulty the amount of "blue sky" being claimed by local broadcasters in their assertions of local coverage.

The only other reference to radio came in the report of H. Galt Braxton, Kinston Free Press, chairman of the Advertising Committee. He recommended that "radio programs be classified as paid advertising, and so marked."

It is difficult to recall, more than two decades later, that radio broadcasting was merely a lusty infant in 1931. Chain broadcasting was only four years old. The first radio news broadcast had taken place barely 10 years earlier. Only a handful of newspapers, some of them SNPA members, had sensed the potentials (friendly and otherwise) in this new medium of communications. Few in the radio industry itself dared more than day-to-day predictions of their future in 1931. Today's experiment often became tomorrow's epoch-marking achievement. If Mr. Anderson's judgment has proved fairly accurate as a long-range prediction, publishers had many an anxious moment before its truth was demonstrated by performance.

Mr. Braxton's recommendation attacked a problem of immediate and growing concern. Since 1927 many newspapers had been publishing radio programs for their news value. That could not be denied, with millions of new radio sets going into American homes every year. (Mr. Anderson's survey had revealed that 85 per cent of the families reached by the investigators owned a radio set, that 47 per cent were listening at the time of the call, but that only 35 per cent of listeners could identify station, program, or sponsor). In those days, newspapers usually published program data as furnished by the stations. These generally included the title of the program and the name of the sponsor, and while editors looked upon this as news, advertising agencies saw it as promotion essential to the success of their clients' radio advertising. The fact that newspapers would publish the sponsor's name in their program listings could be the clinching argument in selling a radio campaign to a doubtful client. Newspaper editorial services were thus being employed for possible undercutting of their advertising structure at a time when every line of advertising was precious. Mr. Braxton's recommendation that the program listings be marked and charged as paid advertising was, indeed, a logical counter by newspapers; it did not prove practical, however, and newspapers found other means of meeting this exploitation.

The recommendation of Mr. Braxton's committee that "the integrity of rate cards be more carefully safeguarded," was a somewhat cryptic reference to another troublesome product of depression. Some large advertisers already were demanding that newspaper advertising rates be reduced to keep them in line with the deflationary trend of the times; others, more subtly, sought lower advertising costs by placing national copy through local dealers at the usually lower retail rates. While a minority of publishers may have thought well of the latter idea as a means of maintaining volume, the prevailing view held that established standards should not be broken down. The Association, in fact, at this meeting adopted a definition of "retail" and "general" advertising (new terms replacing the traditional "local" and "national" or "foreign") which had been accepted a few months earlier by the

American Newspaper Publishers Association. These changes had been proposed by Media Records, Inc., a commercial organization established in 1928 for the accurate measurement of newspaper advertising linage.

The perennial campaign of newspaper publishers for more effective representation of the daily press on the board of the Audit Bureau of Circulations took a new turn in 1931. The SNPA unanimously endorsed a proposal by the International Circulation Managers Association that a newspaper circulation manager be elected to the ABC directorate. Howard W. Stodghill, then circulation manager of the Louisville Courier-Journal and Times, and a past president of the ICMA, became the nominee of the latter organization for the directorship. An outstanding leader in progressive circulation practices, Mr. Stodghill would attain national distinction as a newspaper spokesman during the next decade, in ABC councils and in the tedious hectoring of the newspaper business by Federal agencies.

Mr. Stodghill attended the 1931 ANPA convention, with Emanuel Levi, publisher of the Courier-Journal and Times, partly in the interest of ABC matters and partly to witness a demonstration of a project he had originated several years earlier—the systematic training of newspaper carrier boys in salesmanship.[1]

The demonstration involved two carriers of the Asheville Citizen and Times, who had won a contest for a trophy donated by Robert W. Bingham, publisher of the Louisville newspapers, before the 1931 ICMA convention. The boys were presented to the SNPA meeting by John R. Marks, circulation manager of the Asheville newspapers.

---

[1] Even though this activity did not originate with the SNPA, the fact that an SNPA member took the initiative and received enthusiastic support from Association newspapers deserves mention. Throughout the 1920's and 1930's, newspaper employment of young children as carriers came under frequent attack by private and government welfare agencies. The Louisville Courier-Journal and Times led the way in establishing high standards of character, conduct and scholarship among its carriers. Under Mr. Stodghill's direction the boys (ranging from 12 to 16 years of age) received effective training in salesmanship, collections, and elementary accounting. Their home life, associations and school records were carefully supervised. The immediate benefit to the boys and to the newspapers, demonstrated to the ICMA, caused widespread adoption of the plan throughout the country. In the later agitation for strict limitation on the employment of minors in newspaper circulation work, this welfare activity by important newspapers became the most effective refutation of the argument that newspaper employment was detrimental to children.

Survival in the Lean Years

Gratifying results had been achieved during the previous year by the co-operative selling plan of the St. Petersburg (Fla.) Independent and Times, Charles C. Carr of the Times, and L. C. Brown of the Independent, told the convention. With newspapers all over America sadly contemplating linage losses, the St. Petersburg newspapers had registered a gain of 7 per cent. in general advertising for June 1931, against June 1930. But despite that apparent proof of achievement, the St. Petersburg plan found no immediate imitators.

Another feature which bucked the tide of business gloom came in an address by H. C. MacDonald, who offered many specific hints for increasing display and classified advertising. Among his significant remarks was the report that 40 newspapers offered color printing to advertisers—a trend that would become widespread in the depression years, reach an excellent fruition in a few cities, but fail to rise fully to its potential.

Such were the business features of the 1931 meeting—sparse enough, and possibly indicative of the lack of forward momentum that would characterize nationwide newspaper promotion efforts until near the end of the Thirties. In common with the rest of the business world, newspaper publishers had not yet sized up the full implications of the depression.

For the most part, the 1931 meeting of the SNPA pitched itself on a high note of idealism. Considerable time was spent in paying well merited tributes to two eminent members who had died during the previous year—Major E. B. Stahlman, publisher of the Nashville Banner, and Colonel Robert Ewing, publisher of the New Orleans States. Their names have appeared often in these pages, generally as leaders in a fight for principle or against encroachment on the rights of the press. It was in those terms that their long careers were reviewed by Major John S. Cohen, editor of the Atlanta Journal, and Frederick I. Thompson, publisher of the Mobile Register and News-Item. In a general eulogy of the SNPA dead of 1930-31, the venerable Josephus Daniels, publisher and editor of the Raleigh News & Observer, decried the competition which compelled modern journalism to "subordinate to the things of play the important elements of social and economic life." He recalled the circumstances surrounding the enactment of the Bill of Rights (including the free press guarantee) as a prerequisite to ratification of the Constitution by many of the original States.

"Would it be possible today," Mr. Daniels reflected, "to induce a state to forego the political patronage and preferment inherent in a new government, for the sake of guaranteeing an abstract principle?"

Newspapers which looked upon their operation solely as a business proposition, a source of profits, Mr. Daniels added, forfeit their right to the constitutional privilege and should be placed on the same plane as hucksters of any other merchandise.

Indicative of SNPA membership interest in other things than profit was the reception accorded the report of Prof. William L. Mapel, director of the School of Journalism at Washington & Lee University. This school, then in its seventh year, had been established mainly with funds raised by the SNPA, and its growth had been actively encouraged by the Association. By 1931 its standard of instruction had attained a level which gained it recognition by the Association of Schools and Departments of Journalism—a distinction then enjoyed by but 23 of the more than 200 institutions offering such courses. More than 100 students had elected the journalism course in 1931, Professor Mapel declared, marking a steady expansion of enrolment, in the face of increasingly difficult scholarship and aptitude entrance requirements.

Also from Washington & Lee came Dr. Francis Pendleton Gaines, president of the University, with a definition of the "journalist of tomorrow" that reads two decades later like a remarkable bit of prescience.

"The journalist of tomorrow," declared Dr. Gaines, "must have a background as wide as the interests and the nobler hopes of those he serves. He must have at least a brief insight into the physical sciences and the potent changes of its action and reaction. He must understand the basic movements and the permanent ideals of the social sciences, the trends of economics and the theories of government. He must have a wide fellowship with those minds of all ages and all countries who have crystallized in words the best thoughts of man, or who have set in winsome rhythms man's highest aspirations. He must have some standards of good taste and he must have broad sympathies trained into modes of usefulness.

SURVIVAL IN THE LEAN YEARS

"It may not be too idealistic to say that the journalist must have more than knowledge—he must have a system of professional ethics and he must have a fundamental attitude or a fundamental obligation. He must not only wish to be successful and powerful, but he must want to do the right and he must seek to achieve that which is more satisfying than success or power—some sense of helpfulness."

With false structures of "success" crashing on every side in 1931, the journalists and business administrators of Southern journalism found pleasant relief in addresses which looked both to a glorious past and placed principle above profit and to a future in which helpfulness would be preferred above success and power. In the years ahead, they would demonstrate the intrinsic soundness of the 1931 convention philosophy.

Major Clark Howell, Jr., of the Atlanta Constitution, the third generation of this stalwart Georgia family to win prominence in Southern newspapers affairs, succeeded Mr. Parks as president. His first announcement was a declaration that he believed that the highest office in the Association should be rotated and that he would not be a candidate for a second term, assuming that the membership wished to re-elect him. Mr. Parks automatically became chairman of the board. Walter C. Johnson received another term as treasurer, and Cranston Williams as secretary-manager. James L. Mapes of the Beaumont Enterprise and Journal replaced Major Howell as a trustee of the Association's protection fund.

Directors were chosen as follows:

Alabama, James E. Chappell, Birmingham News and Age-Herald; Arkansas, Kirtland A. Engel, Little Rock Democrat; Florida, Charles C. Carr, St. Petersburg Times; Georgia, Herschel V. Jenkins, Savannah News and Press; Kentucky, Emanuel Levi, Louisville Courier-Journal and Times; Louisiana, Leonard K. Nicholson, New Orleans Times-Picayune; Mississippi, James H. Skewes, Meridian Star; North Carolina, H. Galt Braxton, Kinston Free Press; Oklahoma, E. K. Gaylord, Oklahoma City Oklahoman and Times; South Carolina, F. C. Withers, Columbia State; Tennessee, James G. Stahlman, Nashville Banner; Texas, James L. Mapes, Beaumont Enterprise and Journal; Virginia, M. Botts Lewis, Clifton Forge Review; West Virginia, J. H. Long, Huntington Advertiser and Herald-Dispatch.

Unhappily, the massive prescription of idealism and "chins up" at the 1931 convention had no immediate effect on the national economic malady. The end of 1931 found newspaper revenues 30 per cent or more below those of 1929. All the linage gains that had been piled up in the previous decade had been swept away and advertising volume was back at its 1921 level. Few newspapers, however, had suffered notable loss in circulation. Hopes held as 1932 dawned that the New Year would, at least, mark the end of the debacle, had faded month by month. So when the SNPA gathered again in Asheville for its thirtieth annual meeting, the publishers had no ear for inspirational addresses. Their mood was strictly business. They were fighting a grim rear-guard action with survival itself as the stake.

President Howell set the keynote in his annual report:

"I dare not hazard a guess as to when our trials and tribulations will be lightened; as to when the darkened clouds of business will be shot through with the sunlit rays of returning prosperity. I have no panacea to offer for our ills, either social, political or economic. Eternal vigilance in watching expenses, enthusiastic and constructive salesmanship in producing revenue, and intelligent utilization of our membership in the SNPA will help."

Despite the darkened clouds of business, approximately 80 members and as many guests attended the meeting at Grove Park Inn, July 18-20. Total membership had grown during the year and topped the 200 mark, according to Secretary-Manager Williams. Treasurer Johnson noted only a small decline in receipts and a sizeable increase in expenses, due to increased services called for by the membership in the troubled business situation. Cautiously, he recommended a "readjustment of dues".

On the practical side, Mr. Johnson demonstrated how his newspaper, the Chattanooga News, had tried to keep its budget balanced in the face of steadily shrinking revenue. His picture probably was typical of Southern newspaper operations of the day. With a linage decline of 24.1 per cent during the first six months of 1932 against the similar period of 1931, and a revenue loss of 22.6 per cent, the News had managed to cut expenses 17.6 per cent. Departmental costs had been reduced thus, percentagewise:

Survival in the Lean Years

Administration, 3.1; editorial, 17.2; business office, 2.7; local advertising, 40.0; general advertising, 29.2; classified advertising, 15.3; circulation, 5.9; newsprint, 25.7; ink, 14.6; composing room, 13.4; stereotype, 11.5; pressroom, 16.0.

A maximum cut of 10 per cent had been imposed on salaries. The great drop of 40 per cent in local advertising costs had been effected by gradual reduction of staff from 12 to seven members. People had been separated from the payroll only when it was possible to find other employment for them.

Mr. Johnson cautioned against "improving the looks of the balance sheet" by reduction of depreciation or bad debt allowances. Ample reserves should be maintained for both, he counseled.

Another practical approach to reduction of expenses called upon the new officers and directors to consult with the American Telephone and Telegraph Company on the possibility of abrogating the eight-hour period for transmission of news on leased wires and the institution of a shorter period. Smaller newspapers, especially, found that they could not use more than a small fraction of the report delivered in an eight-hour period. A shorter transmission time would bring a commensurate reduction in costs, it was hoped.

An effort to shore up the crumbling revenue structure appeared in a resolution "noting with genuine regret" a widespread campaign by advertisers to include in contracts a guarantee of circulation, with a pro rata reduction in advertising rates whenever circulation fell below the guaranteed figure. The advertisers' proposal did not provide for higher-than-card rates if circulation went above the guaranteed level. The publishers expressed the fear that "individual newspapers might be placed in the position where they would be compelled to incur unwholesome circulation costs in order to protect their rate structures."

Radio competition, too, at last received official notice from the Southern publishers after several years of sidelong glances. It could no longer be ignored or shrugged off. The three great press associations which served most American dailies with wire news had also felt the depression. Newspaper clients had decreased in number, and many had cut down on the volume of wire service regarded as necessary in prosperous days. At the same time, events in Europe and Asia had demanded broad and expensive reporting—the beginning of Japanese aggression in China, the economic collapse in Central Europe, France and England, the international efforts of President Hoover to stem the worldwide march of financial chaos. Tentatively and warily, the wire services examined the possibility of balancing their budgets by selling news to the broadcasters, who were also discovering an avid public appetite for news via radio. At this stage, the stations were furnishing news as a public service, rarely with advertising sponsorship.

Indignantly, several Southern publishers told the 1932 convention that they had heard news on the radio, by courtesy of one or more of the newspaper wire services, minutes to hours before the same news arrived on their office printer machines. One publisher declared that his newspaper had not received news of the Lindbergh baby's kidnaping in time for publication, although the story had been broadcast several hours before his deadline. After prolonged discussion at two convention sessions, the SNPA formulated this brief resolution:

"Resolved, that the press services be urged to discontinue furnishing news to radio broadcasting stations."

This Canute-like gesture reflected the confusion and division of interest prevalent throughout newspaperdom on the radio news question. A growing number of newspapers, in the South as elsewhere, had acquired broadcasting stations as adjuncts to their publishing operations. It is no secret now that some of them found all of their profits in the depression years coming from radio, with the station earning more than the newspaper lost. These publishers wanted no barriers to the use of press association news for broadcasting; most of them, in fact, regarded news broadcasts under the auspices of the newspaper as effective promotion for the latter. If experience suggests that they were correct in this view 20 years ago, the publishers who not only had no radio station but faced strong competition from a local radio enterprise, found no comfort in their colleagues' complacent attitude toward news broadcasting. The hard fact remained that the commercial news services had a ready market awaiting a radio news report that could be delivered as a relatively cheap by-product of their service to newspapers. The United Press and International News Service sold news as a commodity and did not consider themselves limited to the newspaper market. The Associated Press, a co-operative owned by its members, had to move with more deliberation. Eventually the AP, too, had to get into the radio field to protect its prestige as well as its revenues. The process would keep the entire news field agog for the next three years until a *modus vivendi* was found, and publishers gradually discovered that radio news competition need not be fatal to the printed medium.

The government, too, needed more money. So did the railroads. Uncle Sam again alleged a deficit in postal rates on second-class matter and increased charges on newspapers and magazines. SNPA members, as individuals, registered a mild protest. Enterprising members looked more closely into plans for transporting their newspapers either by baggage cars or in their own trucks. Two SNPA members, in fact,—the Charlotte Observer and the Oklahoma City Oklahoman and Times—built up profitable subsidiaries in truck lines which not only distributed the paper but carried other wares (motion picture films, for example) which required expeditious transportation within the newspaper's circulation fields. Railroad freight rates had been raised during the previous year, adding to the cost of newsprint. Here, too, the remedy proposed by small publishers involved new truck lines for movement of paper from seaports to point of publication.

The newsprint market continued to boil with rumors of price wars that became fact in September, 1932. A cut of $5.50 per ton by Price Brothers Company was countered by International Paper's reduction of $7.00 per ton, bringing the price to $46 base—lower than it had been since the opening of World War I. The price at major Southern points ranged from $46 at seaports to $49 at inland cities. Secretary-Manager Williams believed that the new price would permit newspapers to print larger and better issues, regardless of the trend in advertising volume. That hope was only partially realized, as advertising linage and revenue continued to fall. Newsprint consumption increased nominally, if at all, and the mills had to make additional reductions in their frantic quest of volume before stability was reached.

Political and economic storm clouds banked higher than ever as 1932 slipped into 1933. Franklin D. Roosevelt had scored a shattering victory at the polls in November, and the repudiated Hoover administration found itself practically powerless to deal with the crises that deepened between Election Day and the inauguration of the new President on March 4, 1933. The creeping paralysis of business and banking became total early in the new year.

That was the situation, only dimly foreseen, to which the SNPA committed its new officers and directors at the 1932 convention.

The energetic James G. Stahlman, Nashville Banner, was named president, and his predecessor, Clark Howell, Jr., became board chairman. Walter C. Johnson was returned as treasurer and Cranston Williams as secretary-manager. The new board was constituted as follows:

Alabama, James E. Chappell, Birmingham News and Age-Herald; Arkansas, Kirtland A. Engel, Little Rock Democrat; Florida, G. V. Harper, Miami Herald; Georgia, Herschel V. Jenkins, Savannah News and Press; Kentucky, Emanuel Levi, Louisville Courier-Journal and Times; Louisiana, Leonard K. Nicholson, New Orleans Times-Picayune; Mississippi, James H. Skewes, Meridian Star; North Carolina, Josh L. Horne, Jr., Rocky Mount Telegram; Oklahoma, E. K. Gaylord, Oklahoma City Oklahoman and Times; South Carolina, Roger C. Peace, Greenville News and Piedmont; Tennessee, Adolph Shelby Ochs, Chattanooga Times; Texas, James L. Mapes, Beaumont Enterprise and Journal; Virginia, Powell Glass, Lynchburg News and Advance; West Virginia, J. H. Long, Huntington Advertiser and Herald-Dispatch.

The famed "Hundred Days" of the New Deal had just ended when the SNPA gathered at Signal Mountain Inn, near Chattanooga, for its 1933 meeting, June 26-28. The nation's benumbed business had ground to a shuddering stop as the Roosevelt administration entered office. All banks had been closed by edict of the new President as he rallied the nation to a fresh start. When the banks re-opened and business picked up at elementary levels, the dynamic F.D.R. called upon the Congress for a succession of measures, some of them laying new rails over routes never before traveled by American business. Of chief interest to the publishers assembled at Chattanooga was the brand-new National Industrial Recovery Act, with its numerous and as yet imperfectly understood provisions for employment, minimum wages, maximum hours, and new privileges for organized labor. In the long travail of hammering out workable formulæ of operation under this new legislation, the SNPA would emerge as a major power in national newspaper affairs.

The atmosphere of June, 1933, did not lend itself to dogmatic pronouncements on important policy. It was a time to "wait and see" what would come of the much-mixed broth that was boiling in the New Deal pots. Informal discussions on the floor, in the corridors and on the porches of Signal Mountain Inn, rotated around the portents of the NIRA.

Would the newspaper business as a whole, or in various categories, formulate the codes that the law required? In fact, did that and other provisions of the law apply to newspapers? What was the implication of the NIRA provision that the President might "license" enterprises which did not conform to their industry code? How would such a license apply to the press, in connection with the guarantees under Amendment One in the Bill of Rights? To what extent would the law affect newspapers operating under the Open Shop, as were a dozen or more Southern dailies? How would newspapers adjust their operations to a five-day week?

Those were a few of the myriad questions that SNPA members asked each other in and about the convention. No one had the answers in June, 1933. Some of them, and a host of others, would not be answered when the Association gathered again in 1934. But to their solution the SNPA would contribute mightily in the busy months ahead.

President "Jimmy" Stahlman had put in a busy year. He took seriously the Association's laconic resolution of 1931, "urging" the wire services to discontinue furnishing news to radio stations, and with all of the force that publishers in the whole national field were to see him exhibit during the next seven years, he presented the newspaper case to the Associated Press officers and directors in October. He offered a similar argument before the Inland Daily Press Association in Chicago a few days later, addressed the Pennsylvania and New York Publishers Associations in January and offered a resolution at the AP annual meeting in April. The Associated Press accepted his views substantially—and no man could have done more to obtain agreement to the SNPA thesis. But, as has been indicated, the radio news situation did not lend itself to control either by newspapers or by the co-operative Associated Press. The latter's two commercial rivals were selling news to the broadcasters, at a handsome profit, and newspapers were in no position to command them to desist. President Stahlman continued to carry the newspapers' banner in this battle for several more years and undoubtedly contributed to its eventual decision.

Another resolution adopted in 1931 also received immediate action, President Stahlman appointed a committee headed by Josh L. Horne, Jr., publisher of the Rocky Mount (N.C.) Telegram, to consult with the telephone company on reduced hours for transmission of leased wire news. A rapid canvass of the situation disclosed that no curtailed schedule of hours could possibly satisfy the varying needs of newspapers. Deciding that pressure on the telephone company for that kind of relief would be futile, the committee looked into other phases of the leased wire question. Its members were amazed to find that they were paying up to $20 a month rental for the printer machines on which news was received in their offices. The tariff varied, not always according to an understandable system. They found also that the machines had cost about $600 when they were built by the Morkrum-Kleinschmidt Company, which had sold them to the A.T. & .T. Co. It was quickly apparent to both the telephone company consultants and the publishers that the machines had been paid for many times over, and the telephone people volunteered a reduction in rate. Before the year was out, both sides had determined that the machines should be purchased outright by the newspapers or news services on monthly payments which were considerable less than the old rental charge. And when the vigilant committee learned that the company was building new printers which would make those bought by the newspapers obsolete, the payment was reduced to nominal levels. The ubiquitous Jimmy Stahlman also sat in with this committee's negotiations, which racked up the largest volume of correspondence in 1932-1933 Association affairs. Small as the savings were to individual newspapers, the convention heartily approved the committee's diligence.

Approval also was voiced informally for the new curriculum of the Washington & Lee School of Journalism, which, according to Prof. William L. Mapel, increasingly stressed a broad cultural background rather than training in newspaper techniques. Mr. Mapel brought to the meeting a bundle of testimonials from leading newspaper and news service executives, whose opinion of the new course may be epitomized in the words of one: "We already have a great many more technically perfected newspaper men than we have intelligent ones."

Labor affairs kept Secretary-Manager Williams on the move during the year, serving as arbitrator or counseling members in scale negotiations. While no strikes were reported in SNPA circles during the year, five Southern newspapers (one of them an SNPA member) had established open shop composing rooms. Mr. Williams had also traveled to several cities in which publishers desired information on the co-operative operation plan adopted in 1929 by the St. Petersburg newspapers. His 1933 report named no cities in which this plan or one similar had been put into force, but it is altogether probable that these depression-time conferences planted the seed of co-operative operations that blossomed later in several Southern cities.

The publishers at Chattanooga sensed that they would have to grapple soon with much larger questions than any which had agitated them in recent years. For three months past the Roosevelt Administration had been providing banner headlines almost daily. The Washington correspondents' corps was enthusiastic for and seldom critical of the new President. In general, the publishers also liked the new atmosphere. They liked the feel of powerful engines again throbbing under the deck and the promise of returning prosperity. Some hadn't liked the sleight-of-hand by which the country had been taken off the gold standard. And almost all were uncertain as to the impact of the new NIRA upon business in general and their own craft in particular. But in late June, they could not lay down directive policies for their new officers. They would continue to co-operate in every possible manner with the new administration's efforts to get business and industry into fruitful motion, and await developments in their own field.

To guide the Association in the coming year, they elected James L. Mapes, Beaumont Enterprise and Journal, as president, with Past-President Stahlman as chairman of the board. Walter C. Johnson, again named treasurer, entered his 19th consecutive year as an SNPA executive. Cranston Williams began his ninth term as secretary-manager.

The new board included:

Alabama, James E. Chappell, Birmingham News and Age-Herald; Arkansas, J. N. Heiskell, Little Rock Arkansas Gazette; Florida, Jesse M. Elliott, Jacksonville Florida Times-Union; Georgia, Clark Howell, Jr., Atlanta Constitution; Kentucky, Emanuel Levi, Louisville Courier-Journal and Times; Louisiana, John D. Ewing, Shreveport Times; Mississippi, Birney Imes, Columbus Commercial Dispatch; North Carolina, Josh L. Horne, Jr., Rocky Mount Telegram; Oklahoma, E. K. Gaylord, Oklahoma City Oklahoman and Times; South Carolina, Roger C. Peace, Greenville News and Piedmont; Tennessee, Adolph Shelby Ochs, Chattanooga Times; Texas, W. A. Dealey, Dallas News (upon Mr. Dealey's death in mid-year, F. G. Huntress, San Antonio Express and News, was elected to the vacancy); Virginia, S. L. Slover, Norfolk Ledger-Dispatch and Virginian-Pilot; West Virginia, Robert L. Smith, Charleston Gazette.

Experiments Perilous

Newspaper Honeymoon with New Deal Wanes—Sharp Words Exchanged in Writing Newspaper Industry Code under NRA—SNPA Membership Grows and Dues are Raised 50 Per Cent to Meet New Service Demands—Southern Newsprint Mill Wins Association Approval.

"LIFE IS short, art long, opportunity fleeting, experiment perilous, judgment difficult," wrote the ancient physician, Hippocrates. Scholars differ on the exact meaning of the old Greek words, but the newspaper publishers of America in 1933 and 1934 had a fair idea of the intent. They learned much about experiments perilous and difficult judgment in writing and rewriting the code by which newspapers should be guided under the National Recovery Administration.

This narrative will not attempt to review in detail the tortuous negotiations by which the daily newspapers and the NRA finally arrived at a code. The National Industrial Recovery Act was a frankly new departure in American legislation. It was experimental. It was hastily and imperfectly drafted—an early expression of President Roosevelt's idea of "try something; if it doesn't work, try something else." With its primary aim of getting people back to work in as large numbers as possible and at wages which would give them money to spend in trade channels, nobody quarreled.

That primary aim, however, became complicated with several other objectives before the bill emerged as law. The provision for industrial codes, laudably designed to create equable conditions of competition, in some respects ran counter to the established national tradition against combinations in restraint of trade. The provisions for maximum hours per week at minimum wages undoubtedly had useful applications in some industries which had unscrupulously exploited unskilled working people. At no point did they touch the operations of daily newspapers significantly.

The famous Section 7-A, according to employees the right to organize and bargain collectively with employers through representatives of their own choosing, in one sweep sought to correct a condition that should not have existed in the United States of 1933. Before its philosophy achieved acceptance, it caused many a headache in newspaper circles—relatively few of them in the South.

The act became effective on June 15, 1933. The ANPA board had already called a meeting on June 7 of several of its important committees to consider the law's possible effects on newspapers. Quickly it was decided that the manifold problems presented called for consultation with the major regional and state newspaper associations. To the primary question, "did the law require newspapers to organize under a code?", the volcanic General Hugh A. Johnson, the first NRA administrator, told the Washington correspondents that newspapers would be expected to comply with the law. He would regret that "off-the-cuff" judgment, but was powerless to recall it.

The ANPA Board met again on July 20, in company with representatives of the regional groups. Secretary-Manager Cranston Williams acted for the SNPA. As a first step, the ANPA directed a "survey of wages and hours in the newspaper industry for the purpose of being in position to supply figures to the National Industrial Recovery Administration if they are needed." It also advised publishers not to prepare or subscribe to a code under the Recovery Act "at the present time." The code committee of 25 members began to prepare a code on July 27. A tentative effort to write a code for the "graphic arts industry" blanketing all newspapers and printers under one set-up quickly proved impossible.

In the code committee's first draft, submitted on August 8, it was plain that the publishers wished to preserve as fully as possible the conditions under which they had operated to their own satisfaction over many years.

Although Howard Davis, publisher of the New York Herald Tribune and president of the ANPA, declared that the code draft "in the highest possible degree supports the President's program", the head of the International Typographical Union thought otherwise. Mr. Howard of the ITU objected particularly to the "open shop" clause which read that "no employee shall be required to join any organization to secure or retain employment or to secure the benefits of this code, and the right of every individual to refrain from joining any organization, and the right of employee and employer to bargain together free from interference by any third party, is hereby recognized."

The code draft also exempted newspaper carrier boys from classification as child laborers. It designated editorial workers as "professionals" not subject to the act's provisions for maximum hours and minimum wages. Most important, from the standpoint of the committee, was the re-assertion of the rights guaranteed to the press in the First Amendment to the Constitution. That would remain as the sticking point throughout the next seven months. The law specifically empowered the President to "license" enterprises which did not comply with their industrial code, and that word "license" had a sinister sound to the publishers and their legal advisers. This provision had been written into the law apparently without any thought that it might contravene the free press guarantee in the Constitution. The publishers were advised that, even though Congress could not limit press freedom, the newspapers themselves might waive this constitutional protection by signing a code which included a licensing provision.

Newspaper opinion divided on the temporary code's merits; while most metropolitan newspapers gave it editorial approval, some important dailies thought it failed to measure up to the nation's needs. General Johnson amended its wording on child labor and in the "open shop" clauses quoted above, and approved it on August 15. By the end of August, the NRA was issuing exceptions to newspapers which could not find sufficient skilled help to operate on the code's 40-hour week or which worked under peculiar regional conditions.

With the temporary code in operation, the code committee began drafting a "final" instrument. Late in September, a long series of hearings began. Secretary-Manager Williams, President Mapes, and Board Chairman Stahlman attended these, as well as many other meetings in New York and Washington at which the code was whipped into shape. Two newspaper codes were finally submitted—one by the ANPA and the code committee, and one by the National Editorial

Association, the latter for "non-metropolitan" newspapers, small dailies and weeklies. The small dailies had the option of subscribing to the code which best fitted their requirements.

The final code eliminated much of the matter which had aroused criticism in the temporary draft. The publishers successfully defended their employment of boys as carriers, accepting the provision which forbade the employment of "persons under 16 years of age, except those who are able, without impairment of health or interference with hours of day school". The "open shop" clause was dropped, but the publishers declined to make nationwide provision for the wages and hours demanded by the union leaders, writing into the code the maximum hours and minimum wages prescribed by the law. The offensive "professional" exemption of editorial workers from the law's benefits also came out of the final draft. Instead, the Code Authority was directed to "secure the necessary data and to determine maximum hours and minimum wages for news department workers, and subject to the approval of the administrator, to incorporate its findings in the provisions of this code."

In the President's letter placing the code in effect on March 12, 1934, was a "request" that news department workers be given a five-day 40-hour week on newspapers with more than 75,000 circulation in cities of more than 750,000 population.

The President's order also characterized the newspapers' repetition of the free press guarantee under the Constitution "as pure surplusage." He added "while it has no meaning, it is permitted to stand merely because it has been requested and because it could have no such legal effects as would bar its inclusion."

"Of course," the order continued, "nobody waives any Constitutional rights by assenting to a code. The recitation of the freedom of the press clause in a code has no more place here than would be the recitation of the whole Constitution or of the Ten Commandments. The freedom guaranteed by the Constitution is freedom of expression and that will be scrupulously respected—but it is not freedom to work children, to do business in a firetrap, or to violate the laws against obscenity, libel and lewdness."

Later it came out that this gratuitous insult had been written into the order by General Johnson. To a meeting of the American Society of Newspaper Editors he admitted its authorship, called it "very unfortunate" and "much misconstrued." But millions who had read the reckless statement attributed to the President never heard of its author's regretful apology. It would keynote much of the abuse directed against newspapers in years to come.

With the code in operation, newspapers in the SNPA found that it caused little disturbance in their production routine. The American Newspaper Guild had become strong and vociferous in a number of Northern and Western cities, but by mid-1934 it had made small headway in the South. The President's order, covering newspapers of more than 75,000 circulation in cities of more than 750,000 population obviously did not apply to SNPA members, for no city in SNPA territory had then attained 750,000 population. At the beginning of 1933, the International Typographical Union had decreed a five-day week for its members, in an effort to spread employment opportunities, and Southern newspapers having contractual relations with this union operated under this rule, albeit with some difficulty. By union action, all contracts expiring while the Daily Newspaper Code was under negotiation were held open until the code became final, and many remained in that status when the SNPA met for its 1934 convention at Grove Park Inn, Asheville, on May 21-23. No strikes had been reported in the South during the previous year.

Naturally, code developments impinged on many of the convention discussions. Other aspects of the New Deal also came in for attention. The Business Affairs Committee report, rendered by Charles C. Carr, St. Petersburg Times, noted varying advice given to publishers on income tax liability. Some were told by the Internal Revenue Bureau that contributions to the community chest were no longer deductible as donations to charity, particularly if made by a corporation. The committee had investigated, and believed that this advice was erroneous.

Another recent ruling by the Treasury Department affected newspapers more seriously. Under previous administrations, publishers had fixed the rate of allowance for depreciation on machinery and equipment. The new rule empowered the governmnt to fix that allowance and put it up to the taxpayer to dispute the tax auditors' ruling. Mr. Carr reported that the government expected to pick up about $80,000,000 from corporations during the coming few years through this rule.

Mr. Carr also noted an ominous move in Florida. The state comptroller was attempting to apply a state documentary stamp tax to local and national advertising contracts and orders, on the grounds that they were evidences of indebtedness or promises to pay. The Florida press was fighting the proposal, he said, with prospects of success.

The all-pervading code also affected SNPA finances, according to Treasurer Johnson. Receipts from dues had increased during the year from $12,202.50 to $14,460, thanks to an amendment on dues paid by newspapers with more than 30,000 circulation. Expenses, however, climbed from $12,320.83 to $13,446.21, largely due to the many trips of Mr. Williams to Washington and New York on code matters. Otherwise expenses had been held at rock bottom, Mr. Johnson stated.

This report lit an immediate fuse. Board Chairman Stahlman declared that it was impossible for the Association to operate under existing demands on a $14,000 income. New staff people must be added to help the Secretary-Manager carry the load of the headquarters office. Mr. Stahlman moved the appointment of a committee to revise the dues schedule and provide an income adequate to the Association's work in years to come.

Seconding the motion, H. Galt Braxton, Kinston Free Press, revealed that members of the board of directors and committee chairmen had paid their own travel and hotel expenses, in addition to giving of their time. He urged that provision be made for such outlays in future budgets. The committee was appointed and by the end of the convention had reported a new schedule of monthly dues ranging from $4.00 to $45.00, calculated to provide an annual income of $22,000. The committee recommended employment of a new assistant at headquarters, an increase in salary for Mr. Williams to bring his pay into line with that of similar work in other associations, but ruled out expenses for directors and committee chairmen at regular and special meetings. The new budget received unanimous approval.

Carrying on this generous and progressive spirit, Major John S. Cohen, editor of the Atlanta Journal, expressed the Association's gratitude to "Jimmy" Stahlman in the presentation of a silver service. Mr. Stahlman had served as a director of the SNPA since 1927, Major Cohen stated, and in that and his terms as president and board chairman, "his services have been manifold and useful."

"He made himself a blamed nuisance to me about radio," continued the Major, whose newspaper operated WSB, one of the most noted broadcasting stations in the country, "but he has benefited the newspapers by the fight he made."

Probably the most significant action of the 1934 convention was unpremeditated. It came about after an address by Major George L. Berry, president of the International Printing Pressmens' and Assistants' Union of North America and one of the divisional administrators under the National Recovery Act. After congratulating the publishers upon their long record of amity with his union, and commending the purposes of NIRA, Major Berry turned to the project of the Southern newsprint mill which Dr. Herty had advanced to the Association in 1931. He urged its development as a major contribution by the South to national recovery. The president on motion, requested the resolutions committee to report the next day with a resolution expressing the SNPA view.

When Chairman John D. Ewing read the committee's resolution, approval was general, except for one member. Emanuel Levi, Louisville Courier-Journal and Times, insisted that the resolution include the words "by private enterprise." After a year of close contact with government grasping for the reins of business, Mr. Levi wanted no such control over the newsprint mill project, and his idea prevailed after a brief debate. The resolution as adopted read:

"Resolved, That the Southern Newspaper Publishers Association acknowledge and consider the following facts:

"(a) That the conversion of various kinds and grades of Southern pine into newsprint paper of high quality has been demonstrated by operating tests;

"(b) That there is, because of the possibility of utilizing young growths, and irrespective of the extent of contemplated production, what can be termed an unlimited quantity of Southern pine available within an economic radius of contemplated mill operations;

"(c) That power will be available for the purposes indicated;

"(d) That appropriate millsites at tidewater or on navigable streams, within an economical radius of both timber and power required for such operation, are available, and,

"Be It Further Resolved, That the Southern Newspaper Publishers Asssociation hereby expresses and records its approval of an attempt to develop a plan for the prompt construction by private enterprise of a mill for the purpose of producing newsprint in the South, but designed for the benefit of the entire country; and to that end the President of the Southern Newspaper Publishers Association is hereby authorized and directed to appoint a committee to proceed at once to take the steps which, in the discretion of the committee, are necessary to the accomplishment of the above-named objective, including, but not limited to—

"(1) Formation of a plan of procedure;

"(2) Solicitation of publishers for the purpose of assuring full consumption of the output of newsprint of the proposed unit of the newsprint industry."

That was the mandate which set the association on the paths which have made Southern and national industrial history. Many obstacles lay ahead, but, as related in another chapter, the SNPA committees did not let go or relax in the task until a newsprint mill began production at Herty, Texas, in January, 1940.

Among the eleven deceased members honored by the Memorials Committee was Franklin P. Glass, publisher of the Montgomery Advertiser, president of the SNPA in 1906-1907, and its virtual founder in 1903. He had been active in Southern newspaper ranks for more than half a century. Another SNPA stalwart of earlier years who died during the year was G. J. Palmer, vice-president and business manager of the Houston Chronicle and labor commissioner of the Texas Newspaper Publishers Association. And another whose passing was lamented was Walter A. Dealey, vice-president and general manager of the Dallas News and Journal, who had been elected to the SNPA board in 1933.

The convention ratified the designation of Cranston Williams as SNPA representative on the Daily Newspaper Code Authority, and expressed its satisfaction with the work of Howard W. Stodghill, Louisville Courier-Journal and Times, safeguarding the interests of newspapers and newspaper boys in drafting the NRA code.

A special resolution expressed sympathy and hope for the restoration to health of Col. Walter H. Savory, who was absent from the convention for the first time in nearly a quarter century. Colonel Savory, of the Mergenthaler Linotype Company, had been chairman of the annual golf tournament since its inception at Asheville two decades earlier.[1]

E. K. Gaylord, Oklahoma City Oklahoman and Times, was elected president, and James L. Mapes moved up as chairman of the board. Walter C. Johnson assumed the treasurership for another year, and Cranston Williams again received the board's approval as secretary-manager. The new board included:

Alabama, James E. Chappell, Birmingham News and Age-Herald; Arkansas, J. N. Heiskell, Little Rock Arkansas Gazette; Florida, Jesse M. Elliott, Jacksonville Florida Times-Union; Georgia, Herbert Porter, Atlanta Georgian-American; Kentucky, Emanuel Levi, Louisville Courier-Journal and Times; Louisiana, John D. Ewing, Shreveport Times; Mississippi, T. M. Hederman, Jackson Clarion-Ledger; North Carolina, J. L. Horne, Jr., Rocky Mount Telegram; Oklahoma, Clyde E. Muchmore, Ponca City News; South Carolina, A. W. Huckle, Rock Hill Herald; Tennessee, Adolph Shelby Ochs, Chattanooga Times; Texas, Ted Dealey, Dallas News and Journal; Virginia, S. L. Slover, Norfolk Ledger-Dispatch; West Virginia, Robert L. Smith, Charleston Gazette.

The publishers grew accustomed to operation under the NRA code during 1934 and 1935, and when the SNPA met at Hot Springs, Ark., May 20-22, 1935, an informal poll of the membership indicated that a majority favored a three-year extension of the code after its scheduled expiration on June 16. But the Supreme Court ruled otherwise. The National Industrial Recovery Act was declared unconstitutional on May 27. With it, of course, the codes became a dead issue.

---

[1] During Colonel Savory's disability and after his death, the golf tournament was conducted by Arthur T. Robb and Laurence E. Mansfield, with the assistance of publisher members. Mr. Mansfield has been tournament chairman since the end of World War II.

On the horizon, however, loomed the Wagner Fair Labor Standards Act, which, convention speakers predicted, promised multiplied labor troubles for all industry, including newspapers. The sale of radio news, which had agitated the publishers for several years past and had caused vehement discussions in the 1934 and 1935 meetings of the AP and ANPA found the SNPA in a relative placid mood. The publishers accepted the situation. The majority now believed that sale of news by the wire services to broadcasters held no menace for newspapers—provided that the wire services recognized the newspapers' prior property right to the news and discreetly controlled its sale for radio use.

The Association declined to become excited with Ted Dealey of the Dallas News over the question of "freedom of radio." Mr. Dealey offered a resolution calling upon newspapers to rally to the support of radio stations whose licenses had not been renewed by the Federal Communications Commission. The Dallas publisher, whose newspaper owned (and owns) one of the South's great radio stations, regarded the Commission's action as analogous to Federal interference with a newspaper's publication, and possibly a dangerous precedent. But after a warm discussion, with Mr. Dealey supplying most of the heat, the convention voted to refer the matter to the resolutions committee. There it died.

Major interest in 1935 revolved around the past year's effort to carry out the 1934 resolution favoring construction of a Southern newsprint mill. James G. Stahlman headed the newsprint mills committee, and his strenuous but futile efforts of the previous year were described in detail and with high praise by President Gaylord. The committee made many trips to New York for conferences with engineers and financiers who apparently had every intention of seeing the project to its successful end. A site had been selected and the matter was seemingly within a week of signing a contract when the whole proposition, in the words of Mr. Gaylord, "blew up".

The committee pursued new leads and spent most of the winter persuading their fellow SNPA members to subscribe for sufficient of the mill's prospective tonnage to assure an adequate background for financing. President Gaylord and Chairman Stahlman told the convention that enough tonnage had been guaranteed to assure the construction of a 50,000-ton mill. As told in another chapter, this report was a bit optimistic, but, at top discount, it represented an impressive achievement by Mr. Stahlman's committee. Another testimonial to the committee's interest is the fact that each of its members had subscribed $500 of his own money to pay travel and other expenses. W. G. Chandler of the Scripps-Howard Newspapers contributed $500 for one of his newspapers, represented on the committee, and another $500 for himself. William R. Hearst contributed $1,000. The Association's limited budget did not provide for any such expenditures.

Dr. Herty was present at Hot Springs, too, seconding Mr. Stahlman's narrative. He told the publishers of the tremendous progress that his Savannah laboratory had achieved since his first SNPA appearance four years earlier. Southern pine, he said, could be used not only for newsprint, but for rotogravure, book and writing papers and other cellulose specialities. In his hour-long address, the Savannah scientist again stressed his big idea—that a new paper industry was only one step in the profitable use of the South's land and forest resources. He foresaw an entirely new Southern agronomy rising through the intelligent exploitation of the long-neglected pine forests.

This view was heartily endorsed by two editorial veterans who seldom engaged in the Association's business-office discussions. Tom Wallace, editor of the Louisville Times, long notable for his campaigns against commercial destruction of natural resources and beauty spots, described the South's major problem as the development of its land assets, away from crops that exhaust the soil. J. N. Heiskell, editor of the Little Rock Gazette, expressed similar views.

Both editors poured forthright criticism on the publishers for their "neglect" of editorial discussion in SNPA conventions. Mr. Wallace deplored the excessive attention given by newspapers to syndicated features and promotion schemes, to the neglect of the "rugged individuality, the rugged provincialism which gives the paper singular interest in the area it tries to cover." Advertisers, he declared, recognized these qualities in a newspaper, but they were all too seldom discussed in newspaper meetings. Mr. Heiskell criticized the current custom of front-paging pictures of bullet-riddled gangsters on morgue slabs and other horror pictures, which, he said, "had a brutalizing effect on the public."

On the business side, the publishers were "needled" by Treasurer Johnson for their lack of interest in the Audit Bureau of Circulations.

The committee for which he reported recommended several changes in ABC organization and counseled "it is time that newspaper executives contributed not only their fair portion of money, but their time and ability to this enterprise."

The gradual revival of business received recognition in talks by Robert N. Tate, Western representative of the Bureau of Advertising, ANPA; F. Scott Kitson, comptroller of the Miami Herald; and H. W. Connell, classified manager of the San Antonio Express and News.

The new scale of membership dues instituted at the 1934 meeting had produced more than $20,000 income for the year, Treasurer Johnson stated. Association finances now included a comfortable balance, rather than the deficits of recent years.

That had been achieved in the face of an increase in staff, also ordered in 1934, by the appointment of J. G. Camp to assist Secretary-Manager Williams in labor matters. Mr. Camp had come to the SNPA from the office of the Atlanta Georgian-American, and already had acted for the Association in several contract situations. Reports on labor affairs indicated no prospect of immediate trouble in the South, although the unions' organization efforts were more aggressive than in former years.

The Memorials Committee noted the death of an unusual number of prominent SNPA figures. The list included H. H. Cabaniss, Atlanta Journal, the Association's first president in 1903-1905; Major John Sanford Cohen, editor of the Atlanta Journal, who had served the Association in many capacities since its organization; Adolph S. Ochs, New York Times and Chattanooga Times, an honorary life member of the SNPA and the prime mover in all of its predecessor organizations; and Col. Walter H. Savory, Mergenthaler Linotype Company, also an honorary life member.

Colonel Savory's many years of friendship for the Association were recognized by a vote to name the annual golf tournament in his honor.

Alarmed by increased railroad freight rates that had been established several months earlier, the Association requested the traffic committee to "make a survey of the freight rate structure in the South on newsprint and other pulp and paper products," keeping the membership informed from time to time and making a complete report to the 1936 convention.

Emanuel Levi, Louisville Courier-Journal and Times, was elected president, with Mr. Gaylord taking the seat of chairman of the Board.[2] Walter C. Johnson, Chattanooga News, entered his 23rd consecutive year as an officer, again as treasurer. Cranston Williams was reelected secretary-manager. The 1935-1936 board included:

Alabama, James E. Chappell, Birmingham News and Age-Herald; Arkansas, J. N. Heiskell, Little Rock Arkansas Gazette; Florida, Truman Green, Tampa Tribune; Georgia, Herbert Porter, Atlanta Georgian-American; Kentucky, Fred B. Wachs, Lexington Leader; Louisiana, John D. Ewing, Shreveport Times; Mississippi, T. M. Hederman, Jackson Clarion Ledger; North Carolina, J. L. Horne, Jr., Rocky Mount Telegram; Oklahoma, Clyde E. Muchmore, Ponca City News; South Carolina, A. W. Huckle, Rock Hill Herald; Tennessee, Adolph Shelby Ochs, Chattanooga Times; Texas, Ted Dealey, Dallas News and Journal; Virginia, L. A. Gaines, Jr., Richmond News-Leader; West Virginia, Luther Long, Huntington Herald-Dispatch and Advertiser.

By the middle of 1936, business had climbed well out of the depths of depression. Newspaper circulations, which had never been seriously stricken, moved steadily upward. While advertising linage reports indicated general gains for newspapers, their volume lagged behind the nationwide pace of prosperity. Radio broadcasting, now in its tenth year of chain operation, had taken deep bites into the newspapers' volume of food, drug, and automotive advertising. The situation wrinkled publishers' brows across the nation, and nationwide efforts would soon put new stiffening into organized efforts to restore and maintain the advertising prestige of the daily press.

That was still in the future and only incidentally on the agenda of the SNPA annual convention at Asheville, May 18-20, 1936. The meeting date had been advanced to avoid conflict with the national

---

[2]Emanuel Levi had a relatively brief career as an SNPA officer and director, but he is remembered as one of the mainstays of the newspapers' battle against threatened government encroachments in the mid-1930's. He had been a successful attorney in Louisville before entering newspaper work as general manager of the Louisville Courier-Journal and Times, and his versatile talents were much appreciated by his SNPA colleagues. As noted in this chapter, it was on his insistence that the SNPA laid down the rule that the Southland Paper Mill must be constructed "by private enterprise" rather than by a Federal grant of funds which unquestionably was available. He retired several years ago from newspaper work and is again practicing law.

political conventions, in both of which Southern newspaper leaders had their customary active roles. The Southern press had enjoyed a generally prosperous twelve-month. Of principal concern had been the continued aggressive campaigns of organized labor to obtain newspaper contracts in shops where unions had not existed prior to the New Deal, and to get higher wages and shorter hours under existing contracts. This experience was brand-new to many Southern newspapers, and calls for help flooded into the Association office at Chattanooga. The previous year's meeting in Hot Springs, Ark., (the first Association meeting held West of the Mississippi) had stirred new interest among Southwestern newspapers, with the result that the SNPA, acting with the Texas Newspaper Publishers Association, was opening an office in Dallas. Joseph G. Camp, who had joined the headquarters staff 20 months earlier as Labor Commissioner, moved to Dallas to perform similar duties and to act as executive secretary of the TNPA.[3]

On October 28, 1949, the name of the TNPA was changed to Texas Daily Newspaper Association, effective February 1, 1950. The arrangement between the TDNA and the SNPA was terminated by mutual agreement on October 31, 1951, the TDNA continuing the Dallas office.

At the annual meeting in Fort Worth on February 16, 1952, Ray L. Powers of the Houston Press was elected president, and in April

---

[3]The history of the Texas Newspaper Publishers Association began on January 24, 1921, when 14 daily newspapers were represented at a meeting in Waco which decided to form a permanent organization with an "industrial secretary" to give full time to newspaper labor affairs. The permanent association took form at a meeting in Dallas on March 10, 1921. Newspaper executives present were: A. E. Clarkson, Houston Post; Tom C. Gooch, Dallas Times-Herald; Walter A. Dealey, Dallas News and Journal and Galveston News; Robert H Cornell, Houston Chronicle; P. C. Edwards, Dallas Dispatch; E. S. Fentress, Waco Times-Tribune; B. B. Donnell, Wichita Falls Times; Thomas E. Gaffney, Galveston Tribune; Frank G. Huntress, San Antonio Express and Evening News; Kendall Brooks Cressey, Austin American; W. C. Mayborn, Houston Press; F. A. Colgan, Dallas Dispatch; William P. Hobby, Beaumont Enterprise; George B. Dealey, Dallas News; C. E. Lombardi, Dallas News and Galveston News; W. H. Bagley, Fort Worth Record and Wichita Falls Record-News; and G. J. Palmer, Houston Post.

Mr. Clarkson was elected president; W. A. Dealey, vice-president; Mr. Cornell, secretary-treasurer. G. J. Palmer, vice-president and general manager of the Houston Post, was employed as Special Commissioner (the revised title of "industrial secretary") and he remained in charge of the Houston office until his death on March 9, 1934. Frank R. Ahlgren, of Memphis, succeeded Mr. Palmer and remained until January 10, 1936, when he became editor of the Memphis Commercial Appeal. At this point, the TNPA and the SNPA entered the agreement mentioned above, with the office moving from Houston to Dallas in charge of Mr. Camp.

Experiments Perilous

1952 new Constitution & By-Laws were adopted. The office in Dallas was shortly afterwards moved to Houston at 808 Milam Building, and John H. Murphy appointed full-time secretary-manager. The Association now has over 50 members in Texas compared to 30 in 1952.

This marked a major step forward for the SNPA, adding 16 Texas dailies to the roster and bringing the total membership to 219. The close relationship with the Texas Newspaper Publishers Association was to prove most fruitful in making the newsprint mill an accomplished fact a few years later.

The mill project was still very much alive in May, 1936, but "Jimmy" Stahlman and his diligent committee could report little tangible progress during the previous year. It was not for lack of effort; the project embodied too many apparent risks for investment money, which could find richer opportunities less regional than an unprecedented venture in the deep South. Dr. Herty had continued his research and his missionary work, but the movers for the mill had not yet found the right combination of enthusiasm for the project, technical knowledge, and investment capital.

No tears were shed at Asheville over the year-old passing of the NRA Blue Eagle and the codes. The Wagner Act (Fair Labor Standards Act) and the Social Security Law, both of recent enactment, confronted newspapers (and all other business enterprises) with operating problems never before encountered. Association Bulletins and the Proceedings of the 1936 convention evidence the confidence of SNPA members in the ability of the headquarters office to meet any calls for advice or assistance. The Chattanooga office staff had been increased early in 1936 by the employment of Claude V. Capers, late of the Memphis Commercial Appeal, for the duties performed by Mr. Camp until his transfer to Dallas.

President Emanuel Levi presided at the 1936 convention by request of the Board, even though his newspaper association had shifted from Louisville to Chicago, where he had become publisher of the Herald and Examiner. His annual report emphasized the increased scope of SNPA activities with the establishment of the Dallas office, urged publishers not to enter long-term paper contracts, so that they would be free to subscribe for tonnage of the new Southern mill when it was constructed, and mentioned without comment the new Federal legislation mentioned above.

Labor Commissioner Camp gave the publishers some brief statistics on the national economic situation. The cost of living, he said, was down 15 per cent from the high level of 1929. Newspaper advertising volume had attained only 66 per cent of its 1929 figure. Under union pressure, wage rates had already recovered most of their decline from the high of the boom days and in some cities, basic wage rates were above 1929 figures. He also reminded publishers that they, and all other employers, were paying higher taxes under new social security legislation than they had paid in the era of "prosperity."

Major Powell Glass, chairman of the journalism school committee, presented a report from Prof. O. W. Riegel, director of the Washington & Lee School. Professor Riegel noted that the curriculum established three years earlier had been in effect long enough to justify a report of its success. Graduates of the school were in growing demand, he declared, reflecting both improved conditions in the publishing field and an appreciation of the school's teaching standards. The school was using new temporary facilities for laboratory work, but had the promise of a new building which would place all of its work under one roof.

John A. Brice, Atlanta Journal, reported for the traffic committee. As ordered by the 1935 convention, his committee had gone thoroughly into Southern freight rate questions, in co-operation with other regional traffic bodies and with the traffic division of the ANPA, and he reported that a formal complaint was being prepared for filing with the Interstate Commerce Commission attacking the freight rate structure within the South.

Plans of Tom Wallace for an outstanding editorial affairs program were marred by the sudden death of the scheduled speaker, Clark McAdams, editorial writer for the St. Louis Post-Dispatch. His topic would have been "The Sinister Aspects of Syndicate Journalism," and Mr. Wallace expounded some of the ideas he thought Mr. McAdams would have laid before the convention.

"I assume," said Mr. Wallace, "that he would have discussed what he considered the double-dealing of publishers who employ their editorial columns as alibi testimony in their own behalf and allow political columnists to say—or buy such columnists because they will say—what the publishers don't want to be accused of saying.

"I think he would have discussed also what he considered the sell-out and the false pretenses of some political columnists who, proclaiming themselves independent, and so advertised by vending publishers who know exactly what they want, subordinate their personal views sufficiently to meet the requirements of those whose thirty pieces of silver they pocket.

"He might have discussed—and in a campaign year that might have been interesting—the statement of a drummer for a New York syndicate that a ferociously anti-New Deal columnist sells well in territory in which a majority of the newspapers are nominally for the New Deal, because some publishers hate the New Deal but fearing its popularity among their readers, buy a columnist to enable them to read their own papers with satisfaction, and to point to something in them that will please their fellow clubmen."

Mr. Wallace hinted at an antagonism which was growing between the President and many newspaper owners. The majority of newspapers outside of the South would oppose Mr. Roosevelt for re-election in 1936 (some Southern newspapers did, too). But, like many other national and international situations, this antagonism did not become acute until after the SNPA members had adjourned their 1936 convention. They hadn't given much thought as a group to Mussolini's 1935 invasion of Ethiopia, nor to the ominous revolt of the Japanese military clique against pacifist civilian rule. They had been mildly alarmed by Hitler's February remilitarization of the Rhineland, and some of them would see dread portents in the Spanish civil war that would come in July. No one could have foreseen in May that a King of England would abdicate his throne in December for love of an American woman, nor that the Supreme Court would strike down as unconstitutional many of the New Deal's early acts, and thereby stir up a violent political tumult in 1937. All in all, the prospect was one of continued calm and prosperity when the SNPA committed its 1936-1937 affairs to new officers and directors.

James E. Chappell, editor of the Birmingham News and Age-Herald, assumed the presidency. Since Mr. Levi was no longer eligible for office by virtue of his connection with a non-member paper, Mr.

Gaylord continued as chairman of the board. As expected, Walter C. Johnson received another term as treasurer, and Cranston Williams as secretary-manager. The new board included:

Alabama, Horace Hall, Dothan Eagle; Arkansas, J. N. Heiskell, Little Rock Arkansas Gazette; Florida, Truman Green, Tampa Tribune; Georgia, Herbert Porter, Atlanta Georgian-American; Kentucky, Fred B. Wachs, Lexington Leader; Louisiana, John D. Ewing, Shreveport Times; Mississippi, James H. Skewes, Meridian Star; North Carolina, J. L. Horne, Jr., Rocky Mount Telegram; Oklahoma, Clyde E. Muchmore, Ponca City News; South Carolina, A. W. Huckle, Rock Hill Herald; Tennessee, Adolph Shelby Ochs, Chattanooga Times; Texas, Ted Dealey, Dallas News and Journal; Virginia, L. A. Gaines, Jr., Richmond Times-Dispatch; West Virginia, Luther T. Long, Huntington Advertiser and Herald-Dispatch.

The South Gets A Newsprint Mill

SNPA Committee, Undaunted by Disappointments, Wins Financial and Technical Backing for East Texas Plant—Association Membership Increased—Recession Hits Business, but Publishers Form New Plans for Regaining Lost Advertising Volume—Johnson Succeeds Williams as Secretary-Manager.

"SOUTHERN Newsprint Project Realized."

That headline on *Editor & Publisher's* report of the 1937 SNPA convention at Hot Springs, Ark., May 17-19, may have anticipated the march of events slightly, for nearly three years would pass before Southern newspapers would use newsprint made from Southern pine. But the headline and the dispatch beneath it signalized that "Jimmy" Stahlman's committee had surmounted years of disappointment and discouragement, and that they had at last assembled all the elements of a practical newsprint mill project into a permanent and practical whole.

Many gaps still had to be filled when Mr. Stahlman told the Association of the past three years' work. Publishers would have to come forward with cash investments in addition to pledges of contract tonnage. The Reconstruction Finance Corporation would have to be convinced of the essential soundness of the venture before it would supplement private investment with a loan of government money. This was not known in May, 1937, but the whole picture was one of definite accomplishment. The powerful support given to the committee's efforts by E. M. (Ted) Dealey of the Dallas Morning News, and the intelligent interest shown by Ernest L. Kurth and his associates in the vicinity of Lufkin, Texas, assured that a mill would be constructed in that area. Mr. Stahlman also held high hopes for construction of a mill in the Southeast—hopes that were fully justified by the evident interest of New York banking and engineering groups, but which would be frustrated for several years by the coming of war.

The turning point in the committee's quest had come at the ANPA convention in April, 1937. Nationwide interest of newspaper people in the Southern mill project had been spurred by a recently announced increase of $7.50 per ton by Canadian and Northern United States newsprint mills. The ANPA, stirred by Mr. Stahlman and W. G. Chandler, general manager of the Scripps-Howard newspapers and chairman of the ANPA paper committee, recorded itself emphatically in favor of the SNPA plan and named a committee of its own to further it. This committee was also headed by Mr. Chandler, who had manifested continuous interest in the Stahlman committee's efforts.

That action by the national Association induced the New York financial community to take another look at the Southern plans. It was generally believed in SNPA circles that earlier prospects of financial and engineering assistance from these quarters had been short-circuited by the influence of large Canadian and domestic paper makers; if so, the Southern case now had become too powerful to be longer bypassed. Optimistically, the prospective investors and Mr. Stahlman's committee looked forward to a market in Central and South America for Southern newsprint mills. Even the most optimistic of publishers in 1937 could not have foreseen an annual demand for 6,000,000 tons of newsprint by the United States alone within little more than a decade.

Mr. Stahlman closed his report with an emphatic reference to the doctrine preached from the beginning by Dr. Herty—that the newsprint industry in the South should be an effort of conservation rather than one of destruction.

"The South," he declared, "cannot afford to have such a great national resource destroyed, as has been the case in other sections of the country where timber has been ruthlessly cut and no effort made to reforest. This program in the South will be productive of the planting of millions of heretofore vacant acres of practically useless and worthless land. The cash crop coming from such lands regularly will be a Godsend in certain sections of the South. It is the obligation of the Southern press and Southern industry to protect not only our timberlands, but every other natural resource to the utmost. Any other policy would be suicidal and absurd. . . . A new day is dawning for the South and freedom of American publishers from the domination of Canadian and foreign newsprint interests will shortly be at hand."

New honors had come to Mr. Stahlman as a result of his superb leadership of the newsprint mill campaign. Following the adoption of the ANPA resolution endorsing the Southern mill, that association had named the young Nashville publisher as its President in April, 1937. In his speech of acceptance, he called upon the publishers to get away from the attitude of defeatism that had marked too many acts of press organizations in recent years.

"Never was the time more opportune," he counseled, "for a rededication, a reconsecration to those ideals of public service that have made the press of America great."

The SNPA recognized "Jimmy's" contribution to its progress by presenting him with a plaque in the form of a gilded bronze full-page matrix commemorating his share in the paper mill enterprise. Dr. Herty also received a bronze plaque, characterizing him as "scientist-dreamer-realist", and an honorary life membership in the SNPA. He was the fifth non-member to be so honored in 34 years.

Mr. Stahlman's reference to newspaper "defeatism" before the ANPA had numerous parallels in the convention proceedings at Hot Springs. This phenomenon had many roots, which had been generously watered by events of the previous few months. Mr. Roosevelt's re-election had been opposed by a large majority of the nation's press, including some Southern newspapers. His triumphant return to the White House, with the electoral votes of all but two states, had been widely hailed as a resounding defeat for the "Tory press," and newspapers had come forward with few convincing arguments to the contrary. The press had been put on the defensive also in a strong propaganda campaign for adoption of the so-called Child Labor amendment to the Constitution. This proposal had been adopted by Congress and submitted to the States for ratification in June, 1924. Up to 1932, it had been approved by only three States, one of them Arkansas. By the end of 1937, ratification had been voted by 28 States, including, from SNPA territory, Arkansas, Kentucky, Oklahoma and West Virginia. Affirmative votes of 36 States were needed for adoption.

Private and government welfare agency propagandists used every channel to blame the newspapers for effective opposition to the amendment in the States which had either rejected it or failed to take an action. Newspapers were stigmatized as seeking the protection of the Constitutional free press guarantee in their heartless and harmful exploitation of young children in circulation work. The public seldom learned that Constitutional lawyers considered the proposed amendment a dead letter because it had not been ratified within a reasonable time after its submission. Nor did the public appreciate that important religious bodies, with no economic interest in exploiting children, opposed the amendment because of the unlimited powers it granted to Congress over the lives and education of minors up to 18 years of age. In the prevalent atmosphere of hostility between the New Deal and the press, it was convenient to make newspapers the public villain. The excellent picture that newspapers could offer of their circulation operations employing children reached the public eye only fitfully.

Rancor was kindled anew when the overwhelming majority of newspapers lined up solidly against President Roosevelt's court program, proposed early in 1937. Administration spokesmen, from the President down, lost few chances to attack the "lords of the press" as wilfully blind opponents of essential progress, as representatives "of the country club against the country." Early in 1937, too, the press found itself, inevitably, on the opposite side to the Administration in the epidemic of "sit-down" strikes that plagued the automotive and tire industries. This importation from France was clearly fostered, if not initiated, by Communist elements which had infiltrated some new unions that had come into being under the National Industrial Recovery Act. The "sit-down" appeared to many editors as a clear violation of law, and the press looked to government at all levels for positive affirmative action in protection of property rights. The Administration thought otherwise, let the innovation run its course, and thus maneuvered itself into the place of labor's champion, with the press aligned among the "economic royalists" and "oppressors of labor."

Much of the public hostility to newspapers was engendered by the American Newspaper Guild in Northern and Western cities. Since the Guild had made small progress up to 1937 South of Mason's and Dixon's Line, its part will not be dwelt on lengthily in this history.

The South Gets A Newsprint Mill

Organized under Section 7-A of the National Industrial Recovery Act, the Guild sought a necessary solution of major problems of editorial employees. In 1933, news department workers stood at the bottom of the newspaper payroll. While unionized employees had been able to protect a large part of their earning power, the unorganized reporters, deskmen, and clerks had taken a succession of pay reductions and many of them had lost all employment. Mergers of newspapers had put them on the street with two weeks' pay in their pockets, or possibly none at all. Many of them, under the leadership of Heywood Broun, New York World-Telegram columnist, believed their answer to lie in organization. Their early efforts to unite in a "professional" grouping met frustration in the publishers' code proposals that "professional" employes earning $35 a week be exempt from the code's provisions. In New York City, especially, their efforts at negotiation with newspapers for improved pay and working conditions, generally met evasion or indifference. Gradually but surely the guild movement was driven into the arms of radical labor elements—first of the International Typographical Union, which had long and vainly sought to organize newspaper writers. That plan got nowhere, and a majority of the guild as late as 1936 rejected a proposal of affiliation with the American Federation of Labor. Later the ANG did affiliate with this organization, found only disappointment in the lack of help accorded, and in 1937, shifted its allegiance to the militant Congress of Industrial Organizations.

It was suspected then, and established later, that a small number of Communistic thinkers had worked its way into the Guild's councils. The flames of antagonism that had been kindled by the shortsighted policy of publishers in general were kept glowing by this politically-minded faction. Southern newspapers had fortunately escaped strikes under Guild auspices—strikes which completely stopped publication, and, in several instances, proved fatal to newspaper existence. In any event, the traditional community of interest between management and the writing staff of a newspaper had been shattered in many cities. Newspapers across the country found themselves the target of sniping attacks from within their own ranks. Some editors charged that the sympathy of reporters for organized labor had given the nation distorted and prejudiced stories of the sit-down strikes in Ohio and Michigan—a charge that was never adequately proven.

The South and Its Newspapers

It was in such circumstances that the SNPA heard an address at Hot Springs by Clayton Rand, president of the National Editorial Association and publisher of the Gulfport (Miss.) Weekly Guide. Mr. Rand regarded President Roosevelt's court plan as "a long step toward dictatorship." The court-packing peril also received attention from Giles J. Patterson, Jacksonville, Fla., attorney and member of the joint bar and newspaper committee of the American Bar Association.

Mr. Patterson, a profound student of constitutional law and author of a book on free press rights, told the convention that "American newspapers are our greatest protection against the domination of the country by leaders of temporary majorities."

"To continue to exercise its influence for the good of all the people is the solemn and inescapable duty of the press because of the power it possesses," Mr. Patterson said. "To retain its power, it must possess the confidence of the people. To possess their confidence, it must place adherence to principle above desire for selfish gain, it must live up to its best traditions, it must not become the advocate for special privilege, but must impartially publish all the news. Above all, it must be courageous and fearless.

"Only in this way can it preserve its own freedom, for neither Constitutional guarantees nor decisions of courts can protect from the wrath of the people a press that prostitutes its privileges or offends accepted standards of fairness, of decency, and of morale. If this great freedom perishes, with it will perish all individual freedom."

Dr. Herty also digressed in his talk on Southern newsprint prospects to warn the publishers against possible government regulation of woodlands operations. Such a movement was already well advanced, he said, and its development could cripple the economic progress that proper use of forest resources held for the South. He put it up to newspapers to educate the public and Southern industry toward the protection against ruthless exploitation of natural resources by private enterprise, using common sense, and avoiding the bureaucracy and friction inherent in a government program.

Tom Wallace at this convention produced the "all-star" editorial program that he had had in mind for several years. His guest speakers included Roy A. Roberts, editor of the Kansas City Star; Paul

The South Gets a Newsprint Mill

Bellamy, editor of the Cleveland Plain Dealer, and J. Roscoe Drummond, executive editor of the Christian Science Monitor.

All three were past or future officers of the American Society of Newspaper Editors and held top rating among the nation's newspaper thinkers. Messrs. Roberts and Bellamy, like Mr. Wallace, decried the excessive standardization of newspaper editorial contents, brought about by the publication of nationally syndicated material rather than the carefully developed product of local brains. Mr. Drummond devoted himself to the growing popularity of pictures in newspapers. Declaring that "good news pictures come from ideas rather than from cameras," he advised that editors should "seek pictures which suggestively convey the atmosphere of the news, in addition to literally illustrating the news—illustrations which convey feeling as well as facts."

On the advertising side, this convention marked the initial flickering of a new effort to restore vigor to the promotion of newspapers generally and of the South in particular. The one-time enthusiasm of Southern dailies for co-operative advertising of the region had died more than 10 years earlier, for a variety of reasons noted in another chapter.

An "advertising clinic" at Hot Springs under the leadership of George C. Biggers, Atlanta Journal, and Harry B. Bradley, Birmingham News and Age-Herald, highlighted the widespread apathy that had marked newspaper efforts in recent years and which was reflected in the tardiness with which newspapers were regaining the linage volume they had held in 1929.

Although the South had been comparatively free of labor troubles during 1937, the two offices of the SNPA had had full schedules of conciliation and arbitration among SNPA newspapers and the increasingly active unions. The Dallas office was losing the services of Joseph G. Camp, who had accepted appointment as secretary of the Chicago Newspaper Publishers Association. His place was temporarily filled by Harry B. Adsit, a former publisher of newspapers in West Virginia and other States.

The previous year had seen "Thirty" written to the careers of 13 members, several of them of past or current prominence in SNPA affairs. The necrology list included James L. Mapes, Beaumont

(Tex.) Enterprise and Journal, a past president; Clark Howell, Sr., Atlanta Constitution, one of the founders of the organization in 1903; LeGrand A. Gaines, Jr., Richmond News-Leader, a member of the board for the two past years, and F. C. Withers, Columbia State, who had served nine terms as a director.

In the train of a rising vote of congratulations on the Association's year of great accomplishment, President James E. Chappell turned the gavel over to Ted Dealey, Dallas News, Mr. Chappell becoming the new chairman of the board. Walter C. Johnson, treasurer, and Cranston Williams, secretary-manager, continued their unbroken service in those offices. The new board comprised:

Alabama—Horace Hall, Dothan Eagle; Arkansas—J. N. Heiskell, Little Rock Arkansas Gazette; Florida—Ralph Nicholson, Tampa Times; Georgia—P. T. Anderson, Jr., Macon Telegraph and News; Kentucky—Fred B. Wachs, Lexington Leader; Louisiana—John D. Ewing, Shreveport Times; Mississippi—James H. Skewes, Meridian Star; North Carolina—D. Hiden Ramsey, Asheville Citizen-Times; Oklahoma—Dave Vandivier, Chickasha Express; South Carolina—A. W. Huckle, Rock Hill Herald; Tennessee—Adolph Shelby Ochs, Chattanooga Times; Texas—Bert N. Honea, Fort Worth Star-Telegram; Virginia—Raymond B. Bottom, Newport News Press and Times-Herald; West Virginia—Luther T. Long, Huntington Advertiser and Herald-Dispatch.

Hard times returned to America in 1937.

Around that unpalatable fact the SNPA wove its fabric of accomplishments to and through its 36th annual convention at Edgewater Park, Miss., May 30-June 1, 1938. Falling off in newspaper revenues abated the pressure of new wage negotiations with labor unions. The same cause also brought nearly 40 new members to the SNPA standard, most of them small newspapers which wanted the guidance of successful newspapers in their dose of adversity. Declining business added purpose to national and regional efforts to put newspapers solidly back in the centre of the advertising stage, from which other media had displaced them since 1930. And, finally, the tightening of the financial markets put it up to the publishers themselves to provide the hard dollars needed to bring the Southern newsprint mill to the actual starting line.

The South Gets A Newsprint Mill

"Jimmy" Stahlman was grim-faced and tired when he faced the convention on the morning of June 1. He had spent most of the two previous days and nights, in company with President Dealey and other members of the newsprint mill committee, dragooning publishers into pledging money for the mill's construction, in addition to the tonnage they had previously promised. That job was done. Ground would be broken for the mill near Lufkin, Texas, during July, Mr. Stahlman hoped. Its success, which he believed to be beyond doubt, would lead to the early construction of other mills in the South.

His talk that morning revealed some undisclosed features of the mill campaign and also gave the members a new insight into the character of their committee chairman. Mr. Stahlman told the meeting that he had pledged at the beginning of his efforts four years earlier that he would not take a cent of profit or compensation from the mill after it began operations. He had spent thousands of dollars of his own money, as well as most of his time during the previous three years, toward making the mill a reality. Now, he said, when the question of stock investment by publishers in the project came up, his friends were asking him "What are you going to get out of this thing? How much common stock are you going to get as your slice in this business?"

His answer was "Not one nickel's worth. I will never own a share of stock in any newsprint mill."

"I gave you my pledge," he said, "and I gave it to you honestly, that I never hoped to profit one red cent from anything I had ever done or might do in connection with the development of Southern newsprint. So I haven't signed up for a single share of stock in this mill, and I won't for any other mill, and I want you to know that. I have been fully repaid by the faith that you people have shown, not only in Southern newsprint, but in this particular project, which is the culmination of what I consider the finest effort that has ever been made by the Southern Newspaper Publishers Association."

Only the committee realized at the time how near the mill project had been to another setback when the 1938 convention assembled. It was a $7,000,000 plan, and the backers who had furnished the finance and the technical background had put up something more than $1,000,000 in cash. The mill site and extensive timberlands as well as a half-interest in a railroad were other capital assets. A loan to make up the essential capital had been applied for from the Reconstruction Finance Corporation, and that loan might not be granted, the committee feared, unless the capital structure included a larger sum in cash. Under the "won't take 'no' for an answer" pressure of Stahlman, Dealey, Gaylord and other committee leaders, SNPA members had pledged $429,000 before the convention ended. That closed the financial gap.

Dr. Herty had had money troubles, too. The death of his friend and sponsor, Francis P. Garvan, president of the Chemical Foundation, had deprived him of both spiritual and financial support for his Savannah laboratory. Business depression had dried up other sources of funds. How the courageous old philosopher had met and passed his crisis is told elsewhere in these pages. The SNPA, in a formal resolution, gave full approval to his course. His job, too, was done, and he probably realized that as he faced the meeting. Death would take him before the SNPA met again, but in the concrete wall of the Southland Paper Mills, Inc., in a quondam woodland gap, now named Herty, Texas, there's a bronze slab inscribed with the names of Charles H. Herty and Francis P. Garvan, erected by a grateful Southern Newspaper Publishers Association.

"Jimmy" Stahlman had not underrated the importance of the Association's paper mill effort. In fact, it has proven to be far more important than even he and his enthusiastic colleagues of 1934-1940 could have imagined. Truly, the SNPA had builded better than it knew.

Now the times called for effort in another direction, and again the Association furnished valuable guidance and impetus to a nationwide undertaking.

In the years when the publishers were resisting the Roosevelt Administration on half a dozen fronts and driving hard bargains with the harried makers of paper, the radio and magazines had developed new business. The radio people didn't know the meaning of "depression." They just kept rolling along on the impetus of advertisers' interest in a new medium that might (and often did)

The South Gets A Newsprint Mill

sell merchandise. They and the magazine salesmen used "gadgets" impressively—fancy colored presentations, lantern slides, and other mechanical and theatrical aids—to plant their story firmly in the prospect's mind. Newspapers clung to the system that, on the record, had built them a giant volume of advertising in the 20's, but, as George Biggers told the SNPA in 1938, that system was "as antiquated as the ox-cart and the mustache cup."

Some important newspaper executives had been aware of that for several years and had been striving to form what they called the "United Front" of all newspaper forces interested in getting the press story adequately before the national advertiser. This effort had focused principally on strengthening the twenty-five-year-old Bureau of Advertising of the ANPA by increasing its membership, and providing an income sufficient for research and aggressive selling of the whole newspaper market. That effort would eventually succeed, but it was still far short of the mark in 1938.

The SNPA contribution had its roots in the 1937 "advertising clinic." It visualized an effort parallel with the national Bureau's, through an SNPA Bureau of Advertising that would concentrate on selling the Southern newspaper market. A committee headed by George C. Biggers presented a plan to the 1938 convention that called for the raising of $75,000 a year for three years to finance the operation. Members would be personally solicited by the committee for this fund, the base of individual contributions being the cost of a 5,000-line schedule in the member newspaper. Dave Vandivier, publisher of the Chickasha Express, an SNPA director, and also chairman of the Oklahoma Press Association's advertising committee, had an even more elementary program, calling for extensive work by the individual publisher among the local dealers in his home town, influencing them to demand newspaper advertising support from national distributors.

Present and listening attentively to these proposals was William A. Thomson, who had been director of the Bureau of Advertising, ANPA, since 1913. He told the Association that the Bureau had added 270 new members to its solid core of 350 newspapers and had increased its revenue by about 50 per cent since January, 1938. The Bureau now counted 130 of the 260 SNPA members among its supporters. New promotion methods were being worked out and plans were well advanced for the establishment of a strong selling staff. Mr. Thomson saw no conflict between the larger national plan and the SNPA proposal of aggressive regional selling of newspapers.

Discussion of the Biggers' committee plan by the convention developed some unforeseen difficulties, mainly geographical, and the question was referred to the new Board of Directors. If the committee had not quite reached its objective, it could at the least claim to have stimulated constructive thought on a vital topic, that had been neglected too long.

The persistent Tom Wallace maintained his program of keeping publishers aware of their editorial departments by scheduling three speakers, all from member newspapers. Major James E. Crown, editor of the New Orleans States, had been a major force in the battle against Huey Long and exemplified the "fighting editor" to newsmen the country over. He and Herman B. Deutsch, noted star reporter of the New Orleans Item-Tribune, handed the publishers some strong medicine concerning the current bad public relations of newspapers. Col. Harry M. Ayers, individualistic editor and publisher of the Anniston (Ala.) Star, again found a toothsome morsel in syndicated columns. They were not a healthy substitute for good homemade editorials, he declared.

Labor relations had been handled smoothly during the year, with the business decline lessening the number of union demands for higher pay. Harry M. Adsit continued in charge of the Dallas office, with reported satisfaction to all interests. Claude V. Capers, who had joined the Chattanooga office in 1936, resigned early in 1938 to go with the ANPA Special Standing Committee in Chicago—the second SNPA trained labor expert to progress in his profession within two years. C. W. Tabb had been brought into the Chattanooga office and then transferred to Dallas, and Tom Tanner had been added to the Chattanooga staff in 1938.

One of the pleasant personal surprise touches characteristic of SNPA activities came early in the convention when President Dealey called Victor H. Hanson to the dais. Mr. Hanson recalled the founding of the Association on April 14, 1903 and read the names of the 33 publishers who had attended that Atlanta gathering. Of the number, all but six had died, and of the six survivors only Mr. Hanson remained active in newspaper work.

The South Gets A Newsprint Mill

"Little did any of us present at that first meeting envision the fact that the organization we were launching would become in the short period of 35 years the most effective regional business association in the United States," Mr. Hanson continued. "The growth and development of the SNPA as an organization devoted to the welfare of the newspaper profession in general has been an amazing thing, so amazing that of necessity no one man, or no small group of men, could have been responsible for it.

"Nevertheless, if one man could be singled out who had more to do with its success than any other individual, there could be no question as to his identity. Through his character, his capacity for friendship, his unselfish devotion to the welfare of others, his great ability and his untiring work, Walter Johnson has been an outstanding figure in the SNPA from almost the beginning to the present time."

Mr. Hanson recalled that Walter Johnson had attended the 1904 meeting, missed the next three, and had been present at every convention since 1908 with the exception of the convention in New Orleans in 1913. He noted that Mr. Johnson had rounded out at this convention 25 years of continuous service as an officer of the Association, filling every office with "energy, ability and devotion to duty."

"Many of us feel that such an unusual record, probably without parallel among trade associations and professional organizations, ought to be marked in some special way," Mr. Hanson said. "And so, Walter, it is in grateful appreciation of your service to this organization, in loving tribute to you as a man and as a friend, and in unqualified admiration for you as a newspaper executive and a constructive force in the newspaper world, that I present this silver plaque on behalf of the entire membership of more than 250 Southern publishers of daily newspapers."

Mr. Johnson, unwarned of the occasion, replied briefly and with warmth. He explained his absence from the 1903 organization meeting by the fact that he was helping to establish a new daily in Memphis. And he missed the 1907 meeting because he didn't think an SNPA convention was an ideal spot for a honeymooning couple.

"Carrying on and helping to build the SNPA has been a labor of love to me, as I know it has been to those members who have been active in the Association from those early days down through the years to the present," he commented.

Note should be made also of the first Mechanical Conference of SNPA newspapers held at Birmingham in November. This was an innovation, patterned on the successful meetings of mechanical department executives that the ANPA had been conducting for several years. The initial SNPA conference attracted more than 160 delegates from 11 Southern States, and it devoted itself strictly to its slogan: "A unity of purpose in producing the best newspaper from a mechanical standpoint."

The Texas-Oklahoma Mechanical Conference, which had been meeting for four years, petitioned the SNPA Board for sponsorship by the Association as the Western Division of the SNPA Mechanical Conference and the board granted the request, adding the States of Louisiana and Arkansas to the Western Division. A few publishers who had looked with disinterest on the first meeting in Birmingham received a rebuke from President Dealey for neglecting to pay their mechanical people for their time and travel to the meeting. That would not happen again, for both meetings immediately demonstrated their value to participating newspapers.

The Memorials Committee reported a lengthy list of deceased members, including Mrs. Mary Geddes Stahlman, the mother of James G. Stahlman and E. B. Stahlman, Jr.; Robert Lathan, editor of the Asheville Citizen and a former director; Captain William E. Gonzales of the Columbia State; Judge Robert W. Bingham, publisher of the Louisville Courier-Journal and Times; and Toulmin H. Ewing, of the Monroe News-Star and World.

John D. Ewing, of the Shreveport Times, was elected president, and Ted Dealey succeeded to the chairman of the board. Mr. Johnson began his second quarter century as an officer with his re-election as treasurer, and Cranston Williams entered his 15th year as secretary-manager. The new board of directors included:

Alabama—Ralph B. Chandler, Mobile Press-Register; Arkansas—C. E. Palmer, Hot Springs Sentinel-Record and New Era; Florida—Ralph Nicholson, Tampa Times; Georgia—P. T. Anderson, Jr., Macon Telegraph and News; Kentucky—Barry Bingham, Louisville Courier-Journal and Times; Louisiana—C. P. Manship, Baton Rouge State

The South Gets A Newsprint Mill

Times and Advocate; Mississippi—James H. Skewes, Meridian Star; North Carolina—D. Hiden Ramsey, Asheville Citizen and Times; Oklahoma—Dave Vandivier, Chickasha Express; South Carolina—A. W. Huckle, Rock Hill Herald; Tennessee—Adolph Shelby Ochs, Chattanooga Times; Texas—Bert N. Honea, Fort Worth Star-Telegram; Virginia—Raymond B. Bottom, Newport News Press and Times-Herald; West Virginia—J. H. Long, Huntington Advertiser and Herald-Dispatch.

In presenting this slate for the nominating committee, Victor Hanson recalled that ten years earlier, in the same room and in the same capacity, he had nominated for SNPA president Col. Robert Ewing, father of the 1938-1939 executive.

Long before the Southern publishers gathered for their 1939 meeting at the Hotel Chamberlain, Old Point Comfort, Va., June 15-17, everybody knew that worrisome days were ahead. Adolph Hitler had bulldozed the Great Powers of Europe into accepting his barefaced grabs of Austria and Czecho-Slovakia and the civilized world lived in a state of day-to-day apprehension. Where would the madman strike next? And would his next reach for power be resisted, bringing on another European war, or would Britain and France again knuckle under, postponing the evil day? The uncertainty in Europe helped to hamstring American business during all of 1938 and most of 1939. Newspaper advertising in 1938 fell 13.1 per cent below the 1937 total, with disastrous declines in general and automotive.

Thus circumstanced, publishers were in no mood to put up $75,000 a year for three years to finance the Southern Bureau of Advertising that had been proposed at the 1938 convention. Chairman Biggers had to report that the effort had fallen flat, but he told the 1939 convention of some fruitful individual efforts of his own paper. The task of re-selling newspapers as a primary advertising medium, however, continued to limp for lack of specific, eye-stopping, factual material. As might be expected, the "United Front" in the national field had also made small progress. The inertia of the past ten years was not easily shaken off.

In another important direction, the SNPA had made definite progress. President John Ewing was able to report that the Southland Paper Mill at Herty, Texas, was nearing completion and that it would be delivering newsprint to its contract customers before another year passed. Mr. Ewing's report hinted that the newsprint mill committee might be able to tell the convention of other mill plans, but apparently they had not matured sufficiently for revelation. In fact, war would postpone their realization for more than a decade.

Of overshadowing importance at the 1939 meeting was the departure of Cranston Williams, after 15 years as secretary-manager, and the succession to that post of Walter C. Johnson. The story had been told in part the previous April, at the annual convention of the American Newspaper Publishers Association. Lincoln B. Palmer, general manager of the ANPA, had tendered his resignation because of ill health after 36 years of meticulous and selfless service. He was well past seventy years old and had never recovered his former vigor after breaking his hip in a fall a year previously. The ANPA Board had no difficulty in choosing his successor.

Cranston Williams was the man, if he could be induced to leave the South. In the 15 years of Williams' administration as secretary-manager, the SNPA had taken first rank among regional business organizations. It had grown from 194 to 266 members. Prior to 1916, when Walter C. Johnson was named Secretary-Treasurer, it had been a respected small association of about 60 newspapers, more or less, useful on occasion but self-limited in purpose. Its annual budget during the first 10 years ranged below $2,000, which meant that its accomplishments rested on the shoulders of a few earnest volunteers who gave unstintingly of their time and personal funds when emergencies called for action.

When a headquarters office was established, Mr. Johnson provided office space in the Chattanooga News Building rent free for some eight years.

Williams had quickly learned the ropes from Johnson. Within an amazingly short time, veteran publishers were looking to the young man from Georgia for counsel on management problems. He made himself an expert in labor relations. More and more each year he took over the tasks of Association committees, especially in Washington. His keen intellect rapidly grasped the essentials of a question and marshalled facts into convincing argument. When the SNPA designated him as its representative in the writing and administration of the NRA Daily Newspaper Code (the only non-publisher on the Code Authority), he demonstrated anew the qualities that had endeared him to the Southern publishers.

More important, from the standpoint of the ANPA, Mr. Williams would bring to the national task a fresh viewpoint. Unavoidably, perhaps, the ANPA had become identified by many newspaper people and by important segments of the public, with a stiffly legalistic view of newspaper conduct. Its spokesmen in recent years had been Mr. Palmer and Elisha Hanson, Washington counsel. Both were lawyers and, since their public statements dealt mainly with existing or proposed legislation, the protectively legal note was dominant. It did not make for broad public understanding of the newspaper case, and many publishers were aware of the need of such understanding. Cranston Williams could create it, they believed. With no legal background, he had proven his ability to speak for the Southern press in clear and firm language that the non-legal public could understand and believe.

From every standpoint, the ANPA opportunity was irresistible. A special meeting of the SNPA board was held immediately after the national meetings and the directors, proudly but regretfully, released Mr. Williams from his SNPA obligations. He could proceed to New York on July 1, immediately after the convention at Old Point Comfort. At the convention, the Association adopted a resolution reciting Mr. Williams' many services and expressing hearty gratitude. More practically, "Jimmy" Stahlman, on behalf of the membership, presented the departing executive with a silver pitcher and a check for $1,000.

But, if Cranston Williams' availability was a heaven-sent blessing to the ANPA, his departure left a tremendous gap in the SNPA organization. Where would his like be found?

By a curious turn of events, the successor to Williams was right at hand. He was, of course, Walter C. Johnson, whose continuous service in Association office for more than a quarter century already qualified him as "Mr. SNPA." The directors could have combed the whole nation without finding a man better fitted for the secretary-manager's office.

How a newspaper executive of such widely recognized ability as Walter Johnson's happened to be "at liberty" at this moment of need is not part of the SNPA History. Suffice it to say that internal conditions in the organization of the Chattanooga News were not to his satisfaction during several years of the middle 1930's. He resigned as vice-president and general manager in 1938. A short time afterwards, the News was absorbed by the Chattanooga Free Press. In any case, Mr. Johnson's connection with the SNPA was never broken, and the transition caused by Cranston Williams' departure was effected with no difficulty.

In his final report to the SNPA, Mr. Williams concluded with this paragraph:

"It is a personal pleasure to know that I am to be succeeded by Walter C. Johnson. It was Clark Howell, Jr., who told me first about the SNPA's work and advised Walter Johnson that I was interested in coming with the organization. I shall ever be grateful to Walter Johnson for all of the patience he has displayed in helping me, and I now feel that I can turn back to him the responsibility for direction of the organization, knowing that the SNPA and any other thing in which Walter Johnson is interested is always safe when it is in his hands."

Another who received a well-merited tribute at the Old Point Comfort meeting was Ted Dealey. He was given an engrossed and framed resolution recognizing his indispensable work in bringing the Southland Paper Mill plan to fruition. In his response, Mr. Dealey revealed a few of the crises through which the committee had nursed the project, note of which has already appeared in this narrative.

Mr. Williams reported on other headquarters changes. Tom Tanner had been made SNPA labor commissioner in January and C. W. Tabb had been appointed manager of the Dallas office, after Harry B. Adsit had resigned to join the New York World-Telegram's executive staff. Walter C. Johnson, Jr., who had had vacation experience in the office, would join the organization full-time after his graduation from Duke University where he had in his Junior and Senior years majored in Labor Relations and Economics.

In their second year, the Eastern and Western Mechanical Conferences had proven out beyond expectations. Mr. Williams recommended their continuance so long as mechanical department executives accepted responsibility for planning and directing these technical programs. That condition has been met unfailingly ever since.

The South Gets A Newsprint Mill

A new chairman of the editorial affairs committee, Col. Harry M. Ayers, of the Anniston Star, held to the militant pace established by Tom Wallace. Introducing his program, Colonel Ayers told the convention:

"While the general public apparently has had an apathetic interest in press freedom in this country for some years and while we have seen freedom of the press almost destroyed in our sister democracies, across the seas, it becomes our duty as never before to interpret freedom of the press as something that belongs to all the people and not merely to publishers of newspapers. Moreover, it should be just as much our duty to defend religious freedom as it is our duty to defend freedom of speech through the press or from the political rostrum."

Dr. George Lang, professor of philosophy, University of Alabama, addressed the convention on "Press Freedom as Related to Religious Freedom," recalling the importance of the latter in Colonial days as the base upon which Constitutional guarantees of other freedoms had been reared.

Getting down to earthy economics, Col. Ayers presented Oscar Johnson, president of the National Cotton Council of America, who outlined the importance to the nation of the changing picture of cotton culture in the South during recent years.

The third editorial affairs speaker was Otis Peabody Swift, assistant to the president of Time-Life, Inc., who discussed "The News Picture as a New Instrument of World-Journalism," describing the principles employed by the editors of Life in producing their picture-filled weekly.

Interest of the SNPA in educational problems, especially those pertaining to the press, had a new growth in 1939. Vance Armentrout, of the Louisville Courier-Journal editorial staff, had represented the Association at a meeting called by Casper S. Yost, one of the "founding fathers" of the American Society of Newspaper Editors, and Dean Kenneth E. Olson, of Northwestern University, president of the American Association of Schools of Journalism. The principal journalism schools and the ranking newspaper associations of the country had sent representatives, who proposed a program of co-operation between the press and the educational institutions for the improvement of education for journalism in the United States.

Mark Ethridge, editor and general manager of the Louisville Courier-Journal, reporting this development, proposed that the SNPA approve formation of the new National Council for Professional Education for Journalism and name a representative who would act for the Association (without power to commit the SNPA to expenditure of funds unless previously authorized) and to report annually to the SNPA the Council's progress. A resolution in substantially those terms was unanimously adopted. The SNPA has been continuously represented on this Council. Its work has received many expressions of appreciation from the schools in recent years.

Prof. O. W. Riegel, director of the Washington & Lee School of Journalism, commended the formation of the Council as moving in the direction of the higher professional standards approved by the SNPA. He also thanked the Association for co-operation extended during the year by its manager and directors.

Labor activity during the previous year had been, as usual, undramatic in the South. Newspapers were gradually adjusting their mechanical department operations to a shorter work-week, which, in 1940, would be limited to 40 hours. All unions were pressing organization work, Mr. Tanner reported, and basic wage rates in general were those of 1929, despite the falling off in newspaper revenues. The typographical union was pressing in numerous cities for provision of paid vacations in contracts. The Guild had also made progress in the South and currently had 10 contracts and five "policy notice" arrangements with publishers, none of which provided for the closed shop or the guild shop.

Faced again with the prospect of a shortage of young printers, publishers heard with interest reports of the Southern School of Printing, at Nashville, which it had joined with the ANPA to support many years earlier. It also noted that this organization had assumed the management of the Southwest Vocational School, Dallas, after the latter had announced suspension of operations as a private enterprise. The Texas Newspaper Publishers Association and the American Newspaper Publishers Association contributed toward its support, as an essential source of composing room hands.

Adolph Shelby Ochs, Chattanooga Times, assumed the presidency by unanimous election, and John D. Ewing became the new chairman of the board. James E. Chappell, Birmingham News and Age-

The South Gets A Newsprint Mill

Herald, moved into the treasurer's office so long held by Walter C. Johnson, and the latter was elected by the board as secretary-manager. The new directorate included:

Alabama—Ralph B. Chandler, Mobile Press-Register; Arkansas—C. E. Palmer, Hot Springs Sentinel-Record and New Era; Florida—James L. Knight, Miami Herald; Georgia—George C. Biggers, Atlanta Journal; Kentucky—Barry Bingham, Louisville Courier-Journal and Times; Louisiana—Charles P. Manship, Baton Rouge State Times and Advocate; Mississippi—L. P. Cashman, Vicksburg Herald-Post; North Carolina—Talbot Patrick, Goldsboro News-Argus; Oklahoma—Dave Vandivier, Chickasha Express; South Carolina—A. W. Huckle, Rock Hill Herald; Tennessee—Enoch Brown, Jr., Memphis Commercial Appeal; Texas—Bert N. Honea, Fort Worth Star-Telegram; Virginia—Raymond B. Bottom, Newport News Press and Times-Herald; West Virginia—J. H. Long, Huntington Advertiser and Herald-Dispatch.

Before the Association met in 1940, the face of civilization had changed. The Nazi swastika flew over Poland and most of France and England, almost weaponless, awaited invasion. In the Far East, too, drums were already beating that would call the United States once again to arms. The wars that filled most of the next decade would transform the South from a dominantly agricultural region to a major sphere of the arsenal of democracy. While the guns were thundering around the world, and a secret factory in Tennessee was cooking uranium into new deadliness, the Southern Newspaper Publishers Association continued to look to the long future—South of new wealth and strength in field and factory. While normal Association affairs during the war proceeded through Bulletins and correspondence, rather than annual meetings, this history will glance briefly backward and forward at this far-reaching SNPA program.

Newsprint And A New South

Abundant Southern Forests, Seeded, Tended and Harvested as a Crop Provide Unfailing and Widely Distributed Source of New Wealth—Dr. Herty's Farsighted Pioneer Research Validated by Courageous Support of the South's Organized Publishers.

WHEN a wide ribbon of creamy newsprint paper rolled from the machine of the Southland Mills, near Lufkin, Texas, in January, 1940, a new day arrived for Southern industry and agriculture. The dawning had been deliberately planned—not, like other miracles of industry, a welcome but unforeseen by-product. This dawning had been created by Southern newspaper publishers, hard fisted and profit-minded lumbermen of East Texas, experienced Northern paper manufacturers, and the sound judgment of a Federal government agency. But its foundation rooted in the broad technical knowledge, the encompassing human sympathies and the unconquerable spirit of a frail and aged Georgia scientist—the late Dr. Charles H. Herty.

Another Georgian, Henry W. Grady, had given to the South fifty years earlier from the editorial page of the Atlanta Constitution and from many public platforms, the goal of lifting itself from industrial dependency, of realizing the wealth that lay in its unexplored resources. With the zeal of Grady, Herty combined the secrets of modern chemistry, the scientist's will to buttress theory with fact, and the conviction that in Southern forests lay the key to self-sufficiency for the South and for its millions of citizens.

Year after year during the discouraging 1930's, Dr. Herty hammered his message home to Southern newspapermen. He kept his faith in the attainment of the goal when the widespread poverty of the long depression and the death of his principal source of money had brought his own research work to a seeming dead end. He continued to believe when plan after plan formed by his friends in the SNPA for the commercial proof of his theories failed to attract the essential financial backing. He kept those friends heartened to advance "once more unto the breach, once more," and when he died, in July, 1938, he knew that his efforts were near realization. Had he lived, he would certainly have maintained his campaign for more than one lone newsprint mill as the agency of new Southern prosperity. He would have been pleased, but far from satisfied with knowing that the community in which the Southland Mill operated was named in his honor. He would have continued the fight for the scientifically controlled exploitation of Southern forest resources, under private enterprise, for the well-being of the South and of the nation.

And he would have rejoiced that the Southern Newspaper Publishers Association has made that aim its own during the past decade.

The continuing, if sometimes tenuous, thread of Southern newspaper interest in the establishment of a Southern newsprint industry can be traced directly back to the second meeting of the SNPA in 1904. Probably some of the older men at that meeting remembered ruefully the days when little paper mills dotted the South, as they did other parts of the country. Those early mills had pulped rags collected from the countryside and they made excellent print paper. But their product was costly stuff, upwards of 12 cents a pound in the 1860's and 1870's, and the supply of rags from which its cellulose came never allowed for volume production. Introduction of groundwood pulp had promised cheaper paper since the early 1870's, and newsprint sold in 1904 for less than a fifth of the price of the old rag stock.

Then all but a few of the tiny old paper mills had faded, leaving a skeleton of empty sheds and rusty mill wheels beside idly rushing streams. A few survived and some of them mixed the fibres of Southern trees with rags to produce specialty papers and pulps. None manufactured newsprint, and none would, until January, 1940. Down the intervening years, Southern newspapers, like other Southern consumers, paid out profits to manufacturers, middlemen, and transportation agencies, on almost every article they purchased.

Publishers were grumbling at the "paper trust" when the Southern Newspaper Publishers Association met for the second time in 1904. They had heard that one company in New York was buying financial control of numerous small mills and following the familiar and feared patterns of the new corporate combines in other major industries. What specific grievance irked them is hard to determine from existing records, but it seems probable that the publishers believed the gradual extinction of competition would soon mean higher prices. They heard also that the great Kansas City Star of William Rockhill Nelson had bought a paper mill of its own, assuring it of raw material beyond the control of Wall Street financiers. They wanted to find an answer to the question, "Can Southern Dailies Act Jointly in the Purchase of Paper?" and they sent a distinguished committee to investigate the Kansas City Star's mill enterprise.[1]

Headed by the dynamic Major E. B. Stahlman and including also Frank P. Glass and H. H. Cabaniss, early presidents of the Association, this committee would certainly have returned a positive answer had one then been attainable. But no Southern newspaper of 1904 could match the wealth of Nelson's Star, and Southern newspapers had yet to learn the secret of working together for a great objective. The idea of co-operative buying flickered out.

Southern publishers shared in the formation and operations of the Publishers Buying Corporation in 1920, when many newspapers experienced the desperate plight of inability to buy paper, even at outrageous prices. This co-operative enterprise maintained a corporate existence until 1930, but it ceased effective functions after the paper market broke in 1921-1922.[2] Neither in the South nor elsewhere in America were publishers willing to forego their precious liberty of contract. And in the 1920's and 1930's, there was no reason for them to do so, for paper had become abundant. Demand during the war and after the war had stimulated a flood of new capital investment, mostly in Canadian newsprint mills, which continued to in-

---

[1] The Kansas City Star mill was not an eventual success, principally because of its distance from pulpwood supplies, which had to be shipped to Kansas City. The mill's paper machines were sold to the Spanish River Pulp & Paper Co., and shipped to Espanola, Ont., in exchange for a newsprint contract.

[2] Prime mover in the organization of the Publishers Buying Corporation was William J. Pape, Waterbury (Conn.) Republican and American. In recent years Mr. Pape has resided during the winter at St. Petersburg, Fla.

crease production even after depression had blighted the American market.

The short depression that followed World War I had not run its course, however, when Edward W. Barrett, publisher of the Birmingham Age-Herald, undertook a project that should have advanced Southern paper manufacture by two decades. Newsprint was not abundant in the winter of 1919, when Mr. Barrett and three other gentlemen spent several weeks in the Warrior River section of Jefferson County, Alabama, surveying the spruce pine that grows thickly in that region. Mr. Barrett wanted a new source of pulpwood and he believed that he had found it in this variety of tree, which was not only plentiful in Alabama, but also was remarkably free from resin. The valuable resin and turpentine common to Southern pine varieties, then were believed to debar the use of these trees for paper manufacture. Later Dr. Herty would have plenty to say on that subject, but his day was still more than a decade distant.

Accompanying Mr. Barrett on his timber cruising were C. M. Stanley, then assistant to the president of the Age-Herald Company; Jerry W. Gwin, president of the Jefferson County Board of Revenue and an experienced engineer and contractor, and Robert Clade, a Canadian paper expert. Mr. Stanley, now editor of the Montgomery (Ala.) Journal, recalled the experience in a column written for the Alabama Journal in 1950. The party decided that the Alabama forests held wood enough for a new paper industry and also that spruce pine would make good newsprint. Mr. Barrett's idea, based in part on his father's experience with paper manufacture in a small South Carolina mill, received the expert approval of Mr. Clade.[3]

During December, 1920, it was decided to cut enough trees to make two carloads of pulpwood, which would be shipped to a

---

[3] The first groundwood from Southern trees was used in the mill of the Marietta Paper Manufacturing Company at Marietta, Ga., in 1876, and some of the newsprint thus produced went into the publication of the Marietta Journal, according to the researches of Walter C. Johnson, Secretary-Manager of the SNPA. The superintendent of the mill at that time was John Brabson Shields, who later became acquainted with Mr. Barrett when the latter was a reporter on the Atlanta Constitution staff. Mr. Barrett had known of his father's mill at Bath, S. C., a pre-war paper plant which had been destroyed in the path of Sherman's March to the Sea. The friendship between Barrett, when he became publisher of the Birmingham Age-Herald, and Shields, who retired to the ownership of 3,000 acres of pine woodland near Jasper, Ala., is probably the genesis of Mr. Barrett's interest in pine as a pulpwood.

Northern newsprint mill for the test that would prove or destroy the theory. Cut to standard four-foot lengths, the logs were floated down the Warrior River to Birmingport, and there loaded on flat cars for their journey to Niagara Falls, N. Y.

When the wood reached the Defiance Paper Company at Niagara Falls, the experts pronounced it fully equal to the Northern spruce used for newsprint. Then a strike shut down the paper mill and it was not until May 2, 1921, that the Alabama wood went to the grinders and passed through all the normal processes of newsprint manufacture. The paper arrived in Birmingham in time for publication of a "spruce pine edition" of the Age-Herald on June 20, 1921. Copies of this edition were distributed the next day at the Southern Newspaper Publishers Association convention in Asheville, and Mr. Barrett proudly pointed to its color, strength, and printing qualities. He also called the attention of his publisher colleagues to a front page editorial, which read:

"Today's Age-Herald may mark the beginning of a new epoch of newspaper history in the South. This issue of the Age-Herald is printed upon newsprint paper made from spruce pine cut from the banks of the Warrior River in Alabama. It is the first practical and successful test ever made of manufacturing white paper from the varieties of pine found in the Southern States. The editor of the Age-Herald has long believed that Alabama spruce pine would make white paper because of its freedom from resin and turpentine. To prove his belief he had 50 cords of spruce pine cut last December, floated to Birmingport, loaded on cars and shipped to Niagara Falls. On May 2, the wood was ground and run through the paper machines. The paper upon which today's issue is printed is the result. For many years Northern manufacturers said that Southern iron would not make steel. They said fine cotton goods could not be manufactured in the South. They said high-grade cattle could not be produced here. But the South knew better and proved it. The paper industry bids fair to offer another example. The Age-Herald has shown that it can be done and that there is no reason for the South to remain at the mercy of the Canadian paper producers."

The experimental paper met all the specifications and quality tests then prescribed for standard newsprint. In answering the questions put by publishers at the convention, Mr. Barrett stated that it had a content of 30 per cent sulphite pulp and 70 per cent groundwood, which should have produced a slightly stronger and better sheet than that used by the majority of newspapers. None of the accounts indicate whether the sulphite pulp used in this paper was made from the Alabama spruce pine.

According to Mr. Stanley, the paper used on June 20, 1921, cost 9½ cents a pound, which was considerably higher than the current contract price, but well below the peak prices on the speculative spot market of 1920-21. Much of that cost must be attributed to the expense of shipping two carloads of wood well over 1,000 miles for manufacture. Mr. Barrett said then, and Dr. Herty would later establish, that a Southern mill could obtain Southern wood at less than a third of the wood costs paid by New York and New England newsprint mills. Mr. Barrett also noted that Warrior River coal would be less expensive than Northern fuel.

Mr. Barrett's prospect did not include all of the socio-economic panorama that Dr. Herty would present to the SNPA, but it cannot be questioned that he laid before the publishers a great opportunity. Many of those present at Asheville recognized the possibilities, and wished to prolong the experiments initiated by Mr. Barrett. He refused the offer of remuneration by the SNPA for his out-of-pocket expenses and earnestly counseled his fellow publishers to do in their own localities what he had done in Jefferson County—look over their forests and see whether they included in substantial number trees that would make newsprint. With that information, the SNPA could examine intelligently the possibility of establishing a Southern paper industry. A convention resolution, directing further research, called for reports a "year hence."

Providence willed otherwise. Mr. Barrett's health failed and he died in July, 1922. His promising enterprise was heard from no more. Publishers everywhere found 1921-1922 a time when survival needed all their efforts. Advertising had sharply declined, leaving most newspapers with a high plateau of war-time costs that could not be quickly adjusted to reduced income. Then, too, the urgency had been squeezed out of the paper situation, both by the drop in newspaper demand and the importation of European newsprint. The spur of finding new supplies did not bite so deeply as it had a year or two earlier.

THE SOUTH AND ITS NEWSPAPERS

It may be asked why other publishers of the Birmingham area did not pick up the ball where Mr. Barrett had dropped it. The reasons just mentioned may have been one factor. Another may have been the litigation involving Mr. Barrett with Victor H. Hanson of the Birmingham News; in a bitterly competitive field such as Birmingham was at that time, one publisher's pet enterprise would have been automatically shunned by his rivals. And, apparently, Mr. Barrett's successors on the Age-Herald lacked his personal interest in the Warrior River project. The spruce pines of Alabama flourished without further menace of the pulp-cutter's axes. Mr. Hanson, as will be seen, later took an active part in forwarding the foundation of the South's paper industry.

Even though SNPA records include no allusion to them, we can be fairly certain that publishers considered occasionally the possibility of making paper from Florida grasses, from the bagasse piles of Louisiana's sugar mills, or from cornstalks.[4] Many such ideas were advanced to newspaper associations.

But paper had lost its primary place on the publishers' convention agenda during the late 1920's. Supplies were abundant. Prices had dropped from $90.00 to about $60.00–$65.00 during the fabulous era of advertising and circulation gains prior to 1929. When Dr. Herty first appeared at an SNPA convention in 1931, prices seemed to be rising again, but that trend was shortlived. Canadian mills then could turn out far more newsprint than the depressed United States market could consume.

By that time, Canada had become the major source of newsprint supply for United States dailies. Production of the Dominion's mills had surpassed that of the United States from 1925 onward and new mills and new machines, contracted for in the lush pre-depression days, continued to completion after the rich prospect had disappeared. American publishers in the early 1930's could buy newsprint almost at 1914 prices, and it would appear that Dr. Herty had

---

[4]The Inland Daily Press Association in 1927 heard an enthusiastic description of the cornstalk process of making newsprint and its president, the late John H. Harrison, in 1928 produced an edition of his Danville Commercial News on paper made from cornstalks gathered in the vicinity of that Illinois city. It was good paper, beyond a doubt, but experiments ended with its publication. All too quickly it was realized that while cornstalks (or sugar cane, or certain reedy grasses) make excellent cellulose pulp, the scheme was considered commercially impractical for newsprint.

a thin chance, indeed, of interesting Southern publishers in creating new paper production. A buyer's market still prevailed when the publishers, spearheaded by the SNPA, surmounted the last of their financial hurdles in 1938 and assured the realization of Dr. Herty's vision—a new paper industry in the South, with all that it would eventually imply.

What manner of man was Dr. Herty? What qualities of mind and spirit enabled him to convince publishers of the wisdom, even the necessity, of establishing a new paper industry in the South? How did he convince business men, bankers, and a Reconstruction Finance Corporation management that shied away from loans in any way associated with newspapers, that a newsprint industry would pay out on capital invested and return great, if not immediately tangible, profits to the whole region?

Although this recorder admired Dr. Herty greatly from his first SNPA appearance and listened to him attentively in the auditorium and in private talks for several years thereafter, he finds it difficult to recapture the whole impression. Dr. Herty had the gift of fluent speech possessed by many educated men of the South. He had the easy platform manner of one who had spent many years in the classrooms of great institutions. In his late sixties, he retained the liquid speech of the Georgia coast, not in the least modified by his years of study in Europe and of teaching in other parts of America.

His talks to the SNPA were generally in manuscript, but he seldom referred to the paper in the course of an hour's address. On the table before him he often had a collection of materials to illustrate his verbal descriptions—circular cross-sections of various Southern trees, specimens of pine foliage to differentiate the species, pine cones, laboratory samples of pulp made from a number of different woods, sheets of newsprint to demonstrate comparative strengths, colors, etc. With the well-organized brain of the scientific scholar, Dr. Herty talked the language of his audience, often colloquial, never vulgar. White-haired, thin, and with a light touch of color in the almost transparent skin of his cheeks, he recalled pictures of medieval saints. In his simplicity, vigor, and sincerity of speech, he somehow brought up the image of Will Rogers.

When he first came before the SNPA at Asheville in June, 1931, Dr. Herty already had enjoyed a lifetime of distinction in the realm of chemistry. Born in Milledgeville, Ga., December 4, 1867, Dr. Herty had received his Ph. B. degree from the University of Georgia and his doctorate from Johns Hopkins. He served on the University of Georgia faculty from 1891 to 1899, then studied for two years in Germany. On his return he became associated with the United States Bureau of Forestry, and while there he brought from France the cup which was for about 25 years used for the extraction of turpentine. His innovation both increased the yield and prolonged the life of the trees and he spent 1904 and 1905 with the Chattanooga Pottery Company, manufacturer of the device. He at no time claimed to have invented the cup. It was patterned after those he had seen in use in France. That marked the only commercial association of his long career, and, apparently, it provided him with a financial nest-egg.[5] Shortly afterwards he became head of the chemistry department of the University of North Carolina, later dean of its school of applied science. Even then, his mind had turned to improving the South's economic health by development of its industrial resources, with special attention to naval stores and cottonseed products.

From 1917 through 1921 he was editor of the Journal of Industrial and Engineering Chemistry for the American Chemical Society, and his always busy mind sought the answers to the crucial war-time shortage of dye-stuffs. In 1921, he became president of the new Organic Chemical Manufacturers Association. His principal studies in that era concerned themselves with natural and synthetic pharmaceuticals, a pursuit that brought him into close contact with Francis P. Garvan, president of the Chemical Foundation. The latter had taken over the patents confiscated from German owners during World War I, and Dr. Herty became a consulting advisor on chemo-therapy. As a private consultant, he continued to direct financial eyes toward the South's unexploited resources. Among them, of course, the pine trees ranked high and Dr. Herty had ideas on their industrial uses that conflicted with widely held theories.

---

[5]The naval stores industry did not at first take kindly to the new technique, and Dr. Herty proved to be the company's best salesman. He produced a treasured keepsake of that phase of his career at the 1938 convention of the SNPA, drawing from his billfold a crumpled sheet on which was written in longhand an order from a naval stores firm in New Orleans for one million clay turpentine cups. The Chattanooga Pottery Company, still located in Daisy, Tenn., 15 miles from Chattanooga, now manufactures clay pipes.

Through Dr. Herty's association with Mr. Garvan, the Chemical Foundation in 1931 made a grant of $50,000 for the establishment of the Savannah Pulp and Paper Laboratory. The State of Georgia appropriated $20,000 a year for five years, and the City of Savannah also helped. Dr. Herty had hardly more than begun in this field when he went to Asheville to lay his fundamentals before the publishers. In his 64th year, when many men lay down their tools, this zealot for Southern well-being started a brand new venture from scratch.

He began his Asheville talk in 1931 on the inviting note that he had longed for the day when "we of the South could escape domination of Canadian paper manufacturers, not through artificial means, not through legislation, but from the straight working out of simple economic principles, and through the blessings of sunlight, the creator of cellulose, the characteristic beneficence of our Southern territory from Virginia to Texas."

Then he proceeded to correct prevalent misconceptions about the pines of the South. In word and with specimen cross-sections and foliage, he described the shortleaf or old-field pine of the mountains, the Piedmont and the Coastal Plain; the loblolly pine, common throughout the South and prolific but valueless for naval stores; the longleaf pine, from which most of the fine Southern lumber and most of the naval stores were produced; and the slash pine, about which many false ideas were held.

This misunderstood variety stood high in Dr. Herty's regard. Prolific in seeds, it also grew rapidly, produced a high yield of turpentine, and was widespread in the coastal regions from South Carolina to Louisiana. He urged the publishers to work for experimental tracts of this tree in their own States. He went into considerable detail on the measures of reforestation and fire protection in the Southern States and on the elementary education of young people in forestry.

With proper care the slash pine could make a quickly profitable crop, he declared. In ten years he claimed, this tree begins to yield a profit in pulpwood. Some growers had set out thousands of slash pines in pastures where hogs and cattle were running free. A Georgian had planted alternate rows of pine trees and corn, assuring himself of an annual income while the trees matured. Another was considering alternate rows of pine trees and peanuts. Dr. Herty described cropping methods by which a stand of slash pine could produce an annual harvest of pulpwood in perpetuity, with benefit to the trees which were allowed to grow to commercial lumber sizes.

Then he came to the nubbin of his exposition.

Southern people and Northern paper makers shared the misconception, he said, that longleaf and slash pines were too rich in resin to make paper. It was believed that the resin in the pulp would stick on the paper machine, tear the sheet and throw the machine out of operation. That fear had no basis in fact. It had been thoroughly established that the pines which made the most turpentine contained scarcely more resin than Canadian spruce, a fraction over 1 per cent. The resin associated with the manufacture of turpentine and naval stores was the tree's pathological reaction to the wound inflicted by the manufacturing process. The tree made this resin as a healing medicine for the wounds that were re-inflicted week after week in the turpentine forests. It did not exist in an unwounded tree.

Another common misconception held that the heartwood of Southern pines held too much resin for the manufacture of sulphite pulp. Correct, said Dr. Herty—but no one had ever distinguished between heartwood and sapwood, and heartwood did not begin to form until the tree was about 25 years old. Trees cut to make the samples of paper displayed by the speaker had been found to contain no heartwood. He also showed samples of creamy sulphite pulp made from Southern pine—"as pretty a pulp as was ever seen." Groundwood pulp, he declared, could be made in equally superior quality from the pines of the South.

From that demonstration, Dr. Herty went on to prove that the South, fortunately, could find no market in the North for its pine pulp wood; shipping costs would be impossibly high. Therefore the South would have to manufacture its paper at home, and, according to his figures, the South then used about 600,000 tons of newsprint annually. And Southern wood might be delivered to Southern mills at a cost of about $4.00 per cord, against rates of $14.00 to $16.90 paid by Northern mills.

Newsprint And A New South

"Mills in Canada and New England have to carry some 350,000 acres of land to maintain a perpetual supply of pulpwood for a 100-ton mill," Dr. Herty continued. "In the South you can run on one-tenth of that amount, or 35,000 acres. With more sunlight, warmer climate, and consequent rapidity of growth, we can make as much wood in a year on 35,000 acres as can be made on 350,000 acres in a cooler climate. That is the blessing of the South. That is what sunlight means to us."[6]

While Northern mills were closing down or operating at a loss in 1931, he said, Southern mills on board and kraft paper were suffering smaller losses. He predicted (correctly, as the event proved) that newsprint would soon sell for less than the current $50 price, and he gave the opinion that the South could make and sell newsprint at a profit, if the facts could be ascertained on Southern resources. And he put that task directly up to the publishers. He maintained that careful research would prove that the United States could be not only self-sustaining in pulp and paper, but could export great quantities to the rest of the world.

That was the opening gun of Dr. Herty's campaign, and the shot hit the target fairly. He would appear before succeeding SNPA conventions to report continuous progress. By the end of 1933, his Savannah laboratory produced pulp of good enough quality for shipment to a paper mill at Thorold, Ontario, for manufacture into enough newsprint to run a day's edition for a number of Georgia dailies which financed the shipment costs. This paper contained only Southern groundwood and sulphite pulp, both manufactured by the Savannah Laboratory. It went through the machines of the Beaver Wood Fibre Company, Ltd., without a break at 715 feet per minute and without a trace of resin or pitch. Georgia pine thus established itself as practical raw material for newsprint. Nine daily newspapers testified to the quality of the product by printing their editions of November 20, 1933, on the shipment from Thorold.

How about cost?

Dr. Herty and impartial engineers found that conversion costs and raw materials for a Southern mill making 150 tons per day would

---

[6] Experience has not borne out this enthusiastic estimate by Dr. Herty. Forestry experts consulted by the authors of this History now believe that the rate of growth of Southern trees suitable for pulp is three to four times that of Northern varieties, rather than the 10 times that Dr. Herty cited.

219

total $19.06 per ton. This compared with a current Canadian estimate of $27.90 per ton in Dominion mill operations. Capital charges for the proposed Southern mill were estimated at $12.64 per ton, making a total cost of $31.70. At the nadir of the depression, newsprint sold in New York at approximately $40 per ton, and slightly less occasionally.

Those were depression-time figures, of course, and allowed only 25 cents per ton for taxes. Total investment for a mill making 150 tons a day, or 45,000 tons per annum, was figured at $4,027,500. That dream figure might have been realized had a mill been constructed in the South in 1933. It was not attainable by 1939, when wages, material costs, and taxes had all risen materially above depression levels.

The Canadians took seriously the prospect of Southern competition. Addressing the Canadian Pulp and Paper Association in January, 1934, A. A. McDiarmid, chief engineer of Price Brothers & Co., Ltd., one of the largest producers in the Dominion, declared:

"The paper made from Southern pine to date, indicates the necessity for further study on the problem before it can be established that pulps may be made from this wood that will form, on a commercial basis, a good grade of newsprint. However, with the powerful advantage of indicated lower costs, the unquestionable desire of Southerners for the establishment of industries in their territory, and having regard for all the technical ability active on this problem, it appears reasonable to prophesy that methods will very soon be found to overcome any possible difficulties of successfully manufacturing, on a commercial basis, a merchantable quality of newsprint from these woods."

Southern newspapers everywhere hailed Dr. Herty's demonstration. In June, 1934, Victor H. Hanson, publisher of the Birmingham News, called a meeting of Southern business leaders to discuss the commercial possibilities of a Southern mill. His nephew, Clarence B. Hanson, Jr., who later succeeded him as publisher of the News, soon became prominent in SNPA promotion of the venture.

While no immediate newsprint production resulted from the Birmingham meeting, it deserves more than passing mention in this narrative. The meeting was convoked by Mr. Hanson in association with E. J. Smyer, a prominent attorney of Birmingham, and Thomas

Newsprint And A New South

W. Martin, president of the Alabama Power Company. Among the SNPA members in attendance were: R. F. Hudson, publisher of the Montgomery Advertiser; R. B. Chandler, publisher of the Mobile Register and Press; W. Stuart Mudd, owner of the Tuscaloosa News; F. T. Raiford, publisher of the Selma Times-Journal; Henry P. Johnston, publisher of the Huntsville Times; Col. Harry M. Ayers, publisher of the Anniston Star.

The publishers and other business leaders present organized as the Alabama Conference on Paper Products from Alabama Pine and adopted resolutions calling for intensive promotion of the State's forest products and amendment and enforcement of the State's forest conservation laws.

Even though Dr. Herty's researches had not yet reached their full development, high tribute was paid to his leadership by several of the speakers. The questions involved in the economic use of this great resource were canvassed from every important viewpoint and all answers indicated the necessity and also the probability of early action. Mr. Smyer laid down a detailed legislative program to accelerate the development and concluded with a prophecy that proved more accurate than he had wished.

"In short," he said, "the door of opportunity has been opened wide by Dr. Herty. If we wait, the plants will be located in other sections of the South, and we should act now for the future good of the State."

For one reason or another, the Alabamians did not get the newsprint ball rolling. Texas saw the first Southern newsprint mill in 1940, and Alabama, among the first to comprehend the opportunity, had to wait until 1950 for its first great newsprint mill—the Coosa River Newsprint Company. Within its first two years, its operation had made good all the roseate prophecies of the Birmingham meeting of 1934.

The SNPA at its 32d convention on May 21-23, 1934, had set the stage for the June meeting in Birmingham by adopting a resolution which called for "prompt construction by *private enterprise* of a mill for the purpose of producing newsprint in the South, but designed for the benefit of the entire country."

During 1932-33, the SNPA had been headed by James G. Stahlman, publisher of the Nashville Banner. "Jimmy" had already won recognition throughout Southern journalism as the worthy heir in all respects of his noted grandfather. As an individual and on behalf of the SNPA, he had offered every possible encouragement to Dr. Herty's experiments, and to him was given the task of driving the plan to success. As chairman of the special Newsprint Mills Committee appointed by President E. K. Gaylord, Mr. Stahlman had these able associates: Major Clark Howell, Jr., Atlanta Constitution; Curtis B. Johnson, Charlotte Observer; Junius P. Fishburn, Roanoke Times and World-News; Victor H. Hanson, Birmingham News; Myron G. Chambers, Knoxville News-Sentinel; James L. Mapes, Beaumont Enterprise and Journal; Emanuel Levi, Louisville Courier-Journal and Times; and E. K. Gaylord, Oklahoma City Oklahoman and Times, ex officio.

The committee met at Nashville on July 28, 1934, and agreed to proceed at once with definite plans for a Southern mill. They were starting from scratch. And they would learn during the next three or four years that promises did not always add up to performance. At the outset, they had only the firm conviction that the mill must be built with private capital, not as a government project handed to the newspapers on a silver platter.

As detailed elsewhere in these pages, the spark that actually brought the committee into being was furnished by Major George L. Berry, president of the Pressmen's Union, and in 1934 a prominent factor in the administration of the National Recovery Administration. Major Berry, accompanied by John Coffin of the Hearst Newspapers, appeared at the 1934 convention of the SNPA and in the course of a lengthy address proposed that the SNPA get behind a project to construct a Southern newsprint mill with government funds, which had been generously granted by Congress to President Roosevelt to make the NRA effective. Some SNPA members believe that the President had commissioned Major Berry to put the idea across with the Southern press, but there is no evidence to support that opinion. In any case, the SNPA wanted no such gift of Uncle Sam's money, and they made that emphatically clear in their resolution authorizing the committee's appointment.

Exactly what the committee did during the next three years must be gathered from the memory of the most active participants—and memories do not agree on all details after the lapse of so many years. The details do not appear in the published reports of meetings nor in Association Bulletins, for obvious reasons.

The committee's first contact apparently was with Ernest Rossiter, a New York pulp and paper mill engineer and former Canadian operator, who had substantial contacts with wealthy investors. Mr. Rossiter arranged options on a suitable site for a mill on the Warrior River in Alabama, the scene of E. W. Barrett's experiment with spruce pine in 1919-1921. The committee energetically sought and got commitments from a large number of SNPA members to buy newsprint from the projected mill. During the next two years the committee members traveled frequently to New York to consult with Mr. Rossiter and the engineers who were planning the Warrior River development. By 1936, their efforts seemed to have reached the threshold of success. And then the roof caved in. The prospective investors who had assured Mr. Rossiter of their interest suddenly changed their minds and put their money into other enterprises.

Undaunted by this disappointment, the committee shortly afterward made contact with Alfred I. duPont, a member of the wealthy Delaware family. Negotiating through Mr. duPont's brother-in-law, Edward Ball, the committee obtained a verbal agreement that a mill would be built at St. Joe, Florida, and that the duPont interests would put in some 200,000 acres of timberland as a capital asset. Final details were agreed to at a meeting in Atlanta, and the committee retired at 11:00 P. M. in the belief that the papers would be signed at a meeting the next morning.

Promptly at 9:00 A. M. the full committee assembled—and waited an hour for the appearance of Mr. Ball and his attorney. They finally arrived, with a proposal that knocked the whole enterprise into nothing. This was that the publishers pay several dollars above the market price for the new mill's tonnage. The committee and the publishers who had agreed to buy the projected mill's paper had believed that the price would be at least $2.00 below that of the Northern mills, and the idea of paying a substantial premium above that was wholly unacceptable. The committee members went home, disappointed and baffled. Not for many months did they learn the reason for Mr. duPont's overnight change of mind.

Then it developed that Mr. duPont had consulted one of the banks of New York on the proposition and was flatly told that if he went through with the deal, the bank would not lend another dollar on any of his enterprises. This bank held heavy investments in the bonds of Canadian mills—bonds which were then earning no return and were selling at about 40 cents on the dollar. It wanted no new competition for its suffering Canadian clients, and at that time it was able to stave off the Southern threat. Shortly afterwards, the Hearst Newspapers, which had made tonnage commitments under both the Rossiter and duPont projects, withdrew them. It was common knowledge throughout the newspaper field then that the Hearst interests were heavily in debt to the Canadian paper mills—and the committee deduced that the same banking influences had commanded the repudiation.

Another threat was made directly, Mr. Stahlman recalls, by the head of a newsprint organization with numerous Kraft mills in the South. If the SNPA committee's efforts approached success, he declared, his firm would switch machines in the South from Kraft to newsprint and give newsprint away for as long as it was necessary to convince Southern publishers that it was not to their advantage to construct their own mill. That threat was never carried out, but it added to the committee's frustration.

It may have been about this time—or a bit earlier—that the committee learned about the interest of Ernest Lynn Kurth in its plans for a newsprint mill. Mr. Kurth had extensive forest holdings in East Texas, near Lufkin. Impressive of physique, he was soon to prove that his courage and his grasp of business truths were also on the large (or Texas) scale. Prior to the 1929 market crash he and his associates had planned construction of a 45,000-ton Kraft mill, based on the abundant pine woods of the East Texas coastal plain. When the first gusts of the depression signaled business generally to take in sail, Kurth scaled his plans down to a 27,000-ton mill. That couldn't be financed, either, but Kurth did not quit.

When he was elected president of the East Texas Chamber of Commerce in 1933, Mr. Kurth placed his idea before the chamber, and a committee was appointed to study the project's feasibility. This committee heard of the SNPA plans, and when Mr. Kurth stepped down as president, he became chairman of the Chamber's newsprint mill committee. If he still wavered between Kraft and newsprint, his final decision was influenced by conversations he had during 1934 and 1935 with Richard W. Wortham, Jr., a native of Paris, Texas, who had many friends in Southern newspaperdom. Dick Wortham represented the Perkins-Goodwin Company, of New York, wholesale paper and pulp merchants. Through him, Mr. Kurth was introduced to Albert Newcombe, a director of Perkins-Goodwin Company.

That meeting brought together two essential elements—the owner of timber lands who wanted to make paper and believed that he could find part of the necessary capital, and a 90-year-old organization familiar with newsprint manufacture and marketing, interested in the practical development of the project and willing to assume a share of the investment. Still to be rounded up was the eventual market for the mill's product (the publishers' commitments to the Rossiter and duPont projects had lapsed with their failure) and additional finance.

Then, in 1936, the paths of Mr. Kurth and Dr. Herty crossed. Dr. Herty's success with making practical newsprint from Southern pine had been reported, and the Beaumont Chamber of Commerce invited him to tell his story to a technical forestry group. Mr. Kurth also addressed that meeting, and, hearing Dr. Herty, took fire from the scientist's enthusiasm. They had a long talk after the meeting, in which Captain I. F. Eldridge of the U. S. Forest Service, familiar with Southern forests, also participated. Mr. Kurth had told the meeting of his newsprint mill plans and declared that there should be enough money in East Texas to finance such a mill without going outside.

Mr. Kurth was solidly converted to the newsprint project after a talk with Louis Calder, president of Perkins-Goodwin, who gave his expert opinion that newsprint prices would trend upward over a period of years while Kraft prices would probably go the other way.

Toward the end of 1936, the Perkins-Goodwin officers informed Ted Dealey of the Dallas News that a mill could be constructed somewhere in East Texas if publishers would agree to buy its product. Mr. Dealey, then vice-president of the News, had come up through the editorial side but had a thorough knowledge of the newspaper business. Anything that would help Texas was certain to command his energetic support. He called a meeting of Southwestern publishers in Dallas on January 11, 1937, and Mr. Kurth stated the proposition. Before the meeting ended, 30,000 tons had been pledged. It wasn't enough, but it made a substantial start.

Now the newsprint mill project had these tentative assets: (1) timber lands (2) technical management service (3) a backlog of prospective customers, and (4) some of the money needed for bricks and mortar and machinery. Mr. Newcombe, Mr. Wortham, and Mr. Garvan journeyed to Texas, where the last-named had an old friend and Yale classmate in Wirt Davis, a Dallas banker. Mr. Garvan's Celtic gift of persuasion interested Mr. Davis in the plan, which soon took its first corporate form with $100,000 capital paid in by Mr. Davis and Mr. Calder. Mr. Davis later retired from the enterprise and was replaced on the directorate by J. H. Kurth, Jr. That was a good nucleus—but it didn't grow.

Early in 1937, the depression devils which had been exorcised by President Roosevelt four years earlier once more applied their deadly fingers to the nation's business. Private investors turned a chilly eye to new risks, and the capital that the promoters had in sight fell far short of what was needed. Once more the SNPA committee rejected an offer by the Federal Emergency Relief Association to finance a $5,000,000 mill, with the aim of determining the effect of such an enterprise upon unemployment in the area. The committee, despite its setbacks, was determined to live up to the resolution which prescribed construction by *private enterprise.*

Late in 1937, Mr. Garvan insisted that Dr. Herty make a personal call on Jesse H. Jones, then chairman of the Reconstruction Finance Corporation. Mr. Jones, a Texan and publisher of the Houston Chronicle, might be expected to turn a favorable ear to a plea on behalf of Texas and the newspaper business, presented with Dr. Herty's earnest eloquence. But Mr. Jones took a lot of convincing. In principle and practice, he opposed the loan of RFC funds for any enterprise in which a newspaper or newspapers were concerned. He wanted no part in any possible coercion of the press through government loans.[7]

---

[7] In "Fifty Billion Dollars—My Thirteen Years with the RFC (1932-1945)" By Jesse H. Jones and Edward Angly. The Macmillan Co., N. Y., 1951, Mr. Jones states his views on government loans to newspapers. He also narrates the circumstances of the RFC loan to Southland Paper Mills, Inc., noting succinctly that

Newsprint And A New South

Dr. Herty got his hearing and told his story with the conviction and practical vision that had impressed the SNPA members. He impressed the RFC, too, and paved the way for the many tough-minded sessions that Mr. Kurth had with the RFC before the loan was assured. At the time Dr. Herty approached Mr. Jones, the committee had promised investments in stock totaling $1,500,000. Those pledges, plus the timberlands adjacent to the proposed mill site, were regarded by the promoters as good collateral for an RFC loan. Plans then called for a $7,000,000 company, to construct and operate a newsprint mill of 150,000 tons annual capacity and a Kraft mill of 20,000 tons. But both the RFC and private investors shook their heads. They would go along within reason, but not that deeply. The promoters would have to put up more of their own money and the scale of the operation would have to be reduced to the tonnage proportions for which a market could be assured. Once more, it was up to the SNPA members.

Anyone who was in the company of Ted Dealey or Jimmy Stahlman during late 1937 and early 1938 will recall that those affable gentlemen had no time for light chatter. Mr. Dealey carried the cause to the Texas Newspaper Publishers Association and to SNPA members in the Southwest. Mr. Stahlman, who had stepped from the presidency of the SNPA to that of the American Newspaper Publishers Association, put all of his mettle into gaining pledges of tonnage and financial support from his colleagues in both associations. The crisis was reached when the SNPA met in convention at the Edgewater Gulf Hotel, near Biloxi, Miss., on June 1, 1938, when Mr. Kurth told the committee that the project would fall through unless the publishers matched his own investment of approximately $250,000.

E. K. Gaylord recalls the committee's meeting with a number of publishers considered capable of raising the needed sum. He talked with John McCarrens of the Cleveland Plain Dealer, who was not an SNPA member, but nevertheless pledged $50,000. Mr. Gaylord pledged $60,000 for the Oklahoma Publishing Company, and Ted Dealey committed the Dallas News to a like investment. Barry

---

three loans over a six-year period totaling $8,500,000 had been paid. His own newspaper, one of the most important in Texas, did not buy any of the Southland Mills stock because of his association with the transaction as a lender, and, to his regret, had not benefited as had other Southern dailies through the mill's operation.

Bingham of the Louisville Courier-Journal and Times pledged $30,000 and the $50,000 remainder was raised in smaller amounts from other SNPA members. Sufficient additional tonnage commitments were obtained from SNPA papers, and after two long night sessions, Jimmy Stahlman was able to inform the convention that the goal had been reached.

In the interim, Dr. Herty had been having difficult moments. At the 1937 SNPA convention in Hot Springs, Ark., he was thrilled by the association's award of a plaque recognizing his courageous pioneering. By that time, he was able to show the publishers conclusive proof that newsprint made from Southern pine would stand comparison in every respect with the finest paper made on the American continent. He told the publishers that within the previous year 14 new paper mills had been built or were under construction in the South, representing a capitalization of $80,000,000. A large factor in bringing this new industry to the South had been the conviction that large investments in Southern timber would render a return in perpetuity because of the rapid growth of Southern forests.

He warned, however, that if the Kraft mills and the newsprint mills considered it necessary to buy up large tracts of woodlands for each mill, the South would lose a major benefit of the new industry. Dr. Herty held firmly to his initial creed—that the owner of small farm woodlands should be the primary source of pulpwood, so that the annual cash income would be quickly distributed to all levels. He stood firm, too, against any additional legislation or regulations to control the use of woodlands, and he called upon the publishers to realize their responsibilities in educating the public against increasing government regulation.

"I went all over this 35 years ago," he told the SNPA. "At that time the turpentine operators were cutting big holes in the bottom of the trees to collect the gum. I got up a substitute for that box, a form of cup, and we demonstrated it in 1902 with the Bureau of Forestry in Washington. The trees without a box cut into them would make 23 per cent more gum than trees with the box. No sooner had the news of that gotten around than the same cry went up that has started here, 'we must have legislation! It should be made illegal to cut a box.' I stood out against it. We didn't need legislation. We did need education. What was the result? In three years' time the industry was revolutionized;· box-cutting was a thing of the past. Education had done the work."

Before that meeting adjourned, Dr. Herty was elected an honorary life member of the SNPA, and, in that capacity, he appeared before its 1938 meeting at Edgewater Park. It was his last appearance, and in it he manifested the same steadfast faith that had won the SNPA years before.

He had been through grievously difficult times. Francis P. Garvan had died in the Autumn of 1937 and his passing ended the financial support which the Savannah laboratory had been getting from the Chemical Foundation. Depression had shrunk the resources of that body, and as 1937 ended, Dr. Herty faced the probability that the laboratory doors would be closed on January 1, with its great potential indicated strongly but not yet realized. He "had the feeling of a man buried beneath a mountain of flowers, smothered to death with bouquets, by the tributes of the press. But that didn't take care of the payroll."

Then at the last moment of 1937 came a check for $18,000 from an equipment manufacturer grateful for the laboratory's contribution to the industry. That sum had been raised among the equipment people to tide the laboratory over until permanent financial arrangements could be made. Next, Governor Rivers of Georgia, learning of the laboratory's plight, asked the legislature to make an emergency appropriation of $20,000, in addition to the $10,000 the State already had provided. The legislature complied unanimously. The Doctor's friends in Washington offered to procure Federal appropriations for the institution, but he refused that aid with finality. He wanted no Federal laboratory, with the hostile paper interests of New England and the Northwest in position to hamstring Southern development.

At the suggestion of the Governors of Georgia and Florida and with Dr. Herty's approval, the Herty Foundation was created under Georgia Law to take over the laboratory. Five trustees would administer the ownership of the property, five directors would control its policies. The new entity would be eligible to receive contributions from states or their subdivisions, from individuals and from corporations. Dr. Herty asked for editorial support of the new

Foundation, for which he predicted a glorious future as a high type of educational institution.

Remarking that he had passed his 70th birthday and did not know how long he would be permitted to "nurse this idea along," Dr. Herty ended with an inspiration to new achievement.

"I hope to see the day," he said, "before I drop out of the picture, when we will have a vigorous educational institution combined with a practical every-day research affair making use of the raw materials of the South for the benefit of the people, and through the people, for the benefit of the nation."

Thanking Dr. Herty for his years of unselfish service to the South, Mr. Stahlman closed the session on a note of confidence.

The SNPA adopted a resolution commending the establishment of the Herty Foundation and urging the governors and legislatures of each state in the pine belt to provide financial support.

By that time, Mr. Kurth and his associates had secured 180,000 acres of timberland in the Lufkin area at a fair price. They had also induced the owners of the Angelina & Neches River Railroad, a 30-mile long single-track road running from Keltys through the pine woods to Lufkin and Chireno, to accept stock in the new mill for a half-interest in the line. Mr. Kurth and his East Texas associates, the Perkins-Goodwin interests and the newspaper publishers had subscribed $1,615,000 in cold cash for stock. With the lands and the half-interest in the railroad, the company could now show total collateral of $2,575,000. With that in hand, application was made to the Reconstruction Finance Corporation for a loan of $3,425,000, to be repaid over a period of 10 years. That loan was granted in October, 1938.

Issuance of the corporation's securities was cleared with the SEC in the minimum time of 20 days, despite the somewhat complex ownership structure. The RFC required that construction be placed in the hands of a competent contractor who could furnish a performance bond of $1,000,000, and this work was awarded to the Merritt-Chapman & Scott Corporation of New York. George F. Hardy, also of New York, recognized as an expert in mill design and construction throughout the industry, was retained as consultant engineer. And, although Dr. Herty's premonition in June, 1938, that his days might be short, was tragically verified by his death on July 28, his name lives on in the new mill town three miles from Lufkin, Texas.

Ground was broken for the Southland Paper Mills, Inc., on January 14, 1939, on a site covering 239 acres. Construction began on March 25, and when this author visited the mill on December 14, 1939, all buildings had been completed and boilers and other machinery were going through their warm-up tests. Tom A. Wark, a man of long experience in newsprint manufacture, was brought to Texas from the Watab Paper Company of Sartell, Minn., to be general manager of the Southland mill, and Charles Carpenter, one of Dr. Herty's former laboratory associates, was installed as chief chemist. In its early years the mill used pine logs from adjacent woods at a cost of $4.25 a cord for its groundwood. Its chemical bleached sulphate pulp, of which 15 to 20 per cent is combined with the groundwood pulp, came from the Champion Paper & Fibre Company of Houston. Use of this chemical form departed from the practice of Northern mills, which generally use sulphite pulp for newsprint. Sulphate pulp had been used in Kraft paper for many years, and sulphate pine fibre had been bleached as far back as 1910 at Billingsfors, Sweden, and was in regular use at the Champion Co's plant at Canton, N. C., after 1920. During the 1930's, the Wayagamack Paper Co. had fought and won a test case in the U. S. Courts for the acceptance as "standard newsprint," duty free, of a shipment in which bleached sulphate had been substituted for sulphite. Bleached sulphate was tested by the Herty Laboratory, which confirmed the fact that its manufacture involved less corrosion and less stream pollution than that of bleached sulphite, and that the chemicals used could be recovered.

The Southland Mills opened with a rated capacity of 150 tons daily or about 50,000 tons annually. Its first newsprint came from the paper machine in a sheet 220 inches wide at a speed of 600 feet a minute on January 17, 1940, scarcely more than a year from the date of the turning of the first spadeful of earth for the mill's foundations. The contractors, favored by clement Texas weather, kept 30 to 45 days ahead of their construction schedule. Test runs of the new paper on the presses of the Dallas News, Little Rock Arkansas Gazette and Shreveport Times proved entirely satisfactory.

Editors and readers throughout the South hailed the success and paid well merited tributes to the foresight and the unquenchable fortitude of Dr. Herty. Stands of pine, of many species, and of other trees, suddenly assumed new money importance among the natural assets of all Dixie.

No profit had been anticipated for the Southland Mills in 1940. As in every new operation, "bugs" had to be detected and overcome in daily practice. The net loss for the short year (less than 12 months' production) was $182,271. In 1950, the mill showed net earnings of $3,452,682, on net sales of $16,099,877, after allowing $945,982 for depreciation and depletion, and $3,239,170 for taxes. Production and net sales in 1951 topped the previous year's record. Two newsprint machines produced a total of 130,996 tons and other products, including Kraft board and Kraft pulp, amounted to 32,133 tons—a combined total of 4,351 tons more than in 1950. While net sales increased by $2,568,351, to $18,668,234, net income dropped by $559,508, due wholly to increased taxes.

During 1951, this enterprise added to its timberlands 1,780 acres, at an average cost of $24.56 per acre. Between 1945 and 1951, Southland Mills spent approximately $12,000,000 for additional plant and timberlands, all derived from earnings. The final payment on the company's bank indebtedness was made in 1951, and the firm paid a dividend (its first) to common stockholders in the sum of $856,500 on December 10, 1951.

One more phase of the Southland Mills' development merits notice. As mentioned above, this mill originally purchased its chemical pulp from a Houston firm, which, during the war found itself unable to continue this supply. Southland thus was compelled to construct its owns chemical pulp plant or discontinue operations. The additional capital for this addition was supplied by SNPA members, most of them already large stockholders in the company. The publishers dug into their pockets again to finance the construction of a second paper machine at Southland after World War II.

Brief mention is made on another page of the publishers' success in obtaining the release of raw materials needed for the completion of the chemical pulp mill. The new plant was nearly completed when everything was brought to a sudden halt by the refusal of the pulp and paper section of the War Production Board to permit the purchase of copper and nickel covers for its pulp digesters. The mill had already obtained certificates of necessity for all other mill construction and had laid out the money, some $12,000, for the purchase of these scarce materials.

Ted Dealey, John D. Ewing and E. K. Gaylord journeyed to Washington and had a spirited session with A. G. Wakeman, then head of the pulp and paper division. Mr. Wakeman did not know then that he would be president of the Coosa River Newsprint Company a few years later, and he was completely unsympathetic to the publishers' pleas. He stood on his previous ruling, even though the publishers told him that the digesters were already complete awaiting delivery and that there was no point in melting up the copper-nickel lids for the munitions stockpile.

Undaunted, the publishers went promptly to Senator Tom Connally of Texas and to Donald Nelson, then head of the War Production Board. Mr. Gaylord recalls that Senator Connally carried the case to President Roosevelt. Mr. Wakeman was overruled and the new mill unit went into operation on schedule. Its installation made the Southland a completely integrated paper mill operation, with capacity to meet the needs of a long future.

But long before those pleasing facts had become known, the SNPA had made profitable use of its experience in the promotion and construction of another newsprint mill. The delays in bringing the Coosa River Newsprint Company to operation in Alabama were born only of war's exigencies; once the publishers realized that a concrete opportunity awaited their action, they moved with decision.

Details of the organizations of this mill are related in another chapter. It differed from that of the Southland Mill in some details. First, the Coosa River Mill began with double the capacity of its forerunner, and with ample facilities for expansion. Second, the publishers who bought its common stock were not all members of the SNPA. When members of the Association had invested to the limit of their resources, and contracted for all the tonnage they could consume, the Coosa River mill's needs called for additional work in both of these particulars. Important publishers in other parts of the country eagerly grasped at the opportunity for sound investment and a sure domestic supply of newsprint.

The Coosa River mill, surrounded as it is by forests including many varieties of Southern pine, has experimented and found that Dr. Herty's judgment of 1931 was thoroughly justified. Many different trees can be transformed profitably into woodpulp. Practically all of them, too, reach pulpwood size within 15 to 30 years, assuring a supply in perpetuity for the mill and a continuing steady income for the owners of woodlots and timber stands.

With two successful newsprint mills established by the foresight and initiative of SNPA members, the prospect of investment in Southern operations became much more attractive to outside capital. As noted elsewhere in these pages, several United States and Canadian newsprint operators sent experts into the South to scout possible locations for new mills. Neither the American nor the Canadian paper men, however, became first to build a mill with only the moral, and not the financial, banking of Southern publishers. That achievement fell to a British concern.

The Bowater Organization which had supplied Southern newspapers with paper for many years from its mills in Corner Brook, Newfoundland, decided after World War II that a newsprint mill in the South was an enterprise certain of a profitable future.[8] The company had a list of satisfied Southern customers for all the paper it could sell at that time. Its surveys brought out that Southern family incomes and Southern newspaper circulations had had a relatively greater growth than those in other sections. A mill in the South could supply present and future Southern buyers without the haul of 1,500 to 2,000 miles from the Newfoundland plant, which could then find customers nearer home.

Sites for a mill of the dimensions contemplated by Bowater were no longer so plentiful in the South as they had been 15 years earlier. Since Dr. Herty's early prophecies, more than a score of large paper mills had been built in the Southern States, but except for Southland and Coosa River, none of them made newsprint. They

---

[8]In the research for this chapter, it was learned that the Wall Paper Manufacturers Limited of England had experimented with Southern pine as early as 1906, a quarter century before Dr. Herty appeared on the SNPA scene. The wood had been shipped to England, not for making newsprint but on the possibility that it might make good pulp. It met the test and was used in making letter paper, but the idea was not pursued, and it is unlikely that Dr. Herty had ever heard of the experiment. It was about 1906 also that the Kraft mill at Roanoke Rapids, N. C., one of the first Kraft mills in the South, began the use of Southern pine for its pulpwood.

did, nevertheless, preempt tremendous tracts of woodlands and many of the sites peculiarly adapted to paper mill operation. An English writer has defined the qualifications sought by the Bowaters:

"A flourishing newsprint mill, besides depending on vast timber plantations within a comparatively short haul, ideally requires a large flat site, with freedom to expand, unencumbered by urban building values, but near plentiful labor of high grade, which itself usually means old-established towns; the mill must be well served by road, rail, and waterway—preferably with private sidings and docks—and located near abundant, cheap supplies of coal, electric power or natural gas, or a combination of them; besides all these, its basic need is a generous source of chemically suitable fresh water, of which millions of gallons a day are required."[9]

Bowater found such a place near Calhoun, Tenn., an hour's motor ride from Chattanooga. Sir Eric Vansittart Bowater, chairman of the firm, visited the United States to look over that and other prospects. On his return to England, he obtained government permission to take $15,000,000 from the nation's carefully guarded store of dollars for investment in the American enterprise. From then on, he needed American help, and the SNPA officially, and as individual publishers, did all in their power to forward the project. The big difficulty, with American resources engaged in Korea, was to obtain a "certificate of necessity" which would make available the materials needed for construction and other advantages. With relatively little delay, thanks to the publishers' aid, the Bowaters Southern Paper Corporation received this document, which confers:

"Substantial taxation relief, in the form of accelerated depreciation, when a new factory is built to produce a 'necessitous commodity.'

"Priority in the purchase of controlled building materials and equipment."

This will enable Bowaters to write off over a period of five years 45 per cent of the total capital cost of the plant as estimated by Federal authorities. Sir Eric told an annual meeting of the Bowater Organization in England that "the present-day relatively high

---

[9] "British Initiative Abroad," by Robert Sinclair; published in Spring 1953 issue of *Progress, The Magazine of Unilever Limited*."

costs of construction by comparison with pre-war days will be so reduced as to assure that our new project will be at no disadvantage in this respect, and therefore will be able to operate on a competitive basis with older established mills."

The Calhoun site includes 1,769 acres, bounded on one side by U. S. Highway No. 11. Along another side, at right angles to the road flows the Hiwassee River, a navigable tributary of the Tennessee River. From the Chattanooga-Knoxville line of the Southern Railway, a branch has been built to the paper mill site with provision for adequate sidings. The mill thus has easy transportation by road, rail and water.

The river also provides an abundant supply of the chemically suitable water essential to paper manufacture, and the mill's pumping and filtration plant will produce 25,000,000 gallons of filtered water daily. The mill's storage reservoir will have a capacity of 4,000,000 gallons.

To fill the plant's annual need of 250,000 cords of pulpwood, considerably nearby forest acreage has already been purchased. The management has been at pains, however, to declare that the mill will buy all the pulpwood it can get from farmers and other timberland owners. This policy bears out another of Dr. Herty's dicta—that trees can be an annual cash crop of top importance to the Southern farmer. Bowaters have not overlooked the crop potential either. During 1952 and 1953 the new mills' woods crews planted nine million pine seedlings which will be trees of pulpwood size in about 15 years, and the plan calls for a stepped-up program in the future.

Not counting its own acres of forest lands, Bowaters Southern Paper Corporation represents an investment of $60,000,000. The common stock is all British-owned. Twelve American insurance companies bought the First Mortgage Bonds and five American banks headed by J. P. Morgan & Company have taken up the serial notes. Included are two Southern banks—The Hamilton National Bank of Chattanooga, Tenn., and the Wachovia Bank & Trust Co., of Winston-Salem, N. C.

The mill began making pulp on May 30, 1954. The first paper machine went into production July 12, 1954. The annual capacity of the mill when in full production will be 130,000 tons of newsprint and 50,000 tons of Kraft pulp. All newsprint for the first 15 years' operation has been contracted for by Southern publishers; the Kraft sulphate pulp will be used by other Bowater enterprises or sold.

Employment will be afforded to approximately 750 Tennesseeans in the mill itself, while other hundreds, and perhaps thousands, will find gainful work in the woods operations. It has been estimated that the mill payroll will be $3,200,000 in the first year, and that the outlay for purchased wood will approach that figure. This represents an addition of 60 per cent to the salaries and wages paid in 1952 by Tennessee's forest industries, about $11,000,000.

Of particular interest to SNPA members is the advanced conservation program announced by the new mill. The SNPA has evidenced an accelerating concern with forest and soil conservation throughout the Southern States, and with good reason. It has been stated that 77 out of every 100 acres of forest burned each year in the United States are in the South and that nearly half of these fires are due to human carelessness. Two-thirds of the South's tremendous forests are owned by small proprietors and farmers and it is on these lands that most forest fires are said to start. The 25 per cent owned by industry and the nine per cent in state and national parks or preserves are reasonably well protected from fire.

Late in 1952 Bowaters joined actively in the campaign to educate the owners of the lands from which much of its wood will come. Its trained forestry crews (with equipment comparable to that of the State division of forestry) helped to fight fires wherever they were reported, and took color pictures of the battle. This color film with a dubbed-in sound-track, has been shown to audiences of farmers and landowners throughout East Tennessee, giving them a new viewpoint on forest values and fire perils. Another Bowaters film tells the story of the corporation's tree-planting operation.

Though this concept of forest conservation is not new to the South or to paper makers in other parts of North America, it has been seldom carried to the general public. Industrial practices which devastated the forests of Michigan and Wisconsin half a century ago, leaving behind fire-scarred hills and ghost communities, are not in the book of modern paper manufacturers. They have learned by costly experience that forest conservation and reforestation are fundamentally good business.

It is significant, however, that the Bowaters operation, starting from scratch and with its wood sources in several heavily forested counties of Tennessee, and also in Alabama and Georgia, began the task of educating its neighbors before a wheel turned in the mill. It is a policy which Tennessee newspapers rightly considered worthy of news features. The South's woodlands have ceased to be a vague "natural resource" in the minds of a growing number of Southerners; they are now a source of cash income today and tomorrow, into the limitless future.

It is taking no credit from Bowaters for their intelligent approach to this problem when this History emphasizes the part the SNPA has played for many years, and especially since World War II, in promoting forest and soil conservation. Since the days of Henry W. Grady, Southern leaders have prodded their neighbors to get free from the primitive agricultural economy that ruled the South when the SNPA was born and for many years thereafter. Many influences have been at work during the past five decades to provide the South an income from industry that was worthy of its great resources. Some have been originated by the Federal Government, with the Tennessee Valley Authority as the outstanding example of non-profit operation for the general good. Many have been motivated by the normal desire for private profit, with widely beneficial effects.

The SNPA effort, it may justly be claimed, is in a class by itself. It has provided Southern newspapers with an inexhaustible source of print paper. It has brought completely new industries to areas which would have remained untilled field and idle forest. None of the three mills now operating in Texas, Alabama and Tennessee would have been undertaken unless Southern newspaper publishers had put their brains, their will to achieve, and their dollars solidly behind the first enterprise in the late 30's.

The 1931 vision of Dr. Herty of a prosperous Southern agriculture developed hand-in-hand with new and profitable industry seems well on the road to realization in 1954. Certainly its achievement has been far advanced in the areas around the mills now built or building. Other newsprint mills will be built in the South, even though the newspaper publishers may not give them the initial fillip of investment and tonnage contracts. It is no far-fetched prophecy as this chapter is written to see the South before 1973 as the principal source of all United States-made paper, of every variety.[10] The great progress of the past 10 years that invited the Bowater investment was not born merely of war. It was a final recognition by Americans that the South offered, and still offers, opportunity for the gainful employment of capital and labor matched nowhere else in America.

If the Southern Newspaper Publishers had accomplished no more in its half century than to bring vital new industry to its region and to give the people an appreciation of their resources and capabilities, it would deserve well of the South and of all America. But its officers and members had many other tasks of less impressive proportions during these years of achievement. Succeeding chapters will relate how the SNPA met its responsibilities during World War II and in the momentous years that followed.

---

[10]Some paper and forestry experts believe that the tremendous and almost untouched forests of Alaska hold even more promise for permanent lumber and pulpwood supplies than do those of the South.

Through Fog of War

SNPA Plans Support of New Paper Mills and Other Industries for New Prosperity in South, Also Continues Effort for Improved Newspapers—War-Travel Ban Prevents Annual Conventions in 1944-1945, as Association's Long-Held Hopes Approach Realization.

THE great development of Dixie's newsprint industry just narrated appeared on no crystal ball when the SNPA held its 38th annual meeting, and its first in Texas, at Mineral Wells, May 20-22, 1940. Many of the publishers had detoured to inspect the new Southland mill at Herty, and were delighted with what they saw. Enthusiasm was abundant for duplication of the Southland plant in other sections of the South, but the prospect had been dimmed by events of the previous fortnight. The seemingly invincible German armies had already scattered French and British resistance, and the heroic retreat from Dunquerque was only ten days in the future. Four days before the convention opened, Mr. Roosevelt had told the Congress, "We stand ready not only to spend millions for defense, but to give our service and even our lives for the maintenance of our American liberties." He requested new appropriations totalling $896,000,000 for national defense and laid down what then seemed a fantastic goal of producing 50,000 military and naval aircraft annually.[1]

With such calls upon national production resources, plans for new Southern newsprint mills stood no chance of early realization. Only one such project had taken specific form at that time—a promotion by Gordon Browning, former Governor of Tennessee, of a mill to be located near Savannah, Tenn. This project was not mentioned in the Association's terse resolution, which expressed gratification at the

---

[1] The Public Papers and Addresses of Franklin D. Roosevelt. 1940 Volume. The Macmillan Co., New York, 1941. Pages 198 ff.

successful start of the Southland mill's operation and kept before the Association the long-term goal of expanding Southern industry.

The latter objective received attention in a brilliant address delivered by David E. Lilienthal, director of the Tennessee Valley Authority, before an assembly that crowded the auditorium of the Baker Hotel. Mr. Lilienthal broke the problem of future Southern prosperity down to essentials. The low income earned by Southern families, in comparison with those in other parts of America, could be traced to the South's limited use of its great natural resources. The South produced raw materials, on which it received a relatively low return, for processing in other parts of America or abroad, into manufactures of much greater value. A ton of pulpwood, he pointed out, brought the farmer who cut it $4.00 per ton. To buy an $800 automobile, the farmer had to cut 200 tons of wood. Processed into woodpulp, the wood had a value of $40.00 per ton; when the pulp was made into Kraft paper, its value reached $65 per ton; and when the paper was converted into bags, its value of $150 had multiplied nearly 38 times since the wood left the farmer's truck.

In 1937, he said, the 10 Southeastern States accounted for only 22½ per cent of textile products listed in the Census of Manufactures. Up to that time, he declared, the textile industries which had located in the South were mainly those which produced articles requiring relatively little skilled labor. The South produced 25 per cent of the nation's woodpulp, but only 10 per cent of the paper.

Two major reasons were cited for the South's inequalities and handicaps—inadequacy of industrial research in the South, and the discriminatory structure of railroad freight rates. Dr. Herty's pioneering research was noted as a shining demonstration of what could be done by similar methods for all of the South's potential industry. Mr. Lilienthal's clear analysis of freight rate disadvantages under which the South suffered was an old tale to SNPA veterans of Washington hearings; it highlighted the encouraging fact that the Interstate Commerce Commission and both Houses of Congress were at last looking into the inequalities imposed by interregional freight rate barriers, and, for the laymen, it took the question out of technical language by illustrations that all could understand. His hour-long speech was published, frequently with generous editorial comment, throughout the South, a lusty stroke in the campaign of education of the region to its unused potentials.

Education, in fact, might be called the keynote of the 1940 convention—applied indirectly to the readers of Southern newspapers and directly to Southern newspaper people for the improvement of their service. The only major phase of purely internal concern fell in President Adolph Shelby Ochs's emphasis on recent labor relations trends, and the exposition of these in the report of the Labor Commissioner.

George C. Biggers, of the Atlanta Journal, returned undiscouraged to the task of convincing publishers that drastic departures from established ways must be taken if newspapers were to arrest the steady decline in their prestige and revenue as advertising media. Advertising linage in 1939 marked a near low for the previous decade, topping only the sorrowful record of 1932. Color advertising was available in 112 Southern newspapers, but under such a diversity of rates and regulations that spacebuyers shuddered at the task of making up a newspaper list. The differential spread between retail and national rates had reached dimensions that meant diminishing returns to the national advertiser. The flat rate system for national advertising, so highly vaunted twenty years earlier, no longer fitted the situation, in his opinion (not, however, that of the Advertising Committee). He declared that important executives would welcome a sliding scale based on continuity or volume as a new "club" which agencies could use to get "decent-sized" schedules for newspapers approved by their clients. It was difficult to get an O. K. under existing conditions for more than a 30-day newspaper schedule. His report ended on a prophetic, if sardonic, note:

"Many publishers believe that advertising will have to get much worse before publishers will do a thing about it. In other words, the patient may be well on the way to the morgue before we call in the surgeon."

Things didn't come to that pass, however. Advertising perked up a bit in 1940, and so did the national efforts of newspapers to put new life into their selling methods. The "reform," coming as it did in step with the general revival of industry spurred by defense contracts, had an important role in the revival of newspaper linage.

One of the features of the new sales technique was to be a graphically clear analysis of what people read in newspapers. Editors had been experimenting in haphazard fashion with inquiries of that kind for many years. Dr. George Gallup and other investigators had been seeking a "least common denominator" of reader interest for ten years and Gallup's researches had reached the point where they would be most useful in newspaper selling. At the 1940 convention, the SNPA was treated to a demonstration of this public pulse-feeling.

Jack M. Willem, research director of the Stack-Goble Advertising Agency, Chicago, arrayed numerous graphs to portray the current trends of public interest in news pictures. His study was technical and would have supplied excellent guidance to men whose daily task it was to select and display news pictures. It is doubtful, however, that the publishers brought home much more than general impressions: that sports pictures ranked at the bottom of the table in catching the reader's eye, mainly because few women looked at them; that "leg" pictures drew more attention from women than men; and that scenery and travel pictures held top place, presumably because American readers in early 1940 looked for escape from the horrors of European war. Mr. Willem furnished many technical pointers and emphasized that readers looked for quality and variety in news pictures, no longer for mere novelty.

More "how to do it" instruction came from Mark Ethridge, who had risen meteorically from the managing editor's desk in Macon to vice-president and general manager of the Louisville Courier-Journal and Times. His colleague, Tom Wallace, back at the head of the editorial affairs committee, had assigned him the topic "How to Sell Newspapers Without Pogo Sticks," and Mr. Ethridge prescribed a liberal editorial budget rather than circulation premiums. Under his management, the Louisville newspapers had dropped an insurance plan which had brought in more than 100,000 renewals and 5,000 new subscribers the year before. Circulation department expense had been reduced 14.03 per cent; circulation revenue increased 27.53 per cent. The Courier-Journal's daily average news content was increased from 90 columns in 1935 to 121 columns in 1939, the paper's dress was improved, a new four-color press was installed for comics. Syndicated features were not increased, and an original home-produced magazine replaced a syndicated section. Declaring that "the best dollar is the news dollar," Mr. Ethridge said the newspapers' program was keyed to three principles: "(1) proving that we are good citizens, in spite of being a monopoly; (2) proving that we are interested in the city's prospering; (3) dramatizing our personnel."

Capping the educational side of the program was an exhaustive survey of education for journalism in the South rendered by Herbert Davidson, editor of the Daytona Beach (Fla.) News-Journal. While the South did not have as many journalism courses, in proportion to population, as other parts of the country, Mr. Davidson reported, its "Big Six" university schools and departments ranked among the best in the country. The Washington and Lee School of Journalism, long fostered by the SNPA, had a record enrollment of 127 for the 1940 semester, it was stated by Prof. O. W. Riegel, director.

The typographical and other printing trades unions, as well as the American Newspaper Guild, continued to press organization of Southern newspaper offices. Tom Tanner, Labor Commissioner, reported an increase of five typographical union contracts during the year, bringing the total to 145 cities. The pressmen had contracts in 68 cities, an increase of two; stereotypers, 38, an increase of one; mailers, 16, up three; and photo-engravers, up one, to a total of eight. The guild had lost two contracts during the year, due to the suspension of the Chattanooga News and the operating merger of the Memphis dailies. None of the 12 guild contracts called for the closed or "guild" shop. This union penetration of an area which had been relatively unorganized prior to 1933 had proceeded without measurable disturbance. The SNPA headquarters and labor advisers kept the membership informed on changing union policies, on wage and working conditions provided in existing agreements, and on statistical factors bearing on wage standards. It had noted in 1939-1940 increasing pressure from typographical unions for inclusion of paid vacations under contract agreements, and it advised members that the union as a rule would not currently press for this advantage. Pressmen were urging the inclusion of regulations covering the manning of color presses even upon newspapers which had no such machinery. The object of this move, the SNPA warned, was to establish contract provisions which could be used to union advantage in negotiations with publishers who offered color printing.

Through Fog of War

In the complex chess game of labor relations, the expert advice afforded publishers by the SNPA office proved invaluable. It created an atmosphere of mutual respect in negotiations, provided a balance for publishers without previous experience with union strategy, and constituted a major factor in keeping labor relations in the South on a generally even keel.[2]

The Dallas office, directed by Clarence W. Tabb, had been more than usually busy with wage negotiations, arbitrations, the Western Division Mechanical Conference and the Southwest Vocational School. Mr. Tabb reported that slight current improvement in business indices had been the signal for aggressive demands for wage increases.

Both the Eastern and Western Division Mechanical Conferences had flourished during 1939, several reports indicated. The novelty had not worn off for the mechanical departments executives, nearly 400 of whom had attended the meetings in Chattanooga and Dallas.

Financially, the Association ended the year in excellent shape, according to Treasurer James E. Chappell. The balance on hand was $9,240.68, after expenditures of $33,890.05, and despite the change in the secretary-manager's office with consequent expense at the year's beginning.

Secretary-Manager Johnson recalled his services in all offices of the Association and contrasted the SNPA of 1940 with that of 1924. Then, with a membership of 194, it had a budget of less than $9,000 a year; its present membership totalled 254, with an annual budget of $35,000. In 1924 the Association had a part-time manager and secretary; its current staff numbered eight full-time employees and two completely equipped offices, in addition to a competently manned labor department.

Twenty executives of member newspapers had died during 1939-1940, including Col. Urey Woodson, former publisher of the Owensboro (Ky.) Messenger and an honorary life-member of the SNPA. Only two of the six honorary life members now survived—F. L. Seely, of Grove Park Inn, Asheville, former publisher of the Atlanta Geor-

---

[2]The "protection fund" maintained by the SNPA for ten years against undue union aggression had been dissolved prior to the enactment of the Wagner Fair Labor Standards Act. The balance on hand was returned pro rata to the publishers who had contributed to it.

gian; and Marcellus E. Foster, editor emeritus of the Houston Press and former publisher of the Houston Chronicle.

During recent years, the Association had recognized that publishers of small city dailies had operating problems unlike those of the metropolitan press, and it had encouraged them to hold a group meeting prior to and separate from the main convention. The idea had worked out well and at several past conventions the reports of the small group meeting had been rendered to the whole convention by A. W. Huckle, publisher of the Rock Hill (S. C.) Herald. At the 1940 convention, the nominating committee put Mr. Huckle forward as SNPA president, and he was unanimously elected. No other publisher from a small city had been so honored. (Rock Hill had a 1940 population of about 15,000, and the Herald's circulation was below 10,000). Adolph Shelby Ochs became chairman of the board, James E. Chappell returned as treasurer, and Walter Johnson as secretary-manager. Small city publishers received representation on the new directorate, too. It comprised:

Alabama—Harry M. Ayers, Anniston Star; Arkansas—K. A. Engel, Little Rock Democrat; Florida—James L. Knight, Miami Herald; Georgia—George C. Biggers, Atlanta Journal; Kentucky—Barry Bingham, Louisville Courier-Journal and Times; Louisiana—Charles P. Manship, Baton Rouge State Times and Advocate; Mississippi—L. P. Cashman, Vicksburg Post; North Carolina—Talbot Patrick, Goldsboro News-Argus; Oklahoma—Harrington Wimberly, Altus Times-Democrat; South Carolina—J. M. Blalock, Columbia State; Tennessee—Enoch Brown, Jr., Memphis Commercial Appeal; Texas—Mrs. Oveta Culp Hobby, Houston Post; Virginia—Raymond B. Bottom, Newport News Press and Times-Herald; West Virginia—Walker Long, Huntington Advertiser and Herald-Dispatch.

Following adjournment the convention-goers were guests of Amon G. Carter, publisher of the Fort Worth Star-Telegram, at a rodeo on his Shady Oak Farm near Fort Worth—a thoroughly Texan touch for the first meeting in the Lone Star State.

If the publishers had been able to maintain relative serenity in the face of 1940's alarming events, they had cast it off completely before the SNPA met again in Edgewater Park, Miss., on May 19-21, 1941. In the months between, President Roosevelt had won a third term, opposed by the majority of newspapers, with some once-staunchly

Democratic leaders of the South among them. He had also negotiated the acquisition of numerous offshore bases from Great Britain, as part of a transaction by which the hard-pressed British received 50 old naval vessels. He had recently pushed through Congress the Lend-Lease Act, and many of the newspaper people knew that he had arranged convoy by the American navy for goods en route to Britain.

Early in 1941, Secretary of the Navy Knox had called a meeting in Washington of leading editorial executives and made a bid for informal voluntary censorship of news that might be of use to the Axis. And, in February, the ANPA had called representatives of the principal regional and state associations to New York to consider the function of newspapers in national defense. Before the convention adjourned, news arrived that an American cargo steamer had been torpedoed without warning in the South Atlantic. What remained of 1941 would be a crescendo of the din of war, culminating in the crashing tragedy of December 7—but the men and women meeting on the Gulf Coast in May knew that war was not far from America. Already the Selective Service Act had taken a young man from SNPA headquarters, had curtailed enrollment in the journalism and trade schools of particular concern to the SNPA, and was multiplying the calls from member newspapers on the Association for men to fill various positions.

The smoldering hostility between publishers and the New Deal flared dramatically at two of the 1941 sessions. Harold D. Jacobs, assistant administrator of the Wage and Hour Division, U. S. Department of Labor, lit the match. He was known to many of the members through his more than 30 years' association with the United Press and he had been placed on the program to explain some administrative phases of the Wagner Act.

The ANPA, through its Washington attorney, Elisha Hanson, had contended that the act should not apply to newspapers on the ground that newspaper publication did not constitute interstate commerce. Alleging that Mr. Hanson had advised publishers not to furnish to the Wage and Hour Division payroll records that the law prescribed, Mr. Jacobs ridiculed the attorney's case and truculently told the SNPA membership, "You can be sure of one thing: we are going to get your records."

He also mentioned specifically the Dallas News, which had recently won a decision on the law in the Federal District Court in Dallas, upholding the validity of its individual contracts with employes.

The speaker's belligerent attitude, more than his message, angered the publishers. Ted Dealey of the Dallas News, characterizing the speech as "in very poor taste," declared that Mr. Jacobs had misrepresented the decision of the Dallas judge; that the Dallas News had not only complied with the act, but paid minimum wages more than double those provided by the law. The News had initiated suit against the government, he said, after its normal operations had been disrupted for more than six months by repeated visitations of Wage & Hour Division representatives. The suit called for a declaratory judgment and interpretation of the law which "would tell us whether or not the method used by us in determining wages to be paid was correct." The government's retaliatory suit, he declared, had been punitive in intent, designed to harass the newspaper because of its opposition to New Deal policies.

With several publishers clamoring to be heard, President Huckle entertained a motion for adjournment until the next morning, when the matter could be thrashed out in detail. It was, with Mr. Dealey presenting documentary proof that Mr. Jacobs had not correctly stated the case the previous afternoon. He and Mr. Jacobs exchanged kindly remarks, attesting their long and friendly acquaintance, and Mr. Jacobs disclaimed any intent of deliberate misrepresentation.

This incident was unique in SNPA proceedings. Among themselves, publishers often expressed conflicting views with frankness and emphasis. Never before had a guest speaker been rebuked for "poor taste" or called to account for misstatement. A few guest speakers at recent conventions (generally editors of member papers) had handed the publishers forthright criticism of the industry's policies, without kindling resentment. Publishers had no stomach, however, for a very junior official brandishing Federal power as a threat.

Future generations may find it hard to conceive of the confusion and ill-feeling that came in the trail of the wage and hour legislation. Officially, the ANPA contested both its constitutionality and its application to newspapers. In daily practice, the vast majority of newspapers sought no exemption or special privilege under the law's provisions. SNPA records include many inquiries from publishers for definition of the act's application to a particular condition. They also reveal that the extremely few complaints laid against SNPA members by labor administrators were settled by informal conference and without court action. The fact that they were doing their best to comply with the law and that its minimum wage provisions directly concerned few newspaper employes, made publishers especially resentful of charges of intended evasion.

Numerous publishers were concerned with the broad question of the newspaper's status in interstate commerce. It was not raised in the Dallas News case (which was shortly afterward decided in favor of the News). While the question had never been presented directly to the United States Supreme Court, a mass of analogous decisions seemed to indicate that newspaper publication did not constitute interstate commerce. The Federal Trade Commission case against the SNPA and other groups of the previous decade had been dropped for lack of jurisdiction—but that antedated the jurisprudence of the New Deal. If newspapers were held to be interstate commerce, publishers feared (with reason) that Federal agencies hostile to the press would find new opportunities for persecution, cloaked as investigation. The weight of court decisions during the 1940's tipped the scales against the old legal view—newspapers are now considered as interstate commerce, with consequences that have not all yet been tallied.

Though the general tenor of Southern newspaper labor relations remained untroubled, the Labor Commissioner had the unusual, until then, experience in 1941 reporting five strikes. Three were settled within 24 hours. One, called by the newspaper guild in Monroe, La., ran for eight months. In Raleigh, N. C., where the Times' composing room force struck after fruitless contract negotiations, the paper continued to operate as an open shop. The trend of wages was upward, despite a continued lag in newspaper advertising revenues.

The Association's advertising committee, now under the leadership of Harry Bradley, Birmingham News and Age-Herald, pursued its task of finding why the advertising dollar continued to elude newspapers. Their year's survey of circulations and advertising rates of SNPA members had revealed conditions gruesomely familiar to all space-buyers—no discernible relationship between a newspaper's circulation and its basic advertising rates. The committee reported a hunch, short of a definite conclusion, that this had something to do with the absence of national advertising from newspapers.

The committee also drew on a survey by the Milwaukee Journal, with more comforting results. The Journal, which owned one of the country's most prosperous radio stations, blamed radio for little of its loss in national advertising—more than 2,750,000 lines, or 51 per cent, between 1929 and 1940. More than 1,000,000 lines of the 1929 volume had come from advertisers who had gone out of business. More than half a million lines represented firms no longer active in the Milwaukee market. Nearly a quarter million lines had been transferred to local placement. The paper's own stricter regulation of medical copy had ruled out 150,000 lines. Many of the firms which had disappeared during the depression were automotive and radio advertisers, users of large space. The Milwaukee Journal had long been recognized as both progressive and aggressive in its promotion, and its executives were among the national leaders in efforts to regain newspaper leadership. Mr. Bradley's committee believed that the conditions the Journal had found would be duplicated in the South's large cities, and advised the membership to concentrate on developing new business.

George Biggers told the convention of a new campaign originated by the National Publishers Committee, then appearing in 318 newspapers with copy prepared by the J. Walter Thompson Advertising Agency. Its objectives, as stated by Mr. Biggers, were:

1. To see that every American citizen understands that his political and social freedom depends upon the service rendered to him by his free and uncontrolled newspaper.

2. To point out that in a nation where the individual citizen has the "consumer's right of choice" (the right to spend his money how, when and where he wishes), economic information is just as important as social and political information; hence that newspaper advertising renders a vital service.

3. To show advertisers, by example, the proper use of copy and white space, stressing the importance of continuity in making any message register.

That was a definite start in the right direction. Another step taken during the previous year had been the institution of National Newspaper Week, which had been strongly supported by SNPA headquarters. In these efforts, the newspapers individually and as a national entity, counter-attacked with increasing effectiveness the campaign of criticism and ridicule which had been directed against them since 1933.

Stiffening backbone was also evidenced in the statement of the national, regional and state associations after the New York meeting of February 4, 1941. This was presented by President Huckle and the two directors who had represented the SNPA at the meeting, Enoch Brown, Jr., and George Biggers. It declared:

1. That the newspapers recognize their primary obligation to further national defense in every possible manner.

2. That the newspapers also recognize their essential duty to furnish complete and accurate information compatible with military necessities.

3. That the newspapers in the performance of these obligations bespeak the cordial consideration and co-operation of Federal and State authorities concerned with national defense.

In those three paragraphs stood the newspapers' response to Administration pressure for a voluntary quasi-censorship of news bearing on the national defense. Col. Frank Knox, Secretary of the Navy, (and as a civilian, publisher of the Chicago Daily News), spearheaded the Administration's effort for discreet handling of "war" news. As a lifelong newspaper man, he abhorred the notion of censorship; as the executive charged with preparing the Navy for whatever might happen in a perilous world, he realized the dangers of giving potential enemies full information on American defense measures. Before the SNPA met in 1941, he had called to his side former President James G. Stahlman of the SNPA, who had long held a reserve Navy commission as Lieutenant-Commander. The energetic "Jimmy" was then on active duty in Washington, and would remain in the Navy until the war ended, with the four stripes of a Captain on his sleeve. In 1941, however, he was helping Secretary Knox convince their fellow journalists of the current urgency.

The task wasn't easy. Even with Colonel Knox and Commander Stahlman as spokesmen, the Administration faced the difficulty of convincing the press that its move rested on good faith without ulterior objectives. As individuals, most of those at the New York meeting would probably have agreed with the proposition that news of value to the Axis powers should not be published. Representing their several organizations, they had to maintain the right and duty of the press to inform the public "completely and accurately." Even the appearance of waiving any part of that task must be avoided. So the second paragraph stated the newspapers' "essential duty," to be performed "compatible with military necessities."

That formula was acceptable to all concerned. It came into play when President Roosevelt met Prime Minister Churchill at Argentia, Newfoundland, in August. It guarded news of ship movements in the convoys of Lend-Lease to Britain, and, after June, 1941, to Russia via Murmansk.

After the attack on Pearl Harbor, of course, the censorship became official, though still voluntary in theory. Under both varieties of censorship, the press kept faith, often in heartbreaking circumstances. Early in 1942, for illustration, newspapermen in Southeastern coastal cities saw the horizon ablaze on many nights with the wreckage of ships torpedoed by the U-boats within sight of shore. Their readers knew what was going on, and occasionally criticized the newspapers for suppressing information. Despite frequent grumbles, the news was not published—the Germans got no comfort and no confirmation of the havoc they wrought from the press.

With censorship already evident and war probably not far off, the concern of the publishers for press freedom is understandable. It received another expression from the SNPA when J. N. Heiskell, chairman of the editorial affairs committee, signalized Victor H. Hanson's 40th year as a member presenting him with a bronze plaque engraved:

"Congress shall make no law respecting the establishment of religion, or prohibiting the free exercise thereof; or the abridging of the freedom of speech or the press—United States Constitution."

Experiences under British wartime censorship were related by Arnold Vas Dias, managing editor of the Netherlands Indies News

Agency, Aneta, which had been established in New York after the Nazi invasion of Holland. Mr. Vas Dias had been a London correspondent of De Telegraaf of Amsterdam for 14 years and came to New York to re-establish the news contact with the Netherlands East Indies that had been severed by the German occupation of the homeland. He likened his plight to that of the Memphis Appeal during the War Between the States—fleeing before the advance of a hostile army but keeping alive in city after city. In London, Mr. Vas Dias, as secretary of the Foreign Press Association, had a part in British pre-war conferences on possible censorship. He saw marked similarity in the stages then being passed by the American press with what had happened in London. He believed, however, that the United States had avoided one British error by placing Army and Navy "public relations" (the pre-war euphemism for censorship) under high-ranking officers who could deal as equals with area commanders. He had few faults to find with the British censorship after it had worked out its initial kinks.

Capt. J. Noel Macy, of Westchester Newspapers (Westchester County, N. Y.) had been a familiar guest at SNPA meetings as a director of the Audit Bureau of Circulations. In 1941 he attended as a representative of the War Department Bureau of Public Relations and informed his old friends of what was being done to furnish the press with news of the camps in which several hundred thousand men were receiving military training. The Navy also had a former journalist present in uniform—Lieut. Tyrrell Krum, public relations officer of the 8th Naval District at New Orleans. He asked newspaper support for the Navy's emergency enlistment plan.

But amid all its concern for the immediate future, the SNPA didn't abandon its habit of a long look ahead. Its novel form in 1941 was a symposium on "The Newspaper of the Future," conducted by Dave Vandivier, of the Chickasha (Okla.) Express, with Clark Howell, Atlanta Constitution; C. B. Short, Roanoke Times and World-News; Carl Jones, Jr., Johnson City Press-Chronicle; Jack Langhorne, Huntsville Times, and Ralph Nicholson, Tampa Times.

Most of the amateur seers agreed that newspapers of the coming age would be smaller, better edited, higher-priced and able to hold their own against any kind of competition. Mr. Nicholson predicted higher costs and decreasing revenue, soaring taxes and "punitive legislation not even thought of today." Newspapers should give more thought to their public relations; "we need friends," he averred.

As will be noted shortly, that piece of advice struck home. Events of the next few years, however, made futile any prophetic efforts of 1941. The goals of industrial production for defense set by Mr. Roosevelt had seemed unrealistic in 1940; before 1945 they had been so far distanced that they could be recalled only with wonder that the demands of war had been so grievously under-estimated. To the realization of the nation's war needs and aspirations the South was to contribute on a scale that nobody visualized in 1941. To carry on its next year's work, before the veil was drawn from that future, the SNPA named these officers:

President—Charles P. Manship, Baton Rouge State Times & Advocate.

Chairman of the Board—A. W. Huckle, Rock Hill Herald.

Treasurer—James E. Chappell, Birmingham News and Age-Herald.

Secretary-Manager—Walter C. Johnson.

Board of Directors: Alabama—Harry M. Ayers, Anniston Star; Arkansas—K. A. Engel, Little Rock Democrat; Florida—James L. Knight, Miami Herald; Georgia—W. S. Morris, Augusta Chronicle; Kentucky—Fred B. Wachs, Lexington Herald-Leader; Louisiana—John F. Tims, Jr., New Orleans Times-Picayune; Mississippi—L. P. Cashman, Vicksburg Herald-Post; North Carolina—P. T. Hines, Greensboro News-Record; Oklahoma—Harrington Wimberley, Altus Times-Democrat; South Carolina—J. M. Blalock, Columbia State; Tennessee—E. B. Stahlman, Jr., Nashville Banner; Texas—Mrs. Oveta Culp Hobby, Houston Post; Virginia—C. B. Short, Roanoke Times and World-News; West Virginia—H. C. Ogden, Wheeling Intelligencer and News-Register.

More than 16 months elapsed before the Association gathered at Hot Springs, Ark., for its 40th annual meeting on September 28-30, 1942. For nine of those months the nation had been at war and there had been few occasions for cheering. The United States Navy had turned back a Japanese invasion of Australia in the Spring of 1942, after the Philippines and the Netherlands East Indies had been lost. The Navy had also inflicted heavy damage at Midway in June. The Marine foothold on Guadalcanal was still precarious in late September. In Europe the Germans were battering at Stalingrad and seemed to be moving with their accustomed success toward the oil fields of the Caucasus. General Rommel's Afrika Korps had rolled back the British from Libya in mid-summer and, for all that America knew in September, the Germans were flexing their muscles for the conquest of Egypt. Tokyo had been bombed in April by Lieut.-Col. Jimmy Doolittle's squadron, taking off from "Shangri-La." Many of the newspapermen at Hot Springs knew of tidings that had not yet been revealed to the public—grievous naval losses in the fight for the Solomon Islands that left the Navy with only one able-bodied carrier for many weeks. But not even the best-informed journalists knew that the tide was about to turn. Before another month passed, the Germans in Africa would be on the run. Within two months American and British would land successfully in Morocco and Algiers. Before the end of the year, the Japanese were to concede the loss of the Southern Solomons, and the Germans, a shattering defeat before Stalingrad.

The German submarines, which had inflicted a terrifying toll on shipping along the Atlantic Coast early in 1942, continued to light the horizon with stricken ships and provide news stories that remained unwritten—but dominance in that dread field was passing to the American and British navies.

In the nature of things, the publishers faced pressing war-born problems of their own. The first business transacted by the convention was a telegram to President Roosevelt, with Mr. Manship pledging the loyal support of the Association's 272 members in 14 Southern States toward winning the war. "Your leadership is an inspiration to your countrymen in their hour of greatest peril," the message concluded. Stephen Early, secretary to Mr. Roosevelt, replied in similarly felicitous vein.

Censorship of war news had been established under a voluntary code immediately after the outbreak of war, but as President Manship told the Association, the rights of the public and the press had been carefully safeguarded. Byron Price, former executive editor of the Associated Press, as director of the Office of Censorship, had called to his side men of top reputation for probity and ability in the newspaper field. President Manship himself had assisted Mr.

Price's office and other Federal agencies concerned with news in arriving at sound press relationships. At his instance, each of the Southern States had been represented by an SNPA delegate at a "school" designed to inform newspapers of censorship principles and operations. Despite occasional complaints, the censorship worked well; it suppressed news that would have aided the enemy; it frequently delayed reports of naval losses for the same reason, but the public got the facts without undue delay.

President Manship assured the SNPA that "there can be, there will be, no regimentation of the press, so long as each newspaper in its home community keeps to its place of unselfish leadership for public welfare, and thinks straight and clearly on the great issues that confront us and involve our national life."

The impact of war on industry had caused a continued decline in newspaper advertising, even though many firms with war contracts for their entire output kept their names before the public by "institutional" or public relations advertising. More would do so as the war progressed, with practical encouragement by newspaper associations. The drop in advertising volume was not wholly unwelcome. The War Production Board was already limiting the use of newsprint, and newspapers used their allotments to meet the seemingly insatiable demand of the public for information. Circulations rose throughout the war. Employment and wage levels had not yet been "frozen" in September, 1942, and the newspaper unions continued to push for higher pay. Losses of staff members to the Armed Services had been heavy, but as yet were causing newspapers relatively small inconvenience, due to the publication of smaller papers. The nation's experience with war's demands was still young in 1942.

One situation, however, confronted an SNPA adjunct with immediate danger. E. L. Kurth, president of Southland Paper Mills, Inc., told the convention that the mill at Herty, Tex., might have to close because it could not complete its chemical pulp plant. The mill had been obtaining sulphate pulp from a Houston manufacturer since its establishment in 1940. That source would not be available after January 1, 1943, and the Southland mill had its own chemical pulp plant under construction. This $3,000,000 unit was 89.2 per cent complete, lacking only 140 tons of steel and about $12,000 worth of other commodities. Priorities for these, granted in December, 1941 had expired in June, and their renewal was blocked, the convention was told, by "two War Production Board officials from Northern States." On the urging of John D. Ewing, Shreveport Times, the convention adopted a resolution requesting the War Production Board to grant the necessary priorities. Although the record of the Association does not reveal how it was accomplished, the new chemical pulp unit went into action on schedule. The Southland mill continued to flourish.

When Ralph Nicholson (publisher of the New Orleans Item) advocated a public relations program for newspapers at the 1941 convention, he created a task for a new committee, headed by himself and including several of the strongest members of the Association. This committee rendered no *pro forma* report of "progress." Its program had already gotten under way, aimed at refuting the attacks on newspapers emanating from Washington. The advent of war put an end to that political sniping; newspapers had become an agency to be cherished and praised by the Administration. And Southern newspapers told Mr. Nicholson's committee how they had thrown their resources into forwarding the nation to eventual victory. Newspaperboys were selling war bonds and stamps, and, up to convention time, had produced $44,000,000 from that effort. Newspapers had been the spearhead of the War Production Board's campaign for the collection of scrap metal, rubber, and other scarce and vital materials. Newspaper were publishing, free, display advertisements sponsored by numerous Federal agencies. Under the leadership of Col. Harry M. Ayers, of the Anniston Star, SNPA newspapers were taking full advantage of National Newspaper Week as a promotion opportunity. Mr. Nicholson reported "we have made only a fair start. We haven't solved any problems."

That modest appraisal did not take note of the fact that the SNPA was ready for the turn of the tide in official and public evaluation of newspaper services. Newspapers had instinctively exercised their undiminished power of influencing public action, and the SNPA committee had stimulated them to new, concrete, and timely activity.

Public relations held the convention floor in other aspects. James Wright Brown, Jr., representing *Editor & Publisher*, asked the support and endorsement of the Association for the Memorial to John

Peter Zenger, who had established the free press concept on American soil. The project already had the approval of the ANPA and several other newspaper organizations.

Several naval officers engaged in public relations were introduced by Lieut. Commander Peyton Anderson, president of the Macon (Ga.) Telegraph and News. The Navy also supplied an off-the-record talk by Rear Admiral William Glassford, commandant of the Sixth Naval District, who had commanded the U. S. Naval task forces in the tragically heroic defense of the East Indies the previous winter. Talbot Patrick, former publisher of the Goldsboro (N. C.) News-Argus, described his current activity with the Office of War Information. George W. Healy, Jr., managing editor of the New Orleans Times-Picayune and chairman of the editorial affairs committee, was kept from attending the convention by OWI duties. Clark Howell, publisher of the Atlanta Constitution, had donned the star of a brigadier general in the Army, and upon his resignation as a director of the Associated Press, the SNPA put forward the name of James E. Chappell, editor and general manager of the Birmingham News and Age-Herald, to succeed him on the AP board.

War conditions at home and abroad furnished the topics for several other speakers. Byron Price explained and defended war news censorship, told the members why certain news could not be published, and quoted one newspaperman's verdict as a worthy rule for all newspapers: "There isn't any story in the world that is good enough to justify risking the life of a single American soldier."

Graham Hutton, director of the British Press Service, at Chicago, entertained the meeting with humorous tales of British journalism under the "blitz" of previous years, and of the difficulties of producing newspapers on an allotment of 15 per cent of prewar newsprint tonnage, and that at $140 per ton, with little or no consumer goods available for advertising, with taxes taking 100 per cent of all profits over the 1938 level, with little gasoline or rubber for trucks, with plants either wrecked or in nightly danger of destruction. The papers made money, the public got the news, the government took gigantic tax rceipts—everybody was happy, Mr. Hutton opined, except the advertising manager.

No such curtailment program faced American newspapers at any time during the war, but some trimming of sail was inevitable. Already the SNPA had called off its Mechanical Conferences for the duration of the war. Despite tremendous travel difficulties, the Association would hold its 1943 convention, but abandon those of 1944 and 1945. The annual golf tournament, a feature of SNPA conventions for more than a quarter century, went by the board in 1942 and was not resumed until after the war's end.

Membership totals also suffered briefly from tightened newspaper budgets during 1942, the ranks declining from 268 to 255, according to Secretary-Manager Johnson's report. That trend reversed itself shortly, with the pressure of new Washington regulations and new operating problems making SNPA service a necessity for many newspapers.

The 1942 necrology roll named 12 deceased members, including the two honorary life members who survived from the list of six—F. L. Seely, Sr., of Asheville, N. C., and Marcellus E. Foster, of Houston, Texas.

President Manship, Chairman Huckle, Treasurer Chappell, and Secretary-Manager Johnson were all returned to office. They had in hand many matters the immediate future course of which could not be safely predicted, and the Association wished no midstream swap of leaders. The new board comprised:

Alabama—Jack Langhorne, Huntsville Times; Arkansas—K. A. Engel, Little Rock Democrat; Florida—James L. Knight, Miami Herald; Georgia—W. S. Morris, Augusta Chronicle; Kentucky—Fred B. Wachs, Lexington Herald-Leader; Louisiana—John F. Tims, Jr., New Orleans Times-Picayune; Mississippi—L. P. Cashman, Vicksburg Herald-Post; North Carolina—P. T. Hines, Greensboro News-Record; Oklahoma—Harrington Wimberly, Altus Times-Democrat; South Carolina—J. M. Blalock, Columbia State; Tennessee—E. B. Stahlman, Jr., Nashville Banner; Texas—E. C. Davis, Beaumont Enterprise and Journal; Virginia—Carl B. Short, Roanoke Times and World-News; West Virginia—Robert L. Smith, Charleston Gazette.

Uncle Sam had provided temporary answers to some newspaper problems—and created others—by the third quarter of 1943, when the SNPA convened again at Hot Springs, Ark., September 27-29. The year had demanded an enormous amount of travel and conference by Association officers and kept several new committees busy, in the adjustment of newspaper operations to new government rules. The war news brought sorrow to many families, but it also rang with the cheering notes of eventual victory.

Island by island, the Japanese hold on all of the Solomon Islands and the Southwest Pacific was being pried loose by General MacArthur's forces and a Navy which had recovered its striking power. North Africa and Sicily had been conquered and Allied troops had begun their long and bloody advance up the Italian boot. The German submarines had been driven from the Atlantic Coast and were being harried in mid-ocean by new "killer" forces. Hitler's Wehrmacht, its bright dreams of victory vanished, was falling back on Russia's desolate plains in the face of hosts that no amount of killing seemed to diminish.

On the home front, newspapers had to contend with a genuine shortage of newsprint. The Canadian forests in 1943 had become almost the only source of white paper for the civilized Western world. Canadian paper kept Britons informed on a pittance of the tonnage they had once received from Scandinavia and Finland; it supplied South American dailies which had once looked to Europe for cheap newsprint. The Dominion government and the paper-making provinces expressed alarm at the tremendous drain on their forest resources and told their good American customers frankly that paper had to be rationed. Prices went up, too, by agreement between the newly constituted Publishing and Printing Division of the War Production Board and Canadian government agencies acting for the paper makers.

The new War Labor Board had a speaker at the 1943 SNPA meeting. He expressed satisfaction with the wage rates paid to newspaper mechanical department employees. Under Federal rule, wage rates and employment conditions were practically stabilized for the duration of the war. All newspapers were affected, of course, by the inexorable call of the Armed Services for their young men and women. Smaller newspapers were especially hard hit by the shortage of manpower, due both to the draft and the loss of men to higher-paid war-product enterprises. At least two SNPA dailies had reverted to weekly publication for these reasons in 1943. But, as predicted in the previous year's convention, the services rendered by the Association proved so indispensable to newspapers that the membership total climbed from 255 to 302—passing the 300 mark for the first time.

President Charles P. Manship, concluding an administration covering 28 months—the longest tenure of any SNPA president, brought about by the change in convention dates in 1942 and 1943—had made more than 20 trips to New York and Washington on matters requiring Association attention.

Secretary-Manager Johnson's headquarters put out an unprecedented number of printed and mimeographed bulletins on current matters in addition to its normal routine.

Most of the 40 previous conventions had devoted the greater part of their time to reports of the past year's work and corollary discussion of shop affairs. It was normal for the bulk of the Association's work to carry on through 52 weeks of the year, subject to policies formulated by the annual convention and by the directors' periodic meetings. In 1943, however, most of the convention hours were filled with talks, off the record, by military spokesmen and by former newspaper people engaged in various government war agencies.

The only directive issued in 1943 was highly significant—"that this Association appoint a committee to promote the construction of additional newsprint mills throughout the Southern States to utilize our forest wealth in greater measure and to provide additional employment and an enlarged and dependable supply of essential paper."

Nobody knew when that goal could be attained. No one, indeed, could predict when practical planning could be undertaken. Newspaper executives, like the man in the street, nourished hopes of victory in the nation's world-wide conflict, but not even the military experts of 1943 could set approximate dates for V-E and V-J days. At the moment, American consumers grumbled at the rationing of meat, coffee, sugar, gasoline, the lack of new cars, new washing machines, radios and refrigerators. These minor hardships could not be banished until the war ended.

Southern publishers, however, recognized that the nation's paper supply must be increased as early as possible and that the South offered the most practical area for new development. Alaskan forests, still virgin so far as newsprint products were concerned, might be exploited later; the South, with its immense forest wealth and its geographical convenience to the nation's densest population, could best pick up the load which was already taxing Canadian resources.

Except for that resolution, the 1943 convention devoted itself principally to war-time topics, practically all off-the-record. Their nature can be adequately indicated from the convention program:

"Stabilizing Wages and Settling Disputes," Robert K. Burns, chairman Regional War Labor Board.

"Keeping the Public Informed on the War," Palmer Hoyt, director domestic division, Office of War Information. (Mr. Hoyt, Portland [Ore.] Oregonian executive, after the war became publisher of the Denver Post.)

"Army Public Relations," Major General Alvan C. Gillam, Jr., Commanding General Armored Forces, Fort Knox, Ky., and other officers.

"Newsprint," Matt G. Sullivan, assistant director Printing & Publishing Division War Production Board. (Mr. Sullivan was on leave as general circulation director of the Gennett Newspapers, Rochester, N. Y.)

"War Bond Advertising," Don U. Bridge, special consultant War Finance Division, Treasury Department. (Mr. Bridge had been advertising director of the New York Times before entering war-time service.)

"The Air Offensive Matures," Air Commodore D. L. Blackford, Air Attache, British Embassy.

"Your Navy—on the Battle Fronts and News Fronts," Lieut. Commander W. M. McCarthy, USNR.

"Covering the War Fronts," J. Norman Lodge, Associated Press correspondent, just returned from the Southwest Pacific.

On the record and of flattering topical interest to SNPA members were addresses by J. H. Sawyer, Jr., member of an important newspaper representative firm, and R. S. Tincher, New York Daily News. Their topic, "Newspapers Get Immediate Action," presented facts on the individual and joint achievements of newspapers in arousing mass public response to civilian war objectives. Several members also manifested interest in the "Continuing Studies of Daily Newspaper Advertising," which, initiated by the re-organized Bureau of

Advertising, ANPA, had given newspaper sales forces a new and valuable argument.

Also on the record was the public relations committee report by Ralph Nicholson. This young man had had a background of public relations work for General Motors and other large industrial corporations before becoming part owner of the Tampa Times. In 1941 he had acquired, with financial assistance from International Paper Company, control of the New Orleans Item. The combination of his publishing energy and the general improvement in newspaper advertising and the elimination of an unprofitable Sunday edition had bettered the Item's showing considerably. So his advice fell on attentive ears.

He told the members that there had been less talk about public relations and a great deal more action by newspapers during the past year.

"The war gave newspapers such tremendous opportunities for public service of a nature that could not be duplicated by any other agency, and newspapers took advantage of this opportunity to such an extent that the danger we faced a year or two ago no longer exists," he declared.

"We suggest the advisability of paying more and more attention to our employees," his report concluded. "We should have the best people in the United States getting out our papers, and they should be paid and treated accordingly. Newspapers on the whole are profitable. In my opinion, some employees have not shared to the full measure of their deserts in the profit created by their efforts, teamed with capital and management. These observations apply principally to the non-mechanical departments. More attention to relations with employees will result in better newspapers, that make a more favorable impression on the general public."

This concern with the welfare of non-unionized employees had been expressed repeatedly over the years by SNPA leaders. Pay standards for mechanical department employees had been noted before this convention as generally satisfactory to the War Labor Board. One publisher asked advice of the meeting on how he could proceed before the WLB to obtain an increase in pay for an employee which had been denied several times by the regional board. Mr. Nicholson's advice seemingly was pointed at a target beyond adequate salaries. His own company, he stated, was working out a pension plan. George Biggers stated that he had investigated such pension trusts and advised publishers that they could carry such a plan at lower cost within their organizations than under insurance company rates. A few metropolitan newspapers, notably the Washington Star, had had broad employee welfare plans, including pensions, in force for many years before World War II.

President Manship's "zeal, understanding and thoroughness" in his long administration were rewarded by presentation of a sterling silver punch bowl, ladle and a dozen cups. He became chairman of the board, succeeding Mr. Huckle, and Mr. Biggers took over the executive reins as president. James E. Chappell was re-elected treasurer, and Walter C. Johnson as secretary-manager. The new board included:

Alabama—Jack Langhorne, Huntsville Times; Arkansas—J. N. Heiskell, Little Rock Gazette; Florida—Jesse M. Elliott, Jacksonville Florida Times-Union; Georgia—H. H. Trotti, Atlanta Constitution; Kentucky—Lisle Baker, Jr., Louisville Courier-Journal and Times; Louisiana—John F. Tims, Jr., New Orleans Times-Picayune; Mississippi—L. P. Cashman, Vicksburg Herald-Post; North Carolina—Frank Daniels, Raleigh News and Observer; Oklahoma—E. K. Gaylord, Oklahoma City Oklahoman and Times; South Carolina—J. M. Blalock, Columbia State; Tennessee—E. B. Stahlman, Jr., Nashville Banner; Texas—E. C. Davis, Beaumont Enterprise and Journal; Virginia—Carl B. Short, Roanoke Times and World-News; West Virginia—Robert L. Smith, Charleston Gazette.

For the next three years the SNPA would have to function without an annual convention. Civilian travel was out of the question in 1944. The Navy no longer scraped along with one patched aircraft carrier; for the invasion of the Philippines in October, 1944, it massed 16 fast carriers and 18 light or escort carriers, each of them feeding daily tons of gasoline to their flocks of fighters and bombers. The Red Ball fleet that rolled supplies across France in the summer of 1944 burned gasoline and wore out tires faster than American industry at top speed could furnish replacements. There was little gasoline and no new rubber for civilian use. There was no room on the railroads for convention-goers. Victory over Japan in 1945 came too late in the year for convention arrangements, even had travel restrictions been removed.

The newspaper business as a whole continued to improve its prestige and its financial picture during the war, despite the shortage of articles advertisable to the consumer market. Old problems persisted and new ones arose, mainly concerned with the short supply of newsprint and the difficulties some newspapers had in obtaining a sufficient number of employees. Women moved into many newspaper jobs once considered sacrosanct to males, in all departments. Like their British colleagues, American publishers learned to operate profitably under newsprint restrictions and most newspapers, in fact, earned profits during 1944 and 1945.

The Continuing Studies of Newspaper Reading proceeded under the authority of the Bureau of Advertising, ANPA and under the direction of the new Advertising Research Foundation, a creation of the American Association of Advertising Agencies and the Association of National Advertisers. This unbiased presentation of the newspaper as it appeared to its readers had already influenced profoundly the attitude of large advertisers and their agencies. To a great extent it had helped to break down the indifference with which newspaper advertising had been regarded in 1940.

Through Secretary-Manager Johnson's office and committees named by President Biggers, the SNPA kept its fingers on all that concerned Southern newspapers. Its fight for many years in the interest of equitable freight rates for the South bore long-delayed fruit in an Interstate Commerce Committee decision in early 1945. The SNPA offered its members an analysis of this highly complex situation, with the judgment that though freight rates would generally be higher throughout the country, "the eventual uniformity should give the South equal opportunity."

The newsprint mill committee appointed by President Biggers went to work immediately and spaded away many preliminaries against the day when actual construction could be undertaken.

Throughout the war years, the SNPA conventions had been kept in intimate touch with the problems of educating young people for newspaper work. All journalism schools had offered "accelerated" courses during the war. Most of them had their troubles in filling classrooms, even with women. The American Council on Education for Journalism on which the SNPA was ably represented by Richard Powell Carter, Roanoke (Va.) Times-World Corporation, clearly foresaw that the end of hostilities would bring a great influx of students to journalism schools and departments and took early action to insure the maintenance of high teaching standards. The Council's full program would not be achieved before 1950, but the SNPA and other newspaper associations were working toward its formulation throughout the war years.

Neither did the war hinder the progress of the Southern Newspaper Library. This had been created in 1941, at the instance of Secretary-Manager Johnson, who contributed 100 books from his own shelves. The collection was (and is) housed in the magnificent Chattanooga Library Building, available not only for newspaper people everywhere but for historical research and the eyes of the general public. The Library Committee comprises the past presidents of the Association.

The Association itself maintained a healthy growth during the no-convention years. After the outbreak of war in 1939, the already discouraging state of business in America became worse for several months and some newspapers thought to even the gap between expense and income by saving association dues. Among them were some fairly prominent SNPA members, a fact remarked with some resentment at the succeeding conventions. By 1942, the essential value of SNPA help to publishers had become so widely evident that the membership passed the 300 mark. By 1945, it reached 325—a gain of 101 since 1939. The Association as of July 1, 1945, had the largest daily newspaper membership of any regional group. It included every metropolitan newspaper in the 14 Southern States and others with circulations as small as 4,000 daily. There were still about 80 dailies in the Southern States not in the membership; most of them so small that they might reasonably doubt the probability of getting their money's worth in service for their dues. Within the next five years, practically all of these joined the ranks, in addition to the new enterprises brought into daily publication by the South's industrial expansion.

President Biggers asked to be relieved as president in 1945, and the Association by a mail vote named Carl B. Short, Roanoke Times and World-News. He had been serving as a director and as chairman of the newsprint mills committee when he took office on October 1. Mr. Biggers became chairman of the board. Mr. Chappell continued as treasurer and Mr. Johnson as secretary-manager. The board of directors, largely reconstituted, comprised:

Alabama—R. F. Hudson, Montgomery Advertiser and Alabama Journal; Arkansas—Donald W. Reynolds, Forth Smith Southwest Times-Record; Florida—Norvin S. Veal, Jacksonville Journal; Georgia—Carmage Walls, Macon Telegraph & News; Kentucky—B. F. Forgey, Ashland Independent; Louisiana—John F. Tims, Jr., New Orleans Times-Picayune; Mississippi — L. P. Cashman, Vicksburg Herald-Post; North Carolina—Frank Daniels, Raleigh News & Observer; Oklahoma—Tams Bixby, Jr., Muskogee Phoenix and Times-Democrat; South Carolina—Wilton E. Hall, Anderson Independent and Mail; Tennessee—E. B. Stahlman, Jr., Nashville Banner; Texas—Robert Matherne; Goose Creek Sun; Virginia—William C. Barnes, Martinsville Bulletin; West Virginia—Robert L. Smith, Charleston Gazette; Director-at-Large—Lisle Baker, Jr., Louisville Courier-Journal and Times.

The committee on revision of by-laws presented its report to the Board of Directors on May 28-29, 1945, at the same time that the above slate of the nominating committee was offered. Both reports went to the membership by mail. The by-laws committee proposed an amendment providing for the election of directors in three groups —five each for one-year, two-year, and three-year terms. In order to provide the 15th director (the Association includes 14 states), the amendment called for election of a director-at-large. Lisle Baker had won his nomination and election to the board by outstanding services as chairman of the important committees on business affairs and newsprint-traffic.

President Short died June 14, 1946 and Chairman of the Board Biggers filled out his term as president. Mr. Biggers' report of the three-year interim since the 1943 meeting broadly charted the course ahead—a course that would lead the SNPA into new paths of service to Southern journalism and Southern living.

Economic Renaissance In The South - I

SNPA Seeks Permanence and Expansion of South's Industrial and Social Advances During World War II—Plans Second, then Third, Newsprint Mill and Aggressive Program of Forest Conservation—Calls Publishers to Strengthen Editorial Staffs and Services to Meet Region's New Opportunities.

MANY old SNPA names were missing when the roll was called at the 1946 convention at Edgewater Park, Miss., September 30-October 2. And since this Association had always been one of men and women, rather than of business organizations, the war-time toll of the Grim Reaper received reverent and sympathetic attention at the first post-war reunion. That toll had been grievous, indeed.

President Carl Short had died, literally on duty for the Association. He had responded to a call to Washington against medical advice and knowing that he had a dangerous heart ailment. His end came during the Washington conference on newsprint, on June 14, 1946. Among other honored leaders for whom the SNPA mourned were Past Presidents Victor H. Hanson, W. T. Anderson, and Alfred F. Sanford. There were names of 46 publisher and editor members on the 1946 necrology list, in addition to 104 relatives of members or employees of member newspapers who had lost their lives in the Armed Services. To their memory a tribute was written by Fred Sullens, editor of the Jackson (Miss) Daily News, a master of English prose either in political invective or in graceful and beautifully cadenced sentences to honor departed loved ones.

But however great the concern for the dead, the times summoned the living to new and formidable undertakings. First on the list was the newsprint mill project to which the 1943 convention had committed the Association. Past President Short had headed the 1943 committee and served until his election to the presidency, when the chair was taken by Clarence B. Hanson, Jr., publishers of the Birmingham (Ala.) News and nephew of Victor H. Hanson. Worthily did he carry forward the project that his dynamic uncle had sponsored 12 years earlier. The elder Hanson's death had also caused a vacancy on the newsprint mills committee, which with C. B. Hanson, Jr., as chairman, was constituted as follows:

John F. Tims, Jr., New Orleans Times-Picayune; Charles P. Manship, Baton Rouge State Times and Advocate; James L. Knight, Miami Herald; Ted Dealey, Dallas News; E. K. Gaylord, Oklahoma City Oklahoman and Times; Frank Daniels, Raleigh News and Observer; John D. Wise, Richmond Times-Dispatch and News-Leader; and James G. Stahlman, Nashville Banner.

The committee set itself three tasks: finding an appropriate site for the mill; interesting capital in the project; assuring a market for the mill's product.

Since the Southland Paper Mills at Lufkin, Texas, already served the Southwest, it was determined that the second mill should be located East of the Mississippi, and an appropriate site had been located. It was an ordnance plant at Childersburg, Ala., 35 miles Southwest of Birmingham, and prominent Alabama business people had been investigating its peacetime use since 1944. Surveys indicated that the facilities were best adapted to newsprint manufacture, with power, water, transportation, timberlands and a ready market near at hand.

The committee then met with Donald Comer, chairman of Avondale Mills, and Thomas W. Martin, president of the Alabama Power Company, leaders in the group which had been planning the ordnance plant's future. Both men, it will be recalled, had been prominent in the 1934 meeting at Birmingham, at which a newsprint mill for Alabama had been advocated. Mr. Comer told the SNPA committee that, if the Childersburg site was selected, and if he could have the exclusive co-operation of the Committee, he would undertake organization of company to finance, build, and operate a mill of 100,000 tons annual capacity.

Several members of the 1946 committee had had enlightening experience a decade earlier in the effort to get the Southland Paper

Mills established. They had seen hopes raised high several times, only to be dashed by the last-minute reluctance of prospective investors. Here was a solid proposal, with no more than the reasonable minimum of "ifs." Take it up, now, without debate or delay!

Fortunately, the board of directors was then meeting in Atlanta. Chairman Hanson recommended acceptance of Mr. Comer's offer, and the board on January 27, 1946, adopted this resolution unanimously:

"Resolved, that the Newsprint Mills committee be and hereby is instructed to give its exclusive co-operation to the Comer interests until August 1, 1946, and discontinue any further negotiations with other parties interested in co-operating with the Southern Newspaper Publishers Association for the erection of a newsprint mill in the South."

That resolution, burning the SNPA bridges, called for prompt action. The committee and Mr. Comer succeeded in interesting Edward L. Norton, a prominent Alabama business and philanthropic leader, in the project. On March 18, 1946, the Coosa River Newsprint Company was incorporated in Alabama with Mr. Comer as chairman of the board, Mr. Norton as president, and Mr. Hanson as vice-president, with a strong board of Alabama industrialists and financiers. Under way in Washington were negotiations for the purchase of part and the lease of part of the Childersburg plant. Construction plans would be ready when the site was secured. Negotiations for the technical management of the newsprint mill had not yet reached a stage where discussion of them in public would be wise, Mr. Hanson reported.

Now, what about costs? The Southland Paper Mills had been planned as a $7,500,000 undertaking and an annual capacity of 50,000 tons, it was recalled. Prices had gone up considerably since 1938-1939, and this mill at Childersburg would have double Southland's initial capacity.

Could it be financed?

Mr. Hanson thought that it could. The mill would cost $18,000,000. It would be financed with a bond issue of 60 per cent of the total capital, callable preferred stock 16 per cent, and common stock 24 per cent. The directors of the Coosa River Newsprint Company had already bought $1,000,000 in common stock, raising all the money needed to the present. At Mr. Hanson's urgent instance, 25 per cent of the common stock would be made available for investment by SNPA members.

Mr. Hanson proceeded to remove any remaining "ifs" or doubts in the minds of his fellow publishers. This time there could be no delay of two or three years while the publishers decided whether to back their judgment by their own funds. The Coosa River mill would be built, beyond any doubt, he said. If the publishers invested in 25 per cent of its common stock it would make newsprint. If they didn't share in its financing and later in its control, maybe it would make newsprint—and maybe not. The present investors were the highest type of public-spirited men, but "they are engaged in private enterprise and expect to make a profit." If the publishers did not regard the venture well enough to invest in it, the financial group could find other associates who might not wish to make newsprint. Therefore, "publishers ownership up to at least 25 per cent has ceased to be merely desirable and has become starkly necessary."

The committee requested extension of its authority for exclusive co-operation with the Coosa River Newsprint Company for such time as might be deemed by the directors.

That laid it on the line for the membership. There was at this stage at least $1,080,000 available for publisher investment. E. K. Gaylord, who had had a major part in the financing of the Southland mill, proposed that five publishers tentatively pledge at once to take $100,000 each in common stock and declared that he would be one of the five. That massive bite required some digestion and the convention passed on to less weighty matters.

Chairman Hanson and his committee did not, as they had hoped, get the million and more in pledges for the new mill's common stock at this convention. They did get enough assurances of participation to warrant them in concluding the purchase and lease of the Childersburg plant and in agreeing with the Kimberly-Clark paper interests for the management of the Coosa River Mill.

Those arrangements took the better part of the ensuing year, with Uncle Sam and the publishers negotiating carefully for the transfer of the land and existing utilities. Before the SNPA met again, the cost and capitalization of the mill had been revised upward to $30,-000,000; Kimberly-Clark had taken 25 per cent of the common stock, and arrangements were in process to tie the publishers' 25 per cent of the common in with agreements for the purchase of tonnage. The entire product of the mill would be sold to Southern newspapers.

The paper supply problem, immediate and future, occupied much of this meeting's attention. Secretary-Manager Johnson had, as usual, kept a watchful eye on projected post-war developments in the South. Among them were numerous paper mills, for the manufacturers of other-than-newsprint paper were looking intelligently at the immense Southern forests when Dr. Herty was proving the practicability of newsprint from Southern woods. Numerous Kraft mills had been built in the Thirties. More were coming. Convinced that Southern forests were not, after all, unlimited as a base for industry, Mr. Johnson suggested that Chairman Biggers call the Association's attention to the situation and request appropriate action. Mr. Biggers' annual report put it up to the members in two terse paragraphs. He declared it "imperative that the present supply of raw material for a billion-dollar industry not only be maintained, but that the forests be made to grow more and more wood to meet the increasing demand."

"Every newspaper in the South, daily and weekly," he said, "should join in the economic preservation and utilization of our forest resources."

The resolutions committee headed by Josh L. Horne quoted almost the exact words of the chairman's report, declaring that "in view of the support of conservation and the tree-growing programs being conducted in the several States, the most effective backing is the encouragement of greater development of forest resources by our newspapers."

Adopting that resolution unanimously, the convention also declared:

"We wholeheartedly endorse the soil conservation district movement and urge members to (1) encourage farmers to form districts where districts have not been erected, (2) include soil conservation, as now carried on in these districts, in their community betterment programs, (3) give full support to the work of soil conservation districts, (4) encourage business, industry, and other urban groups to give even greater assistance in the conservation of our land resources, and (5) advocate the teaching of soil conservation in public schools."

That was the opening gun in the campaign which the Association and its individual members have conducted with intelligent persistence during most of the past decade. The Association had declared in 1943 "we dedicate our efforts to democracy in government and in the economic system, and we express our faith and confidence in the system of free enterprise as against socialized undertakings and collectivism."

A decade earlier, the SNPA had specifically provided that the mill eventually built at Herty, Tex., must be developed under private enterprise. Deeds marched with words, action with policy, in the philosophy of SNPA leaders. Committed to private enterprise and against socialized undertakings, the Association, by its campaign for the preservation and wise use of Southern woodlands, set itself in the way of assuring that its chosen way of life should survive and prosper. Southern private enterprise, by its own efforts, must guarantee that forest wealth would be preserved and used for regional and national good, not ruthlessly exploited and destroyed in a generation as it had been in other parts of America. Some benefits are already apparent. With Southern journalism alert to the whole question of conservation and reforestation, these benefits will be multiplied with the passing of human generations.

Much more immediate in the eyes of the 1946 meeting was the problem of adequate supply and reasonable prices for current newsprint needs. The war-time paper shortage, the close co-operation given Federal agencies by publishers, and the frequent contacts newspaper people temporarily in administrative posts had had with the Canadian newsprint manufacturers, all combined, had generated a new atmosphere in the paper market. Big consumers of newsprint, willingly or not, had pared their requirements so that all could have enough paper to keep going. United States publishers in the war years had learned to accept as credible fact the statements of the Canadian paper men that their wood-cutting crews had been depleted by war's demands, and that their mills were, necessarily, furnishing paper to consumers outside of North America. Publishers had even accepted, without undue protest, several war-time increases in price. And William G. Chandler, president of the American Newspaper Publishers Association, quoted Canadian reports at length to the SNPA convention to present the situation in all its grave aspects.

Only three paper machines were idle in all of Canada, Mr. Chandler reported. In July and August, 1946, the Canadian mills were operating at better than 99 per cent of their rated capacity. They were shipping to the United States 81 per cent of their 1946 production. Their product accounted for 78 per cent of United States newsprint consumption; United States mills (including the Southland plant) produced 17 per cent of United States needs, and the remaining five per cent came from other sources. The total tonnage available to United States publishers in 1946 would be only 1 per cent more than they had used in 1941, with circulations considerably increased and advertising in a boom rather than a depression. United States consumption, at current rates, was running so far ahead of potential supply that a prospective shortage of 150,000 tons was foreseen by the Canadians at the year's end.

On the other hand, Mr. Chandler went on to quote, Canada had possible overseas markets for its tonnage at prices far higher than those charged to United States publishers. Scandinavian producers were getting $175 per ton for shipments to South America. Russian and Scandinavian newsprint commanded as much as $300 per ton in China. Great Britain wanted, and had a just claim, to larger tonnage from Canada. So did Australia and the liberated countries of Asia and Europe. The Canadians defended as wholly justified their current price of $85 per ton, New York delivery. The Canadians also pointed out that they might follow the example of United States mills and shift from newsprint to more profitable products.

Turning from the Canadian argument to his own convictions, Mr. Chandler advocated the complete removal of price controls from the newsprint market. Unless the manufacturers were free to charge, and publishers to pay, an adequate price for newsprint, publishers could expect their supply for several years to come to be diminished by diversion to other markets. Canadian producers did not have to obey the rules of the Office of Price Administration, he pointed out; they could sell their product where they pleased, free from the political complications and delays of Federal government regulation. He urged the construction of more domestic mills, and concluded:

"The members of SNPA, a decade ago, showed the foresight and leadership needed in this direction and you are continuing to do it today. The newsprint situation today would indeed be acute throughout the United States but for the mill at Lufkin, Texas, which is a monument to your Association."

Discussion of the question consumed an entire morning session. After four years of government price and tonnage control, some publishers doubted the wisdom of removing these restraints on the paper market. They feared that the "little fellow" would be badly squeezed if metropolitan publishers went after all the tonnage in sight to meet the tremendous potential demand. Briefly, they feared another runaway market like that which followed World War I. Wiser counsel prevailed on this occasion. The SNPA membership considered the situation in all aspects and decided to concur with the ANPA in calling for the lifting of government control of newsprint, and to cooperate with the ANPA in that program.

The ensuing years bore out Mr. Chandler's prediction. Prices of newsprint rose steeply, to the level of $130 per ton for many localities—but the supply met the demand, which increased year after year. Without adding materially to existing plant, the Canadian mills greatly increased total production in the post-war years, while United States publishers, by analogous devices, found ways of getting more printed copies out of every ton of paper. And, as will be seen, the SNPA carried out its program of increasing domestic newsprint production, with the Coosa River mill entering the market in 1950, the Southland mill doubling its product, and the Bowaters Mill in East Tennessee coming to the line as this history is published.

If the publishers in 1946 seem to have acted with greater sagacity and foresight than those of a generation earlier, it must be remembered that the "economic climate" of 1946 differed greatly from that of 1916. Then the publishers had been in conflict for more than ten years with a domestic paper industry that had nearly exhausted its wood supply and was determined to maintain its price advantage by monopolistic price agreements. Neither party offered any basis for amicable agreement on common interests. And in 1916, there was no prospect of manufacturing newsprint from Southern wood.

During the depression, the Canadian newsprint industry passed many troubled years, with no market for a product that had been paced by a decade of booming prosperity in the United States. It was in this era that the SNPA, with strange prescience, planned and built the first Southern newsprint mill—to escape the dominance of Northern and Canadian paper-makers. The South's war-time experience proved salutary for the whole nation, as did that of the mill jointly financed by the New York Times and the Kimberly-Clark Corporation. By 1946, many publishers understood the paper-makers' problems; they also had a better grasp on world market conditions than the publishers after World War I. They accepted a condition that they could not change.

In the South, they also provided for changing it in a manner that would help the Southern press, indeed that of the entire nation, without harm to the interests of the Canadian paper industry. Outraged cries would continue to greet increases in the price of newsprint through the late Forties and early Fifties—but most publishers found the means of paying the price.

Among the means of paying higher paper prices, publishers in 1946 warily contemplated raising subscription carrier-delivered and street sale rates. The three-cent base had been standard for many years, with a scattering of two-cent and five-cent papers. With newsprint at $75 or $80 per ton, not many publishers felt warranted in risking a jump to four cents or five cents per copy. When paper prices reached $100 per ton, as they did shortly after, 1946, higher circulation rates became inevitable. On its own initiative, the SNPA circulation committee had already prepared for this step. Jack Estes, circulation manager of the Dallas News and a past president of the International Circulation Managers Association, reported as committee chairman that three sub-committees had been created, with these assignments:

1. Study of circulation rates and practices, which would give members a fund of information on the technique of raising prices without loss of readers.

2. A check on all State legislation and regulations affecting newspaper circulation operations.

3. An educational bureau, charged with the dissemination of news concerning carrier boy operations.

Economic Renaissance In The South — I

Higher advertising rates also received consideration. So did the question of uniform practice in billing national advertisers when the printed space was less than that ordered, due to shrinkage of matrices in stereotyping. This condition was to cause considerable acrimony between newspapers and advertising interests as publishers took full advantage of mat shrinkage as a paper-saving measure.

Another imperative reason for additional revenue lay in the labor situation, upon which Tom Tanner, Labor Commissioner, and C. W. Tabb, manager of the Dallas office, reported at length. War Labor Board rules had kept wages stable through most of the war period, but in many cities unions had sought and publishers had granted other conditions in lieu of higher wages. These included vacations, additional holidays at penalty rates, pay for holidays not worked, severance pay, sick leaves, and (eternal bugbear of publishers) extension of the "bogus" resetting of advertising mats and plates and other practices that employers denounced as "featherbedding." When wage restrictions were lifted at the end of the war, the unions were determined to hold on to their war-won advantages and get the higher pay indicated by the rising cost of living. Mr. Tabb summed up the situation thus:

"There seems little prospect of publishers successfully resisting further union gains until the present manpower shortage is alleviated or newspapers can obtain equipment which can be operated by workers of a lesser degree of skill and who may be trained in a relatively short period of time."

Only three strikes of notable importance had occurred in SNPA territory during the war. In Birmingham, the newspapers did not attempt to publish during a typographical union strike in July and August, 1945. The San Antonio newspapers had appeared daily using engraved typewritten matter as a substitute for printing over a seven-week period, in the summer and autumn of 1945. Later the same year the St. Petersburg newspapers used photo-engraving for several weeks, then went on an open shop basis with standard printing methods and Teletypesetter equipment. Suit had been filed against the St. Petersburg dailies by the typographical union before the National Labor Relations Board and was still pending.

Teletypesetter equipment was then in use by relatively few newspapers. It would become increasingly popular during the next few years and its development was to reach the point at which wire service copy could go directly from the service printing receivers to the line-casting machine keyboard, without the intervention of either an editor or a machine operator. Several such circuits were placed in operation after 1950 by the three major wire services. The typographical union, which became increasingly truculent in its demands in the late 1940's, resisted this innovation and sought, with some success, to bring Teletypesetter operations within its jurisdiction.

The manpower shortage remained acute in the early post-war years. The Southern School of Printing at Nashville had continued skeleton operation, largely with women students, throughout the war. The Southwest School of Printing at Dallas, also partly supported by the newspapers, had closed its doors for the duration in 1942. Both schools were booming as the SNPA met in 1946. The Nashville school operated in three shifts. The Dallas school solved the problem of new quarters by purchase of trailers, both for instruction rooms and living space.

Both schools were filled by veterans, extending their education under the "G. I. Bill of Rights"; both had difficulty in obtaining a sufficient staff of competent instructors, and both found it hard to keep students for the full course, so great was the demand of printers and publishers for even half-trained help.

Returned veterans also swamped the journalism departments of Southern colleges and universities. Washington & Lee University, which had struggled through the war with seven per cent of its normal enrollment, had maintained the cadre of its journalism department and, in 1946, was ready for the expansion that had been planned in pre-war days. Holt McPherson, of the Shelby (N. C.) Star, had succeeded the indefatigable Richard Powell Carter as chairman of the schools of journalism committee and offered a program for strict maintenance of standards, under supervision of the American Council for Education in Journalism.

As a corollary of its interest in education for newspaper work and of its pioneering in Southern newsprint production, it was natural that the SNPA should investigate the idea of research for better processes of newspaper-making. Chairman Biggers had commented in his report:

"Continued study and research in methods that contribute to successful newspaper operations are essential. We have noted with a degree of satisfaction and pleasure the announcement of the research program initiated by the Texas Newspaper Publishers Association and the appropriation of $30,000 to carry on this work. The ANPA has also become interested in research. There will be no attempt on the part of the SNPA to duplicate the efforts of these organizations. With few exceptions, all members of TNPA are members of SNPA and approximately 100 members of the ANPA are members of SNPA."

A somewhat vague discussion of this idea crystallized in the appointment of a committee to work out plans for an experimental laboratory and to consult other publishers' organizations, individual publishers, and manufacturers.

For the execution of its post-war program, the Association was stronger than at any time in its history. Between 1943 and 1946, the membership had grown from 302 to 360, and Secretary-Manager Johnson looked forward confidently to a roster of 400. Under the frugal management of Mr. Johnson and Treasurer Chappell, the Association had not only lived within its income, but had built up a reserve fund of $37,500. If the latter was still short of the goal of an entire year's expenses, it represented a substantial backlog for emergencies.

Election of new officers did not remove George Biggers from the slate. He reverted to his status as Chairman of the Board when the Association elected E. B. Stahlman, Jr., of the Nashville Banner, as president. James E. Chappell retained the treasury and Walter C. Johnson entered on another term as secretary-manager. In accordance with the amended by-laws only five new directors (all without previous service on the board) were elected as follows:

Charles P. Manship, Jr., Baton Rouge State Times and Advocate; T. M. Hederman, Jr., Jackson (Miss.) Clarion-Ledger; Charles C. Council, Durham (N. C.) Herald-Sun; Roy McDonald, Chattanooga News-Free Press; Charles Hodel, Beckley (W. Va.) Post-Herald and Raleigh Register.

Newsprint and labor, perennial staples of newspaper convention fare, provided a continuous diet throughout 1946 and 1947. As predicted when the publishers asked the lifting of government rules from the sale and distribution of newsprint, prices started their escalator journey. The mills in Canada and the United States turned out an unprecedented tonnage, but it wasn't quite enough for the needs of all. Small city publishers who had shifted from flat paper to rolls found it especially difficult to obtain contract tonnage. Spot market prices skyrocketed, and President E. B. Stahlman, Jr., addressed sharp words in his annual report to publishers who joined in the spot market scramble for paper at any price:

"The purchase of spot newsprint at a fantastic price is not conducive to stabilization of the newsprint price field," he declared. "I cannot help but feel that to continue this would be rendering a disservice to our industry and to our regular suppliers as well. We should not criticize the newsprint manufacturers for failing to meet requirements and for their, comparatively speaking, modest price increase, and in the same breath threaten to break down the entire newsprint price structure by encouraging the purchase of foreign and domestic newsprint at exorbitant prices."

These were not the only critical words in President Stahlman's report to the 45th anniversary convention (the 43rd meeting) of the SNPA at Hot Springs, Ark., September 15-17, 1947.

The whole field of labor relations had been rendered acutely sensitive by the passage of the Labor-Management Relations Act, better known as the Taft-Hartley law. On the national level, the International Typographical Union had laid down conditions which many publishers regarded as impossible of acceptance without violation of the new law. In the absence of judicial interpretation, publishers and labor experts alike were still uncertain of the law's effect upon newspaper operations. To the general subject, Mr. Stahlman spoke thus:

"Not all of the blame for labor troubles can be placed at the door of the unions, for publishers themselves have oftentimes been at fault. Most of the unions with which we deal are extremely proud of the relationship established long ago with the publishers of this nation. Some, whose leaders care little or nothing for the welfare of their individual members, and less about the business success of the publishers with whom they have contracts, will make it extremely difficult to maintain the friendly relationships that should exist. After all, we should be deeply concerned with the well-being and happiness of all our employees, and perhaps the passage of the new labor laws will bring our negotiations back to the local level where they belong."

On the record it is plain that the overwhelming majority of SNPA members did maintain friendly, or at least not hostile, relationships with their union employees. Despite the intransigence of the typographical union toward the Taft-Hartley law, strikes in the Southern territory were fewer in number and of shorter duration than those elsewhere in the country.

The convention heard of a strike against the Beaumont, Texas, newspapers by the typographical union, over the operation of Teletypesetter tape perforators. The papers were published by the photo-engraving process for several days until a new staff of printers could be assembled. Six weeks later, members of the pressmen's and stereotypers walked out as individuals and the papers were forced to suspend for a week. These men were ordered back by their international union presidents, but refused to resume work. Then Major George L. Berry, president of the pressmen, assembled union pressmen from other cities, and barred the illegal strikers from employment at their trade elsewhere. The regular crews returned after a week's idleness. Major Berry's course was commended by C. W. Tabb, manager of the SNPA Dallas office as demonstrating "a great degree of union integrity and responsibility."

Throughout the SNPA territory, union wage rates leaped upward. With the cost of living index 56 per cent above its level for January 1, 1941, hourly wage rates had increased, in some cities, as much as 90 per cent over the pre-war figure. That condition and the steadily upward trend of newsprint prices took most of the joy out of the phenomenal advertising gains that newspapers were recording. Postwar prosperity and the intelligent promotion that organized newspapers had done in recent years were bringing the daily press the highest income it had enjoyed in many years (it would soon pass the 1929 peak) but very few pennies of the new income dollar remained in the till at the year's end.

SNPA conventions, however, have never been notable for throngs at the "wailing wall." The 1947 meeting was no exception. The publishers did their bit of griping at high paper prices, and some of them accurately foresaw trouble ahead in labor relations, but they also had solidly constructive matters to discuss.

Secretary-Manager Johnson reported, for example, that his office had distributed during the year three important manuals for newspaper departments. The Association's advertising committee had prepared and published a practical work entitled, "Newspaper Advertising—How to Write It—Sell It." The editorial committee, in cooperation with the Roanoke Times and World-News, had compiled a "Correspondent's Guide Book." Copies were furnished at cost to members for distribution to their correspondents. And at the instance of the SNPA, the Southern Circulation Managers Association had written and published a "Carriers' Handbook" as a contribution to the welfare and business success of "young Americans who engage in the business of handling a newspaper route."

The Southern Newspaper Library was reported in flourishing condition, with more than 1,500 volumes on file. A catalog would be issued in 1947-1948, the library committee chairman, Past-President A. W. Huckle reported. A project suggested by Past President Charles P. Manship, who had died January 27, 1947, had been realized in the publication by headquarters of a revised roster of the executives of SNPA member newspapers.

Active membership showed a net gain of eight during the year, standing at 368 dailies. The year's expenses had totalled $64,894.92, against receipts of $71,281.84, and Treasurer James E. Chappell was retiring after ten years' continuous service in that office leaving a reserve fund of more than $45,000 on hand. By direction of the Board, headquarters office had acquired additional space, new equipment and additional personnel. Its efficient operation received special commendation in a convention resolution.

The Association's big project, the Coosa River Newsprint Mill, had progressed during the year. Several executives of the paper company and also of the Kimberly-Clark Corp., which had contracted to operate the new mill, were present to describe accomplishments and plans. Two years were to pass before this gigantic enterprise got rolling, but its creation was no longer attended by doubt.

Both of the printing schools, at Nashville and at Dallas, fostered by SNPA interest, continued to attract large enrollments during the year, the convention was told by M. M. Donosky of the Dallas News. Although some of the young people (mostly war veterans) had located with large daily newspapers, the majority had found quick employment with small dailies, weeklies, and job shops.

Journalism schools in the South, with their large post-war rolls, had no difficulty in placing their graduates, Chairman Holt McPherson reported. He asked the Association's continued co-operation with the American Council for Education in Journalism and also called upon newspapers for close relations with schools in their territories. The Washington & Lee School, according to Director O. W. Riegel, was regaining its pre-war momentum, adding to its teaching staff, and bringing an ever-larger number of notable speakers from the publishing field for its lecture programs.

Under the chairmanship of Talbot Patrick (back from the wars to publish the Rock Hill [S. C.] Herald), the committee on research had proposed to the directors that the SNPA undertake a research program covering three years at the cost of $50,000 annually. To that ambitious plan, the directors returned a courteous "no," but told the committee to see what else might be done. They even investigated what the British were working on, especially in the field of improved presswork, and returned a meaty report to the convention. After considerable discussion, the SNPA members decided that such a task ought to be on a national scale. The formal resolution read:

"Whereas, the Southern Newspaper Publishers Association recognizes the fundamental need for a long-range continuing program of research in the field of newspaper publishing to achieve better, quicker and more economical printing, and,

"Whereas, this need is of a national rather than a regional scope, and,

"Whereas, the American Newspaper Publishers Association has initiated a program for mechanical research in the newspaper field, the benefits of which will accrue to all newspapers, and,

"Whereas, this program is at present supported only by ANPA members; now

"Be it resolved, that the American Newspaper Publishers Association be requested to consider development of a long-range research program which may be supported by all newspapers."

A temperate but firm expression of opinion was adopted with respect to the Taft-Hartley Act. The resolution stated:

"Whereas, the Labor Management Relations Act has created the necessity for a readjustment in the relations between employees and employers, and,

"Whereas, it is the conviction of the members of the Southern Newspaper Publishers Association that this can be accomplished in the best interests of both employees and employers, and without impairments of the historic principle of collective bargaining, if both sides enter co-operatively into the spirit of this adjustment, and

"Whereas, it is the further conviction of the members of the SNPA that a prime requisite for industrial labor peace lies in respect for, and compliance with, the law; now

"Therefore, be it resolved, that it is the policy of the members of the SNPA here assembled, that no demands in violation of the provisions of the Labor-Management Relations Act shall be accepted, and that the members of the SNPA will take whatever action they deem necessary to discharge their obligations under the law."

Other resolutions expressed the Association's gratitude to George C. Biggers, Atlanta Journal, who was retiring after three years as president and as chairman of the board; and to James E. Chappell, Birmingham News and Age-Herald, who had asked to be relieved after ten years as treasurer.

Lisle Baker, Jr., Louisville Courier-Journal and Times, was unanimously elected president, with President E. B. Stahlman, Jr., moving into Mr. Biggers' well-warmed place as chairman of the board. Ralph Nicholson, New Orleans Item, succeeded Mr. Chappell as treasurer. Walter C. Johnson continued as secretary-manager. Five directors were elected for three year terms, as follows:

Arkansas—K. A. Engel, Little Rock Democrat; Florida—Charles T. Coffin, Miami News; Kentucky—Lawrence W. Hager, Owensboro Messenger-Inquirer; South Carolina—J. M. Blalock, Columbia State; Director-at-large—Mrs. Oveta Culp Hobby, Houston Post.

Statesmanship of a high order was demanded of the SNPA and its individual members in their labor relations during 1948 and subsequent years. That demand was met, more than adequately. There were strikes—a far larger number than in any comparable period in SNPA annals—but most SNPA members with union relationships maintained them without undue disturbance. The strikes resulted, almost invariably, from the determination of typographical unions to disregard the Taft-Hartley law and to substitute their own "conditions of employment" for the time-honored contract with employers. The majority of SNPA newspapers which had previously contracted with the typographical union continued operations without a contract, usually with higher wages and as much of the old working agreement as complied with the new law. Most local unions wanted peace, too.

That was the state of affairs reported to the 1948 convention, held in St. Petersburg, Fla. (the first SNPA gathering in that State) on November 8-10. Trouble was indicated when the International Typographical Union at its annual convention in August, 1947, adopted a policy of "no contracts" and of defiance both of the Taft-Hartley law and numerous state enactments forbidding the closed shop. Alone among the printing trade unions, the ITU decided to fight the new legislation which it lumped under the description of "slave labor" laws. As a substitute for contracts, it proposed that its members work under union-written conditions of employment which were to be posted in the composing room and which employers were to accept without negotiation. Some of the proposed conditions of employment would have woven into newspaper labor relations several points which had been contested for many years—for example, the "bogus" resetting of advertising received by publishers in plate and matrix form, and compulsory union membership of composing room foremen.

The American Newspaper Publishers Association filed charges against the ITU with the National Labor Relations Board, and the SNPA intervened in this action on behalf of its members, filing broad charges against the ITU and 112 of its subordinate unions. In amended form, the SNPA charges concerned the union's refusal to bargain, its attempted maintenance of closed shops, coercion of local unions in the exercise of their rights under the Taft-Hartley Act, the "bogus" issue and the issue of compulsory membership of foremen.

A temporary injunction restraining the ITU from continuing allegedly unfair labor practices had been issued by Federal District Judge Luther M. Swygert in Indianapolis; an NLRB trial examiner had found the union and its four principal officers guilty on some of the ANPA charges. The case then began its tortuous course through NLRB and court procedure, eventually to produce decisions generally favorable to the newspapers. But that was in the future when the SNPA met.

Relations with other unions continued amicable, under normal contract procedures. Even with the ITU, as stated, the reports to the convention indicated no widespread rupture. On September 1, 1947, there were 146 typographical union contracts with SNPA newspapers. Six of these contracts had been dissolved by strike and two by surrender of union charters. In the 138 remaining offices, 49 "verbal understandings" between publishers and local unions had been reported. In the remaining 89 cities, most operations were proceeding substantially under the terms of the expired contracts, so far as those complied with the law. In Louisville and Dallas, new contracts had been negotiated after the passage of the Taft-Hartley Act.

The publishers heard temperate counsel from Thurman Arnold, former Assistant U. S. Attorney General, who represented the SNPA in the proceedings before the NLRB. He urged newspapers to undertake a campaign of public education on the Taft-Hartley Act's sound purposes, declaring that it was regarded as a "slave labor" law not only by labor organizations, but by many of the general public.

Publishers should show the economic case against the closed shop and the "closed union" which often resulted from it, he said, also against the swallowing up of independent unions by powerful international unions, against coercion which destroyed the autonomy of local bargaining agents, and against the inefficient methods forced on industry by union coercion.

"The SNPA is fighting the battle of the laborites when it shows that domination of local unions by international unions is a combination in restraint of trade," Mr. Arnold argued. "I am the last one to believe in any sort of regulation of labor, but if we are going to have free collective bargaining, we must have some sort of referee."

Economic Renaissance In The South — I

Presiding over the labor relations panel at which Judge Arnold spoke, Richard Lloyd Jones, Jr., publisher of the Tulsa Tribune and World, described working conditions in the newspaper industry as "close to ideal." He predicted a meeting of minds between management and labor on wages and working conditions. Remote as that seemed in the litigation-stirred atmosphere of the moment, it was to be substantially realized in SNPA territory within a comparatively few years.

The long-standing interest of the Association in educating young people for the printing trades achieved new importance, especially for small city newspapers, with the enactment of the Taft-Hartley law. Many of these publishers had not had to deal with organized labor until the middle 1930's, and some of them found, after organization, that the typographical union's restriction on number of apprentices compelled a costly change in their operating methods.

With the tight union shop outlawed by the new Act, the quick training offered by the printing schools in Nashville and Dallas induced several publishers to recruit their short-handed staffs by sending young people for short courses, with the promise of immediate employment on completion. One publisher already had four graduates working, with eight more in school, and a waiting list. Those on the job were getting journeyman's wages after less than two years' employment; underlining again that the schools' purpose was not to break down wage standards but to furnish workmen who were essential to the production of newspapers.

Another angle of trade school education was presented to the meeting in the report of the technical school building recently completed by the International Printing Pressmens' and Assistants' Union at its Tennessee headquarters. George L. Berry, president of that union and a familiar face at SNPA conventions, was quoted as explaining the construction of this "million dollar monument to industrial peace" in these words:

"We have a policy in which we commit ourselves to exhaust all resources for the adjustment of differences by processes of conciliation. If we fail in that, we apply the principle of arbitration. Thus we conserve and husband our might, which ordinarily would go, as in the case of many organizations, to strike benefits in industrial disputes. We use that money to build buildings for education and humanitarian purposes."

Discussion on newsprint mills was brief and fruitful. The Association's committee had been plugging diligently for the last two years to obtain adequate investment of publishers' money in the Coosa River Newsprint Mill, and Chairman Clarence B. Hanson, Jr., told the convention that the committee was still $191,700 short of its goal. That goal, and the cost of the mill, had been revised upward greatly during the past 24 months. Originally, the mill was to have cost $18,000,000 and publishers were to invest about $1,000,000 in its common stock to insure that the plant, when built, would make newsprint.

Mr. Hanson's report was followed by the brief remarks of Ted Dealey, Dallas News, who cited the success of the Southland Mills at Lufkin, and declared that his newspaper would increase its subscription to the Coosa River mill stock. A number of other newspaper executives arose with similar pledges, and two which had not bought any stock climbed aboard the band wagon. The sum raised at St. Petersburg, before and during the convention session, was $300,000, and the total investment of publishers in the mill stood at approximately $10,000,000. The overall cost of the mill would be $32,000,000, it was estimated in 1948.

Mr. Hanson then asked that the newsprint mills committee be dissolved, its task completed. He received a rising vote of thanks, and a resolution declared that the Coosa River mill was "in large measure built upon the energy and enthusiasm, the intelligent advocacy and the unselfish exertion of Clarence B. Hanson, Jr.," and would stand "as monumental testimony to his service."

In addition to the heavy investments by large and small members of the SNPA, the Coosa River mill had received investment support from publishers in Colorado, the District of Columbia, Indiana, Iowa, Missouri, New York, Ohio, Pennsylvania, and Wisconsin.

The Association did not lose sight of an important, if less tangible, objective in its push for the goal of a second Southern newsprint mill. Thomas L. Robinson, publisher of the Charlotte (N. C.) News, reminded the Association of its action of 1946 in favor of conservative and constructive employment of the South's forest resources.

He read the suggestion of Past-President Biggers and the resolution adopted in 1946, and asked that the 1948 meeting confirm that pledge in a new and broader program. This was done, in the following resolution:

"Resolved, that this convention reaffirms its support of the conservation and tree-growing programs being conducted in the several States and urges the members of the SNPA to continue to encourage greater development of our Southern forest resources."

While the SNPA historian has no trouble at all in weighing the importance of resolutions which led to construction of newsprint mills and the use of forest resources, his judgment must be on less sure ground when he tries to evaluate the periodic SNPA outbursts on the editorial performance of newspapers. For several years, readers will recall, the Association had been scolded by its editorial affairs chairmen for a seeming lack of interest in what the writers and reporters did. Such interest had been not at all lacking during the previous decade.

The 1948 convention heard a rousing discussion of journalism and adopted, without discussion, a resolution that must have been read with glee by the numerous critics of newspapers. Nelson Poynter, publisher of the St. Petersburg Times and thus one of the convention's hosts, led an editorial panel on the topic "Does Militant Local Journalism Pay?" Participants were Jenkin Lloyd Jones, editor of the Tulsa Tribune; Ralph Nicholson, editor and publisher of the New Orleans Item, and J. N. Heiskell, editor of the Little Rock Gazette.

Mr. Jones affirmed that such local journalism did pay and he leveled ironic criticism at editors who went in for "Afghanistanism" and "Sacred Cowardice." He defined "Afghanistanism" as the affliction of editors who take a bold stand on issues in far-off places but keep hands off on local questions. And too many newspapers, he declared, have "Sacred Cows" about which nothing is ever printed. Self-censorship, he advised, should meet these three tests:

1. Does it perform a community service?
2. Does it protect the legitimate rights of persons who are blameless?
3. Does it pay off in friendship and respect?

Mr. Nicholson also found in favor of crusading local journalism, as might be expected of a young man who had prospered after seven years in the stormy politics of New Orleans. He counseled that a newspaper must always maintain its reputation for fairness and accuracy (when a newspaper has praised a public man, it can be more effectively biting in critical attacks on him); biased editorials did not convert the neutral reader, and a continuous diet of crusades was not desirable.

Mr. Heiskell summed up his ideas in a scathing resolution, which he moved for adoption under a suspension of the convention rules. As adopted, it read:

"Resolved, by the Southern Newspaper Publishers Association in annual convention at St. Petersburg, Fla., November 8-10, 1948:

"That Southern newspapers as a group fail to recognize the importance of editorial columns; that they pursue a short-sighted and unenlightened policy in the matter of allocating proper and adequate expenditure for editorial writers; that too many publishers make unreasonable demands on an editor's time and resources and thus make their papers suffer in the character and content of their editorials; that publishers habitually fail and refuse to provide sufficient manpower and ability for editorial columns and then complain that editorials are not read and therefore no money should be spent on them; that too many Southern papers place too great a reliance on "canned" editorial matter; and that it is a reproach to Southern newspapers that so comparatively few of them have their own editorial page cartoonist."

In the Soreno Hotel convention hall, there must have been a number of owners, publishers and editors who could have denied the strictures of the courtly Little Rock editor as applying to their own operations. According to the record, however, the motion was seconded by several and carried unanimously.

Tom Wallace, who had done much to vivify the Association's concern with editorial affairs, appeared at this convention in a new role. As editor emeritus of the Louisville Times and president of the Inter-American Press Association, Mr. Wallace urged the Southern press to get better acquainted with the nations of Latin-America. He wanted more North American newspapers to join his association and send reporters and editors to Central and South America to study the people, their customs, their civilization and their progress. (Mr. Wallace didn't tell the SNPA that, after retirement for age from his long service in Louisville, he had learned Spanish and applied himself to the neglected field of closer journalistic relations among the American nations.) His program received approval in this resolution:

"Whereas, Solidarity of the Western hemisphere is necessary to the best development of nations North and South of the Caribbean,

"Resolved, that this convention urges its membership to an active interest in ways and means of improving acquaintanceship between the people of the United States and the people of all the countries South of the United States in this hemisphere, especially exploring opportunities of the press of our South to serve the United States and our neighbors in the farther South."

The resolutions committee, headed at this convention by James E. Chappell of Birmingham, covered considerably more territory than was customary at SNPA conventions. Its other topics included:

Commendation of the two printing trade schools at Nashville and Dallas, with the recommendation that "training be extended to include the other mechanical trades necessary to newspaper production."

Continuation of Association support for the Lee Memorial School of Journalism, with "active participation in its expansion program in whatever ways that are open to us."

Pledging continued support to the American Council for Education in Journalism, encouraging higher standards in journalism teaching.

Commending to the membership encouragement and support of the Booker T. Washington Birthplace Memorial, "to perpetuate the ideals and teachings of Booker T. Washington as a contribution to better race relations, to better understanding of our common problems and to the improvement of effective training of Negroes in the South."

Realizing that very few advertising men can spare the necessary time for doing the high type of training job which they are fully capable of doing, the Association's advertising committee, headed by Loyal Phillips, business manager of the New Orleans Item, produced a sales training manual titled "Newspaper Advertising—How to Write It—How to Sell It." In preparing it, Mr. Phillips was ably assisted by contributions from a number of advertising managers in addition to those from members of the advertising committee. The manual was pronounced the best of its kind that had been printed in many years.

Another undertaking of the same committee was a book titled "50 Successful Newspaper Advertising Ideas." It contained a wide selection of dependable ideas for producing additional linage for newspapers. The book represented the cooperative efforts of some fifty newspaper advertising executives who made contributions in the form of either a suggestion or concrete advertising ideas.

One of the final scenes of the meeting was the reading of a telegram to President Baker from the Southern Historical Association, congratulating the Association on the establishment of the SNPA library. The number of books now included in the collection topped 1650; the catalog promised the previous year had been prepared but not yet published. Despite the absence of a published catalog, Library Chairman Biggers reported that many calls had been made on the library by members and that the broad scope of the collection allowed most of these to be satisfactorily met.

Proceedings of the convention for the first time included a summary of group conferences for publishers of newspapers with less than 10,000 circulation; newspapers of 10,000 to 50,000 circulation; and newspapers of more than 50,000 circulation. All were well attended and devoted themselves entirely to shop topics—the provender that made entire convention programs a few years earlier. These three group sessions in 1948 had been the natural outgrowth of the "small dailies" meetings that had been initiated a number of years earlier. Their popularity in no way hampered the convention's major activities, and they afforded publishers the chance to exchange experiences on a usefully even economic plane.

The convention afforded another pleasant departure from custom—it elected the first woman president of the SNPA. She was Mrs. Oveta Culp Hobby of the Houston Post, already known to the members for several years of useful service as a member of the Board of

Directors. Her executive ability, demonstrated as co-publisher of one of the South's strongest newspapers, had been recognized during the war by her appointment as Colonel commanding the Woman's Army Corps. The SNPA made no fuss over the precedent; it was following custom in choosing from the best available its leader for the coming year, regardless of wealth or sex.

Lisle Baker, Jr., who had presided ably over business and social sessions at St. Petersburg (he was host for the Louisville Courier-Journal and Times at a notable party), automatically became chairman of the board. Ralph Nicholson succeeded himself as treasurer, and Walter C. Johnson as secretary-manager.

New directors were elected for three-year terms as follows:

Alabama—Clarence B. Hanson, Jr., Birmingham News and Age-Herald; Georgia—A. H. Chapman, Columbus Enquirer-Ledger; Oklahoma—Ned Shepler, Lawton Constitution; Texas—M. M. Donosky, Dallas News; Virginia—Carter Glass, Jr., Lynchburg News and Advance; Director-at-large, to fill out unexpired term of Mrs. Hobby—Carl A. Jones, Jr., Johnson City (Tenn.) Press-Chronicle.

Economic Renaissance - II

Coosa River Newsprint Mill Begins Production—Bowater of England Starts Construction of Tennessee Mill, with Moral but not Financial Backing of SNPA—Association's Forestry Program Strengthened—Publishers Give New Attention to Operating Costs, as Korean Conflict Brings Quasi-War Economy.

MRS. Hobby assumed her office within a week after President Truman's astonishing re-election as the nation's Chief Executive—a conjunction which unquestionably influenced the events of her term. To quote one SNPA director, the Stock Market "fell out of bed" immediately after Election Day, and its discouraging trend was reflected in general business conditions. Although most newspapers held even with 1948 in circulation and advertising revenue, and a few registered gains, the forward surge of the post-war years was no longer in evidence. Newsprint remained high in price, but there was plenty available for all newspaper needs without resort to the spot market.

Union labor continued its pressure for repeal of the Taft-Hartley law, pledged by Mr. Truman in his campaign, and also sought higher wage levels. Increases in wages, the SNPA heard, were smaller than in the immediate past—at the rate of $2 to $4 per week, rather than in the $5--$10 range.

Declining or static income, however, combined with high paper prices and a general wage level far above that of pre-war days, plus taxes that bit deeply into profits, confronted all publishers with a steadily narrowing net return.

When the SNPA met for its 1949 convention at Mineral Wells, Texas, October 31--November 2, President Hobby's brief report told the members that "publishers are going to have to become expert business men or prepare to sign promissory notes. If publishers don't survive, their papers will go down with them, and the country is that much worse off. Every time a newspaper folds, another avenue of information is closed to the American people. . . . The margin between success and failure narrows daily. And between these tightening lines, there is increasingly less room for inefficiency caused by laziness, laissez-faire, habit, or even sentiment."

None of these defects appeared in the report of the Association's work for the year. Treasurer Ralph Nicholson had sold the New Orleans Item shortly before the convention and gone to Berlin as assistant to High Commissioner John McCloy, and his report was prepared by Secretary-Manager Johnson. It revealed expenses for the fiscal year of $71,821.91 (an increase of more than 100 per cent over 1939) and an income of $78,044.27 (an even larger increase over pre-war revenue). The reserve fund had been stepped up to a net of $56,666.24. The old problem of delinquent dues no longer existed. Total membership stood at 394, Mr. Johnson reported, with aggregate circlaution of more than 9,200,000 daily, and 7,648,000 Sunday.

Mr. Johnson's office had issued 55 printed bulletins during the year, with a total of 578 pages. Among them were three covering use and conservation of forest lands, and a score (sponsored by the editorial affairs committee) on editorial technique and public service. In addition to the printed bulletins, a total of 597 mimeographed issues went to publishers and newspaper department executives covering all phases of newspaper production. The Association's files included data on almost any question that a member might ask; when answers weren't found in that mine of information, headquarters put out spot inquiries and surveys and turned the results over to the seeker.

On the side of solid accomplishment, the convention viewed new pictures of the Coosa River newsprint mill and were assured by Chairman C. B. Hanson, Jr., that the $32,000,000 mill had been constructed within its budget estimates, on schedule, and would be supplying newsprint to contract customers by January, 1950. SNPA members owned common stock to the amount of $6,207,800 with publishers in other areas holding $3,865,250. Newspaper publishers thus owned more than half of the $18,000,000 common stock that had been issued, with Kimberly-Clark Co., the manufacturing firm which had been retained to administer the plant, owning $6,780,300. Birmingham investors held the remainder of the common, and $14,000,000 in bonds had been placed in the general public market.

Like the Southland Mills of a decade earlier, this Association achievement had been soundly financed, expertly located, and honestly constructed. Its 100,000 tons of newsprint would be an important addition to the North American supply within a year or two when business shook off its 1949 torpor.

While newsprint supply no longer harassed publishers, the SNPA newsprint committee did not let the membership forget the recent past. Its report, prepared by Austin V. Wood, Wheeling (W. Va.) Intelligencer and News-Register, counseled publishers that "a black market in newsprint must never again be tolerated." In isolated cases, some publishers had diverted newsprint into black market channels, Mr. Wood stated, adding "if all of us had consistently and persistently refused to buy at other than the market price, the entire black market would have been eliminated, thereby moving such newsprint as was available into legitimate channels and within reach of all of us."

Conceding that paper manufacturers were entitled to a fair rate of profit, especially in view of their many non-profit years, Mr. Wood argued that current financial statements indicated the ability of numerous mills to reduce prices substantially and still maintain legitimate earnings. He counseled that the SNPA make a concerted effort with the ANPA to obtain relief from high prices when opportunity offered. His report also offered a statistical glimpse at the economic inequalities of the publishers' current operations:

	Average 1935-1939	Year 1948
Federal Reserve Index of Production	100.0	192.0
Labor Dept. Wholesale Price Index	100.0	203.7
Labor Dept. Cost of Living Index	100.0	174.5
Newsprint Price	100.0	232.4
A Newspaper's Indices—		
Composing Room Hourly Wage Rate	100.0	211.0
Advertising Rate	100.0	157.0
Circulation Price	100.0	176.8

Economic Renaissance — II

The report of the Labor Committee, headed by Richard Lloyd Jones, Jr., Tulsa Tribune and World, shed a more encouraging light on the economic scene. Present business conditions, he said, put the burden of proof on labor's representatives in questions involving wage advances. Facts did not now support the case for higher pay, as they did in the three years just after the war.

"Today," he told the publishers, "if you have been insisting on a signed legal contract complying with the Taft-Hartley law, you can have one. If you have wanted Teletypesetters, now you can have them, and in the new Chicago typographical contract, production from them is guaranteed. Finally, if you face a walkout, with hard and thorough advance planning on your part, your regular production schedules can be met with little or no delay."

The typographical union had been fighting a losing battle against the Taft-Hartley law, according to the report of Tom Tanner, SNPA labor commissioner. Chicago publishers had maintained production by various expedients during a strike covering many months and had conceded none of management's prerogatives in its eventual settlement. The typographical union had lost jurisdiction in 14 of the 148 SNPA cities in which it had contracts in 1947, and the publishers in these cities were maintaining publication either by normal printing processes or by numerous makeshifts which had become practical, if not esthetic, in recent years.

The research which had enabled production of newspapers by Varitype in combination with photo-engraving and other processes of preparing the written word for publication had stirred much interest in the machinery field, the convention was told by Talbot Patrick, chairman of the research committee. The Rock Hill Herald publisher had given this subject abundant time during his three years on the committee and he told the convention of many inventions which might be either a boon or a menace to conventional publishing practice. Several processes employed light in the production of a printing surface and while some seemed almost commercial in their progress, none was actually ready for regular newspaper use. He quoted a warning note from a British correspondent, in touch with mechanical research in the United Kingdom:

"If I were concerned with re-equipping a local newspaper, especially a daily, I would very seriously consider gravure or offset, with justifying typewriter composition at first and photo-composing machines later."[1]

The public relations committee had also done some independent investigation of what SNPA newspapers were accomplishing in this activity. Thomas L. Robinson, publisher of the Charlotte News, its chairman, had kept the Association in touch with the public relations work of its members throughout the year and summarized its findings for the convention. Mr. Robinson, introducing himself as a "damyankee from Boston, Mass.," told the convention that he had recently received six pints of real Southern blood as a hospital patient, one of the donors expressing the wish that "this will help a little." He had also picked up something of the South by ringing doorbells of Charlotte News subscribers and asking them questions about the paper, themselves and their ideas of progress. He commended the experiment.

Problems of management and cost accounting naturally held more than usual interest for all publishers, and a panel led by Harry B. Bradley, business manager of the Birmingham News and Age-Herald, thrashed over the American Press Institute's recent findings on these topics.[2]

Participants in the management and cost panel also included Past-President Lisle Baker, Louisville Courier-Journal and Times; Al Dealey, assistant secretary-treasurer, Dallas News; Edward L. Gaylord, secretary, Oklahoma City Oklahoman and Times; and W. Howard Baldwin, vice-president and business manager, Houston Post. With the exception of Messrs. Bradley and Baker, the panel members represented the new generation of SNPA executives—men who were coming to the front in their newspapers and in the Association to assume the responsibilities of their elders. Necessarily, their interest focused on administration. Rules and practices which had been sufficient for their predecessors were likely to fall danger-

---

[1] Although great progress in development of photo-composing machines had been made by both Mergenthaler Lintoype Company and Intertype Corporation, neither had placed its devices in the commercial market up to 1954.

[2] The American Press Institute had been established by the Graduate School of Journalism at Columbia University in 1946. It offered opportunity for specialized study of questions relating to all phases of newspaper operation to men and women actively engaged in Journalism or newspaper management. Generally its seminars included about 24 people, and the proceedings of the more important groups, published by the Institute, afforded a valuable addition to the background of newspaper knowledge compiled by the SNPA and other newspaper associations.

ously short of requirements in an era of evershrinking margins of profit.[3]

From Arno H. Johnson, vice-president and director of media and research of the J. Walter Thompson Company, the convention received an hour-long injection of figures, proving that the business fears of 1949 had been wholly unfounded. Despite their pessimism, commercial firms had actually sold more goods in 1949 than they had in the "good" year of 1948, Mr. Johnson said, and with the application of only 5 per cent more selling force, they could do much better in 1950. He may have been right in his forecast; the irruption of trouble in Korea in mid-1950 threw all calculations and predictions out of balance, and business experienced, if it did not enjoy, a wild boom in the final six months.

On the editorial side, the convention heard Ben McKelway, managing editor of the Washington Star and president of the American Society of Newspaper Editors, warn against a new political attack on press integrity.

"It is especially distressing to hear the President telling the people of this country that their press is not honest," Mr. McKelway said. "That statement is not true. But the same statements, made frequently enough by enough men in high places in Washington, might easily persuade the people that, as they are not getting the truth from the American newspapers, government should therefore put its own men in the press galleries and establish its own news service in order to supply the people with the truth."

He foresaw no immediate threat, but looked upon the establishment of the Voice of America as a State Department news service to other countries, with its own men in the Congressional press galleries, as a possible first step in that direction.

Tom Wallace wasn't scheduled on the program, but the Louisville veteran appeared again with a cogent plea for free press soli-

---

[3] Also indicative of the exigent interest of newspapers in this question was the recent organization of the Institute of Newspaper Comptrollers and Finance Officers, which in 1949, was developing a system of cost-accounting for sub-metropolitan newspapers. This history has noted, on several occasions, the comparative indifference of Southern newspaper executives to analyses of department costs over a period of more than 30 years. In 1949, however, it was reported that 67 SNPA members were receiving the cost and revenue studies initiated in the 1920's by the Inland Daily Press Association. The SNPA was one of six associations co-operating in these studies.

darity in the Western hemisphere. His persistent missionary work got results. A number of prominent SNPA members joined the Inter-American Press Association and John S. Knight, editor and publisher of the Miami Herald (and other important dailies) became president of the organization in 1952.

The long and successful labors of Clarence B. Hanson, Jr., as chairman of the newsprint mills committee, were rewarded by his unanimous election as president for 1949-1950. Mrs. Hobby became board chairman and Lisle Baker, Jr., also automatically, took his place as chairman of the library committee. Myron G. Chambers, Knoxville News-Sentinel, was elected treasurer, and Walter C. Johnson, secretary-manager.

Six directors were elected, Curtis DeLamar, Gadsden Times, filling the Alabama vacancy caused by Mr. Hanson's upward move. Others elected for three-year terms were:

Louisiana—Hunter Jarreau, Alexandria Town Talk; Mississippi—James H. Skewes, Meridian Star; North Carolina—W. K. Hoyt, Winston-Salem Journal-Sentinel; Tennessee—Frank Ahlgren, Memphis Commercial Appeal; West Virginia—Robert L. Smith, Charleston Gazette.

According to his report at the 1950 convention, President Hanson had expected his term to cover the first "normal" year that American newspapers had experienced in much longer than a dog's age. And so it was, until late June, 1950, when the Communists began their tests of American and United Nations strength in Korea. As the SNPA gathered amid the placid luxury of the Greenbrier at White Sulphur Springs, W. Va., October 26-28, 1950, General MacArthur was gaining what seemed to be decisive victories, but the future of the United Nations "police action" could not be foreseen.

Rapid re-arming of American forces threw red signals against most civilian plans for industrial expansion and construction. Consumers thronged to market to buy goods that would certainly disappear again from the stores if the war's dimensions increased. Hunger for news sent circulations soaring. Advertising linage perked up after months of relative quiescence. Responding to the increased demand, newsprint prices began a new climb, with spot market prices reaching for the $200 level. With prices advancing under the spur of panic purchases of both hard and soft goods, organized labor pressed for new wage increases. The stepped-up draft for the armed forces again confronted newspapers with a manpower shortage.

It was natural then, that Mr. Hanson's gavel should fall before a record assemblage for an SNPA convention—534 members, wives and guests, and representatives of supply and equipment firms. The members alone numbered nearly 200—a notable contrast with the preceding convention of the Association at White Sulphur Springs in July, 1923, when total attendance was less than 100. It was in keeping, too, with a frequently observed SNPA custom that the president should conduct the convention with a newly presented gavel—the handle of which came from an old church in Columbia, S. C., and the mallet from the first loblolly pine tree cut on the Coosa River newsprint mill's tract. It was presented by J. M. Blalock, publisher of the Columbia (S. C.) Record.

Reports from the two Southern newsprint mills gave the publishers reason for congratulations. The Southland Paper Mills at Herty, Texas, had its second paper machine in operation for the first time in 1949, and had produced 126,980 tons of newsprint. The Coosa River mill had gone into production on schedule, turning out its first newsprint on January 18, 1950, and was making paper at the rate of 100,000 tons a year on its two machines. Arthur G. Wakeman, executive vice-president of the Alabama mill, had reported that all varieties of Southern pine so far tried had proven satisfactory—thus proving in commercial experience the assertions of Dr. Herty before the SNPA convention of 1931.

The newsprint mills committee, headed by John F. Tims, Jr., New Orleans Times-Picayune, believed that expansion of existing plants should be given first consideration but did not discourage moves for the construction of new mills. Two new enterprises had been proposed since the 1949 convention. One was headed by Paul D. Hammacher of Washington, D. C. and had been looking into prospects in Alabama and Mississippi. Another was being promoted by lumber interests in Southeast Arkansas, but the Korean conflict had put that project on a sidetrack. Uncertainties of Korea and the cold war had also caused the Southland mill to hesitate in the installation of a third newsprint unit at Herty. But the committee looked forward confidently to the day when the mills at Herty and Coosa Pines would be producing newsprint at the rate of 350,000 tons a year.

Mingled with elation over the success of the Association's two paper mills there was continued concern for the permanence of the regional resources upon which the new paper industry rested. Thomas L. Robinson, of the Charlotte News, again reminded the publishers of their previous committments to support soil and forest conservation programs and asked that this convention record itself as favoring a more energetic program, with the full support of SNPA members.

The resolutions committee, of which J. N. Heiskell, Little Rock Gazette, was chairman, offered this double-barreled resolution, which was unanimously adopted:

"Resolved, that the President appoint a committee to urge the Coosa River and the Lufkin plants to install additional machines, and to offer co-operation and any proper assistance to the owners and promoters of the proposed newsprint mills near Prescott, Ark., Naheola, Ala., and any other proposed or contemplated mills in furthering and expediting their projects; and as the need is national and worldwide, that the committee ask the support of other regional newspaper organizations and the ANPA in this very important objective.

"To the end that the South may be self-sufficient in its newsprint needs, we recommend a more intelligent utilization of the two hundred million acres of forest lands and better cultivation of additional waste and idle acres in this area and to thus utilize the tremendous climatic advantages of the area which make possible the growth of certain types of fibrous woods in a fraction of the time necessary in other areas.

"Resolved, that in view of increasing industrialization in the South, SNPA members explore the economic possibilities of fostering fish and wild life in connection with conservation of forests; that we urge the strengthening of all soil and forest conservation programs and pledge support to all national and state organizations that are concerned with conservation."

That resolution had a sequel, as will appear below.

Another resolution, recording the displeasure of the publishers with recent increases in the price of newsprint, was submitted by Mr. Heiskell's committee without approval and referred for further consideration to the newsprint and newsprint mills committees. It was sharply worded, and declared that the "current increases are not based on the need for additional earnings, but rather upon the defenseless position of the newspapers."

As finally adopted, after amendment by the Association's paper experts, the truculent verbiage was stricken out and the SNPA views were expressed in this fashion:

"The Southern Newspaper Publishers Association notes with the keenest concern the substantial increases in newsprint prices which some of the manufacturers have announced to take effect immediately.

"The SNPA does not begrudge the newsprint industry reasonable earnings. It realizes that a financially sound newsprint industry is necessary to insure an ample supply of paper under all conditions.

"The Association is appreciative of the remarkable increase in production achieved by the newsprint industry, which has resulted in large financial benefits to that industry and publishers alike. However, this year, most publishers, in spite of increases in business have had sharp decreases in net profit, while published earnings statements of most newsprint producers indicate larger net profits than in the same period of 1949 and previous years.

"Publishers are profoundly disturbed by downward profit trends in their businesses and are concerned about their ability to continue absorbing increased costs, which, if continued, will operate to the harm of newsprint producers also.

"Therefore, we call upon the industry to consider carefully the effect of these increases on their customers and to justify and explain any increase to the end that the publishers will not be forced to conclude that increases are based largely upon what the traffic will bear.

"In view of these circumstances, the Southern Newspaper Publishers Association in convention assembled goes on record as protesting these increases as apparently being unnecessary, as being immediately harmful to newspapers, as being eventually harmful to newsprint producers and as adding impetus to the inflationary spiral."

Coupled with that diplomatic expression was an additional motion on present and future Southern newsprint mills:

"Since the present rate of consumption of newsprint is far greater than the rate of production, and since Canadian manufacturers do not seem to be interested in building new mills, be it therefore

"Resolved, that the SNPA urges the Southland Paper Mill at Lufkin, Texas, and the Coosa River Mill at Childersburg, Alabama, to install additional newsprint-making machines as soon as possible, in order to increase the production of newsprint in the South, and further be it

"Resolved, that the need for new production of newsprint is so great that the SNPA use its influence and good offices to encourage the building of new mills in the South, and further be it

"Resolved, that the SNPA will endeavor to sell the output of any new machine or mill to member newspapers on a stock participation basis after the new venture has been given the closest scrutiny by the officers and directors of the SNPA and has been approved as a project that the SNPA can unqualifiedly endorse and recommend to its members."

That carefully drawn resolution committed the Association to the support of vitally needed new mills, but it also guarded against use of the SNPA name by promoters out for a quick dollar. Many of the Association's senior members (and not a few of the younger men) had been intimately concerned with the promotion of the Southland and Coosa River mills. With more than a decade of educative experience behind them, they knew the conditions that must be met for thoroughly sound organization of additional newsprint projects—and the SNPA wanted only such enterprises as would combine an abiding concern for the region's broad future welfare with the immediate pursuit of profits. As will be seen, they found these desirable qualifications in the Bowater interests, which within the next two years, advanced proposals for construction of a newsprint mill in Tennessee.

Economic Renaissance — II

Unusual as it was for an SNPA committee to get itself involved in the diplomatic wording of resolutions, Mr. Heiskell's committee provided a second instance at this convention.

While the committee was deliberating its report, James G. Stahlman took the floor at the convention's opening session and without preliminary remarks, tossed this crackling composition to the members:

"Whereas, for a number of years there has persisted and there continues a malicious, determined campaign of smear, vilification, and falsehood against he South as a region, and

"Whereas, no section of the United States of America has experienced such phenomenal growth and development of all its assets—agricultural, commercial, industrial, educational, cultural and spiritual—as has the South during the past 75 years, all without aid of any Marshall Plan, ECA or other assistance outside the ingenuity, brains, ability, and determination of people who have clung to the fundamentals of character in the individual as well as in government, despite the vicious assaults of political mountebanks, sociological crackpots and subversive malcontents, and

"Whereas, no section of the United States holds such potentials for continued progress in the next half-century, and

"Whereas, sporadic efforts of individuals, chambers of commerce, newspapers and other agencies, by reason of their purely local application, do not present the overall story of the advancing South, and

"Whereas, the Southern Newspaper Publishers Association embraces the most effective element for the collection and dissemination of the truth about the South, without which the nation and the world can never know the full story of the South's real worth and her position of leadership, now therefore,

"Be it resolved by the Southern Newspaper Publishers Association in convention assembled, that the President be authorized and directed to appoint a committee to study ways and means of providing an effective and permanent agency within the framework of the SNPA to be charged with the duty of producing, collecting, and distributing information of a local as well as general interest bearing upon the continued progress and development of the South and all its assets of whatever character, to the end that truth may prevail and all the people of a united country may be made familiar with the aims, aspirations, work, resources, and advance of this whole Southern region which acknowledges no equal in potentials and no superior in accomplishment."

The strong-minded Nashville publisher handed his draft to Mr. Heiskell, who shortly thereafter included it with other resolutions offered to the convention for adoption, calling it to the special attention of the meeting. It was adopted, viva voce, without discussion. The prominence of its maker and the scathing language of the preamble commended the resolution to the Associated Press correspondent, who didn't have much else to put on the wires after the opening session. "Jimmy's" masterpiece appeared in newspapers all over the land, with his coruscating description of the South's critics getting far more attention than the resolution's objective.

After the session some of the members had second thoughts. Mr. Heiskell arose before the next day's meeting and reported that his committee had not had opportunity to pass on the wording, which some members considered intemperate. The fact that the AP had sent out the original "fire and brimstone" resolution somewhat complicated the problem. But Mr. Heiskell asked the convention if it wished to consider whether the resolution ought to go into the records as adopted, or if Mr. Stahlman might wish to say something, "in no stronger language than this."

"Jimmy" arose to the occasion, with evidence that his emotional fires burned no less brightly than they had during his presidency 18 years earlier.

"I hate to bore you again," he declared, "but I must defend my ecclesiastical vocabulary. Let me say, as I said yesterday in all honesty, the reason that I brought it up yesterday after apologies to Senator Heiskell and his committee for not having submitted it to him before I brought it to the floor, I had talked the situation over with two past presidents of the SNPA. Of course, they didn't know the language I was going to use in any proposed resolutions, except that they might have suspected that I wasn't going to be anything except typically Stahlman. . . . I have no apologies for the language in the preamble or in the general text. The language which I used was a plain statement of fact, and if there is anybody in this audience who doesn't believe that there has been a continued and deliberate campaign of smear, vilification and falsehood against the South, then he has either been asleep or is unable to understand what has been going on round about. . . . There was no political intent in this thing. It was an effort on my part to focus the attention of the newspaper publishers of the South, and I hope there are still enough in the SNPA with guts enough to express their objections and their opinions about a thing of this kind without fear of treading on somebody's toes either politically or sociologically.

"I then passed the text of the resolution to Senator Heiskell and since the resolution was reported out in all generosity by the Senator for his committee when he submitted his other report and it was adopted by a much larger group than is here present this morning, without a dissenting vote, I say to you in all fairness that the original content of that resolution should stand."

Mr. Heiskell replied that it wasn't a question of fearing to tread on toes, "but of what really is becoming in a resolution that is adopted by Southern newspapers." He asked again whether the members wished to reconsider, and Mr. Stahlman rose to a point of order. The resolution had been adopted unanimously by the full convention and was not subject to revision, he declared. If the members wished to strike it from the record, they could do so by a rescinding vote, but they could not touch it otherwise.

After a brief discussion, the chair sustained the point of order and the resolution stood as adopted. The incident is related at greater length than its influence to date on SNPA activity warrants, because it gives a picture of the informal, man-to-man fashion in which the Association continues to operate. Readers of this volume are aware that not all of the ideas embodied in convention resolutions influence future acts of the Association. Directive resolutions that result from careful thought by the president or a committee on a question have borne fruit, as a rule, in future accomplishments. Resolutions introduced informally and without processing by the resolutions committee have sometimes been adopted, filed and forgotten, occasionally to blaze into new life after several years "in Limbo."

Creation of the two newsprint mills and the Association's consistent policy on forest conservation resulted from the considered action of members who had put their talents, time and money into forming and executing Association policy. The Association's advertising campaign of a quarter century earlier had its origin in resolutions not dissimilar to that of Mr. Stahlman (but without its invective) and the advertising policy was galvanized only by the persistence of several committee members who realized its importance to the South.

On the other side, some resolutions that had been offered and adopted in the early 1920's would have committed the Association to a policy of disciplining members for transgressing certain rules of conduct. By instinct or prescience, the officers of that time ignored these "police powers"; by so doing, they were later able to establish that the Association had not been guilty of actions which might have been found illegal in the Federal Trade Commission investigation of 1925-1931.

The incoming president in 1950-51 appointed a committee in accordance with Mr. Stahlman's resolution, but the committee made no report at the 1951 or 1952 conventions, nor was any requested. That such a committee might have served a useful purpose (and may yet do so) is beyond question. Without any record for guidance, the historian can only surmise that the committee members either disliked the general tone of the resolution or found that its directive was too broad and general for specific action. Whatever the reason, the committee's activity remained "unfinished business" in 1953.

While the several group conferences enabled publishers to air and exchange view on matters of immediate concern, the Association as a whole heard an unusual variety of addresses. Taken *en masse*, they highlighted the increasing complexity of producing a newspaper as the sixth decade of the Twentieth Century opened. It was pointed out by Cranston Williams, general manager of the ANPA, that though the essentials of the trade association's service to its membership had remained fundamentally unchanged for 50 years, the details of those services had ramified greatly. No individual publisher, he said, could hope to keep abreast of the information vital to his business in the fields of credit, labor-management relations, federal, state, and city legislation, government agency rulings, and new technological research.

ECONOMIC RENAISSANCE — II

"The newspaper association is a necessity to efficient and economic production of today's daily newspaper," Mr. Williams concluded. "The newspaper association cannot function without the support, financial and moral, of those executives it is designed to help. The newspaper association works 24 hours a day to foster and protect your interests. Some part of your interest, your co-operation and your contributions should, in return, be given to this creation of yours—your newspaper association—for your benefit."

Even more sharply focused was the shaft of light directed by Robert Spahn, administrative assistant of the Oklahoma City Oklahoman and Times. He headed the new personnel department of those newspapers and argued eloquently for acceptance of that idea by the membership. Labor unions, he said, indoctrinated their young members with the aims and history of their organizations. Few newspaper organizations did a similar job for young people coming into their employment. He described the Oklahoman personnel set-up of nine people, some of them part-time, which was charged with the selection of new employees, testing their aptitudes, safeguarding their health, providing recreation, and, in fine, creating a "team" spirit in the whole enterprise rather than a group of loosely associated departments. Newspapers had lagged behind other industries in this direction, even though newspaper publishing ranked top for the amount of money spent per revenue dollar for labor.

Of somewhat similar concern was the address of an SNPA veteran, D. Hiden Ramsey, general manager of the Asheville Citizen-Times, on "Pension and Retirement Plans." His newspaper was one of a growing number which had established funds of that kind in the early 1940's, and was presently considering expansion of the original benefits to employees. He advised publishers to obtain expert advice in the organization of such plans, emphasizing that it was no field for amateur thinkers.

Advertising prospects and the newspapers' part in them were presented to the convention, respectively, by Frederic R. Gamble, president of the American Association of Advertising Agencies, and Richard W. Slocum, publisher of the Philadelphia Bulletin and immediate past-chairman of the Bureau of Advertising, ANPA.

The two faces long familiar to SNPA gatherings were present in connection with international matters. Tom Wallace repeated his advocacy of stronger participation by United States newspapermen in the works of the Inter-American Press Association, of which he had been elected president. Ralph Nicholson, again an active SNPA member by virtue of his association with the Tampa Times, told of his European impressions after a year in occupied Germany as director of the office of public affairs. His message was not optimistic, and he concluded with a warning: "The time has come for us to recognize that our freedom and our lives are in great peril; that we must be as tough with our friends and as ruthless with our enemies as the circumstances require."

The memorials committee noted the passing during the year of 24 executives of member newspapers, including one past-president of the SNPA—Curtis B. Johnson, of the Charlotte (N. C.) Observer—and three former members of the board—Charles A. Webb, of the Asheville (N. C.) Citizen-Times; Dave Gideon, of the Huntington (W. Va.) Herald-Dispatch; Mason C. Brunson, Sr., Florence (S. C.) Morning News.

K. A. Engel, of the Little Rock Democrat, after many years' service as director and committee chairman, was unanimously elected president to succeed Mr. Hanson, who became chairman of the board. Myron G. Chambers, Knoxville News-Sentinel, was re-elected treasurer; and Walter C. Johnson turned another page in his career as secretary-manager. New directors were elected to three-year terms as follows:

Arkansas—Hugh B. Patterson, Jr., Little Rock Gazette; Florida—R. C. Millar, Jacksonville Times-Union; Kentucky—John B. Gaines, Bowling Green Park City News; South Carolina—H. T. McGee, Jr., Charleston News and Courier; director-at-large, Carl A. Jones, Jr., Johnson City (Tenn.) Press Chronicle. All except Mr. Jones were newcomers to the board.

Hard-working and universally beloved August Engel held the SNPA reins through a year of more than usual uncertainties. Soon after he took office the bright expectations of early victory in Korea had been dimmed by a grim repulse at the hands of great new hosts of Chinese Communists. Hopes rose again as the United Nations forces regained the initiative, resulting in Communist proposals for peace negotiations. These dragged on, month after futile month, and, coupled with the uneasy state of European affairs, offered the nation small prospect of an early return to normal business.

Newsprint prices again rose sharply—16 per cent in little more than a year. Partially as a result of the higher prices, and in part because of a slight decline in advertising linage, the paper shortage that had been feared in 1950 did not take serious proportions. In 1951, publishers had available considerably more paper than they could use. The continued upward trend of paper prices became a source of worry to all newspaper owners, even those who had been most tolerant of the paper-makers' exigencies.

SNPA efforts to enlarge the capacity of the Coosa River newsprint mill had been fruitless in 1950; the management did not wish to risk costly expansion under existing economic circumstances. The Southland Mill, at first reluctant to add to its equipment, had finally applied for the required certificate of necessity to the Federal government and the SNPA applauded its courage. Most promising development in the area of increased paper supply for the South was the near certainty that the Bowater Paper Company, British-owned and with a large newsprint mill in Newfoundland, would construct a new newsprint and Kraft plant in the Calhoun–Charleston, Tenn. area, in the immediate future. Other explorations of the Southern field by United States and Canadian newsprint manufacturers bore no promise of immediate fruit. And for the first time, a substantial group of Southern publishers awoke to the situation of which Secretary-Manager Johnson had warned five years earlier—that manufacturers of Kraft and other papers, but not newsprint, were rapidly preempting the most advantageous mill sites and forest tracts in the South.

When the 1951 convention assembled at Hot Springs, Ark., September 24-26, Southern newspapers were just experiencing the beginning of a technological change that might overshadow all newspaper mechanical developments of the previous half-century. This was the introduction in several Southern States of wire service Teletypesetter circuits which could feed telegraphed matter from the wire editor's desk in New York, Atlanta, or any other central point, directly to the linecasting machine in a newspaper's plant, and operate that machine automatically almost without human aid. No one could yet evaluate all the implications of that innovation, but the number of such circuits offered by the three primary wire services had multiplied week by week since July, 1951.

Relations with the typographical union took on new complications with the widespread adoption of the Teletypesetter circuits, and the ITU had some of its own making by forming a subsidiary to establish newspapers in some of the cities in which it had lost jurisdiction by unsuccessful strikes against newspapers. Although some of these union newspaper ventures would be set up in SNPA territory, this threat of competition caused the publishers small worry at the 1951 convention.

There may even have been some cynically-minded publishers who welcomed the invasion of the newspaper field by an organization which had expert knowledge of only one element of newspaper production. They could have warned the union heads that it was a strategy doomed to heavy financial losses. In a period when the strongest newspapers looked annually at shrinking margins of profit, despite large and steady income, an inexperienced newcomer stood small chance of shaking established competition. By the end of 1952, the International Typographical Union had loaned its Unitype subsidiary $4,000,000 for newspaper enterprises, and had unsuccessfully called upon its membership for a special defense fund assessment.

According to reports of the labor committee and the labor commissioner, SNPA members, in the majority of cities, had sought continuous peaceful relations with the typographical union. After more than four years of union resistance to signing contracts with newspapers, on terms complying with the Taft-Hartley law, the SNPA reported that 66 of its members had such contracts. Approximately half of them gave limited jurisdiction to the union over operation of Teletypesetter installations. Some withheld that control from the union, and some straddled the issue. In other Southern cities, relations with the printers' union continued under verbal agreements. In the five-year period since 1946, the union had lost jurisdiction in 21 out of 148 SNPA cities, almost invariably as the result of unsuccessful strikes against newspapers. Although the previous year had seen scattered strikes of pressmen, mailers, stereotypers, and teamsters, labor-management relations in the SNPA area continued in relative amity.

Economic Renaissance – II

Wages in general had continued their upward trend, at a slower pace than in 1945-1948. The upheaval in prices after the outbreak in Korea had stimulated new pressure for higher pay, in the face of admonitions by the Association's labor experts that current cost of living statistics warranted no rise over established wage standards.

Publishers had often been excited about freedom of the press during the previous two decades—generally about possible consequences of a new law or a judicial or agency decision. The peril to press freedom was more often a legalistic possibility than clear and present.

Now, in 1951, publishers found their freedom to present news of current public interest faced by a genuine, immediate danger, without warrant of any law or decision. In all parts of the country, local officials (mayors, city councils, heads of departments, sheriffs, and police chiefs) were arbitrarily deciding that the facts on such and such a matter should not be made available to the press. Reporters on the trail of rumored shenanigans affecting police matters or municipal contracts suddenly found doors and records closed to them, "in the public interest."

The example had unquestionably been set in war-time Washington, when many matters had to be withheld from publication temporarily to avoid giving vital information to the enemy. Reporters became familiar there with the several grades of "classification" applied to news, and developed methods of cracking the seal on matters that were not genuinely "secret" or "top secret." Newspaper organizations ever since the war had been prying hard at the lids of secrecy on Federal government news, with the strong suspicion that the classifications still essential under "cold war" conditions might be covering much that had little to do with national safety.

In the State and local fields, numerous authorities seem to have taken their cue from the armed services and the Federal bureaus. Subordinate military officers and local police united in several instances to wall reporters and photographers away from the scene of airplane accidents, alleging "security" in justification. That was still prevalent in 1951, but has since been largely eliminated by action of the Air Force commanders. Much more difficult to break through has been the news blockade created by municipal and state officials with something to hide from public gaze. Resort by newspapers to the courts has generally resulted in rulings that made the contested matters public, but sometimes the courts themselves sought to suppress news and to punish editors who violated their orders of suppression.

It was a question on which newspapers could not compromise. By tradition and practice, records affecting public funds and police matters are open to inspection by press and public. Newspapers bent backward in their measures to guard national security, even when that element was difficult of demonstration. They could not tolerate the application of that protection to matters that had not the remotest association with the national defense. They could not grant to state or municipal officers or to the courts the right to seal records as "classified" in the public interest. President Engel, the editorial affairs committee, and the legislative committee brought this question in various phases before the 1951 convention. The resolutions committee touched the matter only obliquely, however, in this statement:

"That we implore our leaders in government to set the example toward restoration of morality in the guidance of our destinies; and that each place the perpetuation of democratic government above political self-interest in order that our way of life may not succumb to socialistic tendencies."

Perhaps the members of the resolutions committee regarded the municipal suppression of news as incidental to the larger issue of corrupt practices in public office. Such matters were much in the public eye in 1951. Perhaps none of the committee members had been directly confronted with the denial of public records to newspapermen; if they had, the resolution might have been expected to deal more specifically with the question. The directors would remedy that defect in the near future.

On the question of newsprint supply and newsprint mills, the committee laid down well-marked lines for association action. It resolved:

"That we commend the Southland and Coosa Mills on pioneering the newsprint industry in the South and demonstrating that good newsprint can be made from Southern pine; that we urge all possible aid and co-operation toward their continued growth and progress;

and that we give our assistance in whatever manner possible to the Bowater Paper Company, and other concerns interested in further development of the industry, looking forward to the time the South shall be self-sufficient as a newsprint source.

"That we should alert Southern publishers to the rapid disappearance of available pulp supplies, advantageously located for the purpose of newsprint production. That the 200,000,000 acres of woodland within our territory, or the advantage of the quick reproduction due to lengthened season of growth cannot successfully of themselves attract newsprint manufacture, and that equally as essential are sites that provide power, fuel and water transportation with competitive delivery prices. That it is the judgment of this Association that every Southern newspaper has an interest in the conservation, development and utilization of our forest resources.

"Because of the great need for newsprint and especially for new production of newsprint, and

"Because newsprint has been declared an essential commodity, and,

"Because Bowater Paper Company desires to erect a new newsprint mill in the South;

"Therefore, be it resolved, That the Southern Newspaper Publishers Association as an Association and as individuals aid Bowater Paper Company in every way possible to obtain a certificate of necessity and later to obtain the necessary steel in order to erect this new newsprint mill at Charleston, Tennessee, and also be it

"Resolved, that the Southern Newspaper Publishers Association appreciates Bowater's coming into the South and encourages Bowater to press through to quick conclusion the plans and erection of this newsprint mill, and pledges the influence and support of this Association to that end."

The Bowater mill would be financed entirely through the company's own resources, without investment by newspaper publishers. Sir Eric Vansittart Bowater, head of the British company, had approved the site near the Hiwassee River in the Calhoun and Charleston area of East Tennessee (about 40 miles northeast of Chattanooga) and had returned to England early in 1951 to obtain permission to bring $10,000,000 out of the country. Additional finance was to be arranged through American institutions. The new Tennessee mill would have an annual capacity of 130,000 tons of newsprint and 50,000 tons of Kraft sulphite, Chairman George C. Biggers told the convention. American officers of the Bowater interest—August B. Meyer, president, and Charles T. Hicks, vice-president, were well known throughout the South. As frequent convention guests, both had carried off occasional golf tournament prizes.

Mr. Biggers noted that the Great Northern Paper Company, which had many Southern customers for paper made at its Millinocket, Me., mills, had examined a site in Georgia and had invited Mr. Biggers to tell the company's board of directors of the state's possibilities. He did, but the board voted that no immediate action be taken. The Anglo-Canadian Paper Co., also important to many Southern newspapers for its Quebec newsprint, had sent timber cruisers and engineers through the South but divulged nothing of its intentions. The White Star Paper Company's project at Prescott, Ark., noted the year previously, was still shelved by excessive construction costs. International Paper Company, largest operator of Southern paper mills, could not be interested by Mr. Biggers' committee in a Southern newsprint plant.

Along that line, the report of T. A. Corcoran, Louisville Courier-Journal and Times, chairman of the newsprint committee, warned that no matter how encouraging the current surplus might be, the long-term outlook for supply was not bright. If foreign demand returned only to its pre-war level, it would amount to approximately 1,000,000 tons and might go as high as 2,500,000 tons if political and exchange limitations were removed. United States demand, particularly, in the South, would show sizeable increases in the immediate future, unless it was inhibited by unsound price practices. He estimated that 10 to 20 new mills would be needed to satisfy these wants. Only two were in the planning stage, one in Canada and the Bowater mill in Tennessee. It seemed to be up to the SNPA, Mr. Corcoran argued, to assure the establishment of additional mills in its territory, to acquire desirable sites and timber stands so that they would be available when "others can be persuaded to construct mills."

Mr. Corcoran's report also urged the creation of a joint committee of newspaper publishers and newsprint manufacturers to consider mutual problems and to develop a better understanding between these interdependent groups.

ECONOMIC RENAISSANCE — II

And the weight of this committee's advice was added to the Association's program, already in effect, of support by individual newspapers to all tree-planting and other conservation programs.

The committee concluded its report by noting that Canadian production had increased 5.6 per cent; United States production, 11.9 per cent (almost entirely that of the two Southern mills), and newsprint imports, mainly from Finland, gained 23 per cent, to a total of 119,492 tons in 1951.

The legislative committee, headed by M. R. Ashworth, Columbus (Ga.) Enquirer-Sun, filled nearly two pages with summaries of legislative or executive actions tending to limit the freedom of newspapers. Suppression of public records ranged from marriage licenses, realty transfers, and building permits to welfare relief rolls and this censorship trend had manifested itself in many localities. Numerous proposals, some of them in effect, for local licensing of newspapers were noted, with the observation that publishers paid the small license tax rather than protest, except in one California locality.

The suit of the Federal government against the New Orleans Times-Picayune, charging violation of the anti-trust act, could affect the operation of some 150 newspapers.

Intimidation and threat of punitive legislation had been noted in two Southern States where newspapers had been aggressive in exposure of corruption and graft.

Congressional curiosity over newsprint market conditions might presage an attempt at return of government control over this commodity, the committee warned.

They also urged publishers to look into the recent Supreme Court decision affecting house-to-house solicitation, with respect to its possible application to carrier boy promotion of circulation. It was a report which should have put publishers on the *qui vive* for encroachments from quarters never before considered.

The SNPA Library enjoyed excellent growth during the year, Mrs. Hobby reported as chairman. It numbered 1,872 volumes, with donations in transit that would put it over the 2,000 mark. Bibliographies had been sent to members and other interested persons, with a gratifying increase in calls for books on its shelves.

Seven dailies had been enrolled during the year, only one suspended, and none resigned, Secretary-Manager Johnson reported. The membership, at 393, stood within seven of the 400 goal that Mr. Johnson had contemplated since the end of the war.

Recognition of changed conditions in the South resulted in mutual agreement between the SNPA and the Texas Newspaper Publishers Association to terminate the joint operation of the Dallas office. It had served its original purposes well. The intimate contacts with Southwestern publishers afforded by the Dallas office had brought many newspapers of Texas, Oklahoma, Louisiana, and Arkansas into SNPA membership. SNPA service had cemented that link solidly. On the other side, the SNPA had given the Texas Newspaper Publishers Association the benefit of its broad experience in labor matters, and had trained the TNPA staff to carry that work forward. The mutual needs that had induced the relationship in 1936 no longer existed; when necessary, the SNPA headquarters at Chattanooga could now serve the entire territory efficiently. C. W. Tabb, who had served as SNPA Labor Commissioner in the Dallas office and also as secretary of the Texas association, had resigned in November, 1950, after 13 years' service, to join the Houston Chronicle.

Change was the subject also of an extraordinary address to the convention by Martin M. Reed, president of the Mergenthaler Linotype Company, on the arresting topic, "Equipment Manufacturers—Parasites or Partners?"

After summarizing the failures both of newspaper equipment manufacturers and of newspaper publishers to give sufficient attention to better methods of making newspapers, Mr. Reed emphasized the importance of the change that was even then taking place in newspaper mechanics. He referred to the "amazing and continuing swing to tape-fed typecasting machines and the concurrent growth of wire circuits for the transmission of pre-composed material." He believed it the most significant production development of the past 50 years, with the possibility that it would reverse the trend toward "newspaper casualties." He warned the publishers, however, that its benefits were not automatic. For machines to turn out three to four times as much type as they have averaged before, they must be kept in good maintenance and repair. Perforator operators must be properly selected and trained—"if anyone thinks he can take theatre ushers and make machine monitors or perforator operators out of them in two weeks, he is in for a sad awakening." To handle copy, tape and type it at the new speed "requires planning, co-ordination and system."

Mr. Reed warned also that the ranks of trained competent technical executives of newspapers were growing "woefully thin." Too few apprentices were being trained in mechanical tasks. Only a handful of men were receiving academic training to fit them for junior executives and eventually top executive posts. No schools were training machinists, who would be of major importance in keeping tape-fed composing rooms in working order. Other industries were attending to similar needs; the great newspaper industry could surely do likewise, if publishers would act in concert.

With production costs assuming life-or-death-importance in newspaper operation, the publishers listened intently to an address by T. Coleman Andrews, president of the American Institute of Accountants, on "The Accounting Problems of Newspapers." He outlined a plan of proper classification of expenses, both by departments and as an over-all operation.

Mr. Andrews, who later became Commissioner of the Internal Revenue Service, was on hand also for the group meeting of newspapers of 50,000 or more circulation.

This group session was marked among other things by the presence of a panel of experts in a variety of newspaper fields—a style which was to be followed at SNPA meetings for several years thereafter.

The 1951 panel was composed of Harry Bradley of Birmingham, Alabama, advertising; D. Hiden Ramsey of Asheville, North Carolina, editorial; J. M. Blalock of Columbia, South Carolina, circulation; Lisle Baker, Jr., of Louisville, Kentucky, management; Bob Millar of Jacksonville, Florida, accounting, and R. L. Jones, Jr., of Tulsa, Oklahoma, mechanical. Chairman and Vice-Chairman of the group were Shields Johnson of Roanoke, Virginia, and W. J. Hearin, Jr., of Mobile, Alabama, respectively.

Most notable of the accomplishments of the group session was the designation of a committee (later referred to by some members as the "3-B" Committee) to examine and recommend procedures for the determination of the cost of producing advertising in newspapers. This "triple B" committee was composed of Messrs. Baker, Biggers and Bradley. The committee directed a detailed study issued in 1952 in pamphlet form, and its work, publicized widely in *Editor & Publisher* magazine, undoubtedly sparked additional interest which led to further studies in this important field.

The pamphlet issued by SNPA in May, 1952, was entitled "Procedures for Determining Cost of Advertising by Newspapers."

Some of the older members of the Association must have thrown their memories back 30 years or more when Edward W. Barrett, Assistant Secretary of State for Public Affairs, stepped to the convention platform. It was in 1921 that his father, then publisher of the Birmingham Age-Herald, had displayed to an SNPA convention the first copies of a Southern newspaper printed on newsprint made from Southern spruce pine—a promise that died with its maker the next year.

The younger Barrett did not have newsprint on his mind, however. His subject was the propaganda war that the American government was waging against Communism in Europe and Asia, and he believed American ideas were slowly winning.

E. K. Gaylord, of Oklahoma City, with nearly a half a century of newspaper experience behind him, added to his already notable contributions to SNPA knowledge by a report of his recent visit to Alaska. The vast timberlands of the Territory, he said, could not be made competitive with Canadian and Southern newsprint manufactures because of the high costs of labor and transportation.

A family name long honored in Southern and national journalism received new lustre when Frank A. Daniels of the Raleigh News & Observer was unanimously elected president. Josephus Daniels, Sr., had taken a prominent part in SNPA deliberations, and his sons had served as directors and committee members. K. A. Engel, of Little Rock, became the new board chairman. Myron G. Chambers, of Knoxville, was re-elected treasurer, and Walter C. Johnson, of Chattanooga, as secretary-manager, entered his 40th year of Association service. New directors for three-year terms were:

Alabama—Harry B. Bradley, Birmingham News and Post-Herald; Georgia—Peyton Anderson, Macon News & Telegraph; Oklahoma—

Economic Renaissance — II

Richard Lloyd Jones, Jr., Tulsa Tribune and World; Texas—Frank Mayborn, Temple Telegram; Virginia—Shields Johnson, Roanoke Times and World-News.

Messrs. Anderson, Jones, and Mayborn each represented a new generation in the conduct of SNPA business. Mr. Anderson had recently purchased complete control of the Macon dailies. The Macon Telegraph had been owned by his family for more than half a century, and the Andersons had also owned part control of the Macon News for the past twenty years. Since 1940, a third-interest in both papers had been held by General Newspapers, Inc., but during the previous year (1951), Mr. Anderson had become sole owner. At 43, he was one of the youngest publishers in the Association. The fathers of Mr. Jones and Mr. Mayborn had also been prominent in SNPA affairs at various periods.

President Daniels and Secretary-Manager Johnson could point with pardonable pride at the 1952 convention to the attainment of several goals during the Association's 49th year. Membership had reached the 400 level—no more, no less. The treasury at last had accumulated the reserve equal to a year's operating costs (some $80,000) after 15 years of striving. The Southern Newspaper Library exceeded 2,100 volumes and the long-desired catalog was about to be published. Over-shadowing all other accomplishments, the SNPA had materially assisted the Bowater Paper Company interests in their plans for a newsprint mill at Calhoun, Tenn., and construction of the mill had been started.

One minor disappointment was reported. The 1952 convention, November 20-22, at White Sulphur Springs, W. Va., did not break the attendance record of 534 members and guests set two years earlier at the same place. Last-minute cancellations due to illness and bad weather brought the attendance down to 505, an increase of more than 500 per cent over that of the first convention at White Sulphur Springs in 1923.

But a year of accomplishment brought no complacency to the men at the Association's head. As Mr. Johnson remarked, "Time marches on and we must continue to keep pace with the advancing South."

To that end, the 1952 program marked a complete departure from established convention practice. The increasing importance of women in newspaper publication gained signal recognition. The publishers were welcomed to West Virginia by Mrs. Frances Ogden Stubblefield, publisher of a number of dailies in that state. The Association's response was made by Mrs. Edith O'Keefe Susong, of Greeneville, Tenn., long a regular convention-goer. And the only address by a non-member featured Mrs. Mark F. Ethridge, wife of the publisher of the Louisville Courier-Journal and Times, with a reputation of her own as an author and wit on newspaper topics.

The ladies also had their own golf contest, as a part of the Association's traditional Walter H. Savory Golf Tournament, which was shifted from its usual second-day spot to the afternoon of the third day, after the completion of convention business.

This convention ran on railroad style schedule, with a time-table in the program. Not novel as a trade association procedure, this was an innovation for the informal SNPA. It was popular, too, as was the Association's first experiences with discussions of its staple topics in the hands of expert panels from within and without SNPA ranks. Routine reports of officers and committees were dispatched on Thursday morning. Following the luncheon at which Mrs. Ethridge talked on "Being the Wife of an Old Newspaperman," the convention divided into the three standard group conferences for small, medium, and large city newspapers.

Friday morning's session gave 45 minutes each to the newsprint and advertising panels, followed by reports of the nominations, resolutions and memorial committees. The afternoon session was devoted to the forestry and editorial panels. Dinner followed a reception by the Bowater Paper Company officials. Evening entertainment took the form of an aquatic show in the Greenbrier Hotel's spacious pool.

On Saturday morning, the entire convention heard the reports of Thursday's three group conferences, a presentation of press-room time and motion studies, a report of the Southern and Southwestern Schools of Printing, and a 45-minute panel on circulation. For the first time in more than 20 years, the convention selected its next meeting place, a choice that traditionally had been left to the Board. President Daniels had named a special committee to canvass the possibilities in advance of the 1952 meeting. With its conventions attracting more than 500 people, the Association had to look early and carefully for adequate quarters. Long ago, it had decided to meet only rarely in the South's large cities. Since the Grove Park Inn at Asheville had been outgrown some 16 years previously the Association had met five times at Hot Springs, Ark., three times at Edgewater Park, Miss., twice each at Mineral Wells, Texas, and White Sulphur Springs, W. Va., and once at St. Petersburg, Fla. For 1953, facing the celebration of its 50th anniversary, the SNPA wanted something new and special, and the choice fell upon Boca Raton, on Florida's ocean coast, in the comfortable month of November.

Reports of the newsprint and newsprint mills committees and the newsprint panel discussions all agreed generally that the supply situation had improved. The price had been increased $5-$10 by various mills in mid-1952, after the publishers had assured themselves that a "plateau" had been attained, and some drew comfort from the belief that the 1952 price level did in fact represent the post-war peak.

D. Hiden Ramsey, Asheville Citizen-Times, who had watched newsprint trends for the Association for many years, cautioned that the "situation does not justify any surrender to complacency." He told the panel that Southern newspapers, with their tremendous circulation growth in recent years, had not reached the saturation point and would continue to need an expanding supply of paper. Any restriction on supply would hit Southern dailies harder than those of other American regions.

Cranston Williams, general manager of the American Newspaper Publishers Association, gave the panel his opinion that it was time to think of a fourth newsprint mill in the South. Another panel member was August B. Meyer, president of the Bowater Paper Company, New York. He declared that inflation and uncertain conditions made it difficult to say where and when and if another Southern mill should be built. He advocated increasing production by existing paper machines, as the Canadian mills had done since the end of World War II. Mr. Meyer expected that the $55,000,000 Bowater plant at Calhoun, Tenn., would be in operation by March, 1954. He also warned briefly that publishers were bringing about higher paper production costs by reducing the width of newsprint rolls as an economy measure. This caution was to be repeated later in 1952 by R. M. Fowler, president of the Newsprint Association of Canada. As a member of the SNPA panel, Mr. Fowler thought that the Canadian mills could meet increased paper requirements during 1953 without difficulty. He also accented the note that the Canadian mills had increased their production by 1,000,000 tons or 85 per cent since the war—and had financed that expansion out of their profits made from paper price levels that irked publishers. "No profits, no expansion," he told the publishers.

Frank Jepson, of Madden, Reeve Angel & Co., of New York, representing European producers on the panel, could see nothing but shortage and the need for more production in the five years ahead. The SNPA newsprint committee, headed by T. A. Corcoran, Louisville Courier-Journal and Times, had commented favorably on the construction of new machines for the Finnish mills (represented by Mr. Jepson) which was expected to add 200,000 tons annually to the supply pool.

George C. Biggers, Atlanta Journal, vice-president of the ANPA and past president of the SNPA and also chairman of the SNPA newsprint mills committee, declared that the American economy was geared to mass production and selling. That called for heavy consumption of newsprint, and it should be maintained, he declared. The British idea of rationing newsprint and limiting newspapers to small editions was profitable to publishers, but it was not adapted to the American way of doing things.

Mr. Biggers' newsprint mills committee reported that, having helped the Bowater mill project to the starting line, it had made no more recent efforts to interest capital in new Southern newsprint mills. This was not a long-range policy, he told the publishers; for the moment, the Southern newspapers could not take on new substantial commitments for purchase of tonnage from mills that might be projected, considering their present agreements with the Southland, Coosa River, and Bowater mills. Mr. Corcoran's committee recommended that the Association continue its interest in new mill construction and the acquisition of potential newsprint mill sites, warning again that other paper interests were moving in on the most favorable locations.

The convention adopted the latter view. After commending the Southland, Coosa River, and Bowater enterprises as making the

"South one of the leading newsprint producers in the United States," the resolution proceeded:

"Be it further resolved, That it is the opinion of the SNPA that despite the splendid progress, there still remains a large potential for further newsprint production in the South, and that it urges the Newsprint Mills Committee to continue its effort to interest new capital in the construction of additional mills and to survey sites for such mills; and to consider whether means should be taken to protect one or more of the sites."

The Association also took cognizance of its newsprint committee's repeated recommendation that a permanent joint committee of newsprint producers and newsprint users be established on a national basis. It endorsed the idea and ordered it transmitted to the ANPA, "in the hope that that organization can take steps to establish such a committee."

And once more the Association reiterated "its strong support of all conservation measures, particularly those concerned with forestry"; members were urged to "continue to give editorial and news support to all measures to that end."

Earlier in 1952, the board of directors had adopted resolutions deploring the increase of $10 per ton announced by Canadian newsprint manufacturers for June 15, and recommending that the price increase be cancelled in the mutual interests of mills and publishers. The newsprint committee had informed the Board that this announcement had come on the heels of a substantial reduction in the price of Scandinavian newsprint to British newspapers. Eastern and Southern U. S. mills announced in late July that they had deferred the proposed rise in price, and later in the year made a $5 to $7 per ton increase effective. Canadian and West Coast Mills, however, adhered to the $10 increase.

The advertising panel devoted most of its time to the relatively new problem of co-operative advertising, upon which newspaper executives held widely varying views. Some regarded it as a device by which national advertising bought its way into newspaper columns at the local rate, which generally was less than the charge quoted for national copy. Other newspaper people, including many of the men charged with selling space, believed that newspaper linage would suffer if this joint purchase of space by national advertisers and their local and retail distributors were restricted. That was the view of E. Julian Herndon, Little Rock Democrat, and Loyal Phillips, St. Petersburg Independent, expressed in the panel discussion. Mr. Phillips, a frequent speaker on advertising topics at SNPA conventions, advised that newspapers put pressure on retailers and district area distributors so that the amount of co-operative advertising in newspapers would be increased. The panel discussion did not evoke any opposing opinions. Ralph Callahan, Anniston Star, declaring that advertising salesmen on smaller papers were inadequately paid, urged the establishment of incentive or bonus programs for advertising staffs.

Views of the editorial panel leaned heavily toward technique. The Board of Directors had looked into the question of news suppression upon which the 1951 convention had expressed itself vaguely, and had decided that more explicit opinions were necessary. It adopted twin resolutions at its mid-winter meeting, held at the Hotel Peabody, Memphis, Tennessee, February 11, 1952, on "Freedom of Information" and "Covenant on Human Rights." These became official actions of the Association by the total endorsement of the convention. They read:

"Freedom of Information—Recognizing the increasing efforts at all levels of government to deprive the public of information about the administration of those offices, members of the Southern Newspaper Publishers Association Board of Directors do hereby resolve to enlist their services in any movement that has for its purposes the resistance of that trend, and particularly do they wish to advise the Freedom of Information Committee of the American Society of Newspaper Editors of their desire to co-operate in every way in its endeavors."

"Covenant on Human Rights—Inasmuch as there is before the United States Senate a United Nations Covenant on Human Rights which presents a serious threat to the basic American freedoms of religion, speech, press, assembly, and petition, and,

"Inasmuch as any signatory to this so-called treaty could suppress those basic freedoms through declaration of emergency, and,

"Inasmuch as the Supreme Court has held that laws implementing treaties are valid, we, the Directors of the Southern Newspaper Pub-

Economic Renaissance — II

lishers Association do hereby resolve that this Covenant on Human Rights, in its present form, be rejected by the United States Senate, and that the members of the Southern Newspaper Publishers Association examine carefully the document and, if they are agreed as to its danger, advise their representative in the Senate."

Both of these matters had been summarized again in the report of the Legislative Committee. This group, of which M. R. Ashworth, Columbus (Ga.) Ledger-Enquirer, was chairman, also repeated its warning that newspapers should not submit to payment of local license taxes; it regarded them as an immediately potential threat to press freedom.

"If we permit licensing, that is granting a privilege to operate newspapers, then we also grant the privilege of having the license taken away, and thereby the permission to publish taken away," the committee warned. In California, a lower court had found such local licensing unconstitutional. The Association did not act upon this phase of the committee's report in 1951 or 1952, possibly because the question was presented in general, rather than specific, terms.

The convention also took no official notice of the recent decision of the U. S. District Court in New Orleans, holding that the sale of advertising at forced combination rates by the Times-Picayune and the Daily States was in restraint of trade and must cease. This decision had been appealed, and the outcome was awaited with concern by many of the membership. Approximately 150 of the Association's 400 newspapers sold their space under some combination arrangement; not all of them, however, maintained the compulsory use of both papers in the combination that was the crux of the government's case in New Orleans.

None of these legal problems came before the editors' panel conducted by Wilbur C. Stouffer of the Roanoke (Va.) World-News. Its theme seemed to be that "good newspapers are read more and longer than ever before, despite pressing requirements on readers' leisure time."

J. Montgomery Curtis, of Columbia University's American Press Institute, advised editors to give more attention to their readers' economic interests—taxes, employment in the community, retail prices, etc. As moderator of a succession of Institute forums of active newspaper people since 1945, Mr. Curtis had amassed a large backlog of information of newspaper practices and needs. He suggested four guides for editorial conduct—circulation figures, letters to the editor, reports from workers in circulation, advertising and news departments, and advertising salesmen's reports on the feeling of their customers on the newspaper's effectiveness as an advertising medium.

Mr. Stouffer stressed the importance of local news. Thomas N. Schroth, managing editor of the militant Brooklyn (N. Y.) Eagle, also addressed himself mainly to the importance of continuous local crusading policies. He was sharply critical of the New York City newspapers in the 1952 Presidential campaign, declaring that only two of the eight dailies maintained an objective viewpoint throughout the contest. He didn't name names. C. W. Orcutt, Knoxville News-Sentinel, keeping to the local theme, repeated the old warning against pet promotions by local advertisers, clubs and friends of the paper's executives. Free publicity must be kept down, he said, so that the paper would have space for legitimate local news. I. William Hill, Washington Star, counseled shorter sentences and shorter stories. Also he advised, "Challenge everything, come up with new ideas, avoid being dull."

Ralph B. Chandler, publisher of the Mobile Press-Register, headed the forestry panel, which also included Charles A. Gillett, American Forestry Products Industries, Inc., of Washington; H. J. Malsberger, Southern Pulpwood Conservation Association, Atlanta; and Charles Hodel, Beckley (W. Va.) Post Herald and Raleigh Register. All spoke on the need for conservation of Southern forests.

Jack Estes, former circulation manager of the Dallas News, who had been appointed SNPA circulation consultant after the 1951 convention, conducted the circulation panel. Other members were: Lisle Baker, Jr., Louisville Courier-Journal and Times; R. C. Millar, Jacksonville Florida Times-Union; James M. Moroney, Jr., Dallas News; W. S. Morris, Augusta Chronicle; Dave Vandivier, Chickasha (Okla.) Express; E. C. Davis, Beaumont Enterprise and Journal; Eugene Worrell, Bristol (Va.-Tenn.) Virginia-Tennessean; Lorentz Steele, Charleston (W. Va.) Gazette, and J. G. Ward, Charlotte Observer.

This was a high-powered panel, for it included a past president and several former directors of the Association. It found that 33 member newspapers had raised subscription prices recently or were in the process of doing so, while 20 newspapers had not effected any increase. Higher prices had resulted in little circulation loss, according to the reports.

Robert H. Spahn, Oklahoma City Oklahoman and Times, who had introduced the subject of personnel management at a recent convention, came back with motion picture studies of the Oklahoman-Times pressroom. They had been used in a recent arbitration hearing, involving the disputed number of men to be assigned to a press. The pictures were aimed to "take some of the mystery out of pressroom operations," Mr. Spahn stated, and they might also be used as a job-training film.

Mechanical department jobs were also the subject of H. F. Ambrose, president of the Southern School of Printing, Nashville, Tenn. As the Association had heard many times before, the number of trained men in newspaper trades was steadily declining, he said. He urged that a demand be created among high school graduates for training as printers, by demonstrating the advantages of the printing trades.

Newsprint questions, higher advertising rates, and television competition were noted as the principal problems before the group meetings. With several publishers reporting that they had adopted narrowed column widths and others considering that economy, agreement was general that newspapers should try to reach standards on the narrower columns and newsprint roll widths, in the interests of their advertisers and of the newsprint manufacturers.

Richard Lloyd Jones, Jr., publisher of the Tulsa Tribune, received unanimous election as president, and Frank Daniels took over the chairmanship of the Board. Myron G. Chambers was re-elected treasurer, and Walter C. Johnson, as secretary-manager. Six directors were named, five for three year terms, as follows:

Louisiana—Chapman Hyams, III, New Orleans Times-Picayune and States; Mississippi—Sumter Gillespie, Greenwood Commonwealth; North Carolina—Thomas L. Robinson, Charlotte News; Tennessee—Charles McD. Puckette, Chattanooga Times; West Virginia—Walker Long, Huntington Advertiser and Herald-Dispatch.

To fill out the unexpired board term of Mr. Jones, the Association chose Edward L. Gaylord, business manager of the Oklahoma City

Oklahoman and Times, and the son of E. K. Gaylord, publisher of those newspapers and a past president of the SNPA.

Messrs. Robinson and Puckette, without previous service as directors, had come to their SNPA newspapers after distinguished service in Northern journalism, Mr. Robinson in Boston and Mr. Puckette in New York. The latter was a native of Sewanee, Tennessee, and a member of a family long distinguished as Southern educators, and had been managing editor of the New York Evening Post and an assistant to the publisher of the New York Times before returning to his native state. Mr. Robinson was an out-and-out New England Yankee, but no unreconstructed Rebel could have been more enthusiastic for the South. Both of the new directors had rendered important service to the SNPA in recent years as committee members —Mr. Puckette as chairman of the Postal Committee and Mr. Robinson as vice-chairman of the Legislative Committee. After their election they continued in these capacities.

The new board met briefly during the convention. Its midwinter meeting, February 28-March 1, 1953, in the luxurious Shamrock Hotel, Houston, adjourned to Oklahoma City, where the directors joined in honoring E. K. Gaylord on his completion of 50 active years in Oklahoma City journalism.

SNPA Marks Golden Anniversary

Record-Breaking Attendance of More than 600 at Boca Raton Convention—50 Years Condensed into 50-Minute Review by President Jones—Trade and Daily Press Hail Occasion—Publishers Warned Against Complacency on Newsprint Supply and Television Competition.

THE 50th anniversary meeting of the SNPA held at Boca Raton, Florida, early in November, 1953, was marked with appropriate ceremony. But the historian cannot resist the observation that the SNPA celebration was only one of the highlights of widespread recognition of the South's enormous progress, socially and economically, during the 50 years of the SNPA.

Three trade journals serving the newspaper and advertising fields were represented at Boca Raton with massive issues. That of *Editor & Publisher,* duly clad in gold, devoted 240 pages to news and advertising development of the truly New South. That of *Advertising Age* gave 80 pages to treatment of the same general subject from another viewpoint. *Southern Advertising & Publishing* appeared in gold with a 90-page edition. Heralded at the convention, but published shortly afterward, was an edition of *Iron Age,* with a 30-page analysis by its editor of the factors which had sent the South industrially far ahead of the rest of America since 1940.

Greeted by a green-and-gold banner as they entered the sumptuous lobby of the Boca Raton Hotel and Club, members and guests were made immediately conscious that the Golden Anniversary was the dominant theme. As they paid their registration fees they were handed a gold-covered convention program, trimmed with the red SNPA emblem designed for the anniversary year. They also received a souvenir lead pencil, gold in color, with the anniversary emblem imprinted on it. The ladies were recipients of a copy of a Souvenir

THE SOUTH AND ITS NEWSPAPERS

Edition of the 976-page "The American Woman's Encyclopedia of Home Decorating," jacketed in gold.

And, at luncheon on November 5, they heard a feature entirely new to an SNPA audience—a 50-minute recorded summary by President Richard Lloyd Jones, Jr., of the Association's half-century of service to Southern newspapers. Mr. Jones had read the draft of this chronicle and decided that it offered some dramatic possibilities. Returning to Tulsa, he composed an amateur script of a radio documentary, tried it out on some Oklahoma newspaper people, then flew to Louisville, where the Louisville Courier-Journal and Times placed the facilities of WHAS at his disposal. Art Sydney, a radio professional of the station, whipped the typescript into regulation form, and Mr. Jones took on the 14-hour task of rehearsing and recording the show. Engineers from the Miami Herald's WQAM put on the taped story at Boca Raton under the title "This is Your Voice," with this introduction by Mr. Jones, after a roll-call of past presidents who are now deceased:

"To the memory of these past presidents of the SNPA this program is respectfully dedicated. On this anniversary date of 50 years, here is the story of an association: the story of the SNPA. Woven into its fabric are the bonds of fellowship, integrity, ingenuity, and hard work. Here today—now in a matter of minutes, we will attempt to recapture the highlights of half a century—the aims, the dreams, the struggle, and, above all, the fulfillment of a purpose: the lighting of a torch ignited by those who have gone before us and handed over to the persons here assembled, ever to be restless, never to be content, seeking relentlessly to improve the service of the press for the welfare of the South and of the people of the Nation."

Stereo slides portrayed SNPA leaders of the past and present, as well as pictures of Southern developments in which the SNPA played an important part. Actors recreated the voices from the near and distant past, including those of Henry W. Grady and Dr. Charles H. Herty. The famous Grady address, in which he described a funeral for which the South had provided "nothing but the corpse and the hole in the ground," was repeated, with interpolated comments illustrative of the South's present ability to furnish all that was necessary to the occasion.

SNPA Marks Golden Anniversary

It was inevitable, of course, that the recording had many references to Walter C. Johnson, concluding with an expression of the Association's gratitude for his long and varied services. And the SNPA tributes to Mr. Johnson did not end with that. In company with other past presidents, he was presented with a plaque setting forth his term of service in that office against an original background—an outline map of the 14 States comprising the SNPA area. When that ceremony was over, Mr. Johnson was again called to the front to receive the original crayon portrait of himself that had been used as copy in an advertisement bought by the board of directors in the special edition of *Editor & Publisher*. Then he received another plaque reproducing the same advertisement in full. Another summons found him receiving a handsome check, with the orders of the board that he take an extended vacation. In a subsequent Bulletin relating these events, Mr. Johnson drily observed that "nothing was said about his having to refund the money if he failed to carry out the orders." And, finally, he received an Elgin watch from a group of friends headed by Garland Porter of *Southern Advertising & Publishing* in token of gratitude for long and friendly co-operation. It was quite a day for the man dubbed by President Jones "Mr. SNPA."

Past presidents who were honored with plaques, besides Mr. Johnson, were: John A. Park, Raleigh Times; Clark Howell, Jr., Atlanta Constitution; James G. Stahlman, Nashville Banner; E. K. Gaylord, Oklahoma City Oklahoman and Times; James E. Chappell, Birmingham News; E. M. (Ted) Dealey, Dallas News; Adolph Shelby Ochs, Chattanooga Times; A. W. Huckle, Rock Hill Herald; George C. Biggers, Atlanta Journal; E. B. Stahlman, Jr., Nashville Banner; Lisle Baker, Jr., Louisville Courier-Journal and Times; Mrs. Oveta Culp Hobby, Houston Post; Clarence B. Hanson, Jr., Birmingham News; K. A. Engel, Little Rock Arkansas Democrat; Frank A. Daniels, Raleigh News & Observer; and immediate past president Richard Lloyd Jones, Jr.

James H. Allison, Wichita Falls Times and Record-News, the senior past president, was unable to attend the convention and his plaque was received for him by Rhea Howard, publisher of those newspapers. Other living past presidents who are no longer in newspaper work, also were awarded plaques. They were: Robert S.

Jones, Asheville, N. C.; Charles I. Stewart, Lexington, Ky.; Arthur G. Newmyer, Washington, D. C.; and Emanuel Levi, Louisville, Ky.

Despite the temptations of Florida's sunny beaches, and despite the birthday parties, the SNPA did accomplish a normal stint of convention business. Twelve new members were admitted, bringing the membership to 412.

Although there was plenty of newsprint available during 1953, the newsprint committee, headed by T. A. Corcoran of the Louisville Courier-Journal and Times and D. Hiden Ramsey of the Asheville Citizen-Times, warned the publishers against complacency. With the completion of the Bowater Southern Paper Mill at Calhoun, Tenn., in 1954, the South would be producing about 377,000 tons of newsprint annually or only one-third of its current newsprint consumption. An increase in European paper use, which is currently far below that of pre-war times, could bring about a serious world shortage, the committee counseled.

The committee informed the convention also that a mill under construction in Louisiana is prepared to give bagasse (sugar mill waste) a thorough test as a pulp material. The committee urged continued SNPA member support of forestry and conservation programs, additional machines at the Southland and Coosa River Mills, and a "serious study of the practicability of SNPA purchasing, or protecting by options, one mill site at least."

The newsprint mills committee did not go along with that final recommendation. In its report signed by Peyton Anderson, Macon Telegraph and News, and Charles P. Manship, Jr., Baton Rouge State Times & Advocate, this committee stated that it had studied sites for mills that could be eventually self-sustaining through pulpwood and timber sales. But, it added, "informed foresters tell us land to support a mill would cost a minimum of $3,000,000. Timber development on the site before it would possibly be self-sustaining would cost another $2,000,000. Your committee does not feel such funds could be raised from the membership at the present time. Nor would it be advisable for the SNPA to operate such an enterprise."

Nevertheless, the committee reported that at least one more mill might be constructed in the South if the publishers would provide contract commitments and investment support as the SNPA members had done for the Southland and Coosa River mills. That proposition had not assumed definite form as this History closed.

Newsprint and forestry engaged the convention's attention additionally through two panel discussions. Mr. Corcoran headed the newsprint panel, which included I. H. Peck, International Paper Sales Co., Montreal; George C. Biggers, Harold S. Foley, Powell River Co., Ltd., Vancouver, B. C.; Ralph Watt, vice president of the Coosa River Newsprint Company; Peyton Anderson, and J. M. Blalock, Columbia State and Record.

Mr. Peck predicted that newsprint demand in North America would reach 6,900,000 tons by 1955, against a total production of 6,800,000 tons in 1953. He believed that the industry could meet the additional need by expansion and improved techniques with existing machines.

Mr. Watt, whose company has done extensive experimenting with Southern woods, predicted that "very shortly, there may be an announcement that hardwoods will be used for making newsprint in the South."

Mr. Ramsey, heading the forestry panel, reported that more than one-fifth of all industrial workers in the South are employed in forest industries. Reuben B. Robertson, Sr., Champion Paper & Fibre Company, Canton, N. C., declared that only 20,000,000 acres, or less than 10 per cent of the South's forests are being managed for sustained yields of pulpwood and lumber, and urged energetic support by the publishers of the SNPA conservation programs. Guyton DeLoach, Georgia State Forester, threw another local light on that picture. Forestry, he said, is now Georgia's biggest business, worth more than $750,000,000 annually. Forestry brought Georgia farmers $167,000,000 in cash income in 1952, he said, more than they received from the sale of corn, cotton, and tobacco crops combined.

The editorial affairs panel, headed by W. C. Stouffer, Roanoke World-News, resolved itself into a discussion of the impact of television on newspapers. Bob Elliott, executive sports editor of the Miami Herald, saw no threat to the press, nor even a battle for survival with television. Both depended upon pictures to whet public interest, he said. James Couey, Birmingham News, said that while newspapers have not lost readers to TV, they have lost reader time. And he called for improved newspaper writing, news coverage, picture presentation by the press if it is to compete successfully for reader attention. Jean Mooney, of NEA Service, Inc., said that TV was doing a better job than newspapers in creating interest among women.

The new complexion of SNPA thinking on labor relations was briefly mentioned in the report of Robert H. Spahn, Oklahoma City Oklahoman and Times, Chairman of the labor committee. In keeping with ideas several times offered by Mr. Spahn himself in recent conventions and by other speakers, publishers were now thinking in terms of time and motion studies to determine manning needs in pressrooms and other mechanical departments. Considerable interest had developed in the scientific training of mechanical department employes by visual aids and other modern training devices. In these related fields, the SNPA had sponsored a clinic at New Orleans during 1953, planned by James L. Knight, Miami Herald, labor committee vice-chairman. This may be considered the most advanced application by newspaper publishers of modern industrial engineering studies to their mechanical operations to the present. Still in the formative stages, it reflects the view that rising labor costs and narrowing profit margins can only be met through the application of more efficient methods to newspaper production, along with more skillful negotiations to permit new and efficient techniques to be introduced into newspaper plants. Naturally, the Teletypesetter operation received considerable attention at the clinic, for Labor Commissioner Tom Tanner reported that the number of these installations in the South had increased from 240 to 264 in the period September 30, 1952-July 31, 1953.

Mr. Tanner's report summarized generally peaceful labor relations during the previous year and pointed to the stable cost-of-living index as justifying no increase in pay for the organized departments.

Chairman K. A. Engel of the Library Committee reported that the Southern Newspaper Library had grown to 2,143 volumes and that the long-promised catalog was nearing completion.

Louis Spilman, Waynesboro (Va.) News-Virginian, chairman of the Schools of Journalism committee, reported on the troubled situation which had arisen during the year on the question of accrediting institutions for education in journalism. Some institutions had objected to the whole principle of accreditation by the American Council on Education for Journalism. As noted earlier, this body included a member of each of the journalism educators associations and also representatives of the SNPA, ANPA, the Inland Daily Press Association and the American Society of Newspaper Editors. The difficulty had been resolved, Mr. Spilman declared, by reorganization of the council on a broader educational association basis and the amendment of its by-laws. New, and presumably acceptable, standards of accreditation of schools had been formulated with no lowering of standards, and Mr. Spilman recommended that SNPA participation in the accreditation program be continued. The SNPA board remained skeptical, however, and, adopting a "wait and see" policy, withheld the annual appropriation of $750 to the council that the SNPA had voted in recent years. Mr. Spilman, who had retired at the convention as committee chairman, continued his advocacy of energetic SNPA participation in the accreditation program. As this History closed, it appeared probable that the SNPA would resume its long-time co-operation in maintaing high standards of instruction for journalism and radio-television.

Loyal Phillips, St. Petersburg Independent, chairman of the public relations committee, recommended that this committee be vested with responsibility for sponsoring National Newspaper Week throughout the SNPA area. In the broad public relations field, he declared that space contributions of SNPA newspapers to rural development projects and youth programs, plus the cash donations of publishers, totalled "considerably in excess of $1,000,000" in recent years.

The finest reporting in the world is done in Washington, the November 6 luncheon guests were told by Ernest B. Vaccaro, who covered the White House for the Associated Press during the Truman administration. Despite the flood of government publicity, he said, most of the news printed by newspapers is the result of enterprising inquiry by reporters.

Harold S. Barnes, director of the ANPA Bureau of Advertising, struck a resounding note of optimism as the 1953 convention's closing speaker. He told the publishers that if they make up a "model blueprint of your community" from available U. S. Census Bureau figures, they can "prove to your advertisers that there's still a rich and unexploited frontier" which they haven't seen because "it's right in their own backyard."

"Too many businesses set their sights too low," Mr. Barnes said. "They think in terms of dollar volume and not in units of production. They've complacently seen their dollar volume roll up each year without investigating their physical volume. Business must be taught to stop taking last year's figures as the only yardstick of progress."

An unusually long list of deceased executives and employees of member newspapers and of their near relatives was offered by the memorials committee, with appropriate resolutions. Among those deceased during the year were John S. Parks, past president of the SNPA, Hugh I. Shott, a former director, Douglas Southall Freeman, editor emeritus of the Richmond News-Leader, Dolph G. Frantz, editor of the Shreveport Journal, John Paschall, editor emeritus of the Atlanta Journal, and Orville E. Johnson, CPA, head of the firm that has audited the association books for more than 25 years.

Among the resolutions adopted one marked the presence at Boca Raton of Evelyn Harris and W. E. Mansfield, the only survivors of those who had attended the original 1903 SNPA gathering. Mr. Harris was then a reporter for the Atlanta Constitution and in later years attended many SNPA meetings as public relations representative of the Southern Bell Telephone Company. Mr. Mansfield in 1903 and for many years afterwards had been Southern sales representative of the International Paper Company.

First on the list of resolutions was one which reaffirmed the association's concern with forest conservation. It read:

"Recognizing the tremendous role that our forest resources play and will play in increasing measure in the economy of the South and in insuring to Southern newspapers an adequate supply of newsprint, we urge the member newspapers to support all measures and agencies that seek to enlarge these resources and foster their wisest use."

Another resolution "rejoiced" at the prospect of early completion of the Bowaters mill at Calhoun, Tenn.

As usual, numerous resolutions expressed the SNPA thanks to the convention hosts, public officials, and the newspapers of Florida, and to all who had contributed to the anniversary convention's success. One thanked Senator Harry F. Byrd of Virginia for the apples he had shipped to the convention from his Shenandoah Valley orchards, another to the Consolidated Book Publishing Co., for the special anniversary edition of Encyclopedia of Home Decorating presented the ladies in attendance at the convention, and to others who had provided gifts and souvenirs.

And the closing resolution, looking to the future, read thus:

"Whereas, the experiments conducted by the Associated Press and the Rocky Mount Telegram clearly demonstrate that the radio transmission of news pictures is entirely practical and can be brought within the economic capacity of the small newspapers; and

"Whereas it is highly essential—notably for the smaller papers—that the fullest development of the wireless method of sending news photographs be speeded up;

"Therefore, be it resolved that the officers, directors, and management of the association be authorized and urged to take the lead in coordinating and quickening the activities of all agencies that are interested in the early institution of a comprehensive and practical system of transmitting photographs to newspapers by wireless."

Peyton Anderson was elected president, and Richard Lloyd Jones, Jr., automatically became chairman of the board. Myron G. Chambers was re-elected treasurer and Walter C. Johnson as secretary-manager.

Max Nussbaum of the Moultrie (Ga.) Observer was elected to the directorship vacated by Mr. Anderson's move to the presidency.

James L. Knight, Miami Herald, was named director-at-large, and other new board members were Loyal Phillips, St. Petersburg Independent; Sam E. Gearhart, Fayetteville Northwest Arkansas Times; Phil Buchheit, Spartanburg Herald-Journal and J. W. Mann, Lexington (Ky.) Herald-Leader. All except Mr. Knight were new to board service.

In Retrospect

INESCAPABLY, the Southern Newspaper Publishers Association was born of the Nineteenth Century. Even the youngest of its founders looked back on a boyhood amid the miseries of Reconstruction, and a young manhood that saw the South raising its head from the wreckage. The progress of the SNPA in the Twentieth Century may be taken as a rough index of what has happened to Southern journalism and to the whole economy of the South since 1903.

The beginnings of the SNPA represented a marked change in the thinking of Southern newspaper owners since the first organization of Southern newspapers was formed. That was the Press Association of the Confederate States, organized in the Spring of 1862 to provide the morning newspapers of the embattled South with telegraphic news. The old link with the New York Associated Press at Louisville had been severed with the opening of hostilities, and makeshifts had filled the interim.

In several respects the war-born Confederate Press Association was remarkable. It laid the groundwork which the co-operative Associated Press largely followed in its reorganization in New York at the turn of the century. For the CPA was truly a co-operative organization, which the old New York Associated Press was not. The CPA was owned by its members and acted in their name in fixing rates for service and in protecting its news from pilferage. Also it put up a strong fight for the interest of newspapers and the right of the public to the news against some Confederate Generals who resented journalistic curiosity. Fragmentary records of this Association came to light a few years ago, and its story was reconstructed in *Editor & Publisher* issues of Aug. 13, 20 & 27, 1949, and, under the pen of Prof. Quintus Wilson, of the University of Utah, in the *Journalism* Quarterly of *Vol. 26, June, 1949*. Like the old soldiers whose heroic tales it told, the Confederate Press Association "faded away" with the war's end, apparently without formal dissolution.

Although the war was quickly followed by a revival of daily and weekly journalism throughout the South, the struggle for existence kept all journalistic energies occupied. The record reveals no effort to form a regional newspaper organization before 1880. On April 15, of that year, the need for improved news service brought together a dozen publishers in Atlanta to form the Southern Press Association. Their guests were important officials of the New York Associated Press and the Western Union Telegraph Company, and the minutes of the meeting, kept by Adolph S. Ochs, then publisher of the Chattanooga Times, record that "arrangements were made for a more extended telegraph service."

The meeting also called for the repeal of duties on print paper and revocation of the patent covering the use of wood-pulp. At that time ground wood was a relatively new constituent of print paper, and the consuming publishers had not yet benefited greatly by the cheaper manufacturing process it afforded.

Membership in the Southern Press Association was limited to newspapers receiving dispatches of the New York Associated Press or of associations connected with that service. SPA records, also fragmentary, indicate the continuing interest of publishers in better news service. Frequent proposals were made that a purely Southern wire news service be organized, to provide a regional supplement to the New York AP dispatches. Nothing came directly of these, and the Southern Press Association seems to have merged its identity with that of the Southern Associated Press, formed on October 29, 1891, to meet a specific crisis in national news service affairs.

The purposes of the Southern Associated Press were "to buy and sell news and to contract with individuals, firms, associations and corporations for its collection, editing, writing, transmission, sale and exchange." A salaried manager was provided, with pay not to exceed $1,200 per year. Only members of the Southern Press Association were eligible to the new group, unless with the written consent of "three-fourths of the executive committee and the nearest shareholder of the Southern Associated Press to the applicant."

At that time the New York Associated Press, the Western Associated Press and the old United Press were locked in a struggle which would destroy the latter and the New York AP. In late 1891, however, both of these wooed the new Southern group with attractive proposals, which were cannily balanced without definite commitments. Eventually, the Southern newspapers, guided by Mr. Ochs and Evan P. Howell, of the Atlanta Constitution, threw their strength to the reorganized Western organization, which became known as "The Associated Press." When that became a fact, the Southern Associated Press ceased as a separate entity.

The years between 1892 and 1898 seem to have passed without meetings of Southern publishers, except for those concerned with the Associated Press. Then the Southern Publishers Association was formed in Atlanta on March 8, 1898, treading the footprints of its predecessors but aiming at a broader field of service. Its fatal defect was limitation of membership to morning newspapers taking the AP service, which barred the numerous evening newspapers then growing in prosperity and importance throughout the South. Professing an interest in all newspaper problems, the Southern Publishers Association also dedicated itself to "co-operation for the development of the material and industrial resources of the South."

This Association met in 1899 and in 1901, with attractive programs but meager attendance. It was apparent that a broader base was needed to bring into active membership the men who were molding a journalism worthy of the New South.

When representatives of 20 morning and evening newspapers met on April 14, 1903 (again at Atlanta) to form the Southern Newspapers Publishers Association, the South that they served was still overwhelmingly rural. No city approached the half-million mark in population, and relatively few had 100,000 souls within their corporate limits. In the States then included in the SNPA (Oklahoma and West Virginia did not join the ranks for several years) either cotton or tobacco provided the bulk of income.

Few mills then turned raw cotton into even the crudest fabrics near the fields where it was grown. Rayon and other chemical fibres were wholly unknown. Cotton moved to New England and Europe, to make fortunes for its processors, but leaving relatively little for

IN RETROSPECT

the farmers and ginners. Scattered factories made furniture from Southern wood, but here again, for the most part, the South had to be content with a relatively small income for its raw forest products. Florida had yet to discover the magic of its sunshine as a source of prosperity. The coal and iron ore in the Southern Appalachians remained largely untouched, for the experts were sure that "Southern iron will not make steel." (They were equally sure 30 years later that Southern pine would not make paper). Development of the South's abundant water power was still elementary and the region would wait many a year before its streams could give electricity to thousands of farms and homes.

The first of the Texas oil fields had achieved nationwide note a couple of years earlier, but not even the most optimistic fortune-seeker could then picture petroleum's impact on the South and the nation. It may be surmised, with almost certainty, that none of the publishers gathered at Atlanta owned an automobile. And, if any did, it is beyond question that none drove to the Georgia metropolis. Then, and for many years afterward, Southern roads (and most others) were surfaced for horse-and-wagon traffic. The automobile is mentioned in SNPA records for the first time in 1907.

Railroad travel in the South in 1903 was adequate for a dominantly rural culture. The Southern Railway System had not yet organized its steel net covering almost all Southern States, but small lines with well-worn equipment and slow schedules shuttled freight and passengers with frequent changes of cars. The telephone, entering its second quarter-century, was steadily adding Southern subscribers, and the SNPA at its 1915 convention heard Pacific Ocean surf breaking in the earphones at each diner's place, over the first coast-to-coast phone line. This was a foretaste of the miracles of radio, but in 1903, Southern editors and newspaper readers who knew of Prof. Marconi's recent transatlantic wireless messages found no application for them in daily life.

If the South was more parochial than other parts of bustling America in 1903, its newspaper people were shedding their indifference to other than local interests. Southern editors and publishers had taken a leading part in the several reorganizations of the Associated Press during the previous 10 years, and they manifested deep concern for the supply of adequate and accurate news of the nation and the world. The editor, rather than the publisher, remained the important factor in Southern journalism, and the South continued to read the crackling and blistering editorials that typified personal journalism. On the other side, Southern readers saw few of the sensational box-car heads that had become familiar in Northern cities late in the Nineties. Not that Southern newspaper people were blind to the circulation-making potentials of the new metropolitan journalism; they were alert to them and, as time passed, they selected for their own such of its elements as would not offend reader sensibilities.

Change was in the air as the SNPA came into being. The long search of newspapers for a machine to accelerate the pace of hand type composition had been rewarded at last with the perfection of the Mergenthaler Linotype. As the new century dawned, every daily in the South had one or more of these machines in operation or was contemplating their purchase. Whether or not the machine fulfilled the claim that it would set five times as much type as a hand compositor, it certainly far outstripped the old technique in output. Unrealized, however, were the fears of the old printers that their jobs would be wiped out. Many of them learned to operate the machine. Others were needed to complete the process of handling the greatly increased output of type on its way to the press. Bigger newspapers became the almost universal result of machine composition.

On the heels of the Linotype's practical development came new presses to take more pages and to whirl them out at ever increasing speed. With them came automatic stereotyping equipment to match the voracity of the new presses for printing plates. If not more than a dozen cities in the South offered immediate markets for the new heavy machinery, the whole newspaper structure felt their impact. Equipment discarded by the big city newspapers found its way to smaller plants, where it represented a parallel degree of progress.

As the SNPA was born, these elements confronted newspapers with a novel set of problems. Comparatively few Southern dailies were unionized in the century's early years, and the typographical union began moving in, to extend its control over the new composing machines. Printers then worked a 10-hour day everywhere in America, and the printing trade unions steadily battled for shorter hours and higher wages as its members' share in the new productivity.

In Retrospect

Gradually the unions attained these objectives. Wages in unorganized cities lagged only slightly behind those where the unions had a foothold. The terse minutes of the SNPA's first decade reveal between the lines the desire of publishers to reach a fair basis of compensation for all employees, in a time of rising income and prices. Again and again, publishers arose in convention to urge that a decent balance be kept between the pay of white collar employees and those in the mechanical departments. And, though few of the SNPA pioneers were admirers of labor organization as such, the majority dealt fairly and amicably with their unionized employees. That has been true throughout the half-century.

Escaping from the old provincialism of the South, the SNPA was not yet ten years old when its membership clearly evidenced the wish to get into broadening stream of business that was creating a flood of new advertising. Men then believed that the magic of advertising could accomplish all things, and, in that spirit, the SNPA voted to spend money to bring the South to the attention of the new national advertisers of the North and West. This resolution was several times repeated before it produced concrete action. Delay came about because the publishers simply didn't know what to say to their prospective new customers. They didn't have the facts about their own operations or about the purchasing power that the Southern market could offer.

It must be remembered that the 20th Century was 15 years old before reliable figures on newspaper circulation or newspaper advertising existed even in rudimentary form. Circulation claims of most publications prior to the establishment of the Audit Bureau of Circulations in 1914 were uniformly unreliable. Even though no conscious exaggeration was present (and it usually was) few publishers had the barest conception of what "net paid circulation" meant. They learned quickly, and SNPA members were among the first to join the ABC in large numbers.

As to advertising, the truth is that most newspaper space was bought rather than sold in the first years of the century. Canny advertisers valued newspaper space much more highly than did most publishers whose bread and butter it was. The advertising group which used newspapers to the best advantage were those selling proprietary medicines. With two, three, or even four daily papers trying to squeeze out a living in a city of a few thousand population, the shrewd medicine advertisers often played one against the other and generally bought some space in all, at ridiculously less than published rates. Since he often paid cash in advance for six months' or a year's advertising, the patent medicine advertiser was heartily welcomed by most newspapers. Quite often he would buy more space than he could use for his own product; the surplus he would broker to other advertisers at a profit, and still at less than the rates on newspaper cards.

No standard unit for sale or measurement of advertising had been generally recognized. Space was sold by the column inch, by the "square," by the nonpareil or brevier line; the agate line was gaining increased acceptance in the larger cities. Until the New York Evening Post began the measurement of New York City newspaper space in 1914, no such service existed. Shortly afterward, the Post included in its reports the measurements of newspapers in a score of other large cities. Until 1928 that remained the only nationwide source of monthly newspaper advertising figures; a broader semi-annual service was instituted by *Editor & Publisher* in 1923.

Inevitably, then, the Southern newspapers of 1909 and later years lacked essential information about their own affairs for an appeal to national advertisers. They, and all other newspapers, suffered other handicaps, too, at that stage. Only a few newspapers then imposed any censorship on the claims of advertisers. *Caveat emptor* was an honored principle. Although medical advertising came in for the heaviest criticism on the score of exaggeration and misrepresentation, it was far from alone in offending against truth. Advertisements of local merchants often took great liberty in describing quality and value of their wares.

The opening decade of the century had witnessed the creation of many great corporations by amalgamation of former competitors under one head. Many of these new giants had to find nationwide markets for their increased production volume, and national advertising in magazines was an attempt to meet that need. It didn't quite fill the bill, for no magazine nor any combination of magazines then adequately covered the expanding American market. But when daily newspapers solicited these accounts, they ran into serious obstacles. The new advertisers and their agencies wanted no association with the "riffraff" that patronized newspapers.

Publishers took that objection seriously. SNPA records of the 1910-1925 period chronicle year after year warnings that newspaper columns must be "cleaned up." Year after year, publishers in growing numbers reported that they had eliminated whole classifications of "objectionable" advertising. Several SNPA members led in the "truth in advertising" crusade of that time and in other moves for improved standards in newspaper conduct. And, as the reform swept forward, the SNPA annually increased its advertising, in the Northern daily and trade press and in its own columns, to attract new business to the South. It was one of the first and most potent factors in opening the undeveloped Southern market.

The SNPA was also among the first newspaper associations to gauge the importance of specialized education to the future welfare of journalism. No school of journalism existed in 1903; proposals of Joseph Pulitzer for a comprehensive course of study in that year lay dormant until his death in 1911 made a large sum available for endowment of a school at Columbia University. In the meanwhile, journalism schools had been started at the University of Missouri and several other institutions, and their teachers were groping for the right policies and techniques in the 1920's.

The SNPA entered the education picture by voting to raise an endowment fund for a journalism school at Washington & Lee University, Lexington, Va., in 1921. General Robert E. Lee had courageously but prematurely attempted to establish studies for journalism at this institution in the late 1860's, and the SNPA proposal struck a popular chord. The Association has kept an affectionate eye on this school since its establishment and has also been strongly represented on national bodies concerned with curriculum and teaching standards of journalism schools throughout the country.

In the equally important area of training young people for the printing trades, the SNPA has also exercised enlightened leadership. When the typographical union limited the employment of apprentices at a level which publishers considered perilous to the future manning of their shops, the SNPA encouraged the establishment of schools teaching the rudiments of printing. Most of the "graduates" of these schools completed their training in newspaper plants, and some eventually found their way as union journeymen into SNPA offices. Although the Association resisted efforts by the typographical union to get a voice in the schools' conduct, it also refused to countenance the concept that the schools were hostile to union organization.

As this history has often noted, Southern newspapers and their employees generally got along with a minimum of friction. Most cities represented in the SNPA of 1953 had no unionized newspaper employees 50 years ago. By 1920, however, union contracts existed in most of the large Southern cities and union organization spread throughout the South during the next 20 years, accelerated, of course, by the New Deal legislation of 1933-1936.

Even though the typographical union lost jurisdiction in about 20 per cent of SNPA cities during the late 1940's because of its refusal to work under the Taft-Hartley law, prolonged strikes were few in the South. Common sense and moderation on both sides avoided extremes in most localities. That followed the pattern of the early SNPA days. While some strong-minded publishers early in the century regarded unions as intruders in the conduct of business, the majority sought fair and amicable relations.

During the past 20 years, the SNPA has supplied expert advice on labor relations to members desiring it. It also provided up-to-date information on wage scales and wage trends to the entire membership. Through the Labor Department and the Headquarters office, publisher members have been advised of their rights and responsibilities under complex labor legislation of recent years, and the net result has been excellent. Newspaper employees in the South, organized or not, have shared, with a fair degree of equity, in the increased prosperity of newspapers.

What the SNPA has done for Southern industry and for the conservation of natural resources has been told at length in these pages. Fifty years ago, the seed of these recent accomplishments existed in the minds of Southern newspaper people to a far greater extent than they did in the consciousness of national industry or of the public at large.

In Retrospect

The SNPA was mindful of the public interest as well as of newspapers' economic advantage when, long ago, it approved the proposed creation by President Theodore Roosevelt of the Appalachian and White Mountain Forest reserves. It was again guarding the public welfare as well as that of its members when it repeatedly recorded itself in recent years as supporting all measures for the preservation of Southern forests and Southern soil. The results of that advocacy will be more evident when the SNPA celebrates its centenary than they are today.

One facet of the modern SNPA, however, would have been strange to the founders. That is the prominence of ladies in Association social and business affairs. There had been women in Southern journalism in the Nineteenth Century, to be sure. Mrs. Eliza Jane Poitevent Nicholson had ably succeeded her husband as publisher of the New Orleans Picayune. In 1903, Dorothy Dix Gilmer was already carving out the newspaper career which would bring her nationwide fame during the next 50 years. But these were exceptions. It was rare in most Southern newspaper offices for women to hold responsible posts, and it is not strange that the attendance records of the first 15 years of SNPA conventions mention no women.

In a day when motor travel was a perilous adventure and railroads a hot and dusty ordeal, wives and daughters were content to let Father take the convention trips alone. Not until the SNPA turned away from the large cities and held its meetings in the cool comforts of Grove Park Inn at Asheville did the ladies appear on the convention scene.

They weren't numerous at first, and Mrs. Walter C. Johnson, wife of the secretary, had a fairly easy time as unofficial entertainment chairman. But not many years passed before Mrs. Johnson needed the help of a busy committee. Their program usually included sightseeing drives to scenic spots in the Great Smoky Mountains, an afternoon of cards, an inspection of the palatial George Vanderbilt estate at Biltmore, and a bit of shopping for homespun cloth and other handicraft products of Biltmore Industries. Later, evenings of musical entertainment and dancing arranged by the ladies' committee were features of SNPA conventions.

Nor were publishers' wives and daughters the only ladies at the conventions. Supply and equipment men also brought their ladies for a pleasant vacation; occasionally, one or more of the syndicates sent a feminine representative. Most important, some of the publishers were women.

According to SNPA records, Mrs. Lois K. Mayes, publisher of the Pensacola Journal and News, was the first woman named to be Association's directorate. For several years, Mrs. Mayes and Mrs. Edith O. Susong, publisher of the Greeneville (Tenn.) Sun, were regular convention attendants. The first woman to become president of the SNPA was Mrs. Oveta Culp Hobby, co-publisher of the Houston Post, after she had served several years as a director; and of recent memory is the entertainment provided at the White Sulphur Springs convention in 1952 by Mrs. Frances Ogden Stubblefield, publisher of several West Virginia newspapers.

Like many of the changes that the Association has witnessed in its first fifty years, this sharing of effort by women underscores the fact that the South now marches step for step with other parts of America. The war-born sectional differences that were nearing their end in 1903 were, for the most part, gone and forgotten in 1953. The South still has its own cultural flavor and it still has problems rooted in its past that await complete solution. Beyond any doubt, these are much nearer solution today than they were 50 years ago.

In a physical sense, Southern newspapers are on a par with their contemporaries elsewhere in America. Their plants are modern. So is the thinking of their publishers and editors. Innate conservatism has not blocked genuine progress. Editorially, Southern newspapers have maintained through this half century of change the place of strong public influence that they held in 1903. They have kept a prudent, but firm, step ahead of their readers and of many Southern political spokesmen.

Thanks in large part to sagacious newspaper guidance, marching with industrial and agricultural progress, the people of the South no longer need listen to head-shaking plaints that "the South is the problem child of America." Rather, within the brief span of half a century, the South has become the scene, the reservoir, and the barometer of the nation's destiny.

So closes this summary of the first 50 years of effective newspaper organization in the Southern States. No claim is made, or can be,

In Retrospect

that the SNPA has been responsible for the tremendous economic, political, and social gains that have been recorded in the Southland since 1903. The latent power of the South had been recognized many decades earlier. But it cannot be gainsaid that the SNPA, by promoting sound business practices among its members, strengthened them mightily for the task of guiding the South to its destiny; nor can it be denied that the SNPA directly brought to fruition projects of gigantic importance to Southern prosperity.

Impressive as the South's accomplishments have been, it is clear from these pages that the Southern Newspaper Publishers Association does not regard its task as completed. The repeated emphasis in Association speeches and resolutions on the South's still unrealized opportunities is not mere lofty rhetoric or Southern oratory. It speaks for the spirit which guides the more than 400 newspapers in the Association of 1953, even as it led the newspapers of their fathers and their grandfathers from material poverty half a century ago to the relative luxury of the present.

That spirit does not prize material prosperity or wealth as primary objectives; they are means to the end of preserving and expanding the value of our national culture that intelligent Southern people have always held dear. The South has at last freed itself—in no small measure, thanks to its enlightened journalism—from the poverty, illiteracy, and prejudice that were its dreadful legacy from war. In 1953, the entire region stood upon the threshold of a renaissance holding unlimited promise for the political, social, economic, and spiritual progress of the American nation.

Epilogue

"The South and Its Newspapers," marking the first half-century of the SNPA, goes to press at the moment when Walter C. Johnson announces his retirement as secretary-manager. While that act is not factually part of the SNPA history, 1903-1953, it seems appropriate to one who has been associated with Mr. Johnson in its preparation that the end of his long services should be made a permanent part of this record. On that point, he has not been consulted, for good reason.

The frequent notice that this history has, of necessity, given his SNPA activities, is not to his liking. Again and again, while the book was in gestation, he protested to this collaborator that it was "too much Johnson." Be that as it may, no history of the SNPA could have been written with less notice of W.C.J. As others have truly, if tritely, said, he has been indeed "Mr. SNPA."

This association will go forward. Its second half century should far surpass the achievements of 1903-1953, with continued benefits to the entire South. The foundation has been strongly laid. While Walter Johnson was by no means unique in advancing the policies that have made SNPA strong and useful, his more than 40 years of continuous service in office have enabled him to do more than most to make deeds march with words, action with resolution.

Finally, at no juncture in this task of writing "The South and Its Newspapers" has it been possible for the signer of this page to express publicly his feelings toward his co-author. Let it be said now that a long newspaper career has provided no more pleasant experience than this has been. As many throughout the South know well, Mr. Johnson combines his professional ability with tenacity of purpose and with true Christian understanding and love of his fellow man. Without his diligence and patience in preserving the early story of the SNPA, this book could not have been undertaken. Without his kindly guidance at every stage of its preparation and his never-failing friendship, the work must have fallen far short of its objective. To both the Association and to the man who has been its balance wheel for so many years, this friend wishes many more years of fruitful living.

ARTHUR T. ROBB

INDEX

A

Adler, H. C., Chattanooga Times, a n a l y s i s newspaper publication costs, 58; chairman labor committee 1928, 141

Adsit, Harry B., acting labor commissioner SNPA Dallas office, 1937, 193; in charge at Dallas, 1938, 198; to New York World-Telegram, ------

Advertising—SNPA voted to advertise South to advertisers of North and West, 1909, 24; co-operative campaign planned, 1910, 27; SNPA members advocate refusal of advertising with fraudulent or incredible claims, 1911, 33; restriction and penalty rates advocated for medical and alcoholic beverage advertising, 1911, 33; SNPA appropriation of $400 for advertising, 1912-13, 36; SNPA pledged monthly page in Printers Ink, 1913, 39, gains cited from "clean-up" of newspaper advertising c o l u m n s, 1913, 39; four-point advertising program proposed by committee, 1914, 42; truth-in-advertising campaign, 1914, 48; first full year of SNPA advertising reviewed and new plan ordered, 50; new financial basis for SNPA advertising, 55; advertising campaign approved and expanded, 1916, 61; campaign used 33 full pages in trade papers, 1917-18, 76; AAAA seeks SNPA co-operation in standardizing commission practices, 1919, 80; newspaper linage doubled between 1914 and 1919, 78; SNPA advertising nearly $20,000, 1920-21, 85; newspaper linage declined, 1921, 101; S N P A committee recommended withholding commissions f r o m "non-recognized" agencies, 1 0 1; SNPA advertising faltered during 1921-22, 107; revived, 1923-24, 122; SNPA policy on agency relations stated, 1923, 116; SNPA reported $21,000 available for 1925-26 advertising, 133; SNPA campaign terminated 1926-27, 136; SNPA policy on agency commissions revised, 1927, 138; SNPA adopts new definitions of "retail" and "general" advertising, 1930, 146, 155; St. Petersburg plan for eliminating "cutthroat" sales competition reported, 1930, 146; clinic to overcome apathy in newspaper promotion, 1937, 193; SNPA Bureau of Advertising proposed, 197; failed to win support, 201; ANPA Bureau of Advertising strengthened, 197; United Front stimulated newspaper selling, 242; Advertising limited by World War II impacts, 256

Advertising Age, 50th Anniversary convention edition, 1953, 331

Advertisers Audit Association (forerunner of Audit Bureau of Circulations) 44

Ahlgren, Frank, Memphis Commercial Appeal, director, 1949-52, 300

Alabama Conference on Paper Products from Alabama Pine, 1934, 221

Alabama spruce pine used for newsprint, 1921, 96; 212

Allen, Charles H., Montgomery Advertiser, advertising committee, 1916-17, 60; 1918-19, 76; second vice-president, 1917-18, 67; 1918-19, 76; chairman business affairs committee, 1923-24, 111

Allison, James H., Nashville Tennesseean-American (later with Fort Worth Record and Wichita Falls Times and Record-News), adverti s i n g committee, 1916-17, 61;

355

1918-19, 76; executive committee, 1916-17, 61; 1920-21, 88; first vice-president, 1917-18, 67; 1918-19, 76; president, 1919-20, 82; honored as past president at 50th Anniversary convention, 1953, 333

Ambrose, H. F., Southwest School of Printing, addressed 1952 convention, 329

American Assn. of Advertising Agencies, SNPA co-operation with, 1919-25, 80; 101; 116; 138

American Council for Education in Journalism, SNPA co-operation with, 206; 266; 283; 291; SNPA withholds support 1953, pending settlement of disputed issues, 337

American Inter-Regional Newspaper Council, 1924, 131

American Newspaper Guild, organized 1933, 173; inactive in South, 1937, 190; reported 10 contracts and five "policy notices" with Southern newspapers, 1939, 206

American Newspaper Publishers Assn., 7; 170; endorsed SNPA newsprint mill project, 1937, 187

American Press Institute, cost-finding survey, 1949, 298

American Publishers Conference, SNPA co-operation with, 1922-25, 109; 115; 123; 140

American Society of Newspaper Editors, Canons of Journalism, 1923, 104

American Telephone & Telegraph Co., coast-to-coast talks featured SNPA 1916 convention, 61; unable to change news transmission schedules at SNPA committee request, 1932, 166; reduced rentals of printer machines, 1932, 166

Anderson, Eugene, director Macon School of Printing, 1920, 87

Anderson, P. T., Macon Telegraph, chairman Audit Bureau of Circulations committee, 1920-21, 88; director, 1928-29, 141

Anderson, Peyton T., Jr., Macon Telegraph & News, director, 1937-38, 194; 1938-39, 200; 1951-54, 320; U. S. Navy, 1942-45, 258; chairman newsprint mills committee, 1952-53, 334; newsprint panel, 1953, 335; president, 1953-54, 339

Anderson, W. T., Macon Telegraph, executive committee, 1914-15, 51; acting president, 1914-15, 52; president, 1915-16, 56; executive committee, 1916-17, 62; 1917-18, 68; 1918-19, 77; proposed school for training printers, 1919, 81; chairman printing schools committee, 1920-21, 88; defended operation of Macon School, 1924, 121; death reported, 1946, 268

Andrews, T. Coleman, president American Institute of Accountants, on newspaper accounting systems, 1951, 319

Angelina & Neches River RR, half-interest to Southland Paper Mills, Inc., 230

Arendell, F. B., Raleigh News & Observer, SNPA founder, 9

Armentrout, Vance, Louisville Courier-Journal, SNPA representative conference on education for journalism, 1939, 205

Armstrong, Collin, sought continued SNPA co-operation with AAAA, 86

Arnold, Thurman, SNPA counsel in NLRB hearings, 286; addressed 1948 convention, 286

Ashworth, M. W., Columbus (Ga.) Enquirer-Sun, chairman legislative committee, reported efforts to suppress local news, 1951, 317; local press licensing efforts opposed, 1952, 327

Associated Press, New York, 1901, 7; 343

INDEX

Atkinson, Charles D., Atlanta Journal, SNPA founder, 9; urged SNPA support for Audit Bureau of Circulations, 1914, 49; executive committee, 1915-16, 56; 1921-22, 103

Audit Bureau of Circulations, prediction of, 1911, 35; organized, 1914, 49; officers on SNPA programs, 58; 67; 86;—SNPA endorsed proposal for newspaper circulation manager as ABC director, 1931, 156

Ayers, Col. Harry M., Anniston Star, on syndicated columnists, 1 9 3 8 , 198; editorial chairman, 1939, 205; director, 1940-41, 246; 1941-42, 254; 221

B

Bagasse, as pulp material, 214; to be used by Louisiana mill, 1953, 334

Ball, Edward, negotiations for Southern newsprint mill, 223

Baker, Lisle, Jr., Louisville Courier-Journal and Times, director, 1943-45, 264; director-at-large, 1945-46, 267; president, 1947-48, 284; board chairman, 1948-49, 293; cost-finding and management panel, 1949, 298; circulation panel, 1952, 328; honored as past president at 50th annniversary convention, 1953, 333

Baldwin, W. Howard, Houston Post, cost-finding-management p a n e l , 298

Barksdale, Mrs. W. W., Clarksdale (Tenn.) Leaf-Chronicle, director, 1922-23, 110

Barnes, Harold S., ANPA Bureau of Advertising, addressed 1953 convention, 337

Barnes, W i l l i a m C., Martinsville (Va.) Bulletin, director, 1945-48, 267

Barrett, E d w a r d W., Birmingham Age-Herald, SNPA founder, 9; produced Birmingham Age-Herald edition on paper from Alabama spruce pine, 1921, 90; 211; death reported, 1922, 92

Barrett, Edward W., Jr., Asst. Secretary of State for Public Affairs, addressed 1951 convention on U. S. propaganda abroad, 320

Barton, Leslie M., Chicago Daily News, on ANAE advertising code, 146

Basham, Thomas E., co-operation with SNPA advertising campaign, 1920, ——

Beaver Wood Fibre Co., 249

Bell, Frank G., Savannah News, executive committee, 1909-10, 26; 1915-16, 56; special paper committee, 1916, 60; first vice-president, 1916-17, 61; president, 1917-18, 67; 1918-19, 76; chairman traffic committee, 1920-21, 88; executive committee, 1919-20, 82

Bellamy, Paul, editor Cleveland Plain Dealer, addressed 1937 convention, 193

Benson, John, president AAAA, on free publicity and advertising rates, 145

Berry, Major George L., president International Printing Pressmens and Assistants Union, on sanctity of newspaper-union contracts, 1923, 113 proposed SNPA s p o n s o r Southern newsprint mill with Federal funds, 1934, 175; 222; ended illegal strike a g a i n s t Beaumont newspapers, 281; commended by SNPA Labor Commissioner, 281; labor relations policy of Pressmens Union, 1948, 287

Biggers, George C., Atlanta Journal, chairman advertising clinic, 1937, 193; chairman committee on SNPA Bureau of Advertising, 1938, 197; local advertising successes reported, 1939, 201; director, 1939-40, 207; 1940-41, 246; criticized newspaper sales methods, 197; SNPA repre-

357

sentative national defense policy meeting, 1941, 251; president, 1943-45, 264; board chairman, 1945-46, 267; acting president, 1946, 267; board chairman, 1946-47, 279; urged SNPA join in "economic preservation and utilization of forest resources," 272; commended by SNPA, 1947, 284; comment on newsprint demands of U. S. economy, 1952, 324; newsprint panel, 1953, 335; honored as past president at 50th Anniversary convention, 1953, 333

Bingham, Barry, Louisville Courier-Journal and Times, director, 1938-39, 200; 1939-40, 207; 1940-41, 246; investor in Southland Paper Mills, Inc., 228

Bingham, Robert W., Louisville Courier-Journal and Times, donor of carrier-boy trophy, 1931, 156; death reported, 1938, 200

Birmingham Age-Herald, Alabama spruce pine edition 1921, 90

Bixby, Tams, Jr., Muskogee Phoenix & Times-Democrat, director, 1945-48, 267

Blackford, Air Commodore D. L., RAF, addressed 1943 convention 262

Blalock, J. M., Columbia State, director 1940-41, 246; 1941-42, 254; 1942-43, 259; 1943-45, 264; 1947-50, 284; newsprint panel, 1953, ⸺

Blondell, J. A., Baltimore Sun, on accounting systems, 144

Bottom, Raymond B., Newport News Press and Times-Herald, director, 1937-38, 194; 1938-39, 201; 1939-40, 207; 1940-41, 246

Bowaters Organisation, investigated Southern mill sites, 311; located new mill near Calhoun, Tenn., 323; early experiments with Southern pine footnote 234

Bowater, Sir Eric Vansittart, 235

Bowaters Southern Paper Corporation, organized to build Calhoun mill, 234; forestry and fire protection operations, 236-237; financial and operation details 236

Bowen, J. W., Birmingham Age-Herald, chairman labor committee, 1923-24, 111

Bradley, Harry B., Birmingham News and Age-Herald, chairman advertising clinic, 1937, 193; chairman advertising committee, 1940-41, 249; chairman cost-finding-management panel, 1949, 298; director, 1951-54, 320

Braxton, H. Galt, Kinston Free Press, director 1923-24, 111; 1924-25, 125; 1931-32, 159; proposed radio programs be charged as paid advertising, 154; proposed directors and committee heads be paid for travel expense on SNPA business, 174

Brice, John A., Atlanta Journal, director 1925-26, 131; 1927-28, 139; chairman traffic committee, 1936, 184

Bridge, Don U., war finance division, Treasury Dept., addressed 1943 convention, 262

Brown, Enoch, Jr., Memphis Commercial Appeal, director 1939-40, 207; 1940-41, 246; SNPA representative national defense policy meeting, 1941, 251

Brown, James Wright, *Editor & Publisher*, advertising plan offered 1914, 53

Brown, James Wright, Jr., *Editor & Publisher*, proposed SNPA endorse John Peter Zenger free press memorial, 1942, 257

Brown, Lew B., St. Petersburg Independent, on joint St. Petersburg advertising sales plan, 1930, 147

INDEX

Brown, L. Chauncey, St. Petersburg Independent, director 1928-29, 141; 1929-30, 145; 1930-31, 150

Brown, Robert W., Louisville Times, chairman executive committee, 1908-09, 22; vice-president, 1910-11, 28; president, 1911-12, 35; executive committee, 1912-13, 37; 1913-14, 40; 1915-16, 56

Brueggehoff, Louis N., Shreveport Times, SNPA founder, 9

Brunson, George W., Greenville (S. C.) News, secretary-treasurer, 1911-12, 35; 1912-13, 37; executive committee, 1913-14, 40

Brunson, Mason C., Charleston News & Courier, executive committee, 1910-11, 28; death reported, 1950, 310

Bryan, John Stewart, Richmond News-Leader, airplane edition to 1923 SNPA convention, 117; associated with S. E. Thomason in purchase of Chicago Journal and Southern newspapers with paper company funds, 1930, 148

Bryan, Walter G., Atlanta Georgian, advertising committee, 1916-17, 61; 1918-19, 76; executive committee, 1917-18, 68; 1918-19, 77; publisher New York American, 1919, 85

Buchheit, Phil, Spartanburg Herald & Journal, director, 1953-56, 339

Bureau of Advertising, ANPA, organized 1913, 45; strengthened 1938, _____

Burch, A. W., Charlotte Observer, chairman photo-engraving school committee, 1920-21, 88; school reported unnecessary, 1921, 97; executive committee, 1921-22, 103

Burleson, Albert C., Postmaster General, denounced by SNPA members for attacks on newspapers, 1919, 79

Burns, Robert E., commended SNPA newspaper wage policies, 1943, 262

C

Cabaniss, Henry Harrison, Atlanta Journal, SNPA founder, 9; temporary secretary, 6; president, 1903-04, 8; 1904-05, 12; appreciation of (footnote) 13; guest of honor at 25th Anniversary convention, 135; death reported, 1935, 180

Calder, Louis, Perkins-Goodwin Co., 225

Caldwell, J. P., Charlotte Observer, vice-president, 1907-08, 20; president, 1908-09, 22; death reported, 1912, 37

Callahan, Ralph, Anniston Star, advertising panel, 1952, _____

Camp, Joseph G., labor assistant SNPA Staff, 1935, 180; SNPA labor commissioner at Dallas, 1936, 182; report on economic situation, 1936, 184; to Chicago Newspaper Publishers Assn., 1937, 193

Campbell, P. H., Macon Telegraph, SNPA founder, 9

Canadian reciprocity, favored by SNPA, 31; effect on U. S. paper industry, 32

Capers, Claude V., SNPA labor commissioner, 1936, 183; to ANPA special standing committee, 1938, 198

Carr, Charles C., St. Petersburg Times, report on joint advertising sales plan, 1931, 157; director, 1931-32, 159; report on Florida effort to impose stamp tax on newspaper contracts and orders, 1934, 173; income tax questions, 1934, 173

Carter, Amon G., Fort Worth Star-Telegram, host to SNPA at Shady Oak Farm, 1940, 246

Carter, Richard Powell, Roanoke Times-World Corp., SNPA representative American Council for Education in Journalism, 1944, 266

Cashman, L. P., Vicksburg Herald & Post, director, 1928-29, 141; 1929-

359

30, 145; 1939-40, 207; 1940-41, 246; 1941-42, 254; 1942-43, 259; 1943-45, 264; 1945-46, 267

Censorship, World War II, Secretary Knox appeals for voluntary censorship of news that might aid Axis, 251; SNPA and other newspaper groups statement of national defense news policy, 251; SNPA President C. P. Manship helped make regulations workable, 255; C. P. Manship reported regulations protect public and press, 256

Chambers, Myron G., Knoxville News-Sentinel, newsprint mills committee 222; treasurer, 1949-50, 300; 1950-51, 310; 1951-52, 320; 1952-53, 329; 1953-54, 339

Chapman, A. H., Columbus (Ga.) Enquirer-Sun, director, 1948-50, 293

Chappell, J a m e s E., Birmingham News and Age-Herald, chairman advertising committee, 1 9 2 3-2 4, 111; director, 1930-31, 150; 1931-32, 159; 1932-33, 164; 1933-34, 168; 1934-35, 177; 1935-36, 181; president, 1936-37, 185; board chairman, 1937-38, 194; treasurer, 1939-40, 206; 1940-41, 246; 1941-42, 254; 1942-43, 259; 1943-45, 264; 1945-46, 267; 1946-47, 279; commended by SNPA, 1947, 284; honored as past president at 50th Anniversary convention, 1953, 333

Chandler, Ralph B., Mobile Register & Press, director, 1938-39, 200; 1939-40, 207; 221; chairman forestry panel, 1952, 328

Chandler, William G., Scripps-Howard Newspapers, endorsed SNPA mill project to ANPA, 1937, 187; as A N P A president, addressed SNPA on newsprint situation, 1946, 274; advocated removal of newsprint price controls, 1946, 275

Charlotte Observer, truck line for transport of newspapers and other commodities, 1931-32, 163

C h e m i c a l Foundation, aided Dr. Charles H. Herty research, 216; 226

Childersburg, Ala., site for Coosa River Newsprint mill, 1946, ____

Child Labor, regulation in dispute in NRA code negotiations, 1933, ____

Child Labor Amendment, approved by 28 States, 1937, ____

Circulation, discussed at 1914 convention, 45; SNPA support of ABC, 58; 67; 96; higher rates considered to meet rising costs, 1946, 276; studies by Jack Estes, 276

Clade, Robert, Alabama spruce pine experiment, 211

Clague, Stanley, managing director Audit Bureau of Circulations, at SNPA conventions, 86; 96

Clarke, Elmer E., Little Rock Arkansas Democrat, executive committee, 1912-13, 37; 1913-14, 40; 1914-15, 51; 1915-16, 56; 1916-17, 62; 1919-20, 82; director, 1922-23, 110; 1923-24, 111; 1924-25, 125

Clarkson, A. E., Houston Post, executive committee, 1909-10, 26; acting secretary, 42; 1914-15, 51; director, 1926-27, 134

Clemens, William M., M e m p h i s News-Scimitar, (later with Birmingham News and Knoxville Journal-T r i b u n e), executive committee, 1910-11, 28; 1911-12, 35; 1912-13, 37; secretary-treasurer, 1913-14, 40; plea for broader functions and higher pay for secretary-treasurer, 1914, 43; re-elected, 1914-15, 56; 1915-16, ____; code for editorial conduct of newspapers, proposed 1924, adopted 1925, 124

Code of Editorial Conduct, adopted by SNPA 1925, 126; text of, 126

Coffin, Charles T., Miami News, director, 1947-49, 284

INDEX

Coffin, John, Hearst Newspapers, 222
Cohen, Major John S., Atlanta Journal, general chairman news and legislative committees, 1 9 2 3-2 4, 111; report on Lee Memorial School of Journalism endowment, 1925, ...; eulogy of Major E. B. Stahlman and Col. Robert Ewing, 1931, 157; award of silver service to James G. Stahlman, 1934, 174; death reported, 1935, 180
Comer, Donald, chairman Avondale Mills, chairman of the board of Coosa River Newsprint Co., 194, 269
Connell, H. W., San Antonio Express & News, addressed 1935 convention 180
Continuing Studies of Newspaper Advertising, 262; 265
Coosa River Newsprint Co., 233; organized 1946, 270; officers, 270; financing completed by publishers' investments, 288; mill near completion, 1949, 295; operation started, 1950, 301
Corcoran, T. A., Louisville Courier-Journal & Times, chairman newsprint committee, 1951, 316; predicted world-wide newsprint shortage, 316; proposal that SNPA acquire and protect newsprint mill sites, 316; 334
Couey, James, Birmingham News, editorial panel, 1953, 335
Council, Charles C., Durham Herald-News, director, 1946-49, 279
Crown, Major James E., New Orleans States, addressed 1938 convention, 198
Curtis, J. Montgomery, director American Press Institute, editorial panel, 1953, 327

D

Dallas News, court decision on validity of individual contracts with employees, 1941, 248

Dallas office, SNPA-TNPA, opened, 1936, 182; joint operation terminated, 1951, 318
Daniel, Charles, Atlanta News, SNPA founder, 9
Daniels, Frank A., Raleigh News & Observer, director 1 9 4 3 - 4 5, 264; 1945-46, 267; newsprint mills committee, 1946, 269; president, 1951-52, 320; board chairman, 1952-53, 329; honored as past president at 50th Anniversary convention, 1953, 333
Daniels, Josephus, Raleigh News & Observer, Secretary of the Navy, 1913-20, 80; addressed 1925 convention, 126; called for revival of ancient editorial virtues, 1927, 135; eulogized SNPA dead, 1931, 157
Daniels, Josephus, Jr., Raleigh News & Observer, director 1922-23, 110
Davidson, Herbert, Daytona Beach News-Journal, chairman journalism schools committee, 1940, 244
Davis, E. C., Beaumont Enterprise & Journal, director 1942-43, 259; 1943-45, 264; circulation p a n e l, 1952, 328
Davis, Howard, New York Herald Tribune, ANPA president, on NRA code, 170
Davis, John, Albany (Ga.) Herald, on aid to farmers, 1924, 124
Davis, Wirt, Southland Paper Mills, Inc., 225
Dealey, Al, Dallas News, cost-finding and management panel, 1949, 298
Dealey, E. M. (Ted), Dallas News, director, 1934-35, 177; 1935-36, 181; 1936-37, 1866; on "freedom of radio," 1935, 178; Southland Paper Mills, Inc., 187; president, 1937-38, 194; gained Texas support for Southland Paper Mills, Inc., 227; board chairman, 1938-39, 200; SNPA tribute, 1939, 204; defended Dallas News a g a i n s t

361

charges by convention speaker, 248; newsprint mills committee, 1946, 269; urged publishers to invest in Coosa River mill, 1948, 288; honored as past president at 50th anniversary convention, 1953, 333

Dealey, W. A., Dallas News, director, 1933-34, 168; death reported 176

Defiance Paper Co., 91; 212

DeLamar, Curtis, Gadsden (Ala.) Times, director 1949-51, 300

DeLoach, Guyton, forestry panel, 1953, 335

Deutsch, Herman B., New Orleans Item-Tribune, addressed 1938 convention, 198

Dodge, Philip T., president Mergenthaler Linotype Co., pledged $2,000 for Lee Memorial School of Journalism, 1923, 112; as president International Paper Co., advised publishers not to rely heavily on European newsprint supplies, 113

Donosky, M. M., Dallas News, on post-war revival of Southern printing schools, 1947, 282; director, 1948-51, 293

Dowd, W. Carey, Charlotte News, advertising committee, 1915, 54

Dowd, W. Carey, Jr., Charlotte News, director 1928-29, 141; 1929-30, 145

Drummond, J. Roscoe, Christian Science Monitor, addressed 1937 convention, 193

Duerson, M. K., Lynchburg News & Advance, executive committee, 1906-07, 19; 1907-08, 20; 1915-16, 56; 1919-20, 82; 1925-26, 132

duPont, Alfred I., prospective investor in Southern newsprint mill 223

E

Early Southern newspaper associations, 1862-1900, 340-342

Editor & Publisher, plan for SNPA advertising campaign, 53 special 50th Anniversary convention edition, 1953, 331

Education, SNPA funds aided establishment of printers school at Macon, Ga., 1919, 87; 94; 122. SNPA raised endowment fund for Lee Memorial School of Journalism, Washington & Lee University, 1921-23, 99; endowment fund completed, 1923, 112; additional schools for printers, 1923, 122; contract with Macon school cancelled, 1924, 122; Southern School of Printing, Nashville, 1924-53, 122; 130; SNPA associated with other newspaper groups and journalism educators to maintain high standards, 206; SNPA directors withheld funds from American Council for Education in Journalism pending adjustment of disputed accreditation issues, 1953, 337

Elias, Don S., Asheville Citizen-Times, director, 1930-31, 150

Ellard, Prof. Roscoe B., director Lee Memorial School of Journalism, 131

Elliott, Bob, Miami Herald, editorial panel, 1953, 335

Elliott, Jesse M., Jacksonville Times-Union, director, 1933-34, 168; 1934-35, 177; 1943-45, 264

Elliott, W. A., Jacksonville Times-Union, executive committee, 1915-16, 56; 1916-17, 62; 1917-18, 67; 1918-19, 77; second vice-president, 1919-20, 82; first vice-president, 1920-21, 87; president, 1921-22, 103; director, 1922-23, 110; 1923-24, 111

Engel, K. A., Little Rock Arkansas Democrat, director, 1929-30, 145; 1930-31, 150; 1931-32, 159; 1932-33, 164; 1940-41, 246; 1941-42, 254; 1942-43, 259; 1947-50, 284; president, 1950-51, 310; board chairman, 1951-52, 320; honored as past president at 50th Anniversary convention, 1953, 333

INDEX

Estes, Jack, Dallas News, newspaper circulation and public relations factors, 1946, 276; SNPA circulation consultant, 1951, 328; chairman circulation panel, 1952, 328

Estill, Col. J. H., Savannah News, SNPA founder, 9; executive committee, 1905-06, 16; death reported, 1907, 20

Ethridge, Mark, Louisville Courier-Journal & Times, proposed SNPA support for National Council for Professional Education for Journalism, 1939, 206; described Louisville newspapers' circulation gains through editorial improvement, 1940, 243

Ethridge, Mrs. Mark, addressed 1952 convention, 322

Ewing, John D., Shreveport Times, resolution that ownership of newspapers by power or paper interests is contrary to sound public policy, 1929, 142; director, 1933-34, 168; 1934-35, 177; resolution favoring construction of Southern newsprint mill, 1934, 175; director, 1935-36, 181; 1936-37, 186; 1937-38, 194; president, 1938-39, 200; board chairman, 1939-40, 206; death reported, ———

Ewing, Col. Robert, New Orleans Daily States, SNPA founder, 9; executive committee, 1903-04, 8; 1904-05, 12; 1905-06, 16; 1921-22, 103; director, 1923-24, 111; 1924-25, 125; president, 1927-28, 138; 1928-29, 141; board chairman, 1929-30, 144; 1930-31, 150; death reported, 1931, 157

Ewing, Toulmin H., Monroe News-Star & World, death reported, 200

F

Fair Labor Standards Act (Wagner Act) presented new labor problems, 178

Federal Emergency Relief Administration, offer of financial aid rejected by SNPA newsprint mills committee, 226

Federal Trade Commission, fixed newsprint price, 1917, 69; filed suit against SNPA et al alleging restraint of trade, 120; background of suit, 119; reports on, 1926, 132; 1927, 137; suit dropped for lack of jurisdiction and as groundless against SNPA, 1930, 145; revealed purchase of newspapers with paper company financial aid, 1929-30, 140; 141; 149

Felkel, Herbert, St. Augustine Record, director, 1926-27, 134; 1927-28, 139

Ferguson, Premier G. H., of Ontario, formed Newsprint Institute of Canada, 1930, 148

Finlay, James F., SNPA counsel in Trade Commission suit, 125; 132

Fishburn, Junius P., Roanoke Times-World Corp., director, 1926-27, 134; 1927-28, 139; 1928-29, 141; 1929-30, 145; newsprint mills committee, 222

Florida newspapers resist state stamp tax on advertising orders, 173

Foley, Harold S., Powell River Co., Ltd., newsprint panel, 1953, 335

Forestry, SNPA endorsed creation of forest reserves, 1908, 22; SNPA resolutions sought editorial support for all movements concerned with forest and soil conservation, 1946-53, 272; 288; 338

Forgey, Col. B. F., Ashland (Ky.) Independent, director 1945-46, 267

Foster, Edgar M., Nashville Banner, SNPA founder, 9; executive committee, 1903-04, 8; 1904-05, 12; 1905-06, 16; special paper committee, 1904, 11; vice-president, 1906-07, 18; president, 1908, 20; advertising committee, 1909, 24;

executive committee, 1908-09, 22; 1910-11, 28; 1912-13, 37; 1913-14, 40; 1914-15, 51; 1915-16, 56; 1916-17, 61; 1917-18, 67; 1918-19, 76; chairman program committee, 1920-21, 88; general chairman business office committees, 1923-24, 111; death reported, 1926, 133

Foster, Marcellus E., Houston Chronicle, executive committee, 1917-18, 68; 1918-19, 77; first vice-president, 1919-20, 82; president, 1920-21, 87; executive committee, 1921-22, 103; director, 1924-25, 125; 1925-26, 132; (with Houston Press), 1927-28, 139; death reported, 1942, 259

Foster, M. Stratton, director, 1926-27, 134

Fowler, R. M., Newsprint Assn. of Canada, addressed 1952 convention, 323

Freedom of the press, issue in NRA code negotiations, 1933-35, 169; discussed by Giles J. Patterson, 1937, 192; seen menaced by local censorship and licensing efforts, 1951-52, 313; 317

Free Publicity, discussed by SNPA 1921, 94; by C. P. J. Mooney, 1926, 133; condemned by SNPA resolution 1929, 143

Freeman, Douglas Southall, Richmond News-Leader, (footnote) 1921, 98; death reported, 1953, 338

Fry, Wilbur W., N. W. Ayer & Son, on "The Newspaper and National Advertising," 1915, 54

G

Gaines, Dr. Francis Pendleton, president Washington & Lee University, on "The Journalist of Tomorrow," 1931, 158

Gaines, John B., Bowling Green (Ky.) Park City News, director, 1950-53, 310

Gaines, LeGrand A., Jr., Richmond News-Leader, director, 1935-36, 181; 1936-37, 186; death reported, 1937, 194

Gamble, Frederic R., president AAAA, on newspaper advertising, 1950, 309

Gannett, Frank E., financed Teletypesetter development, 1929, 144

Garvan, Francis P., assisted Dr. Charles H. Herty's research, 216; 226; death reported, 1938, 196; 229; memorialized by plaque at Southland Paper Mills, Inc., 196

Gaylord E. K., Oklahoma City Oklahoman and Times, executive committee, 1920-21, 88; 1921-22, 103; director, 1922-23, 110; 1923-24, 111; 1924-25, 125; 1925-26, 131; 1926-27, 134; 1927-28, 139; 1928-29, 141; 1929-30, 145; 1930-31, 150; 1931-32, 159; 1932-33, 164; 1933-34, 168; president, 1934-35, 177; aided in financing Southland Paper Mills, Inc., 1935-38, 196; 227; board chairman, 1935-36, 181; 1936-37, 185; director, 1943-45, 264; newsprint mills committee, 1946, 269; proposed to invest $100,000 in Coosa River Newsprint Co. stock, 1946, 271; report on Alaskan pulpwood resources, 1951, 320; honored by SNPA board on completion of 50 years in journalism, 1953, 330; honored as past-president at 50th Anniversary convention, 1953, 333

Gaylord, Edward L., Oklahoma City Oklahoman and Times, cost-finding and management panel, 1949, 298; director, 1952-54, 329

Gearhart, Sam E., Fayetteville Northwest Arkansas Times, director, 1953-56, 339

Geddes, Sir Auckland, British Ambassador to U. S., urged Southern press to "enroll in cause of world peace," 1920, 87

INDEX

Georgia dailies printed on Southern paper (newsprint) _____
Gideon, Dave, Huntington (W. Va.) Herald-Dispatch; director, _____; death reported, 310
Gillam, Major Gen. A. C., Jr., USA, Army public relations, 1943, 262
Gillespie, Sumter, Greenwood Commonwealth, director 1952-55, 329
Gillett, Charles A., American Forestry Products Industries, Inc., forestry panel, 1952, 328
Gilt Edge Newspapers, 1913, 44
Giovannoli, Harry, Lexington Leader, executive committee, 1917-18, 68; 1918-19, 77; report on printing schools, 121; director, 1923-24, 111; 1924-25, 125; 1925-26, 131; 1927-28, 139
Glass, Carter, Jr., Lynchburg News & Advance, director 1948-51, 293
Glass, Franklin Potts, Montgomery Advertiser (later with Birmingham News), SNPA founder, 5; association with earlier Southern newspaper groups, 5; temporary chairman, 6; secretary-treasurer, 1903-04, 8; 1904-05, 10; 1905-06, 16; president, 1906-07, 18; saluted by USS Alabama in Hampton Roads, 20; president American Newspaper Publishers Assn. (footnote) 5; (newsprint) 149; death reported, 1934, 176
Glass, Powell, Lynchburg News & Advance, director 1930-31; 150; 1932-33, 164; report on Lee Memorial School of Journalism, 184
Glassford, Rear Adm. William, USN, addressed 1942 convention, 258
Golf Tournament, Walter H. Savory Memorial, proposed by F. L. Seely, 1915, 55; Walter H. Savory appointed chairman, 1925, 132; discontinued during World War II, 259; ladies in competition, 1952, 322

Gonzales, Capt. William E., Columbia State, on objectionable advertising, 11; death reported, 1938, 200
Grady, Henry W., Atlanta Constitution, 332; 208
Graustein, Archibald R., International Power & Paper Co. (1929) 142
Graves, John Temple, Atlanta News, SNPA founder, 9
Gray, F. G., Atlanta Journal, special newsprint committee, 1904, 11
Gray, James R., Atlanta Journal, SNPA founder, 9; executive committee, 1906-07, 19
Great Northern Paper Co., fair sales policy toward newspapers (footnote) 32; examined mill site in Georgia, 1951, 316
Green, Truman, Tampa Tribune, director 1935-36, 181; 1936-37, 186
Groover, C. I., Columbus (Ga.) Enquirer-Sun, SNPA founder, 9
Group conferences at conventions, 246
Gwin, Jerry W., 211

H

Hager, Lawrence W., Owensboro Messenger-Inquirer, director, 1947-49, 284
Hager, W. Bruce, Owensboro Messenger-Inquirer, director 1929-30, 145; 1930-31, 150
Haldeman, Bruce, Louisville Courier-Journal, SNPA founder, 9
Hall, Harold, with William LaVarre, purchased Southern newspapers with paper company assistance, 1929, 141
Hall, Horace, Dothan Eagle, director 1936-37, 186; 1937-38, 194
Hall, Wilton E., Anderson Independent & Mail, director, 1945-47, 267
Halstead, W. R., Atlanta Constitution, presented plan for advertising the South, 1914, 41; 50; vice-president, 1914-15, 51; resigned, 52

365

Hammacher, Paul D., investigated newsprint mill possibilities, 301

Hanson, Clarence B., Jr., Birmingham News & Age-Herald, chairman newsprint mills committee, 1945, 269; vice-president Coosa River Newsprint Co., 1946, 270; financial needs for Coosa River mill, 1946, 270; additional financing of Coosa River mill, 1948, 288; commended by SNPA, 1948, 288; director 1948-50, 293; president, 1949-50, 300; board chairman, 1950-51, 310; honored as past president at 50th anniversary convention, 1953, 333

Hanson, Elisha, ANPA counsel, criticized by SNPA members, 1930, 148; denied Fair Labor Standards Act applied to newspapers, 247

Hanson, Victor H., Montgomery Advertiser, (later with Birmingham News) SNPA founder, 9; discussed agency relations, 1904, 11; secretary-treasurer, 1906-07, 18; 1907-08, 20; 1908-09, 22; 1909-10, 26; 1910-1911, 28; vice-president, 1911-12, 35; president, 1912-13, 37; executive committee, 1913-14, 40; 1914-15, 51; 1915-16, 56; 1916-17, 61; 1917-18, 67; 1918-19, 76; 1919-20, 82; board chairman, 1923-24, 111; 1924-25, 125; director, 1925-26, 131 1926-27, 134; 1927-28, 139; 1928-29, 141; 1929-30, 145; convoked Alabama Conference on Paper Products from Alabama Pine, 1934, 220; newsprint mills committee, 222; presented plaque to W. C. Johnson, 1938, 198; received plaque commemorating 40 years' membership, 1942, 252; death reported, 1946, 268

Harding, President Warren G., wrote Marion Star code of ethics, 104

Hardy, George F., 230

Harper, G. V., Miami Herald, director 1932-33, 164

Harris, Evelyn, honored at 1953 convention, 338

Harrison, J. C., Augusta Chronicle, executive committee, 1920-21, 88

Harrison, John H., Danville (Ill.) Commercial News (newsprint) ____

Hasbrook, Charles P., Richmond Times-Dispatch, executive committee, 1921-22, 103

Healy, George W., Jr., New Orleans Times-Picayune, chairman editorial affairs committee, 1942, 258

Hearst, William R., contribution to newsprint mill committee 1935, ____; tonnage commitment of Hearst newspapers withdrawn, 224

Hederman, Thomas M., Jackson (Miss.) Clarion-Ledger, executive committee, 1920-21, 88; 1921-22, 103; director, 1922-23, 110; 1924-25, 125; 1934-35, 177; 1935-36, 181

Hederman, Thomas M., Jr., Jackson Clarion Ledger, director, 1946-49, 279

Heiskell, J. N., Little Rock Arkansas Gazette, executive committee, 1920-21, 88; 1921-22, 103; director, 1933-34, 168; 1934-35, 177; 1935-36, 181; 1936-37, 186; 1937-38, 194; 1943-45, 264; for development of Southern land resources, 1935, 179; criticized newspapers for gruesome pictures, 1935, 179; editorial panel, 1948, 289; charged Southern newspapers do not recognize importance of editorial page, 1948, 290; presented 40-year membership plaque to Victor H. Hanson, 1942, 252; proposed resolution that two Southern newsprint mills increase capacity, that SNPA encourage new mills, and pledge support to all forest and soil conservation movements, 1950, 303

Hemphill, J. C., Charleston News & Courier, SNPA founder, 9; executive committee, 1903-04, 8; 1904-

INDEX

05, 12; president, 1905-06, 16; executive committee, 1906-07, 18; 1907-08, 20; 1908-09, 22

Herndon, E. Julian, Little Rock Arkansas Democrat, advertising panel, 1952, 326

Herty, Dr. Charles H., urged publishers to investigate practicability of establishing Southern newsprint industry, 1931, 154; (newsprint) ------; pressed plea for Southern mill, 1934, 179; urged education, not legislation, in conservation of Southern forests, 1937, 192; (newsprint), 208; financial difficulties, 1938, 196; 229; biography, 215; met Ernest L. Kurth, 1936, 225; called on Reconstruction Finance Corporation, 1937, 226; elected honorary life member SNPA, 189; final appearance before SNPA, 196; 229; death reported, 231; memorialized in plaque at Southland Paper Mills, Inc., mill, 196

Herty, Texas, site of Southland Paper Mills plant, 176

Herty Foundation, 229

Hill, I. William, Washington Star, editorial panel, 1952, 328

Hines, P. T., Greensboro News-Record, director 1941-42, 254; 1942-43, 259

Hinman, F. W. R., Jacksonville Times-Union, executive committee, 1908-09, 22; 1909-10, 26; 1911-12, 36; 1912-13, 37; vice-president, 1913-14, 40; president, 1914-15, 51; died in office, 1914, 52

Hitt, George W., Indianapolis Star, addressed 1911 convention, 35

Hobby, Mrs. Oveta Culp, Houston Post, director 1940-41, 246; 1941-42, 254; C o l o n e l commanding Women's Army Corps, 1943-45, 293; director-at-large, 1947-49, 284; president, 1948-49, 292; b o a r d chairman, 1949-50, 300; honored as past-president at 50th Anniversary convention, 1953, 333

Hodel, Charles, Beckley (W. Va.) Post-Herald and Raleigh Register, director, 1946-49, 279; forestry panel, 1952, 328

Holderby, A. R., Jr., Richmond Times-Dispatch, SNPA founder, 9; executive committee, 1903-04, 8; 1904-05, 12; special newsprint committee, 1904, 11; executive committee, 1912-13, 37; 1913-14, 40; 1914-15, 51

Holland, W. W., Spartanburg Herald & Journal, executive committee, 1919-20, 82; director, 1926-27, 134

Holliday, J. R., Atlanta Constitution, SNPA founder, 9; chairman SNPA advertising campaign committee, 36; executive committee, 1912-13, 37

Honea, Bert N., Fort Worth Star-Telegram, director, 1937-38, 194; 1938-39, 201; 1939-40, 207

Hook, E. B., Augusta Chronicle, SNPA founder, 9

Horne, Josh L., Rocky Mount Telegram, director 1932-33, 164; 1933-34, 168; 1934-35, 177; 1935-36, 181; 1936-37, 1866; chairman committee to seek reduced news transmission hours from A. T. & T. Co., 1932-33, 166; experimental radio transmission of news pictures, 1952-53, ------

Howard, Charles P., president International Typographical Union, criticized publishers' draft of newspaper code, 1933, 170

Howell, Clark, Sr., Atlanta Constitution, SNPA founder, 9; called first meeting to order, 6; chairman Lee Memorial School of Journalism endowment fund committee, 1921, 98; urged unity among publishers in dealing with labor unions and advertisers, 40; d e a t h reported, 1937, 194

367

Howell, Major Clark, Jr., Atlanta Constitution, director 1922-23, 110; 1923-24, 111; 1924-25, 125; 1926-27, 134; 1929-30, 145; 1930-31, 150; president, 1931-32, 159; "no panacea" for depression woes, 1932, 160; board chairman, 1932-33, 164; director, 1933-34, 168; newsprint mills committee, 222; in "Newspaper of the Future" symposium, 1941, 253; Brigadier General, AUS, 1942-45, 258; honored as past-president at 50th Anniversary convention, 1953, 333

Howell, Evan P., Atlanta Constitution, active in organizing Associated Press, 1891, 342

Hoyt, E. Palmer, Office of War Information, addressed 1943 convention, 262

Hoyt, W. K., Winston-Salem Journal-Sentinel, director 1949-51, 300

Huckle, A. W., Rock Hill Herald, director 1934-35, 177; 1935-36, 181; 1936-37, 186; 1937-38, 194; 1938-39, 201; 1939-40, 207; president, 1940-41, 246 SNPA representative at national defense policy conference, 1941, 251; board chairman, 1941-42, 254; 1942-43, 259; honored as past-president at 50th Anniversary convention, 1953, 333

Hudson, R. F., Montgomery Advertiser and Alabama Journal, director 1945-46, 267; 221

Hume, Frederic W., American Publishers Conference, on postal legislation, 1922-25, 109; 115; 123

Humphrey, William E., Federal Trade Commission, defended newspapers against fellow commissioners, 1926, 133

Huntress, Frank G., San Antonio Express & News, director 1933-34, 168

Hutton, Graham, British News Service, on British war-time newspapers, 1942, 258

Hyams, Chapman, III, New Orleans Times-Picayune & States, director, 1952-55, 329

I

Imes, Birney, Columbus (Miss.) Commercial Dispatch, director 1933-34, 168

Inland Daily Press Assn., reports on newspaper costs, 43; invited SNPA to joint meeting, 1925, 123

Institute of Newspaper Comptrollers and Finance Officers, 1949, 299

International Power & Paper Co., financed purchase of newspapers, 141

Intertype Corporation, exhibited machinery 1916 convention, 57; supplied machines to printing schools, 94

International Printing Pressmens & Assistants Union of North America, labor relations policy, 1949, 287

International Typographical Union, campaign for 44-hour week, 93; attacked publishers' draft of Daily Newspaper Code, 1933, 170; "no contract" policy under Labor-Management Relations Act, 1947, 285; jurisdiction lost through strikes against SNPA newspapers, 297; financed competing dailies against newspapers in cities where ITU lost jurisdiction through strikes 312

Iron Age, Southern progress edition, 1953, 331

J

Jacobs, Harold D., assistant administrator Wage & Hour Division, U. S. Department of Labor, in controversy with SNPA members, 1941, 247; 248

Jarreau, Hunter, Alexandria (La.) Town Talk, director 1949-51, 300

Jeffress, E. B., Greensboro News, executive committee, 1919-20, 82

INDEX

Jeffries, W. H., Birmingham Age-Herald, executive committee, 1907-08, 20; 1909-10, 26

Jenkins, Herschel V., Savannah News, director, 1931-32, 159; 1932-33, 164

Jepson, Frank, Madden-Reeve Angel & Co., need for added newsprint production, 1952-57, 324

Johnson, Arno H., J. Walter Thompson Co., declared 1948-49 business fears lacked foundation, 299

Johnson, Curtis B., Knoxville Sentinel (later with Charlotte Observer), executive committee, 1907-08, 22; 1908-09, 22; vice-president, 1909-10, 26; president, 1910-11, 28; on Southern Agriculture and industry potentials, 1911, 34; advertising committee, 36; chairman, advertising committee, 1914, 41; executive committee, 1911-12, 36; 1912-13, 37; 1913-14, 40, 1014 15, 51; 1916-17, 61; 1917-18, 67; 1918-19, 76; newsprint mills committee, 222; death reported, 310

Johnson, Gen. Hugh A., NRA administrator, declared newspapers must comply with National Industrial Recovery Act by organizing under code, 170; regretted insulting characterization of newspapers in Presidential order promulgating Daily Newspaper Code 1934, 172

Johnson, Oscar, president National Cotton Council of America, addressed 1939 convention, 205

Johnson, Orville E., SNPA auditor, death reported 1953, 338

Johnson, Shields, Roanoke Times-World Corp., director 1951-54, 321

Johnson, Walter C., Memphis News-Scimitar, 1904 (footnote), 12; later with Chattanooga News, executive committee, 1913-14, 40; 1914-15, 51; advertising committee, 1915, 54; second vice-president, 1915-16, 56; acting secretary, 1916, 57; secretary-treasurer, 1916-17, 61; 1917-18, 67; 1918-19, 76; 1919-20, 82; 1920-21, 88; 1921-22, 103; 1922-23, 109; 1923-24, 111; 1924-25, 125; declared SNPA business requires full-time manager, 111; presented with watch and locket, 1924, 121; president, 1925-26, 131; board chairman, 1926-27, 134; treasurer, 1927-28, 139; 1928-29, 141; 1929-30, 144; 1930-31, 150; 1931-32, 159; recommended higher dues, 1932, 160; reported how Chattanooga News budgeted for depression, 1932, 160; re-elected treasurer, 1932-33, 164; 1933-34, 167; 1934-35, 177; new dues schedule successful, 1935, 180; re-elected treasurer, 1935-36, 181; 1936-37, 186; 1937-38, 194; awarded plaque for 25 years' service as officer or d i r e c t o r, 1938, 199; re-elected treasurer, 1938-39, 200; secretary-manager, 1939-40, 202; 1940-41, 246; 1941-42, 254; 1942-43, 259; 1943-45, 264; 1945-46, 267; studied increased demands on Southern forests, 1946, 272; publication of adtising, editorial a n d circulation manuals, 1946-47, 282; re-elected secretary-manager, 1946-47, 279; 1947-48, 284; 1948-49, 293; 1949-50, 300; 1950-51, 310; 1951-52, 320; 1952-53, 329; 1953-54, 339; honored as past-president at 50th anniversary convention, 1953, 333

Johnson, Walter C., Jr., SNPA headquarters staff, 1939, 204

Johnson, Mrs. Walter C., entertainment chairman, SNPA conventions, 349; presented with silver service for interest in SNPA, 1924, 121

Johnston, Henry P., Huntsville Times, 221

Jones, Carl A., Jr., Johnson City Press-Chronicle, "Newspaper of the

Future" Symposium, 1941, 253; director-at-large, 1948-50, 293; director, 1950-53, 310
Jones, Jenkin Lloyd, Tulsa Tribune, editorial panel, 1948, 289
Jones, Jesse H., Houston Chronicle, chairman Reconstruction Finance Corporation, 226
Jones, Richard Lloyd, Jr., Tulsa Tribune and World, described working conditions on newspapers as "close to ideal," 1949, 297; chairman labor committee, 1949, 297; director, 1951-54, 3 2 1 ; president 1952-53, 329; b o a r d chairman, 1953-54, 339; composed "This Is Your Voice," 50th Anniversary convention feature, 332; honored as past president at 50th Anniversary convention, 1953, 333
Jones, Robert S., Asheville Citizen, executive committee, 1911-12, 36; 1912-13, 37; 1913-14, 40; 1914-15, 51; acting vice-president, 1914-15, 52; vice-president, 1915-16, 56; president, 1916-17, 61; executive committee, 1917-18, 68; 1918-19, 76; honored as past president at 50th Anniversary convention, 1953, 333
Journalist's Creed, written by Dean W a l t e r Williams, University of Missouri (1922), 104

K

Kansas City Star, newsprint mill, 12; footnote, 210
Kelley, T. J., Atlanta Constitution, SNPA founder, 9
Kelly, Harvey J., warned against inordinate union demands, 1929, 143
Kellogg, H. N., chairman ANPA special standing committee, conferred with SNPA members on labor conditions, 1920, 87
Kimberly-Clark Paper Co., management of Coosa River Newsprint Co., 1946, 271; purchased 25 per cent of common stock, 272
Kitson, F. Scott, Miami Herald, addressed 1935 convention, 180
Knight, James L., Miami Herald, director 1939-40, 207; 1940-41, 246; 1941-42, 254; 1942-43, 259; newsprint mills committee, 1946, 269; director-at-large, 1953-56, 3 3 9 ; management clinic, 1953, 336
Knight, John S., Miami Herald, president Inter-American Press Assn., 1952, 300
Knott, Eugene, Louisville Post, SNPA founder, 9
Knox, Secretary of the Navy Frank, voluntary censorship of news that might aid Axis powers, 1941, 251
Koenigsberg, M., International Feature Service, addressed 1918 convention, 71
Koester, George R., Greenville Piedmont, director, 1923-24, 111
Kohn, Alex B., Charleston Evening Post, paper committee, 1916, 60
Kohn, George M., SNPA advertising campaigns, 56
Korean hostilities complicated U. S. industrial situations, 1950, 300
Kurth, Ernest Lynn, planned paper mill near Lufkin, Texas, 187; 224; met Dr. Charles H. Herty, 225; organized Southland Paper Mills, Inc., 225; obtained loan from Reconstruction Finance Corporation, 230; delay in construction of chemical pulp unit, 1942, 257
Kurth, J. H., Jr., Southland Paper Mills, Inc., 225

L

Labor, new machines confronted publishers with momentous changes at turn of century, 4; 344; discussed at early SNPA conventions, 11; shortage of printers, 1919, 78; W. T. Anderson proposed that SNPA

INDEX

help establish schools for training printers, 1919, 81; Macon School of Printing established 1919, 87; approved for SNPA aid, 1920, 87; SNPA considered school for photoengravers, 1920, 87; decided such school unnecessary, 1921, 97; SNPA endorsed eight-hour day for printers, 93; SNPA pledged continued support to Macon School, 1921, 94; SNPA authorized appointment of special standing committee and employment of wage consultants, 1921, 102; SNPA renewed contract with Macon school, investigated others, 1923, 112; SNPA subsidy to Macon School discontinued, 1924, 122; SNPA labor department approved, 1928, 141; labor department discussed, 1929, 143; labor department report, 1930, 150; SNPA protection fund organized, 1930, 153; few labor disturbances reported in SNPA territory, 1930-31, 153; aid to members in labor troubles, 1930-31, 153; unions reported aggressive in organizing Southern locals, 1936, 180; "sit-down" strikes criticized by newspapers, 1937, 190; SNPA and Texas Newspaper Publishers Assn. established Dallas office, 1936, 182; increased union activity reported by two SNPA labor offices, 1937, 193; recession abated union wage pressures, 1937, 194; SNPA protection fund dissolved (footnote) 245; five strikes against SNPA newspapers, 1940-41, 249; wages and manpower under war-time regulation, 1943-46, 260; union wages rose sharply after World War II, 277; three major strikes against SNPA newspapers during World War II, 1946, 277; wage trends and living costs in SNPA territory, 1946, 277; International Typographical Union resisted Labor-Management Relations (Taft-Hartley) Act, 1947, 280; strike against Beaumont newspapers settled by Major George L. Berry of Pressmens Union, 1947, 281; SNPA called upon unions to comply with Taft-Hartley Act, 1947, 284; I.T.U. adopts "no contract" policy under Taft-Hartley Act, 1947, 285; I.T.U. "no contract" policy produced unusual number of strikes in SNPA territory, 285; SNPA joins ANPA in charges against I.T.U. before National Labor Relations Board, 1948, 285; status of union-newspaper contracts in South, 1948, 286; majority of SNPA newspapers maintained contractual or verbal agreements with unions, 1951, 312; I.T.U. publishing competitive dailies in cities where it lost jurisdiction through strikes, 312; modern industrial engineering principles applied for improvement of newspaper production, 1953, 336

Lang, Dr. George, addressed 1939 convention, 205

Langhorne, Jack, Huntsville Times, "Newspaper of the Future" Symposium, 1941, 253; director, 1942-43, 259; 1943-45, 264

Lanston Monotype Machine Co., exhibited machinery at convention 1916, 58

Lathan, Robert, Charleston News & Courier, executive committee, 1915-16, 56; 1916-17, 62; 1921-22, 103; director, 1925-26, 131; won Pulitzer Prize for best editorial of 1924, addressed 1925 convention, 126; death reported, 1938, 200

LaVarre, William, with Harold Hall, bought Southern newspapers with paper company assistance, 1929, 141

Lea, Col. Luke, Nashville Tennessean, promotion plan for South, involving SNPA co-operation with railroads and utilities, 1928, 140; fails for lack of press support, 1929, 143

Lee, Dr. Alfred McC. Lee, journalism schools, (footnote), 98

Lee, General Robert E., journalism instruction at Washington & Lee University, 1867, 97

Lee Memorial School of Journalism, Washington & Lee University, SNPA approves establishment of, 99; SNPA members pledged $50,000 toward endowment fund, 1923, 112; recognized by Associations of Schools and Colleges of Journalism, 1931, 158; progress reported, 131; 166; 184; 278; record enrolment, 1940, 244 pre-war momentum regained, 1947, 283

Levi, Emanuel, Louisville Courier-Journal and Times, director, 1931-32, 159; 1932-33, 164; 1933-34, 168; 1934-35, 177; insisted that Southern newsprint mill be constructed "by private enterprise," 1934, 175; newsprint mills committee, 1934, 175; 222; president, 1935-36, 181; continued as president through 1936 convention, after becoming Chicago Herald & Examiner publisher, 183; honored as past president at 50th Anniversary convention, 1953, 33

Lewis, M. Botts, Clifton Forge (Va.) Review, director 1931-32, 159

Lilienthal, David M., director Tennessee Valley Authority, addressed 1940 convention on essentials for Southern progress, 241

Lodge, J. Norman, Associated Press war correspondent, addressed 1943 convention, 262

Long, Col. J. H., Huntington (W. Va.) Herald-Dispatch and Advertiser, director 1929-30, 145; 1930-31, 150; 1931-32, 159; 1932-33, 164; 1938-39, 201; 1939-40, 207

Long, Luther T., Huntington Herald-Dispatch and Advertiser, director, 1935-36, 181; 1936-37, 186; 1937-38, 194

Long, Walker, Huntington Herald-Dispatch and Advertiser, director, 1940-41, 246; 1952-55, 329

M

Macon School of Printing, established under SNPA auspices, 1919, 87; reported successful, 1920, 87; 94; 112; SNPA discontinued subsidy, 1924, 121

Macy, Capt. J. Noel, War Department public relations program, 1941, 253

Malsberger, H. J., Southern Pulpwood Conservation Assn., forestry panel, 1952, 328

Mann, J. W., Lexington Herald-Leader, director 1953-56, 339

Mansfield, Laurence E., co-chairman and later chairman Walter H. Savory Memorial Golf Tournament, (1934) 177

Mansfield, W. E., International Paper Co., addressed 1904 convention, 12; comment on E. W. Barrett newsprint experiment, 1921, 91; honored at 50th Anniversary convention, 338

Manship, Charles P., Baton Rouge State Times and Advocate, director, 1938-39, 200; 1939-40, 207; 1940-41, 246; president, 1941-42, 254; 1942-43, 259; aided in organiation of World War II censorship, 255; declared regulations protect rights of press and public, 256; board chairman, 1943-44, 264; awarded sterling silver punchbowl set by SNPA, 1943, 264; made 20 trips to Washington and New York on SNPA business during record 28 months' administration, 1943, 261; newsprint mills committee, 1946, 269; death reported, 1947, 282

372

INDEX

Manship, Charles P., Jr., Baton Rouge State Times and Advocate, director, 1946-47, 279; vice-chairman newsprint mills committee, 1953, ____

Mapel, Prof. William L., director Lee Memorial School of Journalism, 1931, 158; new curriculum, 166

Mapes, James L., Beaumont Enterprise & Journal, executive committee, 1919-20, 82; director, 1928-29, 141; 1929-30, 145; 1930-31, 150 1931-32, 159; 1932-33, 164; labor department report, 1930, 150; trustee SNPA protection fund, 1931, 159; president, 1933-34, 167; board chairman, 1934-35, 177; newsprint mills committee, 222; death, 1937, 193

Marietta Paper Manufacturing Co., 211

Marks, John R., Asheville Citizen-Times, directed prize-winning carrier boy team, 1931, 150

Marshall, John, Great Northern Paper Co., comment on E. W. Barrett newsprint experiment, 1921, 91

Martin, Thomas W., Alabama Power Co., associated with Coosa River Newsprint Co., 1946, 221; 269

Massengale, St. Elmo, attended 1906 convention, 19; addressed 1907 convention on agency relations, 20; prepared 1916 SNPA advertising campaign, 61; praised for co-ordination of SNPA advertising, 1918, 76

Matherne, Robert, Goose Creek (Texas) Sun, director 1945-46, 267

Mayborn, Frank, Temple (Texas) Telegram, director 1951-54, 321

Mayes, Mrs. Lois K., Pensacola Journal, first woman on executive committee, 1919-20, 82; 1920-21, 88; 350

McCarrens, John S., Cleveland Plain Dealer, invests in Southland Paper Mills, Inc., 227

McCarthy, Lieut. Commdr., W. M., USNR, addressed 1943 convention, 262

McClellan, George A., Jacksonville Metropolis, executive committee, 1914-15, 51

McCormick, Medill, Chicago Tribune, addressed 1907 convention, 20

McDiarmid, A. A., Price Bros. Co., Ltd., on Southern newsprint, 220

McDonald, H. C., on newspaper color advertising, 1931, 157

McDonald, Roy, Chattanooga News-Free Press, director 1946-47, 279

McGee, H. T., Jr., Charleston News & Courier, director 1950-53, 310

McKelway, Ben, Washington Star, president American Society of Newsaper Editors, warns of new political attacks on press integrity, 1949, 299

McKenney, R. L., Macon News, SNPA founder, 9, special paper committee, 1916, 60

McPherson, Holt, Shelby (N. C.) Star, chairman journalism schools committee, program for maintaining high standards, 1946, 278; on SNPA co-operation with American Council for Education in Journalism, 1947, ____

Mechanical conferences initiated by SNPA, 1938, 200; suspended during World War II, 1942, ____; resumed, 1946, ____

Media Records, Inc., definitions of "retail" and "general" advertising, 1931, 156

Mergenthaler Linotype Co., exhibited machinery 1916 convention, 57; supplied machines to Macon School of Printing, 1919-24, 94

Merritt-Chapman & Scott Corp., constructed Southland Paper Mills, ____

Meyer, August B., president Bowater Southern Paper Mill Corp., 323; advocated increased production by

373

existing machines rather than new newsprint mills during inflationary period, 323

Mickle, E. B., director Southern School of Printing, Nashville, 1925, 130

Miller, F. H., Montgomery Journal, SNPA founder, 9; executive committee, 1921-22, 103; director, 1922-23, 110

Millar, R. C., Jacksonville Times-Union, director, 1950-53, 310; circulation panel, 1952, 328

Milton, George Fort, Sr., Knoxville Sentinel (later Chattanooga News) executive committee, 1906-07, 18; annual prize for best editorial promoting international peace, 1926, 133; 144

Mooney, Charles P. J., Memphis Commercial Appeal, addressed 1913 convention, 38; addressed 1925 convention, 126; director, 1925-26, 132; discussed free publicity, 1926, 133; death reported, 1926, 134

Mooney, Jean, NEA Service, editorial panel, 1953, 336

Moore, Daniel D., New Orleans Times-Picayune, executive committee, 1912-13, 37; 1913-14, 40; 1914-15, 51; 1915-16, 56; 1919-20, 82; paper committee, 1916, 60; second vice-president, 1916-17, 61

Moore, Thomas H., ANPA Bureau of Advertising, on government advertising, 1919, 80

Moore, V. C., Raleigh News & Observer, executive committee, 1919-20, 82

Morgan, Wiley L., Knoxville Sentinel, director 1924-25, 125; secretary-treasurer, 1925-26, 131; 1926-27, 134; reported adverse effect of newspaper consolidations on SNPA dues income, 135; retired from newspaper work, 1927, 138

Morkrum-Kleinschmidt Co., manufacturer of telegraph printers, 1933, 166

Moroney, James M., Jr., Dallas News, circulation panel, 1952, 328

Morris, W. S., Augusta Chronicle, director 1941-42, 254; 1942-43, 259; on circulation panel, 1952, 328

Muchmore, Clyde E., Ponca City News, director 1934-35, 177; 1935-36, 181; 1936-37, 186

Mudd, W. Stuart, Tuscaloosa (Ala.) News, 221

N

National Council for Professional Education in Journalism, supported by SNPA, 1939

National Industrial Recovery Act, 1933, 164; newspaper code negotiations, 169; 170; 172; declared unconstitutional, 1935, 177

National Newspaper Week, supported by SNPA, 1941, 1953

National Publishers Committee, paid campaign to improve newspaper public relations, 1940-41, ____

National Recovery Administration, NRA code negotiations, 164; 169; 172

Nelson, William Rockhill, Kansas City Star, 12; 210

Nevin, James B., Atlanta Georgian, presided at 25th Anniversary banquet, 135

Newcombe, Albert, 225

Newmyer, Arthur G., New Orleans Item-Tribune, "truth-in-advertising" movement, 1914-17, 67; SNPA advertising campaign, 1919-20, 85; executive committee, 1917-18, 68; 1918-19, 77; 1920-21, 88; second vice-president, 1921-22, 103; plan for reorganization of SNPA, 1922, 106; advocated strict enforcement of rules on advertising commissions,

INDEX

1922, 106; board chairman, 1922-23, 109-110; president, 1923-24, 111; 1924-25, 125; board chairman, 1925-26, 131 honored as past-president at 50th Anniversary convention, 1953, 333

New printing processes, 1949, 297

"Newspaper of the Future," symposium, 1941, 253

Newsprint—major topic at 1904 convention, 10; 1908 convention demands repeal of duty on woodpulp and paper imports, 22; SNPA urged approval of Canadian reciprocity treaty, 1911, 31; publishers alarmed by rise in newsprint prices, 1916, 59; special paper committee appointed, 1916, 60; SNPA asks Federal control of newsprint production, distribution and prices, 1917, 64; War Industries Board restrictions on paper use, 1917, 69; Federal Trade Commission fixed news print price, 1918, 69; paper prices skyrocketed after lapse of war-time regulation, 80; spot market price at $200, contracts, $100, 1919, 84; Publishers Buying Corp. formed, 1920, 84; SNPA co-operated with ANPA in drastic economies, 85; runaway paper market reached peak and slowly declined, 1921, 100; conservation measures continued, 1923, 115; SNPA asked State Department to protest Canadian ban on pulpwood exports, 115; Newsprint Institute of Canada organized by Premiers of Quebec and Ontario, 1929, 148; International Paper Co. withdrew preferential price to Hearst Newspapers, offered contracts at $62, 148; price structure disorganized as Canadian mills fight for tonnage in depressed U. S. market, 1930, 149; Dr. Charles H. Herty shows SNPA the possibilities of a Southern newsprint industry, 1931, 154; Canadian mills continue price war, 163; SNPA approved construction of Southern newsprint mill by private enterprise, 1934, 175; Stahlman committee's efforts to finance Southern mill met repeated disappointments, 183; J. G. Stahlman reported successful financing of Southland Paper Mills, Inc., 187; Southland Paper Mills Inc., in operation, 1940, 208; Southland Paper Mills, Inc., added chemical pulp unit, 232; War Production Board restrictions on paper consumption, 1942, 256; serious shortages, 1943, 260; SNPA called construction of additional Southern newsprint mills, 1943, 261; SNPA and ANPA asked removal of newsprint price controls, 1946, 275; SNPA approved construction of Coosa River Newsprint Co, mill, pledging tonnage and investment, 1946, 270; circulation prices raised to meet paper costs, 276; newsprint prices rose, but supply reported nearly adequate, 1946-47, 280; SNPA members pledged $300,000 for Coosa River mill, 1948, 288; other publishers invest in Coosa River mill, 1948, 288; Coosa River Newsprint Co. mill in operation, 1950, 301; Korean hostilities sent spot market paper price to $200, 300; Bowaters Organisation examined mill site near Calhoun, Tenn., 311; SNPA promised aid and encouragement to Bowaters mill, 315; Bowaters Southern Paper Corp. mill under construction, 1953, 323; prices and supply seen at peak, 323; current and future newsprint conditions, 1952, 324; SNPA committee reports adversely on plan to purchase future mill sites, 1953, 334; Bowaters Calhoun mill in operation, 1954, ------

375

Nichols, M. R., Atlanta Constitution, SNPA founder, 9

Nicholson, Leonard K., New Orleans Times-Picayune, director, 1926-27, 134; 1927-28, 139; 1928-29, 141; 1929-30, 145; 1930-31, 150; 1931-32, 159; 1932-33, 164

Nicholson, Ralph, Tampa Times, director, 1937-38, 194; 1938-39, 200; "Newspaper of the Future" symposium, 1941, 253; purchased New Orleans Item, 1941, 257; chairman public relations committee, 1941-42, 257; newspapers and national war effort, 1942, 263; improved newspaper public relations, 1943, 257; treasurer, 1947-48, 284; 1948-49, 293; editorial panel, 1948, 289; sold New Orleans Item and went to Berlin on diplomatic mission, 1949, 295; report on European conditions, 1950, 310

Norton, Edward L., president Coosa River Newsprint Co., 1946, 270

Nussbaum, M. E., Moultrie (Ga.) Observer, director, 1953-55, 339

O

Ochs, Adolph Shelby, Chattanooga Times, director, 1932-33, 164; 1933–34, 168; 1934-35, 177; 1935-36, 181; 1936-37, 186; 1937-38, 194; 1938-39, 201; president, 1939-40, 206; board chairman, 1940-41, 246; honored as past president at 50th Anniversary convention, 1953, 333

Ochs, Adolph Simon, Chattanooga Times (later publisher New York Times), secretary Southern Press Assn., 1881, 341; active in organizing Associated Press, 1891, 342; deplored large-size newspapers, 1919, 10; addressed 1925 convention, 126; honorary life member, 1925, 130; death reported, 1935, 180

Ogden, H. C., Wheeling Intelligencer and News-Register, director 1941-42, 254

Oklahoma City Oklahoman and Times, organized express Co. to distribute newspapers and other commodities, 1932, 163

Olson, Dean Kenneth E., Northwestern University, president American Assn. of Schools of Journalism, sponsored joint conference on education for journalism, 1939, 205

Orcutt, C. W., Knoxville News-Sentinel, editorial panel, 1952, 328

O'Shaughnessy, James, executive secretary AAAA, urged standard newspaper practice on agency commissions, 1919, 80; addressed SNPA on Federal Trade Commission suit, 1926, 132

P

Palmer, Charles E., Hot Springs Sentinel-Record and New Era, director 1938-39, 200; 1939-40, 207

Palmer, G. J., Houston Post, vice-president, 1905-06, 16; executive committee, 1912-13, 37; 1913-14, 40; 1915-16, 56; 1916-17, 62; paper committee, 1916, 60; on labor department, 1929, 143; death reported, 1934, 176

Palmer, Lincoln B., manager ANPA, 1903, 7; addressed 1918 convention, 71; report on Federal Trade Commission suit, 1926, 132; retired as ANPA general manager, 1939, 202

Pape, William J., Waterbury (Conn.) Republican, addressed 1920 convention on Publishers Buying Corp., 84; footnote, 210

Park, John A., Raleigh Times, advertising committee, 1912, 36; executive committee, 1915-16, 56; 1920-21, 88; director, 1925-26, 131; president, 1926-27, 134; board chairman, 1927-28, 138; 1928-29,

Index

141; honored as past president at 50th Anniversary convention, 1953, 333

Parks, John S., Fort Smith Southwest American and Times-Record, director, 1925-26, 131; 1926-27, 134; 1927-28, 139; 1928-29, 141; warned SNPA against joining railroads and utilities in Southern promotion campaign, 1928, 140; president, 1929-30, 144; 1930-31, 150; on business depression, 1931, 152; board chairman, 1931-32, 159; death reported, 1953, 338

Patrick, Talbot, Goldsboro News-Argus, director, 1939-40, 207; 1940-41, 246; in government service, 258; publisher Rock Hill Herald, proposed SNPA undertake research program, 1947, 283; report on new printing processes, 1949, 297

Patterson, Giles J., addressed 1937 convention on press freedom, 192, 310

Patterson, Hugh B., Jr., Little Rock Arkansas Gazette, director, 1950-53

Peace, B. H., Greenville (S. C.) News, executive committee, 1920-21, 88; director, 1927-28, 139

Peace, Roger C., Greenville News & Piedmont, director 1932-33, 164, 1933-34, 168

Peck, I. H., International Paper Sales Co., newsprint panel, 1953, 335

Pendleton, C. R., Macon Telegraph, SNPA founder, 9

Pension plans, discussed by 1943 convention, 264; report by D. Hiden Ramsey, 1950 convention, 309

Perkins-Goodwin Co., 225

Phillips, Loyal, St. Petersburg Independent, advertising panel, 1952, 326; chairman public relations committee, 337; director, 1953-56, 339

Porter, Herbert, Atlanta Georgian-American, director, 1934-35, 177; 1935-36, 181; 1936-37, 186

Postal Rates, SNPA opposed increase in second-class rates, 1912, 37; wartime postal rate increase denounced as unfair, 65; Major E. B. Stahlman and F. W. Hume on proposed rate increase, 1924, 123; SNPA demands repeal of war-time postal rates, 1927, 138; President Ewing reported new law restored 1920 schedules, 1928, 140; Frederick A. Tilton, Third Assistant Postmaster General, on rates, 1930, 147; second class postage increased as revenue measure, 1931, 163

Potts, Major Allen, Richmond News-Leader, director 1922-23, 110; 1923-24, 111; 1924-25, 125

Powers, W. C., Great Northern Paper Co., on war-time paper prices, 1918, 72

Poynter, Nelson, St. Petersburg Times, chairman of panel "Does Militant Local Journalism Pay?", 1948, 289

Poynter, Paul, St. Petersburg Times, non-competitive advertising sales plan with St. Petersburg Independent, 1930-31, 147

Press Association of the Confederate States, 1862, 340

Press Freedom, issue under NRA code negotiations, 1933, 1934, 171; threatened by local news censorships, 1950, 313; SNPA protested local censorships and licensing, 1951, 317

Price, Byron, Associated Press, director Office of Censorship, 1942, 255; 258

Printers Ink, published first SNPA advertising campaign, 27; 36; 40; 51; 61

Printing Schools, first established under SNPA auspices at Macon, Ga., 1919-20, 81; 87; 94; 112; SNPA

377

cancelled contract with Macon School, 1924, 121; Southern School of Printing, Nashville, 122; 206; Southwestern Vocational School, Dallas, 206; establishment of technical school by Pressmens Union commended, 1948, 287

Protection Fund organized by SNPA, 1930, 153; dissolved, 1936, 245

Publishers Buying Corp., 1920, 84; 210

Puckette, Charles McD., Chattanooga Times, director, 1952-55, 329

Pulitzer, Joseph, New York World, plan for journalism instruction, 97

R

Radio broadcasting, first discussed, 1922, 109; publishers' experiences with newspaper-owned stations, 1929, 144; discussion, 1931, 154; stations buying news service from wire associations, 1932, 161; SNPA resolution urged press services to cease selling news to broadcasters, 1932, 162; President Stahlman sought support of other newspaper associations in fight against radio news, 165; SNPA discusses "freedom of radio," 1935, 178; radio news competition regarded as inevitable, 1935, 178; radio advertising in severe competition with newspapers, 1936, 181; radio transmission of news pictures, experiment commended, 1953, 339

Raiford, F. T., Selma Times-Journal, 221

Raine, Gilbert D., Jr., Memphis News-Scimitar, (footnote) 17

Ramsey, D. Hiden, Asheville Citizen-Times, director 1937-38, 194; 1938-39, 201; on "Pension and Retirement Plans," 1950, 309; declared Southern newspapers have not reached saturation point in circulation and need more newsprint, 1952, 323; vice-chairman newsprint committee, 1953, 334; chairman forestry panel, 1953, 335

Rand, Clayton, president National Editorial Assn., addressed 1937 convention, 192

Rankin, Leland, Richmond News-Leader, executive committee, 1907-08, 20

Rapier, Paul E., Mobile Register, SNPA founder, 9

Reconstruction Finance Corp., aid sought for construction of Southland Paper Mills, Inc., 1937, 225; loan for Southland mill considered, 230; loan of $3,425,000 granted to Southland mill, 230

Reed, Martin W., Mergenthaler Linotype Co., addressed 1951 convention, 318

Reeder, Ross A., Miami News, director 1924-25, 125

Reid, Whitelaw, New York Tribune, on special instruction for journalism in 1872, 97

Research, SNPA committee to investigate practicability of newspaper production research, 1946, 279; referred to American Newspaper Publishers Assn., 1947, 283

Reynolds, Donald W., Fort Smith S. W. Times-Record, director 1945-46, 267

Rhodes, Rufus N., Birmingham News, SNPA founder, 9; executive committee, 1903-04, 8; 1904-05, 12; 1905-06, 16; 1906-07, 18; vice-president, 1908-09, 22; president, 1909-10, 26; death in office, 26

Riegel, Prof. O. W., director Lee Memorial School of Journalism, 184; on journalism education standards, 206

Robb, Arthur T., golf committee, 1934, 177

Roberts, Roy A., Kansas City Star, addressed 1937 convention, 192

INDEX

Robertson, Reuben B., Sr., Champion Paper & Fibre Co., forestry panel, 335

Robinson, Thomas L., Charlotte News, urged more energetic support of forest conservation programs, 1948, 288; chairman public relations committee, 1949, 298; on support for conservation, 1950, 302; director, 1952-55, 329

Rogers, Jason, New York Globe, addressed 1914 convention on newspaper selling, 44; proposed "federal" form of national newspaper organization, 1918, 72; accounting system, 1919, 81; Publishers Buying Corp., 1920, 84

Rogers, S. S., Chicago Daily News, ANPA president, addressed 1906 convention, 17

Roosevelt, Franklin D., President of the United States, 1932, 163; re-elected, 1936, despite newspaper opposition, 185; increasing newspaper antagonism toward, 189; "court-packing" program resisted, 1937, 190; re-elected 1940, 246

Ross, John, Charlotte Observer, executive committee, 1909-10, 26

Rossiter, Ernest, effort to finance Southern newsprint mill, 223

S

St. Petersburg (Fla.) Independent and St. Petersburg Times, plan to minimize destructive sales competition, 1929-31, 147, 157; typographical union strike, 1945, 277; sued by union before National Labor Relations Board, 1946, 277

San Antonio Express & News and San Antonio Light, typographical union strike, 1945, 277

Sanford, Alfred F., Knoxville Journal-Tribune, advertising committee, 1909, 24; executive committee, 1909-10, 26; 1910-11, 28; 1911-12, 36; vice-president, 1912-13, 37; president, 1913-14, 40; executive committee, 1914-15, 51; 1916-17, 61; 1919-20, 82; legislative committee, 1918-19, 75; death reported, 1946, 268

Savannah Pulp & Paper Laboratory, organized by Dr. Charles H. Herty, 217; ownership transferred to Herty Foundation, 229

Savory, Col. Walter H., Mergenthaler Linotype Co., on training operators, 1919, 81; chairman SNPA golf tournament, 1925, 132; honorary life member, 1927, 139; SNPA expressed hope for his recovery, 1934, 177; golf tournament named in his memory, 1935, 180

Sawyer, J. H., Jr., addressed 1943 convention, 262

Schroth, Thomas N., Brooklyn Eagle, editorial panel, 1952, 328

Screws, Major W. W., Montgomery Advertiser, addressed 1906 convention, 17

Seely, Fred L., Atlanta Georgian, executive committee, 1909-10, 22; proprietor Grove Park Inn, Asheville, 1915, 55; proposed SNPA golf tournament, 55; honorary life member, 55; rules for guests' conduct at Grove Park Inn (footnote) 90; death reported, 1942, 259

Seitz, Don C., New York World, praised Southern press leadership at 1914 convention, 44; (footnote) 46

Shepler, Ned, Lawton Constitution, director, 1948-50, 293

Sherrill, J. B., Concord Tribune, director, 1927-28, 139

Shields, John Brabson, 211

Shott, Hugh I., Bluefield Telegraph & Sunset News, director 1927-28, ——; death reported, 1953, 338

Short, Carl B., Roanoke Times-World Corp., in "Newspaper of the Future" symposium, 1941, 253; di-

379

rector 1941-42, 254; 1942-43, 259; 1943-45, 264; chairman newsprint mills committee 1943, 267; president, 1945-46, 267; died in office, 267; 268

Shutts, Frank B., Miami Herald, director 1925-26, 131

Siegling, R. C., Charleston News & Courier, director 1922-23, 110

Skewes, James H., Meridian Star, director 1927-28, 139; 1930-31, 150; 1931-32, 159; 1932-33, 164; 1936-37, 186; 1937-38, 194; 1938-39, 201; 1949-51, 300

Slack, E. Munsey, Johnson City (Tenn.) Staff, executive committee, 1920-21, 88

Slocum, Richard W., Philadelphia Bulletin, addressed 1950 convention, 309

Slover, S. L., Norfolk Ledger-Dispatch, executive committee, 1917-18, 68; 1918-19, 77; director, 1933-34, 168; 1934-35, 177

Smith, James J., Birmingham Ledger, SNPA founder, 9; executive committee 1912-13, 37

Smith, Robert L., Charleston Gazette, director 1928-29, 141; 1933-34, 168; 1934-35, 177; 1942-43, 259; 1943-45, 264; 1945-46, 267; 1949-51, 300

Smith, Ross C., Birmingham Age-Herald, SNPA founder, 9

Smyer, E. J., 220

Southern Advertising & Publishing, 50th Anniversary edition, 1953, 331

Southern Associated Press, 1891, 4; 341

Southern economics, 1903, 4

Southern Historical Assn. commended SNPA for establishment of Southern Newspaper Library, 1948, 292

Southern newspaper labor policies, 1903-53, ——

Southern Newspaper Library, 1941, 266; 282; 292; 336

Southern Newspaper Publishers Association, founded 1903, 3; draft of organization, 6; at Nashville, 1904, 10; at Charleston, 1905, 15; at Montgomery, 1906, 17; at Richmond and on SS Pocahontas, 1907, 19; at Charlotte, 1908, 21; at Birmingham, 1909, 24; at Mobile, 1910, 26; new by-laws adopted, 28; at Louisville, 1911, 30; at Knoxville, 1912, 36; at New Orleans, 1913, 38; at Atlanta, 1914, 42; at Asheville, 1915, 52; at Asheville, 1916, 57; at Asheville, 1917, 63; regular Bulletin service began 1917, 74; at Asheville, 1918, 69; undivided support pledged to President Woodrow Wilson, 1918, 70; dues increased to $40 annual maximum, 74; co-operative advertising campaign supported by 85 newspapers, 1918-19, 77; at Asheville, 1919, with Southern Division of Associated Press, executive council of American Assn. of Advertising Agencies, and Southern Council of AAAA, 77; offered good wishes to President Wilson on his mission to Europe, 79; permanent headquarters established at Chattanooga, 83; at Asheville, 1920, 83; membership reached 230, 83; dues raised to $75 annual maximum, 83; at Battery Park Hotel, Asheville, 1921, 90; membership reached 250, 90; Federal law on newspaper ownership and circulation statements approved and government audits of disputed circulation claims urged, 96; postponement of postal rate increases approved, 97; at Grove Park Inn, Asheville, 1922, 106; new organization plan and standards of business conduct adopted, 107; at Greenbrier Hotel, White Sulphur Springs, W. Va., 1923, 110; West Virginia newspapers admitted to

INDEX

membership, 110; new organization plan in operation, 110; at Asheville, 1924, 118; appointment of full-time manager approved, 121; Cranston Williams appointed manager, 125; at Asheville, 1925, 125; at Asheville, 1926, 132; 25th Anniversary at Atlanta, 1927, 134; dues increased to $250 annual maximum, 135; at Edgewater Gulf Hotel, Edgewater Park, Miss., 1928, 139; at Asheville, 1929, 142; resolution condemned newspaper ownership by power or paper interest as contrary to sound public policy, 142; at Asheville, 1930, 145; at Asheville, 1931, 152; at Asheville, 1932, 160; shorter news transmission periods sought as economy measure, 161; efforts to break newspaper rate structures resisted, 161; at Signal Mountain Inn, Chattanooga, 1933, 164; at Asheville, 1934, 173; resolution for construction of Southern newsprint mill by private enterprise adopted, following proposal of government aid for project by Major George L. Berry, 175; 221; newsprint mills committee organized, 176; ......; at Hot Springs, Ark., 1935, 177; newsprint mills committee rejected financing of mill by Federal Emergency Relief Administration, 226; at Asheville, 1936, 182; Dallas office opened in co-operation with Texas Newspaper Publishers Assn., 182; newsprint mills committee encountered stiff opposition to mill project, 183; at Hot Springs, Ark., 1937, 187; at Edgewater Gulf Hotel, 1938, 194; SNPA Bureau of Advertising proposed, 197; Mechanical conferences initiated, 200; members pledge final needed sums for financing Southland Paper Mills, Inc., 195; at Hotel Chamberlin, Old Point Comfort, Va., 1939, 201; SNPA Bureau of Advertising plan dropped, 201; ground broken for Southland Paper Mills, Inc., 231; Cranston Williams resigns to become general manager American Newspaper Publishers Assn., 202; Walter C. Johnson appointed secretary-manager, 202; at Mineral Wells, Texas, 1940, 240, Southland Paper Mills Inc., in operation, 231 at Edgewater Gulf Hotel, 1941, 246; SNPA and other associations in statement of newspapers' national defense policies, 251; at Hot Springs, Ark., 1942, 254; pledge of loyal support of 272 SNPA members to President Roosevelt in conduct of war, 255; release of critical materials for completion of chemical pulp unit Southland Paper Mills, demanded, 257; at Hot Springs,, Ark., 1943, 259; membership passed 300, 261; resolution adopted for construction of additional newsprint mills in Southern States, 261; annual conventions suspended for duration of World War II, 264; amended by-laws provide new terms for directors, 267; at Edgewater Gulf Hotel, 1946, 268; directors approved Alabama offer to organize newsprint mill at Childersburg, Ala., 270; removal of newsprint price controls asked, 275; resolution adopted urging member newspapers to encourage greater development of Southern forest resources, 272; soil conservation and conservation of Southern land resources endorsed, 288; at Hot Springs, Ark., 1947, 280; membership increased to 360, 279; headquarters office expanded, 282; full compliance with Labor-Management Relations Act pledged, with call upon unions for similar stand,

284; newspaper research held national rather than regional association project and referred to ANPA, 283; at St. Petersburg, Fla., 1948, 285; Southern printing s c h o o l s asked to extend training to include other newspaper trades, 287; 291; three group conferences, according to circulation, initiated, 292; support of Booker T. Washington Birthplace Memorial commended as "a contribution to better race relations," 291; at Mineral Wells, Texas, 1949, 294; membership increased to 394, 295; at Greenbrier Hotel, White Sulphur Springs, W. Va., 1950, with record attendance of 534 members and guests, 300; strong resolution adopted for increased newsprint production in South and more intensive support of conservation measures, 3 0 2 ; newsprint manufacturers asked to consider publishers' economic problems, recent price increases protested as harmful to both newspapers and paper manufacturers, 303; new newsprint mill projects to be encouraged, after approval by officers and directors, 304; Coosa River Newsprint Co. mill in operation, 300; at Hot Springs, Ark., 1951, 311; at W h i t e Sulphur Springs, W. Va., 1952, 321; membership reached 400, 321; newsprint mills committee advised to encourage further mill development and "to consider whether means should be taken to protect one or more mill sites," 324; members again urged to give editorial and news support to all forestry conservation measures, 325; resolutions define SNPA position on "freedom of information" and call for U. S. rejection of United Nations' proposed "covenant of human rights,"

326; 50th Anniversary convention at Boca Raton, Fla., 1953, 331; newsprint mills committee reported unfavorably on SNPA acquisition of potential newsprint mill sites and woodlands as economically impracticable, 334; experiments with domestic radio transmission of news pictures approved and its rapid development urged, 339

Southern Press Assn., 1880, 341

Southern Publishers Assn., 1898, 342

Southern School of Printing, Nashville, 122; 130; 206; 278; 282

Southern spruce pine, used for newsprint 1921, 90

Southland Paper Mills, Inc., 196; 201; 208; 231; 232; 269; 301

Southwest School of Printing, Dallas, 122; 206; 278; 282

Spahn, Robert H., Oklahoma City Oklahoman and Times, on need for training newspaper personnel in history and aims of their organizations, 309; motion picture study of press operations, 329; chairman labor committee, 1953, 336

Spilman, Louis, Waynesboro News-Virginian, c h a i r m a n journalism schools committee, recommended continued SNPA participation in American Council for Education in Journalism, 1953, 336

Stahlman, Major, E. B., Nashville Banner, defined practical newspaper advertising policy, 1904, 11; special paper committee, 1904, 12; (footnote), 12; chairman postal committee, 1917, 70; argued for fair second-class rates, 70; report on publishers unsuccessful postal rate fight, 79; recommended retention of Federal law requiring newspaper ownership and circulation statements, 1921, 96; d i r e c t o r, 1923-24, 111; chairman traffic committee, 1923-24, 112; warned SNPA

INDEX

not to join railroads and utilities in promotion campaign for the South, 140; death reported, 157

Stahlman, E. B., Jr., Nashville Banner, director, 1941-42, 254; 1942-43, 259; 1943-45, 264; 1945-46, 267; president, 1946-47, 279; labor relations under Taft-Hartley Act, 1947, 280; rebuked publishers for spot market newsprint purchases, 1947, 280; board chairman, 1947-48, 284; honored as past president 50th Anniversary convention 333

Stahlman, James Geddes, Nashville Banner, director, 1927-28, 139; 1928-29, 141; 1929-30, 145; 1930-31, 150; 1931-32, 159; president, 1932-33, 164; board chairman, 1933-34, 167; fought newspaper battle against radio news, 1933, 165; received silver service from SNPA, 174; chairman newsprint mills committee, 1934, 178; 187; _____; ANPA President, 1937, 189; success in financing Southland mill, 1937, 187; plaque from SNPA, 1937, 189; announced complete success of Southland Mill financing, 1938, 195; refused profit for self and paper in Southern mill financing, 1938, 195; aide to Secretary of the Navy, with rank of lieutenant commander, on active duty throughout war, retiring as captain, 251; newsprint mills committee, 1946, 269; offered and defended resolution against "malicious, determined campaign of smear, vilification and falsehood against the South as a region," 305; honored as past-president at 5th Anniversary convention, 1953, 333

Stahlman, Mrs. Mary Geddes, death reported 1938, 200

Stanley, C. M., on E. W. Barrett spruce pine experiment, 211; column on Barrett experiment, 211

Steele, Lorentz, Charleston Gazette, circulation panel, 1952, 328

Stewart, Charles I., Lexington Herald, chairman paper conservation committee, 1918, 71; executive committee, 1919-20, 82; chairman newsprint committee, 1920-21, 88; advocated higher advertising rates and consideration of every means for creating a Southern newsprint industry, 1920, 85; newsprint conditions reported better, 1921, 100; second vice-president, 1920-21, 87; first vice-president, 1921-22, 103; president, 1922-23, 109; retiring from newspaper work, elected honorary life member, 1923, 115; honored as past president at 50th anniversary convention, 1953, 333

Stockton, T. T., Jacksonville Times-Union & Citizen, SNPA founder, 9; executive committee, 1903-04, 8; 1904-05, 12; 1905-06, 16; 1906-07, 18

Stodghill, Howard W., Louisville Courier-Journal & Times, demonstrated carrier training methods, 1931, 156; commended by SNPA 1934, 177

Stone, Melville E., Associated Press, addressed 1911 convention, 30

Stouffer, Wilbur C., Roanoke World-News, chairman editorial panel, 327; 335

Stouffer, W. W., Louisville Post, director 1922-23, 110

Stubblefield, Mrs. Frances Ogden, welcomed SNPA to West Virginia, 322

Sullens, Major Frederick R., Jackson (Miss.) News, director 1923-24, 111; 1925-26, 131; 1926-27, 134; chairman memorial committee, 1946, 268

Sullivan, Matt G., War Production Board, addressed 1943 convention, 262

383

Sullivan, W. B., Columbia Record, advertising committee, 1915, 54; executive committee, 1916-17, 62

Sulphate pulp, first used for newsprint by Southland Paper Mills, Inc., 231

Supply and Equipment representatives at 1906 convention, 19; machinery exhibited for first time, 1916, 57

Susong, Mrs. Edith O'Keefe, Greenville (Tenn.) Democrat-Sun, executive committee, 1921-22, 103; addressed 1952 convention, 322

Swift, Otis Peabody, Life Magazine, addressed 1939 convention, 205

T

Tabb, C. W., Chattanooga headquarters staff, 198; assigned to Dallas office, 1938, 198; ——; reported increased union activity, 1940, 245; rising wage trends, 1946, 277; commended Major George L. Berry for "union integrity and responsibility" for ending strike against Beaumont newspapers, 1947, 281; joined Houston Chronicle, 1950, 318

Tanner, Tom, Chattanooga headquarters staff, 1938, 198; SNPA Labor Commissioner, 1939, 206; ——; number of union contracts increased, 1940, 244; I.T.U. "losing battle" under Taft-Hartley Act, 1949, 297; labor conditions, 1953, 336

Taschereau, Premier L. A., of Quebec, organized Newsprint Institute of Canada, 1930, ——

Tate, Robert H., ANPA Bureau of Advertising, addressed 1935 convention, 180

Taylor, E., Miami Herald, executive committee, 1921-22, 103

Telegraph printers, adjustment of rentals obtained by SNPA, 1933, 166

Teletypesetter, exhibited by Southern Bell Telephone Co., 1929, 144; used by St. Petersburg newspapers during typographical strike, 1945-46, 277; general description, 1946, 278; circuit service by major wire services, 1951, 311; circuits operative in 1953, ——

Tetrick, W. Guy, Clarksburg (W. Va.) Exponent, director, 1923-24, 111; 1924-25, 125; 1925-26, 132; 1926-27, 134

Texas Daily Newspaper Assn. (formerly Texas Newspaper Publishers Assn.) (footnote), 182

Texas Newspaper Publishers Assn., in Dallas office operation with SNPA, 1936-50, 182; 318; brief history of, (footnote), 182

Texas-Oklahoma Mechanical Conference, sponsored by SNPA as Western division, 1938, ——

"This Is Your Voice," 50th Anniversary convention feature, 332

Thomas, W. E., Roanoke Times, executive committee, 1916-17, 62

Thomason, S. E., associated with John Stewart Bryan, in purchase of Chicago Journal and Southern newspapers with paper company aid, 148; chairman ANPA paper committee, defends self against charge of neglecting publishers' newsprint interests, 1930, 148

Thompson, Frederick I., Mobile Register, executive committee, 1910-11, 28; 1911-12, 35; 1920-21, 88; member Federal Trade Commission, 133; eulogy of Major E. B. Stahlman and Col. Robert Ewing, 1931, 157

Thomson, James M., New Orleans Item-Tribune, advertising committee, 1909, 24; executive committee, 1913-14, 40; legislative committee, 75

INDEX

Thomson, William A., director ANPA Bureau of Advertising, addressed 1938 convention, 197

Tilton, Frederick A., Third Assistant Postmaster General, addressed 1930 convention on postal rates, 147

Tims, John F., Jr., New Orleans Times-Picayune, director 1941-42, 254; 1942-43, 259; 1943-45, 264; 1945-46, 267; newsprint mills committee, 1946, 269; chairman newsprint mills committee, 1950, 301

Tincher, R. S., New York Daily News, addressed 1943 convention 262

Tompkins, D. A., Charlotte Observer, SNPA founder, 9; executive committee, 1903-04, 8; 1904-05, 12; 1905-06, 16

Traffic Committee, constituted in 1923, 114; 141; 180; 184

Trotti, H. H., Atlanta Constitution, director 1943-44, 264

Turner, R. E., Norfolk Virginian Pilot, executive committee, 1920-21, 88

U

United Press, 1891, 342

V

Vaccaro, Ernest B., Associated Press, addressed 1953 convention 337

Vandivier, Dave, Chickasha (Okla.) Express, director 1937-38, 194; 1938-39, 201; 1939-40, 207; proposed newspaper promotion plan 1938, 197; conducted 1941 symposium on "Newspaper of the Future," 253; circulation panel, 1952, 328

Vas Dias, Arnold, Netherlands East Indies News Agency, on British war censorship, 1941, 252

Veal, Norvin S., Jacksonville Journal, director, 1945-46, 267

W

Wachs, Fred B., Lexington Leader, director 1935-36, 181; 1936-37, 186; 1937-38, 194; 1941-42, 254; 1942-43, 259

Wakeman, Arthur G., War Production Board, in controversay with SNPA committee on materials for Southland Mills chemical pulp unit, 233; executive vice-president Coosa River Newsprint Co., 1950, 301

Wallace, Tom, Louisville Times, asked development of Southern land resources, 1935, 179; criticized neglect of individuality of Southern newspapers, 1935, 179; on "sinister aspects of syndicated journalism," 1936, 184; "all-star" editorial program, 1937, 193; chairman editorial affairs committee, 1937-38, 198; pleads for free press solidarity in Western hemisphere, 1948, 299; president Inter-American Press Assn., 1948, 290; urged U. S. newspapers to become better acquainted with Latin-America, 1948, 290; repeated plea, 1950, 309

Walls, Carmage, Macon Telegraph & News, director, 1945-46, 267

Ward, J. G., Charlotte Observer, circulation panel, 1952, 328

Waring, Thomas T., Charleston Evening Post, executive committee, 1905-06, 16

Washington & Lee University, endowment fund for Lee Memorial School of Journalism raised by SNPA, 99; 112

Watson, Roy G., Houston Post, director, 1922-23, 110; 1923-24, 111

Watt, Ralph, vice-president Coosa River Newsprint Co., 1953, 335; predicted use of Southern hardwoods for pulpwood, 335

Watterson, "Marse Henry," Louisville Courier-Journal, addressed 1911 convention on journalistic decency, 30

Webb, Charles A., Asheville Citizen-Times, director, 1926-27, 134; report on ANPA open shop division, 1929, 143; death reported, 1950, 310

Weston, Samuel P., directed ANPA imports of European newsprint, 1920, 100; (footnote), 137

West Virginia, added to SNPA territory, 1923, 110

Whitman, Russell R., managing director Audit Bureau of Circulations, addressed SNPA, 58; 67

Williams, Cranston, SNPA manager, 1924, 125; 1925, 131; secretary-manager, 1927-28, 139; 1928-29, 141; 1929-30, 144; 1930-31, 150; 1931-32, 159; 1932-33, 164; 1933-34, 167; 1934-35, 177; 1935-36, 181; 1936-37, 186; 1937-38, 194; 1938-39, 200; SNPA representative Daily Newspaper Code Authority, 1933-35, 170; general manager ANPA, 1939, 202; addressed 1950 SNPA convention, 308; advised SNPA to consider fourth newsprint mill, 1952, 323

Williams, Dean Walter, University of Missouri, "Journalist's Creed," 104

Willem, Jack E., survey of news picture interests, 1940, 243

Wimberly, Harrington, Altus (Okla.) Times-Democrat, director 1940-41, 246; 1941-42, 254; 1942-43, 259

Wintersmith, J. B., Louisville Courier-Journal, advertising committee, 36

Wise, John D., Richmond Times-Dispatch and News-Leader, newsprint mills committee, 1946, 269

Withers, F. C., Columbia State, advertising committee, 1912, 36; executive committee, 1912-13, 37; 1917-18, 68; 1918-19, 77; director, 1924-25, 125; 1928-29, 141; 1929-30, 145; 1930-31, 150; 1931-32, 159; death reported, 1937, 194

Women in Southern journalism, 1903-53, 322; 349

Wood, Austin V., Wheeling Intelligencer and News-Register, chairman newsprint committee, denounced black market operations, 296

Woodson, Urey, Owensboro Messenger, Legislative committee, 1918, 75; chairman legislative committee, 1920-21, 88; executive committee, 1920-21, 88; 1921-22, 103; director, 1926-27, 134; 1928-29, 141; honorary life member, 1929, 145; death reported, 1940, 245

World War I, SNPA pledged full support to President Wilson, 1918, 70

World War II, imminence in 1930's caused sharp decline in U. S. business, 1939, 201; conquest of France stirred U. S. to enormous defense spending, 1940, 240; defense efforts increased, 1941, 247; advertising dropped, 1942, 256; SNPA pledged support to President Roosevelt, 255; SNPA officers and committees on frequent trips to Washington and New York, 259

Worrell, Eugene, Bristol Virginian-Tennesseean, circulation panel, 1952, 328

Wortham, Col. Louis J., Fort Worth Star-Telegram, legislative committee, 1918-19, 75; advocated training of Linotype operators in public vocational schools, 81

Wortham, Richard W., Jr., (newsprint), 225

Y

Yost, Casper S., past-president American Society of Newspaper Editors, sponsored joint conference on education for journalism, 1939, 205

Z

Zenger, John Peter, SNPA endorsement sought for Memorial to commemorate his establishment of free press principle on American soil, 257

SOUTHEASTERN MASSACHUSETTS UNIVERSITY
Z479.J6 1974
The South and its newspapers, 1903–1953